Perceptions of the European Union's Identity in International Relations

This book examines the perception of European Union's identity by the main actors in international relations.

Analysing issues related to public discourse in third countries as demonstrated by, amongst others, their political elites, civil society, and think-tanks, the book highlights a 'normative gap' with regard to the European Union's self-definition/perception and its perception in the international environment. It also shows that the European Union's perception of normative power in international relations is not shared consistently by the main principal actor yet is differentiated relative to geographical area and scope of activities undertaken by the EU. It demonstrates that the perception of the EU's normative identity is a source of the crisis of the European Union as an effective and significant player in the international arena.

This book will be of key interest to scholar and students of European Union politics, European politics/studies, European integration, identity politics, and international relations.

Anna Skolimowska is Head of the Department of International Relations at the Institute of Political Science at the Cardinal Stefan Wyszyński University (UKSW), Poland.

Critical European Studies
Edited by Yannis A. Stivachtis
Virginia Tech, USA
Formerly co-edited with Hartmut Behr
Newcastle University, UK

European Identity Revisited
New Approaches and Recent Empirical Evidence
Edited by Viktoria Kaina, Ireneusz P. Karolewski and Sebastian Kuhn

Discourses and Counter-discourses on Europe
From the Enlightenment to the EU
Edited by Manuela Ceretta and Barbara Curli

The Democratic Quality of European Security and Defence Policy
Between Practices of Governance and Practices of Freedom
Evangelos Fanoulis

Lobbyists and Bureaucrats in Brussels
Capitalism's Brokers
Sylvain Laurens

Europeanization as Discursive Practice
Constructing Territoriality in Central Europe and the Western Balkans
Senka Neuman Stanivuković

The Criminalisation of Communism in the European Political Space after the Cold War
Laure Neumayer

Conditionality, EU and Turkey
From Transformation to Retrenchment
Rahime Süleymanoğlu-Kürüm

Perceptions of the European Union's Identity in International Relations
Edited by Anna Skolimowska

For more information about this series, please visit: www.routledge.com/series/ASHSER-1421

Perceptions of the European Union's Identity in International Relations

Edited by Anna Skolimowska

Routledge
Taylor & Francis Group
LONDON AND NEW YORK

First published 2019
by Routledge
2 Park Square, Milton Park, Abingdon, Oxon OX14 4RN

and by Routledge
52 Vanderbilt Avenue, New York, NY 10017

Review: Prof. Joanna Starzyk-Sulejewska, University of Warsaw

Routledge is an imprint of the Taylor & Francis Group, an informa business

British Library Cataloguing-in-Publication Data
A catalogue record for this book is available from the British Library

Library of Congress Cataloging-in-Publication Data
A catalog record for this book has been requested

ISBN: 978-1-138-54385-0 (hbk)
ISBN: 978-1-351-00562-3 (ebk)

Typeset in Times New Roman
by Apex CoVantage, LLC

Contents

Tables

Contributors

Olga Barbasiewicz, Institute of Middle and Far East Studies, Faculty of International and Political Studies, Jagiellonian University in Kraków (Poland), PhD, is Assistant Professor in the Institute of Middle and Far East Studies, Faculty of International and Political Studies, at Jagiellonian University in Krakow. She has a PhD and M.A. in Political Science as well as an M.A. in Japanese Studies. She held the JASSO scholarship and studied International Relations at Tsukuba University in Japan. In her current research, she focuses on memory politics and Japanese-Korean relations regarding the alliance with the U.S. She gives lectures at Japanese, Czech, Lithuanian, German and Hungarian Universities.

Olga Barburska, Centre for Europe, University of Warsaw (Poland), PhD – graduated from the Institute of International Relations, University of Warsaw. Since 1997 she has been Associate Professor at the Centre for Europe, University of Warsaw. Dr Barburska is Specialist in European Studies and International Relations; her main fields of research interests are: history of European integration, political and social dimension of European integration; and the European Union's foreign policy (especially the EU's Eastern policy). She is a visiting professor, coordinator and participant of various international research projects as well as the author, co-author and editor of over 30 publications, including books in Polish, English and Ukrainian: *Eastern Dimension of the EU's Foreign Policy: Achievements and Problems* (2016); *Past and Presence of European Integration. Poland's Perspective* (2015); *Eastern Policy of the European Union: Success or Failure?* (2014); *History of European Integration* (2013); *Introduction to European Studies: A New Approach to Uniting Europe* (2013); *Poland in the European Union: First Experiences. Selected Political, Legal and Social Aspects* (2008).

Adrian Corpădean, PhD in History, is Associate Professor of European Integration within the Department of International Relations and Vice Dean of the Faculty of European Studies in Cluj-Napoca, Romania. He is author of several books and articles on European integration, the Romanian diaspora during communism, and countries from the Western Balkans. Dr Corpădean is interested in: history of European enlargement, institutional communication, project cycle management, European institutions and decision-making in the EU.

Laura Maria Herţa, PhD in History, is Associate Professor of International Relations and Head of Department of International Relations at the Faculty of European Studies in Cluj-Napoca, Romania. Author of several books and articles on the history of Yugoslavia and the wars in Former Yugoslavia, as well as author of chapters and articles tackling EU as normative power. She is interested in war studies and security studies, humanitarian intervention, the Balkan region, South Caucasus, and Central and East Africa.

Iwona Janczyk is a PhD candidate at Warsaw School of Economics. She is both an economist (Finance – WSE and Management in International Business – Community of European Management Schools, CEMS) and political scientist (International Relations – University of Warsaw), interested in development economics, government policies towards FDI, food security, international competitiveness of countries and International Financial Institutions. She has gained work experience in the private and public sector, and in the academic community. In her PhD thesis she analyses the impact of large-scale farmland acquisitions on food security in chosen African countries, also looking for the best solutions how to maximize the development impact of investments in these countries.

Anna Masłoń-Oracz, PhD, Warsaw School of Economics (Poland), is a lecturer at Warsaw School of Economics. She is a political scientist, economist and an expert in the area of EU foreign policy, with particular focus on the global trade policy and transatlantic relations (EU, US, Africa). Dr Masłoń-Oracz is a member of the International Women's Forum and Vice-President of Polish European Community Study Association. As a business-oriented researcher, Dr Masłoń-Oracz has conducted analyses on how clusters influence regional development competitiveness from the smart specialization perspective. She is also involved in international projects in many countries in Africa concerning women empowerment, development of SME's and regional innovation system (RIS) to enhance the role and importance of RIS in economic development and growth.

Ana Pantea is a lecturer in the Department of International Relations at the Faculty of European Studies in Cluj-Napoca, Romania. Author of *Between I and Thou. Introduction to Everyday Intersubjecitvity* (Eikon, Cluj-Napoca, 2011) and *Fragmented Communities* (Cluj-Napoca, 2018), both in Romanian. She is interested in conflict resolution in Asia, Chinese foreign policy, BRICS.

Beata Piskorska (dr hab./PhD), Institute of Political Science and Foreign Affairs at the Department of International Relations, The John Paul Catholic University of Lublin (Poland). Works as a Professor in Institute of Political Science and Foreign Affairs at the Department of International Relations, The John Paul II Catholic University of Lublin, Poland. Her main research interests include: European integration, mainly foreign policy of the EU, European Neighbourhood Policy, international relations in the region of East European countries, and soft power in international relations. She is an author of the following publications: *Soft Power in the European Union Policy toward Eastern Partnership countries*, Lublin 2017; *Eastern Dimension of the European Union policy*, Toruń 2008; *European Union and Russia. A Road towards new relations*, Lublin 2012; *Ukraine after parliamentary election 2012: pro-European perspective*, Lublin 2013.

Bartosz M. Rydliński, Institute of Political Science, Cardinal Stefan Wyszyński University in Warsaw (Poland). Obtained PhD in Political Science, teaches at the Institute of Political Science at Cardinal Stefan Wyszyński University in Warsaw and works for "Amicus Europae" Foundation of the former Polish President Aleksander Kwaśniewski. Dr Rydliński was an EASI-Hurford Next Generation Fellow at the Carnegie Endowment for International Peace and a visiting scholar at Georgetown University's Center for Eurasian, Russian and East European Studies (CERES) in 2014.

Anna Skolimowska, PhD in Political Science, Institute of Political Science, Cardinal Stefan Wyszyński University in Warsaw (Poland) is Associate Professor of International Relations and Head of Department of International Relations at the Institute of Political Science of Cardinal Stefan Wyszynski University in Warsaw, Poland. She is author and editor of: *Constructivism in the European Studies* (Warsaw 2013), *Theories and Methods in the European Studies* (Warsaw 2013), *European Union as an international organization* (Warsaw 2014) and *European Union as a Normative Power Actor* (Warsaw 2015). Her interests are theories and methods in the study of the European Union, the EU's external relations, and institutionalization in the contemporary international relations.

Şerban Văetişi, PhD in Cultural Anthropology, lecturer in the Department of International Relations at the Faculty of European Studies in Cluj-Napoca, Romania is author of: *Writing Culture and the New Ethnographic Theories* (Cluj-Napoca, 2008) and *American Communities. Cultural Forms and Community Strategies* (Cluj-Napoca, 2018), both in Romanian. He is interested in globalization and postcolonial studies, political geography, urban studies, and Transatlantic and Latin American studies.

Acknowledgements

I would like to thank everyone who contributed to the process of the book preparation: scientists from many Polish universities (Cardinal Stefan Wyszyński University in Warsaw, Warsaw University, Jagiellonian University, Warsaw School of Economics, The John Paul II Catholic University of Lublin) as well as of foreign universities (The Babeş-Bolyai University in Cluj-Napoca, Romania). Such a variety of scholars allowed, though partly, to present the Central and Eastern European perspective on the issue of the European Union's identity in the international relations.

The book was supported by the Cardinal Wyszyński University in Warsaw (Institute of Political Science, Faculty of Historical and Social Sciences) and the by The Konrad-Adenauer-Stiftung in Poland.

Abbreviations

AAs	–	Association Agreements
ACP	–	African, Caribbean and Pacific Group of States
ASEM	–	Asia-Europe Meeting
BRT	–	EU-Japan Business Round Table
CAN	–	Andean Community
CAO	–	Cabinet Office
CARDS	–	Community Assistance for Reconstruction, Development and Stabilisation
CARICOM/ CARIFORUM	–	Caribbean Community
CELAC	–	Community of Latin American and Caribbean States
CFSP	–	Common Foreign and Security Policy
CIS	–	Commonwealth of Independent States
CTF	–	Consultative Task Force
DCFTA	–	Deep and Comprehensive Free Trade Agreements
EaP	–	Eastern Partnership
EBC	–	European Business Council
ECCK	–	European Chamber of Commerce in Korea
EEC	–	European Economic Community
EEU	–	Eurasian Economic Union
ENP	–	European Neighbourhood Policy
EPA	–	Economic Partnership Agreement
EPA	–	Euronest Parliamentary Assembly
ESS	–	European Security Strategy
EU	–	European Union
EUROMED	–	Euro-Mediterranean Partnership
EUSR	–	European Union Special Representative
FPA	–	Foreign Policy Analysis
FTA	–	Free Trade Agreement
FOCAC	–	Forum on China-Africa Cooperation
ICC	–	International Criminal Court
IEBL	–	Inter-Entity Boundary Line

AAs	–	Association Agreements
IFOR	–	Implementation Force
IR	–	International Relations
ISIL	–	Islamic State of Iraq and the Levant
JAES	–	Joint Africa-EU Strategy
JETRO	–	Japan External Trade Organization
JIIA	–	Japan Institute of International Affairs
KITA	–	Korea International Trade Association
NAFTA	–	North American Free Trade Agreement
NEPAD	–	New Partnership for Africa's Development
NPE	–	Normative Power Europe
NPT	–	Non-Proliferation Treaty
MDG	–	Millennium Development Goal
METI	–	Ministry of Economy, Trade and Industry
MOFA	–	Ministry of Foreign Affairs of Japan
ODA	–	Official Development Assistance
OSCE	–	Organisation for Security and Cooperation in Europe
PIC	–	Peace Implementation Council
RCEP	–	Regional Comprehensive Economic Partnership
SAA	–	Stabilisation and Association Agreement
SEECP	–	South-East European Cooperation Process
SFOR	–	Stabilization Force
SICA	–	Central American Integration System
SMP	–	Strategic Modernisation Partnership
SPA	–	Japan-EU Strategic Partnership Agreement
TPP	–	Trans Pacific Partnership
TTIP	–	Trans-Atlantic Trade and Investment Partnership
UNASUR	–	Union of South American Nations
UN	–	United Nations
VLAP	–	Visa Liberalisation Action Plan
WTO	–	World Trade Organization

1 Introduction

Theoretical and methodological background of the survey

Anna Skolimowska

Since its inception in 1993 – when the provisions of the Treaty of Maastricht came into force – the European Union (EU) has become an important player in political international relations. Previously, since late 1950s, the European Communities developed economic relations with most countries and regions of the world through a series of strategic partnerships or various types of international agreements. For this reason the European Union is an active player in international diplomacy, promotion of human rights, trade, development and humanitarian aid, and it cooperates with multilateral organizations. She is present in many regions of the globe: Africa, Asia, Latin America and the Caribbean, North America, etc. The EU is represented through approximately 140 delegations and offices around the world.

After the provisions of the Treaty of Lisbon came into force, the European Union's character in the international relations changed even more. In Article 47, the Treaty gave it for the first time a legal personality in the international relations. Moreover, the Treaty in Article 21 points at the EU's guiding principles on the international scene:

> The Union's action on the international scene shall be guided by the principles which have inspired its own creation, development and enlargement, and which it seeks to advance in the wider world: democracy, the rule of law, the universality and indivisibility of human rights and fundamental freedoms, respect for human dignity, the principles of equality and solidarity, and respect for the principles of the United Nations Charter and international law.[1]

The character of the European Union in the international relations is determined by its legal status, instruments of foreign and external relations as well as of its capabilities, mainly economic ones. This formal institutional approach however seems insufficient to understand the complex and geographical differentiation of the EU's external activity. What seems to be missing in such an approach refers to the identity and informal issues of the European Union's external presence. This gap is even more visible when reading official documents on the EU's foreign relations, in which there is an attempt to answer the following question: what kind of identity, understood as self-identification – should the EU acquire in the relations with the third countries?

Searching the literature dedicated to the topic of the European Union's presence in the international relations one can only find few studies on the EU's identity at the global stage.[2] Researchers more often pay attention to the problem of Europe's Common Foreign and Security Policy (CFSP) or the regional involvement in many parts of the globe.[3] What seems to be missing, however, are the studies of the European Union from the outside perspective. Scientists possess knowledge of the way in which third parties perceive not only everyday activities and policies of the European Union and its institution around the globe, but what is becoming more and more expected are the analyses of the EU's identity perception and its possible influence on EU's self-identification. It is the effect of Constructivist assumptions and their growing popularity not only within European Studies but also within International Relations over the last decade.

What was defined in Maastricht terminology as the Common Foreign and Security Policy has been one of the most compelling factors in helping shape the EU's external image and the perception of its identity held by the rest of the world, constituting the lens through which it is identified and evaluated by outsiders worldwide. Perceptions of the European Union have mostly been studied from an internal perspective, producing a wide range of contributions on topics such as EU's self-identification, Euroenthusiasm or Euroscepticism inside the European boundaries. On the other hand, external perceptions of the European Union are still an underexplored territory: empirical data are often patchy and fragmented and few theoretical studies have been published.[4] One of the pioneers in this field is 'The EU through the Eyes of the Asia-Pacific' project (APPP) based at the National Centre for Research on Europe, University of Canterbury, New Zealand, led by Martin Holland and a project on 'The External Image of the European Union' led by Sonia Lucarelli of the University of Bologna in the framework of the GARNET.

The purpose of the book is to show the perception of the European Union identity in international relations by 'others' (third countries' political elites, civil society, think tanks etc.) and the meaning of third parties' discourse on the European Union's identity in international relations, especially for the narration on its identity in international relations.

The objective of the book is to fill the gap existing in the literature, thereby presenting a wide and consistent review of the existing surveys addressing the external perceptions of the EU. The innovative character of the survey refers to the theoretical assumption of normative European Union's identity and discursive practices in the third countries that legitimate (or not) narration among third parties and thus influence European Union self-identification.

In this respect, it is however worth noting that the book is still quite limited in time and space, with some areas not being covered and many surveys and specific questions being fragmented. Moreover the contributors are aware of restrictions coming from discourse analysis as a main method of the survey. Huge methodological advantage is to stay at the level of discourse treated as a source of objective knowledge on reality.

The book consists of two general parts. The first one will analyze the identity issue of international relations' actors. It seeks to answer the following question: how to analyze and what is the cognitive value of the identity concept in International Relations and within the European Studies.

The second part of the book will contain specific case studies of the perception of EU's external identity reflected in the discursive practice of selected countries of the word, such as United States of America (American think-tanks' analyses of the EU's global specificity); the Russian Federation (an analysis of political actors as well an academic community perception of the European Union); the Balkan countries as well as the countries of the Eastern Partnership and their perspective of the EU envisaged in their public and civil discourse; the African region and its attitude towards Europe; and East Asian (South Korean and Japanese perception of the European values), Indian and Latin America perception of the European Union's global identity.

Theoretical assessment

The survey is grounded in the post-modern variant of Constructivist perspective of International Relations. The point here is the value of that version of Constructivism with its assumption of the possibility to reach knowledge about the reality on the basis of the analysis of the ideational elements of this reality, such as: language, beliefs, imaginations, etc.

Referring to post-modern variant of Constructivist perspective is expected to give a better understanding of the way in which third countries discursively (de-)construct European Union's identity in the international relations and if it has the ability to change EU's internal discourse on her international identity.

The theory should be able to simultaneously explain others' perceptions of the European Union's identity. The aspiration is not to explain the detailed EU global activity or every third country's policy towards Europe but that of answering the questions: what kind of Europe do they see and if/how this image meets discourse and actions of the European Union on her identity?

It is assumed that in the last ten years the most dominant discourse on European Union's identity at the global stage refers to the idea of normative power. The phenomenon of normative power should be understood as the ability of one international entity to exert its ideological influence on other members of international relations (described by the notions of 'power over opinion' and 'ideological power'). Therefore, the concept itself is not founded on the analysis of the economic resources held by the EU in international relations. It rather refers to its ability to diffuse Europe's legal and political standards, ideas, discourses and integration standards, and to shape the international environment with the use of such tools. The innovative and original character of the concept of the European Union as a normative power was built on the assumption that the power of the EU in international relations does not lie in its military capabilities or economic resources, but stems from the importance of the ideas, standards and values underlying the project of European integration.[5]

The research will be embedded in the Constructivist perspective of International Relations. It assumes that social reality is the product of social interaction. The perception of the actors of this reality, their roles and identities are shaped not only by internal factors (political culture, actors' expectations, role discourse), but also by external factors. It is here that the expectations about the role and identity of the European Union are articulated by third parties. This specific external impulse should lead to a unique way of defining and redefining the European identity in the international relations.

The book will be divided into several parts. The first one will provide an analysis of the theoretical as well as methodological challenges while studying the European Union's identity and its perceptions in the international relations. In the second, empirical part of the book, the case study analysis will follow. This will be an analysis of public discourse, public opinion research, and analysis of think-tank opinions on the role and identity of the European Union in selected parts of the world: Russia, the United States, the countries of the Eastern Neighborhood, African states, and countries of the Far East. These are only selected cases, on the basis of which the question concerning the acceptance of the European Union's normative identity will be asked.

Constructivists' assumptions regarding international reality as well as agents' identities within the International Relations are quite promising, especially when it comes to the understanding of the behavior, interest and policies of an actor in the international scene. The concept of identity introduced by Alexander Wendt constitutes a revolution in the way of understanding interactions among international actors. According to Constructivism, identity is developed, supported and changed in the process of interactions among actors of the international relations – in this sense it is socially constructed.[6] Therefore identities also have variable and fluxional nature depending on the character of participants of international relations in specific time and place.

According to Constructivism, identity is regarded as a product of social and political actions. It is used to highlight the process and the interactive nature of the development of the collective understanding. Thus, two characteristics are important for the Constructivist view of identity. First, identity is a 'contingent product' of social and political action, and second, it is understood as a ground or basis for further action.[7]

The aim of this study will be to analyze the perception of the European Union in selected countries/regions of the world. The perception will be defined here as:

- discursive shaping of the European Union's image (statements by representatives of political elites, EU image in local media, think tanks, civil society);
- articulating expectations of its role in the region (similarly, in statements by representatives of political elites, the EU image in local media, think tanks, civil society); and
- perception of the normative identity of the EU in international relations – whether third countries recognize this role, whether they consider it an expected element of European identity in international relations or rather articulate another narrative of the EU.

Hypothesis

It is assumed that the European Union – since its beginning, in 1993, under the Maastricht Treaty provisions – has developed its identity and role in international relations as a normative actor. Scholars have described this phenomenon by using the concept of the normative power (Normative Power Europe, NPE), a concept developed by Ian Manners in 2002. Normative power refers to the European Union's ability to spread the norms and standards of European integration into the international community. Such norms and standards are ruled by the following principles: respect for human dignity, liberty, democracy, equality, the rule of law, and respect for human rights (TEU, Article 21); they should convey the legal, economic, social, political, and cultural norms elaborated during the European integration process.

When it comes to the perception of the European Union's identity it is assumed that the way in which EU constructs her own identity takes under consideration others' image of herself. In other words, the main assumption of the survey is that discourse on EU's identity in third countries/parties should share an idea on normative character of the European Union in international relations.

The research is devoted to finding answers to the following questions: what is the content of the dominant discourse on EU's identity among the European elites?; what is the content of the public discourse on EU's identity in the third countries?; is the declared and up to date discourse on the European Union identity in the international relations as a normative actor reflected among political elites, public opinion, and civil society in third countries?; does it change in time/under what circumstances?; could it have a possible impact on a way in which EU changes its discourse on international identity?

Applied methodology

Methodologically contributors refer to a discourse analysis. It works on official documents, media analysis, speech acts, think-tanks analysis, elite interviews and archival research. The book aims to examine how the perceptions of the European Union's identity and role in the international relations are distributed worldwide in third countries public, civil as well as media discourse.

Since the 1990s, the application of discourse analytical approaches has boomed in International Relations. It posits that 'things' – objects, subjects, states, living beings, and material structures – are given meaning and endowed with a particular identity through language.[8]

Constructivist scholars have largely drawn on discourse analytical methods in the pursuit of different research agendas. To make it simple, Constructivist scholars have mainly focused on identity and norms. Among different Constructivist variants post-modern Constructivism emphasizes the inter-subjective process which underpins common norms and defines social structures. In Constructivist accounts, social norms have 'communicative, rather than merely referential functions', ones that 'guide, inspire, rationalize, justify, express mutual expectations'.

Through discursive interactions agents endogenously construct social reality. In turn, the structural context contributes at re-shaping agents' preferences and identities.[9] To explain dynamics of discursive interactions, Constructivists largely refer to Habermas' distinction between communicative and strategic action: the latter type is oriented at gaining hegemony in discursive practices, the former strives to gain recognition and build consensus. Accordingly, discursive processes sustaining the making of common norms seldom rely on authoritative interpretation. The focus on consensus-building, rather than power, explains the ideational character of interpretative Constructivism.

This posture generally recalls one of locating the speaking subjects in a wider discursive field. Yet, in some empirical analyses, the Copenhagen School narrowed down the scope of the analysis to the particular national contexts. O. Waever suggested relying on the distinction among discursive fields to unfold discursive productions in and of Europe. The first layer is a 'state-nation core concept'; the second, 'the relational position' of states 'vis-à-vis Europe' and the third expresses 'the kind of Europe which is promoted through discourses'.[10] Much of the actual textual work is about tracing the development of a few key concepts, their historical origins, their transformations, and not least their constitutive relationship to other concepts.

Understanding discursive systems makes it possible to predict in the following way: if the dominant system seems to be well functioning, if no major pressures or anomalies are present, one can take this system as basis and make rather precise and strong predictions; if the system is under pressure, one cannot take the specific system as such as premise but only move one level down and say: what other combinations are possible on the basis of the deeper elements? And if the crisis is tough, then move down one more level.

Applied methodology refers to O. Waever's concept of the discursive fields. The first step is to define the character of core European identity discourse among European Union's political elites (High Representative for Common Foreign and Security Policy, President of the European Council and academics). The second chapter of the book will be dedicated to the issue of European identity construction in the international relations as well as of the perceptions of the EU by others and the intersections between them.

The second step will be to examine the relational position of third states towards European identity. For that reason empirical case studies will be provided. The special emphasis will be put on public discourse analysis in selected third countries to set the image of European Union's identity there and to answer the question of what kind of Europe they see. In the third step an attempt to evaluate the third parties' discourse on European identity and its impact on the European identity will be taken.

Notes

1 *Consolidated version of the Treaty on European Union*, C 326/15, 26.10.2012.
2 See H. Larsen, 'The EU as a Normative Power and the Research on External Perceptions: The Missing Link', *Journal of Common Market Studies*, vol. 52, no. 4, 2014,

pp. 896–910; S. Lucarelli and L. Fioramonti, *External Perceptions of the European Union as a Global Actor*, London, Routledge, 2010; R. Kuźniar, 'Międzynarodowa Tożsamość Europy (UE)', in E. Haliżak and S. Parzymies (eds.), *Unia Europejska Nowy Typ Wspólnoty Międzynarodowej*, Warsaw, Oficyna Wydawnicza ASPRA-JR, 2002.

3 See for example D. Milczarek, *Pozycja i Rola Unii Europejskiej w Stosunkach Międzynarodowych. Wybrane Aspekty Teoretyczne*, Warsaw, Centrum Europejskie Uniwersytetu Warszawskiego, 2003; D. Milczarek, 'Rola Międzynarodowa Unii Europejskiej Jako "Mocarstwa Niewojskowego"', *Studia Europejskie*, vol. 1, 2013; Ch. Hill and M. Smith, 'International Relations and the European Union: Themes and Issues', in Ch. Hill and M. Smith (eds.), *International Relations and the European Union*, Oxford, Oxford University Press, 2011, pp. 3–21.

4 S. Braghiroli and L. Salini, 'How Do the Others See Us? An Analysis of Public Opinion Perceptions of the EU and USA in Third Countries', *Working Paper*, vol. 33, 2014, http://openaccess.city.ac.uk/13676/1/tw_wp_33.pdf, (accessed 25 June 2018), p. 33.

5 I. Manners, 'Normative Power Europe: A Contradiction in Terms?', *Journal of Common Market Studies*, vol. 40, no. 2, 2002, p. 239.

6 A. Wendt, *Social Theory of International Politics*, Cambridge, Cambridge University Press, 1999, p. 70.

7 R. Brubaker and F. Cooper, 'Beyond "Identity"', *Theory and Society*, vol. 29, 2000, p. 8.

8 L. Hansen, *Security as Practice: Discourse Analysis and the Bosnian War*, London, Routledge, 2006, p. 18.

9 S. Guzzini, 'Reconstruction of Constructivism in International Relations', *European Journal of International Relations*, vol. 6, no. 2, 2000, pp. 147–182.

10 O. Waever, 'European Integration and Security: Analysing French and German Discourses on State', in D. Howarth and J. Torfin (eds.), *Discourse Theory in European Politics: Identity, Policy and Governance*, New York, Palgrave Macmillan, 2004, pp. 33–67.

Bibliography

Braghiroli, S. and L. Salini, 'How Do the Others See Us? An Analysis of Public Opinion Perceptions of the EU and USA in Third Countries', *Working Paper*, vol. 33, 2014, http://openaccess.city.ac.uk/13676/1/tw_wp_33.pdf, (accessed 25 June 2018).

Brubaker, R. and F. Cooper, 'Beyond "Identity"', *Theory and Society*, vol. 29, 2000, pp. 1–47.

Checkel, J., 'Constructivist Approaches to European Integration', *Arena Working Paper*, vol. 6, 2006, www.sv.uio.no/arena/english/research/publications/arena-working-papers/2001-2010/2006/wp06_06.pdf, (accessed 25 June 2018).

Consolidated version of the Treaty on European Union, C 326/15, 26.10.2012.

Diez, T., 'Constructing the Self and Changing Others: Reconsidering Normative Power Europe', *Millennium: Journal of International Studies*, vol. 33, no. 3, 2015, pp. 613–636.

Diez, T., 'Normative Power as Hegemony', www.euce.org/eusa/2011/papers/7l_thomas.pdf, (accessed 23 August 2015).

Guzzini, S., Reconstruction of Constructivism in International Relations', *European Journal of International Relations*, vol. 6, no. 2, 2000, pp. 147–182.

Hansen, L., *Security as Practice: Discourse Analysis and the Bosnian War*, London, Routledge, 2006

Hill, Ch. and M. Smith, *International Relations and the European Union: Themes and Issues*, in Ch. Hill and M. Smith (eds.), *International Relations and the European Union*, Oxford, Oxford University Press, 2011, pp. 3–21.

Johansson-Nogués, E., 'Is the EU's Foreign Policy Identity an Obstacle? The European Union, the Northern Dimension and the Union for the Mediterranean', *European Political Economy Review*, vol. 9, 2009, p. 27.
Kuźniar, R., 'Międzynarodowa Tożsamość Europy (UE)', in E. Haliżak and S. Parzymies (eds.), *Unia Europejska Nowy Typ Wspólnoty Międzynarodowej*, Warsaw, Oficyna Wydawnicza ASPRA-JR, 2002.
Larsen, H., 'The EU as a Normative Power and the Research on External Perceptions: The Missing Link', *Journal of Common Market Studies*, vol. 52, no. 4, 2014, pp. 896–910.
Lucarelli, S. and L. Fioramonti, *External Perceptions of the European Union as a Global Actor*, London, Routledge, 2010.
Manners, I., 'Normative Power Europe: A Contradiction In Terms?', *Journal of Common Market Studies*, vol. 40, no. 2, 2002, pp. 235–58.
Manners, I., 'The Concept of Normative Power in Word Politics', *DIIS Brief*, May 2009, http://pure.diis.dk/ws/files/68745/B09_maj_Concept_Normative_Power_World_Poli tics.pdf, (accessed 25 June 2018).
Milczarek, D., *Pozycja i Rola Unii Europejskiej w Stosunkach Międzynarodowych. Wybrane Aspekty Teoretyczne*, Warsaw, Centrum Europejskie Uniwersytetu Warszawskiego, 2003.
Milczarek, D., 'Rola Międzynarodowa Unii Europejskiej Jako "Mocarstwa Niewojskowego"', *Studia Europejskie*, vol. 1, 2013, pp. 33–54.
Nicolaïdis, K. and R. Howse, 'This is my Eutopia. . . .: Narrative as Power', *Journal of Common Market Studies*, vol. 40, no. 4, 2002, pp. 767–792.
Waever, O., 'European Integration and Security: Analysing French and German Discourses on State', in D. Howarth and J. Torfin (eds.), *Discourse Theory in European Politics: Identity, Policy and Governance*, New York, Palgrave Macmillan, 2004, pp. 33–67.
Wendt, A., 'Anarchy Is What States Make of It: The Social Construction of Power Politics', *International Organization*, vol. 46, no. 2, 1992, pp. 391–425.
Wendt, A., *Social Theory of International Politics*, Cambridge, Cambridge University Press, 1999.
Zehfuss, M., 'Constructivism and Identity: A Dangerous Liaison', *European Journal of International Relations*, vol. 7, no. 3, 2001, pp. 315–348.

2 Constructivist perspective on identity issue in International Relations

Anna Skolimowska

Introduction

Since the 1980s ('Constructivist turn') International Relations (IR) scholars have paid increasing attention to identity issue. More projects and books on the importance of identity are being prepared. Yosef Lapid and Friedrich Kratochwil even point out the return of the identity issue to the theoretical reflection on the nature of the international relations.[1]

There is no coherent definition of the identity concept however. It is becoming an important element to understand international relations and to explain continuity and variability of this reality. Following the thought of Alexander Wendt, one of the most prominent representatives of Constructivism in IR, it is claimed that state's interests are shaped by their identities, which change with time; the natural phenomenon of identity more and more increasingly becomes a subject of scientific thought.[2]

Popularity of the identity issue in International Relations derives from the growing popularity of Constructivism among theoreticians during the last three decades. It allows researchers to analyze the intangible aspects of the political reality such as: norms, values, discourses or ideas and also the phenomenon of identity, which is a peculiar product of these intangible elements. The interest in the identity issue within International Relations may also derive from a peculiar socialization of the thought on the international reality. The socialization of the International Relations was to make studies more focused on the social context of international politics.

The aim of this analysis is to evaluate scientific value of Constructivism in explaining international relations – especially the identity issue. This goal will be achieved by answering the following questions: what is the character of the concept of identity in the International Relations? What is the explanatory value of this phenomenon? Does Constructivism and the idea of identity proposed by it enable explanation of the international reality? What is the difference between the two strands of Constructivism in their attitude towards the identity issue in International Relations?

It is assumed that Constructivism is best suited to explain the identity issue in International Relations among other approaches (i.e. Neorealism or Neoliberalism) due to its characteristics: ideational ontology and special attention on epistemological matters. 'Social' character of the Constructivism allows us to undertake the reflection on soft elements of international reality like i.a. identity issue. The analysis will be made by using qualitative methods – by identifying the phenomena of identity in the works of the main representatives of Constructivism in International Relations.

The chapter will be divided into three sections. The first will touch the phenomenon of identity in Social Science in general. Genesis and way of its conceptualization will be shown. The second part of the chapter will be analysis of the genesis and specificity of Constructivism in the IR. It will allow to point at the novel character of Constructivism explanation of the international reality. The third part of the chapter will contain Constructivist way of explaining the identity issue in IR. Main works of Constructivist scholars will be presented.

This analysis makes it possible to understand the theoretical thought over the phenomenon of identity within the frames of International Relations.

Constructivist turn in International Relations

Studying identity of the international actors was preceded by theoretical activity undertaken by scholars of the social sciences in the United States not later than the 1960s when the concept of individual identity was developed.[3] Identity is understood here as something that people/social groups have; they pursue it or they should have it. It is a trait that meaning should be sought and discovered.[4] Within the frames of the social sciences the concept of identity joins such basic social categories as social class, race, ethnic background, sex, disability and sexuality, showing the connection between psychological and social processes in given societies or political communities.[5] The research on identity constitutes basis for deeper thoughts on the nature of new and appearing social and cultural forms as well as on the influence of globalization, trans-nationality, post-colonialism and multiculturalism on social and political processes.

Scholars of International Relations took the concept of identity to explain actions and behaviors of the states. Interest in identity issues was possible due to the popularity of Constructivist paradigm within IR in the 1980s ('Constructivist turn'). Constructivism was an answer to changes in the international reality at that time: decreasing importance of state independence as a result of globalization processes, increasing economic and social importance of scientific knowledge, shift of power, etc. These facts made researchers understand that science does not depend on subjects it concerns but rather it shapes them. This statement was valid especially in the context of the Cold War, which was about to finish soon. Theories such as Neorealism or Neoliberalism were neither able to predict the upcoming change nor understand its core later on. This cognitive pessimism of ontological background subsequently moved on to epistemological matters spreading doubt in the positivistic paradigm of science.[6]

Together with the Constructivist turn in International Relations issues of identity became increasingly taken up in the process of explaining the nature of international reality. This kind of perspective was about to touch many more aspects of these processes as it is concerned with analyzing the social dimension of the international relations. This peculiar socialization of the international relations was to pay more attention to the social context of international politics. Representatives of Constructivism (Alexander Wendt, Nicolas Onuf, Friedrich Kratochwil) questioned both ontological and epistemological assumptions of the foregoing theoretical approach within the frames of International Relations. They underlined the importance of ideas, norms, institutions and identity for international politics and indicated correlation of agents and structures.[7] The substance of the Constructivist turn in International Relations was to abandon the foregoing theoretical assumptions, which were found insufficient for understanding the reality. The Constructivist perspective was inspired by changes based on Social Sciences such as Philosophy or Sociology.[8]

Constructivism assumes that the character of international relations cannot be analyzed without its context. The analyzed elements are: beliefs, ideas, opinions, and discourses. There are two standpoints within this approach. The first, rooted in Humanities, refers to hermeneutics and phenomenology. It pursues understanding of the meanings that people relate to social activity. It assumes epistemological positivism and uses hermeneutical methods in research. The second is more radical – it rejects cognitive positivism, even declaring scientific nihilism. The first standpoint is called Poststructuralism; the second, Postmodernism.[9]

The reason behind the popularity of Constructivism in the International Relations in the 1980s, mainly in the USA, was also connected to the geopolitical situation of those times. Not only was the end of theories declared then, but also the 'end of history', as stated by Francis Fukuyama. The historical context (i.e. the end of the Cold War) and discussions among researchers of the International Relations (especially Neorealists and Neoliberals) prepared ground for Constructivism, which became especially popular among researchers from the USA. Europe was dominated by the thought on international relations developed by the English School, which analysis of interstate interactions focused on their roles in international relations.

The term 'Constructivism' was introduced to International Relations by American researcher Nicholas Onuf. He used it for the first time in his book *World of Our Making: Rules and Rule in Social Theory and International Relations*[10] published in 1989. Other representatives of this strand are i.a. Peter Katzenstein, Friedrich Kratochwil and Alexander Wendt.

The Constructivist perspective states that the theory of international reality and its studies should be based on solid ontological and epistemological basis. Representatives of this strand ask new questions concerning the role of identity, norms in forming of national interests, character of processes of institutionalization and global management, and also the social construction of international regimes. The Constructivist debate within the frames of International Relations is held on the levels of metatheory and the theory of international relations.

The genesis of Constructivism in the International Relations should be sought in the context of the third inter-paradigm debate between Rationalism and

Reflectivism. It concerned both ontological and epistemological matters within IR theories. The extreme positions were to be reconciled by Constructivism. That was Alexander Wendt's ambition.[11] The appearance of Constructivism in the International Relations was related to four factors: an attempt to reassess the concept of world theory and politics; the already mentioned inability of traditional approaches to catch the essence of changes in world politics at the end of the 1980s and the beginning of the 1990s; and the appearance of a generation of young researchers, who spotted the necessity to change the foregoing paradigms.[12]

The changes introduced to International Relations by Constructivism are called the 'Constructivism turn'. Its essence is accepting positivistic epistemology together with inter-subjective ontology and opening epistemology to interpretationism. Turn in the ontology consists in becoming open to ideation factors in researches of the international reality. Constructivism is not a unified strand, however. There are two basic strands: conventional and post-modern.

Conventional Constructivism perceives states as a principal level of analysis for international political theory. Moreover, it is assumed that international reality has intersubjective rather than material character. States' interest and identities are constructed by the structure rather than given exogenously.[13] This strand, which dominates mainly in the USA, concentrates on the meaning of norms and identity in shaping the international politics (ideational ontology). Researchers of this strand assume the positivistic epistemological orientation stating the need to build bridges between different theoretical approaches. The research comprises mainly of quality and case-study methods. They assume that the truth about the world can be discovered through objective research procedure. They are theoretically inspired by sociology, institutionalism and theory of organization. They do not pay much attention to meta-theoretical matters. They use the so-called process-tracing method in their research.[14] This strand is represented i.a. by Jeffrey Checkel, Joseph Jupille, and James Caporaso.

Post-modern Constructivism is most popular in Europe. It deals with the language in shaping the social reality. The main analytical category here is the power of discourse. From epistemological perspective these researchers refer to post-positivism. They ask questions concerning the possibility of a certain event happening. For example: instead of the question of what factors caused interests of a state in international relations to be changed the Constructivists concentrate on the background of the event and on language constructions (discourse) which accompanied the change. In their researches they refer to induction methods and focus on the process of reconstruction of the state's interests. They concentrate on the language in the context of reproduction of identity in the social world. These Constructivists use mainly the method of discourse analysis. They are theoretically inspired by language studies performed on the basis of the social theory i.a. by the following researchers: Jürgen Habermas, Pierre Bourdieu or Jaques Derrida.[15]

All this shows that Constructivism is not a unified standpoint: it is divided between those who perceive Constructivism as a tool either for explaining or understanding the international reality.[16] The preceding typology also proves that within the International Relations Constructivism differs not only in the subject aspect, but also in the object one – due to the research tradition in which it is embedded. However in the Anglo-American tradition of Political Sciences Constructivism has the positivistic form. Researches of this strand state the possibility to reach an objective truth about the reality constructed socially with empirical research methods. Cognition here has the form of explaining the reality.

The continental (European) tradition of Constructivism has the post-positivistic form.[17] Researchers of this strand deny the existence of objective truth about reality, as it is influenced by subjective understanding and interpretations. Language is the only tool which makes it possible to reach it. Cognition here has the form of understanding the reality.

Constructivists, despite different epistemological strands, claim that the majority of, or even all significant elements of the international politics result from detailed social conditions and historical processes, not from inevitable consequences deriving from human nature or the nature of society. The most well-known contemporary Constructivists are: Nicholas Onuf (*World of Our Making: Rules and Rule in International Relations*, 1989), Alexander Wendt (*Social Theory of International Politics*, 1999), John Ruggie (*Constructing the World Polity: Essays on International Institutionalization*, 1998) and Martha Finnemore (*National Interests in International Society*, 1997).

Constructivists state that the objective social reality does not exist. The social and political world are intangible objects and they do not exist outside of human consciousness. The international system is not anything external towards a person. It exists as inter-subjective awareness among people, it is a product of a man and has ideational character. It constitutes a set of ideas, a collection of thoughts, a system of norms developed by specific people in a specific place. Inter-subjective character of international relations enables studying them with scientific methods, both in a positivistic and post-positivistic sense.[18]

Constructivists use analytical categories from the areas of sociology, psychology or philosophy, which widens the theoretical discourse within the international relations.[19] Using such sources causes the fact that the Constructivists' thought naturally concentrates on individuals and groups rather than on states, international organizations or other actors of international politics. It is thanks to Constructivism that the international reality started to be perceived and studied in the categories of social reality. Assumptions of Constructivism are as follows: the structures of human association are determined primarily by shared ideas rather than material forces, and that the identities and interests of purposive actors are constructed by these shared ideas rather than given by nature.[20]

Constructivism has been best developed by the American political scientist Alexander Wendt in his work entitled *Social Theory of International Politics*. It is divided into seven parts including sociological and philosophical analysis of the social construction of international reality – the core of Constructivist perception of international relations.

Wendt's thesis is based on criticism of opinions of Keneth Waltz, the author of *Theory of International Politics* (1979), which includes synthesis of Neorealism; and Robert Keohane, the author of *After Hegemony* (1984),[21] who is considered to be the father of contemporary Neoliberalism in the theory of international relations.

Regarding the basic Neorealistic paradigm, Wendt indicates errors in this type of thinking. He claims that it too hastily rejects the fact that states are causative subjects and they have human traits such as intentionality, rationality, and interests.[22] Neoliberals in turn quickly reject the opinion that international relations are state-oriented, which leaves space for adversaries of Neorealism.

The second part of Wendt's book concerns the process of international politics. The author claims that this structure is created, reproduced and even modified under the influence of interactions among its states. The author calls them agents of international politics. The model of these interactions assumes that states (as entities with anthropomorphic traits as: interests, identity, needs, desires) choose specific behavior as response to external stimulus. It leads to their identity becoming real and subsequently to establishing their interests and consequently to choosing a specified behavior. The author indicates four factors which can lead to changes in relations among states within the structure. These are interdependence, homogenization, self-restraint and common fate.[23]

Neorealists and Constructivists agree that states strive to survive and be safe. But what form of security policy derives from it? Do states try to become as powerful as possible, or are they rather satisfied with what they have? Wendt states that we can learn by studying identity and interests, because they are shaped as results of interactions among states, which create group meanings being a construction, according to which the future activities are organized. Through participation in this structure, actors can better understand their identities, their role in the system and expectations towards them.

Identity issue according to Constructivism

Constructivism as a paradigm is divided into conventional and post-modern variants as mentioned before. These two strands aren't in agreement on the identity issue and differ when referring to this topic. Nevertheless according to Constructivist scholars the idea of identity is crucial for understanding the international reality. It is derived from Social Psychology, especially from the theory of social identity. Social groups define themselves based on sets of ideas. These ideas can be articulated directly through a discourse or indirectly by common symbols, codes or signs. The purpose of these ideas is to create a definition of the given social group as a community separate from others. Members of such a group are convinced about the existence of a common base on which they create 'imagined community'.[24]

Constructivism is willing to undertake the issue of identity as it pays attention to the states giving them human attributes, like intentionality, rationality, and interests.[25] From this perspective it is easy to understand why identity is such an important element to explain states' behaviors in the IR. Despite many strands of Constructivism within the paradigm there is a strong belief in explaining the value of the identity concept.

According to conventional Constructivism, represented by leading representative Alexander Wendt, identity is at base a subjective or unit-level quality, rooted in an actor's self-understandings. Wendt defines identities as relatively stable, role-specific understandings and expectations about the self.[26] However, the meaning of those understandings will often depend on whether other actors represent a given actor in the same way, and to that extent identity will also have an intersubjective or systemic quality. Two kinds of ideas can enter into identity; in other words, those held by the Self and those held by the Other.[27] Therefore identity comprises of two types of ideas: self-perception and perception of others towards the given subject. In this aspect identity is constituted by internal and external structures towards the given subject. Alexander Wendt lists several types of identity:

a personal or corporate – such identities are constituted by self-organizing structures, which make actors/states distinctive from the others. It requires consciousness and memory of sameness. It is the basis for other types of identities. Wendt indicates the existence of the phenomenon of corporate identity, which he relates to a set of internal traits which self-organize the given political community. These are: individuals acting in the given community, physical resources, opinions and institutions.[28] Corporate identity is an intrinsic and self-organizing identity that constitutes actor individuality. It is motivational energy to engage in action or interaction. The corporate identity of the state generates four basic interests: (1) physical security, (2) ontological security in relationships to the world, which create a desire for stable social identities,[29] (3) recognition as an actor by others, above and beyond survival (autonomy), and (4) development for better life at the collective level;

b concerning the type – identity which exists integrally with an actor and depends on the actor's traits (political system – for example democratic states, monarchies, etc.). Actor may have multiple types of identities depending on its characteristics;

c concerning the role – it is identity which can exist only in relation with others, because it is the others who legitimize it and give meaning to it;

d collective identity – such an identity is related to the process of identification, i.e. considering self-image in the eyes of others during the process of constructing own identity.[30] Within this category an individual marks his/her similarity to others in the group. It can be understood as sameness itself deriving from characteristics of the given subject or as subjective feeling, experience or perceiving own similarity towards other members of the given group. Such identity reveals itself with the attitude of solidarity or common actions with other group members. From this perspective the difference between the concept of identity as an analytical tool and the social attitude is often unclear.

The concept of identity introduced by Wendt constitutes a revolution in the scope of understanding interactions among subjects of the international relations. It assumes that identity is developed, supported and changed in the process of interactions among them, and international relations themselves are socially constructed. Therefore identities also have variable and fluxional character depending on the participants of international relations in the given time and place.

Alexander Wendt emphasizes that identities vary by issue, time and place. He points at the three mechanism throughout which the identity is being formed:

a structural contexts – inter-subjective systemic structures of regional or global international systems constitute interaction contexts that facilitate the emergence of dynamics of collective identity formation. They consist of the shared understandings, expectations, and social knowledge embedded in the international institutions in terms of which states define their identities and interests;[31]
b systemic processes – Wendt points out the two systemic processes important for identity construction: rising interdependence (understood as rising domestic interactions or feeling of the common threat) and transitional convergence of domestic cultural and political values. Both encourage collective identity formation and thus they lead to greater sensitivity of actors to each other;
c strategic practice – Wendt derives them from a symbolic interactionism and explains that actors form their identities through interactions by learning; an important role in this process is played by behavioral and rhetorical strategies.[32]

In Wendt's way of explaining identity phenomenon there is a fundamental role of the states–structure interplay. Wendt's analysis focuses on state interaction in which identities are defined and sustained or changed. They are not given but are developed and sustained or transformed in the process of interaction. He points at the inter-subjective elements of the structure like expectations and social knowledge that are embedded in the international institutions. Wendt emphasized that they help to understand identities as characteristics of actors, and the actors form their own interests on this basis: identities are the basis of interests. According to Wendt, the daily life of international politics is an ongoing process of states taking identities in relation to others, casting them into corresponding counter-identities, and playing out the result.[33]

Wendt argued that identities structure relations between states within the international politics. Moreover identities refer to who or what actors are. They designate social kinds or states of being. Interests refer to what actors want. They designate motivations that help explain behavior. Interests presuppose identities because an actor cannot know what it wants until it knows who it is, and because identities have varying degrees of cultural content so will interests.[34]

Thus we can distinguish six qualities for the Constructivist usage of the term:

- identity is constructed and therefore is dependent on agents that construct it;
- identity is a dynamic concept and is consequently dependent on the social context and the agents;

- identity rests on a 'tradition' in which it has a particular legitimacy of its own, and therefore it has a particular relation to history;
- identity sustains a close relation to the system of political values in which it takes place;
- identity is based on drawing borders producing in-group and out-group biases. Therefore, 'self' finds itself with 'other'; identity possesses a center.[35]

Martha Finnemore in her book *National Interests in International Society and The Purpose of Intervention*[36] emphasized that given norms are created at the international level and later by the discursive practices spread among member states. Within this process works a logic of appropriateness. States have accommodated their presence in the international structure according to the norms of the international cooperation and led to the new understanding of their interest.

Another representative of the Constructivist paradigm, Ted Hopf, says that identities are necessary, in international politics and domestic society alike, in order to ensure at least some minimal level of predictability and order. Durable expectations between states require inter-subjective identities that are sufficiently stable to ensure predictable patterns of behavior.[37] Moreover the identity of a state implies its preferences and actions in the international arena. A state understands others according to the identity it attributes to them, while simultaneously reproducing its own identity through daily social practice. The producer of the identity is not in control of what it ultimately means to others; the inter-subjective structure is the final arbiter of meaning.[38] Conventional constructivism accepts the existence of identities and wants to understand their reproduction and effect.

According to the post-modern strand of Constructivism, identity reveals hidden structures of hegemony among the participants of IR. It uses critical social theory to specify some understanding of the origin of identity. Critical theory's approach toward identity is rooted in assumptions about power. Critical theorists see power being exercised in every social exchange, and there is always a dominant actor in that exchange. Unmasking these power relations is a large part of critical theory's substantive agenda.[39]

The post-modern strand of Constructivism is represented i.a. by Roxanne Doty who perceives foreign policy as a socially constructed domain.[40] She explores how subjects of foreign policy are socially constructed via discursive practices. She assumes that discourse produces identities and positions them vis-à-vis one another. Doty develops then a Discursive Practice Approach (DPA) that emphasized the linguistic construction of reality. Within this interpretation an inherent element of the linguistic practices is power constructed by particular discourses. Thus the power is productive of subjects.[41]

At that point Doty's work refers to Michael Foucault's works on the meaning of discourse as a social construct created and perpetuated by those who have the power and means of communication.[42] Foucault holds that truth, morality, and meaning are created through discourse. Discourses, in Foucault's work, are ways of constituting knowledge, together with the social practices, forms of subjectivity and power relations.[43] Discourse transmits and produces power. Discourses are about what can be said and thought, but also about who can speak, when, and with what authority. They embody meaning and social relationships, they constitute both subjectivity and power relations. In addition, discourses are not about objects; they do not identify objects, they constitute them and in the practice of doing so conceal their own invention. Discourses exist both in written and oral forms and in the social practices of everyday life. As observed by Foucault, language plays a powerful role in reproducing and transforming power relations along many different dimensions (of class, culture, gender, sexuality, disability and age, etc.).[44]

Foucault's idea regarding the discourse has influenced international relations literature, especially among the post-modern strand of Constructivist scholars. The idea is that behavior takes place in social contexts, which consist of communications, a discourse being one of its essential elements. The separation of speech and action in foreign policy would then be misleading. Indeed, in foreign policy either partially or entirely, speech and action are integrated.

The linguistic approach addresses a question: how do possible policy makers generate a particular decision? In other words, analyzing foreign policy within this discursive practices approach is an activity that calls for attention to the extent to which conditions make policy makers possible to decide and act accordingly.[45]

The post-modernist strand of Constructivism is useful for the study in terms of finding out how foreign policy makers perceive other actors in world politics, which in turn leads to how they will act in response to its dynamics. In relation to the creation of the inside or the self, post-modernists offer the way in which foreign policy officials or the state governments obtain foreign policy legitimacy of their publics.

Referring to the idea of Discursive Practice Approach by Constructivist scholars aims to contribute to better understanding of the identity phenomenon in the international relations literature. They assume that identity is a socially constructed phenomenon. Conventional Constructivists view this construction via the systemic relation of agents and structure whereas post-modern Constructivists give language and discourse a fundamental role in creating and changing the scope of one's identity. Both face methodological challenges as pointed out in the chapter.

Another post-modern scholar referring to the identity issue is William E. Connolly. Connolly emphasizes that identity is relational and collective and is defined through the collective constituencies identified by others. It might be tightly or loosely demarcated in the dimension of its breadth. An identity can also vary along the dimension of depth. No identity is the true identity because every identity is particular, constructed and relational. A conception of identity is both historically contingent and inherently relational.[46]

Conclusion

The concept of identity in the International Relations was borrowed from social psychology, especially the theory of social identity.[47] It states that social groups define themselves based on a set of ideas. These ideas can be expressed directly through discourse or indirectly by common symbols, codes or signs. The purpose of these ideas is to create definitions of the given social group as a community different from other groups. Members of such group are convinced about the existence of a common base on which they create an 'imagined community'.[48]

Within the frames of the International Relations the subject of identity of participants of international relations was first taken up together with the appearance of Constructivist researchers in the 1980s. From this moment a tendency to take up this subject in research and referring to a scientific approach which would include ideational elements of the international reality (norms, values, rules) can be seen, including the matters of identity.

The substance of the Constructivist turn in the International Relations was to abandon the foregoing theoretical assumptions, which were found insufficient for understanding the reality. The Constructivist perspective within the frames of the International Relations was inspired by changes based on Social Sciences such as Philosophy or Sociology. Constructivism claims that the social reality exists only due to an agreement among persons and it has a subjective character. From this perspective the reality is variable and unsustainable. Constructivists also claim that it usually has a local character, not a global one, and it is limited in time.

More and more frequent attention of researchers focused on the matters of identity seems to fulfill the postulate expressed by Martin Wight regarding the need to supplement the thought on international relations not only with material factors but also with ideational ones.[49]

In Constructivism, identity is regarded as a product of social and political actions. It is used to highlight the process and the interactive nature of development of the collective understanding. Thus, two characteristics are important for the Constructivist view of identity. First, identity is a 'contingent product' of social and political action, and second, it is understood as a ground or basis for further action.[50] Identity thus is a dependent variable conditioned by international environment.

Also for post-modernist scholars, identity is an important element for understanding the international reality. Post-modernist scholars deny the notion of objective truth: truth and knowledge of reality depends on our perception and representation of reality. In its state-centric analysis, Constructivism sees states as an individual or agent determined by norms, practices and identities. Post-modernism, however, goes further by providing alternative historical narratives to the formation of states and identity concepts. By engaging in their deconstruction, post-modernism is able to question these concepts that the Constructivism paradigm accepts as given, hence engaging more critically with the norms and practices that it describes.

Notes

1 Y. Lapid and F. Kratochwil, *The Return of Culture and Identity in IR Theory*, Boulder, CO, Lynne Rienner, 1996.
2 A. Wendt, *Social Theory of International Politics*, Cambridge, Cambridge University Press, 1999.

3 R. Brubaker and F. Cooper, 'Beyond Identity', *Theory and Society*, vol. 29, no. 1, 2000, pp. 1–47.

4 Brubaker and Cooper, 'Beyond Identity', p. 1.

5 Examples of such works are: M. Wetherell (ed.), *Identity in the 21st Century. New Trends in Changing Times*, Basingstoke, Palgrave Macmillan, 2009; J. McLaughlin, P. Phillimore and D. Richardson (eds.), *Contesting Recognition Culture, Identity and Citizenship*, Basingstoke, Palgrave Macmillan, 2011.

6 S. Guzzini, 'Reconstruction of Constructivism in International Relations', *European Journal of International Relations*, vol. 6, no. 2, 2000, p. 151.

7 Ch. Reus-Smit, 'Konstruktywizm', in S. Burchill et al. (eds.), *Teorie Stosunków Międzynarodowych*, Warsaw, Książka i Wiedza, 2006, p. 278.

8 A. Skolimowska, 'Konstruktywizm Jako Teoria Integracji Europejskiej', PhD Thesis, Cardinal Stefan Wyszyński University in Warsaw, 2013, p. 133.

9 M. Bevir and R.A.W. Rhodes, 'Teoria Interpretacjonistyczna', in D. Marsh and G. Stoker (eds.), *Teorie i Metody w Naukach Politycznych*, Kraków, Wydawnictwo Uniwersytetu Jagiellońskiego, 2006, pp. 131–132.

10 Nicholas Onuf is a retired professor of international relations at the University of Florida. He is an author of: N. Onuf, 'A Constructivist Manifesto', in K. Burch and R.A. Denmark (eds.), *International Constituting Political Economy, International Political Economy Yearbook*, vol. 10, 1997, pp. 7–18; N. Onuf, 'Constructivism: A User's Manual', in V. Kubálková (ed.), *International Relations in a Constructed World*, London, M.E. Sharpe, 1998, pp. 58–78; N. Onuf, 'Worlds of Our Own Making: The Strange Career of Constructivism', in D. Puchala (ed.), *Visions of International Relations*, Columbia, University of South Carolina Press, 2002, pp. 119–141; N. Onuf, 'Parsing Personal Identity', in F. Debrix (ed.), *Language Agency and Politics in a Constructed World*, New York, M.E. Sharpe, 2002, pp. 26–50.

11 Wendt, *Social Theory of International Politics*, p. 2.

12 Reus-Smit, 'Konstruktywizm', p. 278.

13 A. Wendt, 'Collective Identity Formation and the International State', *The American Political Science Review*, vol. 88, no. 2, 1994, p. 385.

14 It is a research method in which a researcher accompanies the researched phenomenon to discover its hidden meanings. Using this method helps to identify the process, i.e. mechanisms and relations among independent variables and the effect of dependent variables. Process-tracing forces the researcher to consider alternative ways leading to the given phenomenon taking place – this method offers the possibility to draw more than one possible way of evolution of the given phenomenon.

15 J. Checkel, 'Constructivist Approaches to European Integration', *Arena Working Paper*, vol. 6, 2006, www.sv.uio.no/arena/english/research/publications/arena-working-papers/2001-2010/2006/wp06_06.pdf, (accessed 2 June 2018), p. 7.

16 A. Wiener, 'Constructivist Approaches in International Relations Theory: Puzzle and Promises', *Constitutionalism Webpapers*, vol. 5, 2006, p. 13.

17 The term post-modernism refers generally to a collection of philosophers including M. Foucault, J. Derrida and J.F. Lyotard, who were concerned with the deceptive essentialist discourses of the modern era and their consequences for the advancement of knowledge. When applied to IR, post-modernism is usually identified with the 'post-positivist' theories which also condemn mainstream IR for the uncritical nature of its assumptions. The post-modernist emphasis on textuality, however, has led critics to find post-modernism guilty on the charge of complete nihilistic relativism. By denying the possibility of an objective reality and by declaring any theory of IR a fabrication with no legitimate grounding, it seems to possess no mechanism with which to assert one theory over another. F. Krause Dornelles, 'Postmodernism and IR: From Disparate Critiques to a Coherent Theory of Global Politics', *Global Politics Network*, www.globalpolitics.net/essays/Krause_Dornelles.pdf, (accessed 25 June 2018), p. 10.

18 R. Jackson and G. Sørensen, *Wprowadzenie do Stosunków Międzynarodowych. Teorie i Kierunki Badawcze*, Kraków, Wydawnictwo Uniwersytetu Jagiellońskiego, 2012, pp. 269–270.
19 Before, the main inspiration for researchers of international relations were law, natural science or economy.
20 Wendt, *Social Theory of International Politics*, p. 1.
21 R. Keohane, *After Hegemony Cooperation and Discord in the World Political Economy*, Princeton, Princeton University Press, 1984.
22 Wendt, *Social Theory of International Politics*, p. 9.
23 A. Wendt, 'The Agent-Structure Problem in International Relations Theory', *International Organizations*, vol. 3, no. 41, 1987, pp. 343–363.
24 M. Marcusen et al., *Constructing Europe? The Evolution of Nation-State Identities*, in T. Christiansen, K.E. Jørgensen and A. Wiener (eds.), *The Social Construction of Europe*, London, Sage Publications, 2001, p. 102.
25 Wendt, *Social Theory of International Politics*, p. 10.
26 Wendt, *Social Theory of International Politics*, p. 21.
27 Wendt, *Social Theory of International Politics*, p. 224.
28 Wendt, 'Collective Identity', p. 385.
29 Ontological security is understood as a constant feeling of identity: being aware of aims, preferences and interests, which in turn give possibility of further actions in the international environment.
30 Wendt, *Social Theory of International Politics*, pp. 222–228.
31 Wendt, 'Collective Identity', p. 389.
32 Wendt, 'Collective Identity', pp. 390–394.
33 Wendt, *Social Theory of International Politics*, p. 21.
34 Wendt, *Social Theory of International Politics*, p. 231.
35 A. von Busekist, 'Uses and Misuses of the Concept of Identity', *Security Dialogue*, vol. 35, no. 1, 2004, p. 82.
36 M. Finnemore, *National Interests in International Society and the Purpose of Intervention*, New York, Cornell University Press, 1996.
37 T. Hopf, 'The Promise of Ted Hopf Constructivism in International Relations Theory', *International Security*, vol. 23, no. 1, 1998, p. 174.
38 Hopf, 'The Promise of Ted Hopf Constructivism', p. 175.
39 Hopf, 'The Promise of Ted Hopf Constructivism', p. 185.
40 R. Doty, 'Foreign Policy as Social Construction: A Post-Positivist Analysis of U.S. Counterinsurgency Policy in the Philippines', *International Studies Quarterly*, vol. 37, no. 3, 1993, pp. 297–320.
41 Doty, 'Foreign Policy as Social Construction', p. 302.
42 M. Foucault, *The Archaeology of Knowledge and the Discourse on Language*, New York, Panteon, 1972, p. 49.
43 Foucault, *The Archaeology of Knowledge*, p. 49.
44 V. Pitsoe and M. Letseka, 'Foucault's Discourse and Power: Implications for Instructionist Classroom Management', *Open Journal of Philosophy*, vol. 3, no.1, 2013, p. 24.
45 I.G. Wahyu Wicaksana, 'The Constructivist Approach Towards Foreign Policy Analysis', *Indonesian Journal of Social Sciences*, http://citeseerx.ist.psu.edu/viewdoc/download;jsessionid=67085141520E0D0CF4AF8948E0CD9CD8?doi=10.1.1.465.6017&rep=rep1&type=pdf, (accessed 25 June 2018).
46 W.E. Connolly, *Identity\Difference,* Minneapolis-London, University of Minnesota Press, 1991, pp. 45–46.
47 Brubaker and Cooper, 'Beyond Identity'; E. Erikson, *Identity: Youth and Crisis*, New York, W.W. Norton Company, 1968.
48 M. Marcusen, et al., 'Constructing Europe? The Evolution of Nation-State Identities', in T. Christiansen, K.E. Jørgensen and A. Wiener (eds.), *The Social Construction of Europe*, London, Sage Publications, 2001, p. 102.

49 M. Wight, 'Why Is There no International Theory?', in H. Butterfield, M. Wight and H. Bull (eds.), *Diplomatic Investigations: Essays in the Theory of International Politics*, London, Allen & Unwin, 1966, pp. 17–34; M. Wight, 'Western Values in International Relations', in H. Butterfield, M. Wight and H. Bull (eds.), *Diplomatic Investigations: Essays in the Theory of International Politics*, London, Allen & Unwin, 1966, pp. 89–131; M. Wight, 'The Balance of Power', in H. Butterfield, M. Wight and H. Bull (eds.), *Diplomatic Investigations: Essays in the Theory of International Politics*, London, Allen & Unwin, 1966, pp. 149–175.

50 Brubaker and Cooper, 'Beyond Identity', p. 8.

Bibliography

Bevir, M., and R.A.W. Rhodes, 'Teoria Interpretacjonistyczna', in D. Marsh and G. Stoker (eds.), *Teorie i Metody w Naukach Politycznych*, Kraków, Wydawnictwo Uniwersytetu Jagiellońskiego, 2006, pp. 131–152.

Brubaker, R. and F. Cooper, 'Beyond Identity', *Theory and Society*, vol. 29, no. 1, 2000, pp. 1–47.

Checkel, J., 'Constructivist Approaches to European Integration', *Arena Working Paper*, vol. 6, 2006, www.sv.uio.no/arena/english/research/publications/arena-working-papers/2001-2010/2006/wp06_06.pdf, (accessed 25 June 2018).

Connolly, W.E., *Identity\Difference*, Minneapolis-London, University of Minnesota Press, 1991.

Czaputowicz, J., *Zastosowanie Konstruktywizmu w Studiach Europejskich*, Warszawa, Wydawnictwo Uniwersytetu Warszawskiego, 2016.

Doty, R., 'Foreign Policy as Social Construction: A Post-Positivist Analysis of U.S. Counterinsurgency Policy in the Philippines', *International Studies Quarterly*, vol. 37, no. 3, 1993, pp. 297–320.

Erikson, E., *Identity: Youth and Crisis*, New York, W.W. Norton Company, 1968.

Finnemore, M., *National Interests in International Society and the Purpose of Intervention*, New York, Cornell University Press, 1996.

Foucault, M., *The Archaeology of Knowledge and the Discourse on Language*, New York, Panteon, 1972.

Guzzini, S., 'Reconstruction of Constructivism in International Relations', *European Journal of International Relations*, vol. 6, no. 2, 2000, pp. 147–182.

Hopf, T., 'The Promise of Ted Hopf Constructivism in International Relations Theory', *International Security*, vol. 23, no. 1, 1998, pp. 171–200.

Jackson, R. and G. Sørensen, *Wprowadzenie do Stosunków Międzynarodowych. Teorie i Kierunki Badawcze*, Kraków, Wydawnictwo Uniwersytetu Jagiellońskiego, 2012.

Keohane, R., *After Hegemony Cooperation and Discord in the World Political Economy*, Princeton, Princeton University Press, 1984.

Krause Dornelles, F., 'Postmodernism and IR: From Disparate Critiques to a Coherent Theory of Global Politics', *Global Politics Network*, www.globalpolitics.net/essays/Krause_Dornelles.pdf, (accessed 25 June 2018).

McLaughlin, J., P. Phillimore and D. Richardson (eds.), *Contesting Recognition Culture, Identity and Citizenship*, Basingstoke, Palgrave Macmillan, 2011.

Marcusen, M., et al., *Constructing Europe? The Evolution of Nation-State Identities*, in T. Christiansen, K.E. Jørgensen and A. Wiener (eds.), *The Social Construction of Europe*, London, Sage Publications, 2001, pp. 101–121.

Onuf, N., 'A Constructivist Manifesto', in K. Burch and R.A. Denmark (ed.), *International Constituting Political Economy, International Political Economy Yearbook*, vol. 10, 1997, pp. 7–18.
Onuf, N., 'Constructivism: A User's Manual', in V. Kubálková (ed.), *International Relations in a Constructed World*, London, M.E. Sharpe, 1998, pp. 58–78.
Onuf, N., 'Parsing Personal Identity', in F. Debrix (ed.), *Language Agency and Politics in a Constructed World*, New York, M.E. Sharpe, 2002, pp. 26–50.
Onuf, N., 'Worlds of Our Own Making: The Strange Career of Constructivism', in D. Puchala (ed.), *Visions of International Relations*, Columbia, University of South Carolina Press, 2002, pp. 119–141.
Pitsoe, V. and M. Letseka, 'Foucault's Discourse and Power: Implications for Instructionist Classroom Management', *Open Journal of Philosophy*, vol. 3, no. 1, 2013. pp. 23–28.
Reus-Smit, Ch., 'Konstruktywizm', in S. Burchill et al. (eds.), *Teorie Stosunków Międzynarodowych*, Warszawa, Książka i Wiedza, 2006, pp. 269–296.
Skolimowska, A., 'Konstruktywizm Jako Teoria Integracji Europejskiej', PhD Thesis, Cardinal Stefan Wyszyński University in Warsaw, 2013.
Skolimowska, A., *Konstruktywizm w Studiach Europejskich*, Warszawa, Oficyna Wydawnicza Łoś-Graf, 2013.
Wahyu Wicaksana, I.G., 'The Constructivist Approach Towards Foreign Policy Analysis', *Indonesian Journal of Social Sciences*, http://citeseerx.ist.psu.edu/viewdoc/download;jsessionid=67085141520E0D0CF4AF8948E0CD9CD8?doi=10.1.1.465.6017&rep=rep1&type=pdf, (accessed 25 June 2018).
Wendt, A., 'The Agent-Structure Problem In International Relations Theory', *International Organizations*, vol. 3, no. 41, 1987, pp. 335–370.
Wendt, A., 'Anarchy Is What States Make of It: The Social Construction of Power Politics', *International Organizations*, vol. 46, no. 2, 1992, pp. 391–425.
Wendt, A., 'Collective Identity Formation and the International State', *American Political Science Review*, vol. 88, no. 2, 1994, pp. 384–396.
Wendt, A., *Social Theory of International Politics*, Cambridge, Cambridge University Press, 1999.
Wetherell, M. (ed.), *Identity in the 21st Century. New Trends in Changing Times*, Basingstoke, Palgrave Macmillan, 2009.
Wiener, A., 'Constructivist Approaches in International Relations Theory: Puzzle and Promises', *Constitutionalism Webpapers*, vol. 5, 2006, pp. 1–27.
Wight, M., 'The Balance of Power', in H. Butterfield, M. Wight and H. Bull (eds.), *Diplomatic Investigations: Essays in the Theory of International Politics*, London, Allen & Unwin, 1966, pp. 149–175.
Wight, M., 'Western Values in International Relations', in H. Butterfield, M. Wight and H. Bull (eds.), *Diplomatic Investigations: Essays in the Theory of International Politics*, London, Allen & Unwin, 1966, pp. 89–131.
Wight, M., 'Why Is There no International Theory?', in H. Butterfield, M. Wight and H. Bull (eds.), *Diplomatic Investigations: Essays in the Theory of International Politics*, London, Allen & Unwin, 1966, pp. 17–34.
Zehfuss, M., *Constructivism in International Relations, The Politics of Reality*, Cambridge, Cambridge University Press, 2002.

3 In search of academic tools to evaluate the European Union's identity on the global stage

Anna Skolimowska

Introduction

Research related to the subject of foreign policy of the European Union (EU) reveals two major tendencies.[1] The first refers to the researchers examining the roles of the EU in international relations and distinguishing perspectives of normative power,[2] civilian power,[3] *soft power*[4] etc. The second research tendency consists in examining the matters of perception of the role in international relations agreed to by the European Union.[5] It mainly concerns the analysis of the way the external entities, i.e. states, international organizations or state organizations, perceive the definition of the EU's identity in international relations accepted by itself. It derives from the Constructivist assumption that the role of the EU in external relations is a result of not only its narration and its own definition of its identity and role, but is also a result of this role being recognized by other participants of international relations.

The purpose of this chapter is to show the manner in which researchers, especially the representatives of Constructivism, analyze the role and identity of the EU in external relations within the frames of International Relations and European Studies. The chapter especially focuses on the search for analytical perspectives of that role and identity among the third parties.

The character and the role of a given subject of international relations constitutes an effect not only determined by the definition accepted by it but also is a subject to acceptance of such features and actions of the external environment derived from them.

The chapter analyzes the manner in which the European Studies approach the matter of identity of the EU in the international relations. It concerns answers to the following questions: what is the definition of the EU's international identity but more importantly what is the perception of this identity among external entities? In the third part of the chapter an analysis of the Constructivist way of explaining the phenomenon of the EU's identity will be undertaken.

It is assumed that due to the extraordinary and atypical character of the European Union in international relations it fosters a particular definition of its own international identity. It is a definition of a normative actor promoting the values and rules of the European project in international relations and aiming at regulating its international environment with non-military instruments of foreign policy. The level and scope of the executed politics within the concept of normative power are conditioned by legitimization of that attitude of the European Union by external entities.

The identity of the European Union in European Studies

It is assumed that the EU develops an understanding of its identity as a result of its involvement in international relations. From this perspective the EU's identity should be the reflection of the international order at the given time. The identity of the European Union evolves and depends on the traits of the international environment at the given time.

European Studies have elaborated a number of tools for the analytical approach to the identity and the role of originally the European Communities and at present the European Union in terms of international relations, which provides a clear proof of the existence of a true diversity and great multitude of instruments available in the research on this phenomenon. The most popular concepts include: civilian power, soft power and normative power.

The concept of civilian power, which has been used to characterize the role of the European Communities/the European Union in the world since 1970s, was taken from international relations. It denotes the character of those international entities which foreign policy depends, inter alia, on: accepting the necessity to cooperate with other participants at the international stage (the idea of multilateralism), using non-military instruments (mainly the economic ones) for the security of own interests and readiness to establish transnational structures to solve the appearing problems. Foreign policy of civilian powers refers to economic, diplomatic and cultural means and is not based on military power. The European Communities – due to lack of own military resources – were perceived as civilian power. This manner of analyzing the role of European Communities in the world was developed by F. Duchêne.[6] This approach underlined the role of the European Communities as an entity performing foreign policy based on: economic instruments (common trade policy, development aid, humanitarian aid etc.) with the significant role of non-state actors (the European Commission) and based on intermediation of international organizations – mainly the United Nations. Such role of the European Communities derived from the foregoing logic of the European integration, which developed the fastest in the area of *low politics*. The 1970s was the first time the idea of coordinating foreign policies of the member states of the Communities within the frames of the European Political Cooperation began. Furthermore during the time of the Cold War power race the role of the European Communities as a civilian power seemed to be the only one that was possible.

The concept of the European Union as a civilian power presently constitutes one of the main analytical categories related to the role of the EU in international relations. The civilian power of the European Union is expressed in the dominance of diplomatic cooperation in the context of solving international problems; the superior importance of economic means in attaining targets of foreign policy; and referring to transnational institutions for reaching the targets of foreign policy.[7]

As far as the issue of the role and identity of the European Union in international relations is concerned, the researchers have so far devoted particular attention to the concept of normative power that was developed by Ian Manners, a supporter of the theory of social Constructivism.[8] Manners presents a proposal of the theoretical approach to the way in which the European Union shapes the international environment (by changing its standards and norms), not as much with the use of material instruments (such as military power, economic or legal measures), but through the power of attractiveness of the European project to the third parties encoded in European standards, values, principles and procedures. The policy conducted within such framework towards the external environment is referred to as normative, i.e. promoting the standards, values and principles of the European project in the international sphere with the use of specific political instruments (soft instruments). The conception of social constructivism aims at explaining, inter alia, the reasons for the differences in the way the role and the identity of European Union are perceived by the third states.

The normative aspect of the European Union in international relations indicates its ability to shape standards and norms of the European integration in international environment such as: human dignity, freedom, democracy, equality, state under the rule of law, respect of for human rights. This set includes legal, economic and socio-political norms developed during the European integration and the norms set forth inter alia in the Charter of the United Nations, the Helsinki Final Act, and the Paris Charter or the Universal Declaration of Human Rights. They constitute the uniqueness of the European project and have power to influence the external environment. The normative power of the EU is based on spreading the previously mentioned normative system in relations with third parties. It is achieved through:

- self-acting spread – the European norms spread in third countries without the EU's participation;
- communication strategies – informational actions of the EU;
- procedural activities – institutionalization of relations with the EU;
- transfer – reciprocal benefits in relations between the EU and other states;
- EU's presence in other states;
- cultural diffusion processes of learning the EU norms by third parties.[9]

The normative presence of the European Union in international relations is aimed at changing norms, standards and rules of international politics. This presence is related to the European Union's capacity of influencing the external environment not only with economic instruments (as in the case of the civilian power) but also with the power of attractiveness of the European project for third parties. The instrument for promoting European norms and values consists in persuasion. If the third parties find the European values attractive of persuading, the institutionalization of reciprocal relations appears and political dialogue concerning conditions of cooperation begins. Actions of the European Union for promoting own values are performed through a number of policies (i.e. development assistance, trade, policy of claims etc.). The most important channel of transmission of norms and European values is the political dialogue with third parties. It is related to the need of its institutionalization, for example in the forms of: association agreements, European Neighborhood Policy or strategic partnership. It is accompanied by the process of socializing its participants. The normative aspect of the EU is of ideational character (connected with ability to establish and sustain norms, European values through soft instruments: dialogue, persuasion), not the material one (connected with the economic, military resources held or the population potential). The purpose of the normative foreign policies is to shape the international environment with law, international regimes or organizations. The instruments for normative policies used by the entities in international relations are of the following characters: economic, diplomatic, cultural and social (without the military component). The normative instruments in foreign politics refer to: equal partnership, persuasion, cooperation, conditionality or using sanctions. Legal and political norms developed in this way bind all participants of this process. The normative means of foreign politics must be in accordance with the norms of the international law.

The normative foreign policies are performed within the frames of the international law and it uses means stipulated by it to implement strategies. Legitimization of such policies is constituted by pursuing enhancement of the international law, international institutions and promoting the normative structure of international relations by redeeming and respecting external and internal legal obligations assumed by states.[10]

Formulated at the beginning of the 2000s, the concept of the identity of the European Union as the normative power in international relations became an increasingly popular theoretical tool used by the researchers, which leads to the elaboration of the basic assumptions of the theory. Yet currently this concept faces a certain crisis, reflected both in the criticism towards its theoretical standpoint and in the attempts to falsify it or to transform it deeply. The criticism comes not only from the part of the representatives of the alternative paradigms (such as the political neo-realist school), but also from the environments traditionally supporting the theory.[11] More often the term 'regional normative power' appears to be appropriate for the EU. It points at the limited group of countries where perceptions of EU's normative identity is present. The second challenge relates to the problem of how to support the idea of normative power Europe concept in the regions where major economic or political actors are involved (for example in Asia).

The role of the European Union in international relations according to Constructivism

The Constructivist explanation of the role of the European Union in international environment stems from the claim of its normative influence on third parties.

The result of such a way of thinking on external relations is the concept of the normative role of the European Union in international relations developed by Ian Manners.[12] The role of the European Union in this variant is based on the founding rules of the European project, such as: peace, democracy, human rights, rule of law. Constructivists indicate socialization as the driving force of the process of executing its normative role by the European Union.[13] Socialization is understood as a process pursuing spread of the European order and model throughout the world by bringing the third parties and partners round to its own ideas and norms. It is a mechanism based on the logic of adequacy. The European Union 'teaches' the third parties European rules and values. The external entities accept and follow these rules, if they are convinced that the rules are reasonable and valid and also if they accept the European Union itself. The mechanisms of Europeanization through socialization are easier: when Europeanized entities are in a new or uncertain situation, they identify themselves with or aspire to join the European Union. It is a deliberative process depending on the intensity of contacts between the parties. The process of socialization of the third parties is facilitated by conformity of these states with the European norms, values and rules.[14]

The issue of the role of the European Union in international relations is researched e.g. by Charlotte Bretherton and John Vogler in their work entitled: *The European Union as a Global Actor*.[15] The authors claim that the European Union is not a typical actor in international relations. They call it *multiperspectival policy* being in the process of constant construction. This process is conditioned both by internal and external factors. Furthermore, the European Union is an international community based on values, which it has transformed into an ability to act as a normative actor of international relations. This can be seen through the following forms of its international activity: promotion of human rights, sustainable development, development assistance and humanitarian actions. The EU is able to act in international relations on its own developing policies in this area independent from its member states. The authors refer to constructivist categories of analyzing international politics and roles played by international entities. To achieve that they use the following concepts: opportunity, presence and capabilities.[16] The concept of opportunity refers to conditions created by external environment for the European Union within the scope of executing its role. These conditions are understood here as a process of interpretation of ideas and giving social sense to the actions on the international stage. This perspective towards the chances created for the EU in international relations refers to the research on the discursive process of constructing its international identity by the external environment. These 'meta-narrations', important for constructing its role, are: globalization, co-dependence, the end of the Cold War or the terrorist attack of 11th September 2001. Relating to the discourse on globalization the Constructivists claim that it created a chance for the European Union to play a more significant role in international relations as within its frames it is common to state that states become less effective facing the challenges connected to it. Therefore possibilities for actors like the EU who act on behalf of the member states have been created.

In relation to the concept of the EUs' presence in international relations Ch. Bretherton and J. Vogler understand it as an ability to influence external entities, shape their behavior and practices of actions. They underline that this presence increases in time together with subsequent enlargements and intensification of the European integration. The level of this intensification also performs the legitimizing role and reflects the effectiveness of its political system.[17]

The concept of resources relates to the internal possibilities of external actions of the European Union. They are understood as the ability to form effective external policies and possess adequate political instruments of international influence. They are constituted by: European values, internal legitimization of actions towards the external environment, ability to form priorities and form policies (the concepts referring to the level of institutional coherence of external actions) and the ability to use instruments of foreign policy (negotiations, diplomacy, economic and military means).[18]

Constructivists see the external actions and the role of the European Union in the categories of the process of forming a political community, which Knud Eric Jørgensen called 'the diplomatic republic of Europe'.[19] According to the representatives of the Constructivist theory the process of forming the foreign policy is not constituted by negotiations over the level of execution of interests of states but rather by the phenomenon of evolution of interests and identity of member states participating in external actions of the European Union. The external actions of the European Union are seen here not only as a result of rational calculation of interests of the states but as a process of forming and changing the identity of actors participating in it. Constructivists claim that the European Union is, without doubts, a global actor of international relations and its peculiar presence and role is connected with providing new meanings and with performing new actions on the international stage.

Ben Tonra, a constructivist, claims that the European Union is a new type of participant of international relations, a kind of multi-aspect construct, which through its global activity changes the meaning and perception of foreign policy of the member states. It is also a new type of participant of international relations and a new type of power.[20] EU is able to change the scope and content of foreign policy of its member states due to the fact that there has been a collective context created for: institutionalization of cooperation within the scope of foreign affairs, the manner of exchange of information, setting the schedule of political events and the manner of making decisions. It is a phenomenon known as Brusselization or Brussels inter-governance. These concepts relate to the process which resulted in the national policies being formed in the European context.[21]

Perception of the EU in international relations – some theoretical aspects

The external image of the European Union has become a popular topic within European Studies in recent years. Major research projects have provided general insight into external perceptions of it.

The first systematic study of the external perceptions of the EU was carried out by Martin Holland, Natalia Chaban, Jessica Bain, Katrina Status and Paveena Sutthisripok.[22] The main focus of the study was put on Asia and the Pacific elites and their views on the European Union. The goal of the survey was to identify the comprehensive range of perceptions of and attitudes towards the EU that exist in Asia-Pacific public discourse in: media (print media, newspapers, magazines), public opinion and political elites in New Zealand, Thailand and Australia. The survey took place in 2005 and a total of 71 Asia-Pacific business, political and media elite members were interviewed. Political elites were identified as current members of national parliaments representing different political parties. Media elite were identified as editors/news directors and lead reporters of the media outlets that were established as the national leaders in the EU coverage. Business elite were identified as members of national business round tables, and other official business networks. The study used two questionnaires – one for business and political elites, and another one for media elites. The question order rotated depending on the flow of conversation. Each interview lasted on average 45 minutes.[23] The study utilizes qualitative interpretative methodology capitalizing on its strong insight and interpretation. To improve the reliability of this particular attitudinal research, the collected data was analyzed using content analysis methodology incorporating cognitive semantics tools. The employed methodology revealed the categories that 'mapped' the 'EU' concept via re-construing mental 'schemata' of the concept. Elite interviewees were asked to rate the importance of the EU to their country at present as well as in the future when compared to other significant actors. In terms of its importance the EU was not perceived to be the most important counterpart in any of the three Asia-Pacific countries: Australia was perceived to be the leading counterpart by New Zealand interviewees, the USA was seen as a priority in importance for Australian elites, and Asia led in the perceived importance among Thai respondents. The image of the European Union was usually connected to the image of: bureaucracy, Brussels, economic power, rationalization, prosperity, huge market, trade, trade barriers, economic protectionism, inward looking market.[24] None of the elites perceived the European Union a s a normative power. The image was rather materialistic and connected to the economic/civilian nature of the European project.

The second study of the topic of the Europe's identity perception abroad was taken by Sonia Lucarelli and Lorenzo Fioramonti in 2010.[25] The starting point of the survey was the following hypothesis: the way in which the EU is perceived by other countries is likely to have a direct bearing on its success as a player in the international arena. What the world thinks of the EU is therefore an important factor in facilitating or opposing the achievements of EU-sponsored policies. Comprehending the perceptions of the EU can help gauge the extent to which the Union is seen as a credible and consistent actor in global politics. Furthermore, they can also help assess the extent to which the European 'soft power' is still a reality in the eyes of citizens around the world. Moreover, external images might tell us something on the degree of the EU's effective communication skills, which, according to the Middle Eastern diplomat mentioned in the incipit, is not high.[26] In a way perceptions can be seen as 'early warning systems' for an actor such as the EU, which is still in the process of establishing itself as a credible international focal point. What this literature has not done so far is to investigate the impact and effectiveness of the EU's performance on the images that it projects of itself abroad: no systematic research has been conducted on 'external views' worldwide. The failure to investigate external images not only results in a gap in the literature that deserves to be filled, but it might also have/have had important practical repercussions. We share the view that common identity for the Europeans can only be political, grounded in the set of social and political values and principles that Europeans are ready to recognize as theirs, that make them feel like a political group. According to this view, culture, history, policies and institutions are the frameworks in which the interpretation of political values takes place, thereby giving meaning to political identity. The country studies identify images of the EU in the United States of America (USA), Russia and China, Iran and Lebanon, Israel and Palestine, Mexico and, finally, India, Brazil and South Africa. These countries were selected as they represent a diverse range of perspectives, which might allow for interesting generalizations while providing a good approximation of the whole range of global perspectives. The perception analysis is organized around four different groups: public opinion, political and business elites, civil society and the media. This methodological set-up proved quite useful in order to identify different images of the EU in the various groups, based on the conviction that different stakeholders within the same country might hold a diverse range of opinions about the EU from 2006 to 2008.

The previously mentioned surveys show that European Union identity and its perception abroad is not a clear category. Europeans officially create the perception of the EU as an example of civilian or even normative power in the international relations while the perception within the global partners might be different. It is rather an image of Europe as a trading partner than global 'force for good' and a promoter of universal values of humanity. For some regions (i.e. Australia or New Zealand) the European Union is an important partner but still in the shadow of USA. From this perspective it is fair to say that EU is not a global superpower but rather a regional power or even a sectoral power when it comes to economy and trade. Normative discourse is not so much present outside the world (except countries of the nearest neighborhood).

Identity can be said to be constructed as a consequence of a two-step process. First there is a formation of a 'Self'. Second, the Self is shaped in its relation to a set of specific and generic 'Others' in the social context in which the Self is inserted. In the second part of the process, the collective Self is shaped in its contact with Others. Identities can, in this sense, be said to only truly acquire meaning when they come into contact with Others inside a determined social context. Moreover 'we-ness' and its resulting collective agency can be said to be successful when Others accept and welcome such identity/agency. If on the contrary outsiders' balance sheet of that identity/agency is mostly negative, then this is a sign of that the Self is not adequately constructed for its social context and/or has not been adequately molded to fit into the environment in which it is inserted.[27]

Constructing of the EU's identity

The Constructivist explanation of the identity of the European Union in the international environment becomes popular since the 90's of the 20th century when the European Union appeared on the map of political international relations after Treaty of Maastricht provisions came into the force. The interest in the identity issues emerged from the analysis of the European Union's growing political role in the IR that could not be described using the known tools for analyzing states' foreign policy since the EU is not a state and does not conduct state-like foreign policy. For that reason scholars needed to develop and search for new tools for describing the EU's character in the IR.[28] Some scholars referred to the idea of the role or actorness of the European Union, whereas the more Constructivist-oriented though of the EU as a specific political community that develops its own international identity.

We can distinguish three Constructivist strands when it comes to European identity: conventional, post-modern and critical.[29] The conventional Constructivist scholars ask questions about the factors that influenced the identity change of the European Union in the international relations. They explore how the identity of the EU is constructed in the course of social interaction; through encounters with other actors; and in the context of the external environment of institutions and events, which enable and constrain EU action, acquired through internalization or socialization by the citizens of the Union.

The European Union from the beginning searched her own identity in the international relations. It should be noted that the expression of her identity is EU's foreign policy. The European Union is present in international relations by external economic relations (within the framework of the Common Commercial Policy, rendered development assistance, cooperation with third countries, humanitarian aid, etc.) and the foreign policy conducted within Common Foreign and Security Policy (CFSP). Institutionally, the character of European integration is twofold: communitarian/supranational (for economic cooperation) and intergovernmental (for cooperation under the CFSP). Although the Treaty of Lisbon unified the structure of the European Union by eliminating its pillar structure – which is an expression of the preceding logic – in relation to external relations, their specificity has been preserved. Integration in the scope of CFSP has a different organizational and decision-making framework than in the context of economic relations. Making decisions here is in the nature of agreements and compromises between member states, and is not done at the level of the European institutions independent from them. The European Union's role in foreign affairs is to coordinate the positions of member states and establish strategies and an agenda for joint action. This area of European integration consists of the cooperation of sovereign member states in foreign matters, which is expressed by leaving unanimity as the main method of making decisions and limiting the role of supranational institutions (*Treaty on European Union*, 2009, Title V).

Important elements in the foreign relations of the European Union are the activities undertaken by member states as part of national foreign policies. In accordance with the provisions of the Treaty of Lisbon, cooperation in the field of foreign affairs between member states has an intergovernmental character and is not in conflict with national foreign policies.[30] The spaces of communication, negotiation and deliberation are institutions in which the member states coordinate their foreign policies and strive to develop a common European position. These include the European Council and the Council of the European Union. The implementation of the adopted arrangements rests on the shoulders of the High Representative for Foreign Affairs and Security Policy, the President of the European Council and the member states.

Based on the preceding claims regarding the specific nature of the European Union's foreign relations, it can be noted that they differ from the national foreign policy model. Activities on the European Union forum (in particular under the CFSP) involve the coordination, negotiation and setting of joint strategies, positions and actions by the member states.

EU's foreign policy is fragmented, and its meaning disputed. Different national and institutional actors converge in the making of international discourses about international activity (i.a. European Council, Council of the European Union, High Representative of the Union for Foreign Affairs and Security Policy).

In 2003 the first of the political documents, containing the self-definition of the European Union's identity in international relations, was prepared (*European Security Strategy*, 2003). This document contains an indication of the civil and normative nature of European identity. It emphasizes the challenges for European security, such as terrorism, the availability of weapons of mass destruction, organized crime, the weakening of the state system and the privatization of the armed forces. Europe's response to these challenges was to increase the potential to mobilize all necessary civilian resources in crisis and post-crisis situations. It was mainly about civilian instruments (soft) such as increasing diplomatic capabilities, better exchange of intelligence information between member states and partners, increasing the number of civilian missions or strengthening the EU's operational capabilities within NATO in the field of crisis management. The strategy assumed cooperation with neighboring countries in the democratization process and economic issues. The document also contains an indication of the reference to international law and the United Nations system as guarantors of the order of the international trace.

The European Security Strategy of 2003, however, did not respond either to the content or the form of the challenges and threats which the European Union and its members faced at that time. In 2015, the European Council entrusted the High Representative with the task of developing a new global EU strategy in the field of foreign and security policy. It was determined that member states expected such a document to be produced by June 2016. Many entities took part in the process of reflection on the directions and assumptions of the new global strategy of the European Union. Not only European institutions (including the European Parliament), national parliaments, expert circles (from Poland it was, inter alia, the Polish Institute of International Affairs), but also civil society.

The effect of this process was the development and presentation of the assumptions of the global EU strategy in the field of foreign and security policy in June 2016. The new document entitled: *Common vision, joint action: A stronger Europe – The global strategy for the foreign and security policy of the European Union*, includes the assumptions of the new global strategy of the European Union in the international relations:

> The strategy is to express the ambition of the strategic autonomy of the European Union. We live in times of existential crisis, both within the European Union and outside it. Our Union is at risk. Our European project, which brought unprecedented peace, prosperity and democracy, is now being questioned. In the east, the European security order has been violated, and terrorism and violence are afflicting North Africa and the Middle East, as well as Europe itself. Growth is not keeping pace with demographic change, security tensions in Asia are getting worse and climate change is causing further distortions.

Analyzing the philosophy of new strategic assumptions of the European Union in international relations, one can point to the evolution of thinking about the role of the EU in the world and the emergence of reflection on the need to develop real instruments of international influence. This evolution, in relation also to the Strategy from 2003, is expressed in the departure from the idealistic vision of the international environment and the role that the European Union should play in it. Until now it was a role described as a 'normative actor'.

Meanwhile, the new strategic document from 2016 draws attention to the concept of 'principled pragmatism' as a philosophy of EU external relations. It means that the actions of the European Union in the international environment will be the result of a realistic assessment of the environment, to which it will respond with more adequate external policy instruments. The document focuses not so much on instruments of soft international influence such as economic instruments, promotion of democracy, human rights, institutionalization of cooperation, but clearly emphasizes the need to authenticate the EU's position in external relations by means of military external policy instruments:

> Priority issue is investing in security and defense in particular. In order to be able to respond to external crises, build the potential of our partners and guarantee the security of Europe, a full spectrum of defense capabilities is necessary.

The strategy devotes much space to issues related to the need to strengthen the European defense dimension and build independent forces capable of defending and guaranteeing European interests in the world. There are numerous references to the idea of multilateralism and the reform of global governance proposal for the area, which could compete, for example, with the Russian offer.

Conclusion

The EU and the process of European integration in foreign policy matters are contested discursive fields[31] with an open and heterogeneous discursive environment, where the very existence of a minimum of cultural homogeneity is a matter of discussion.[32] Throughout its evolution, the main scholars of European integration have used a variety of terms to describe the EU (and previously the European Community), such as 'civilian power' and 'normative power'.

The extraordinary character of the European Union in international relations is a challenge for scholars of both international relations and European Studies. The studies devoted to the external activities of the European Union face this challenge. On one hand, there are many analyses of the Common Foreign and Security Policy or external economic activity. On the other hand, there are only a few analyses of the problem of the EU's identity in the global stage and, what is more important, on the perception of this identity among external actors. When it comes to the identity issue, the normative power concept was a popular theoretical perspective used by scholars. With time, however, it seems to be losing its analytical validity. Some modifications of the concepts have appeared, such as the term 'regional normative power' presented by H. Larsen.

European Studies lack, however, the profound and complex studies on the perception of the European Union's normative identity – or any other form of identity – among third parties. According to the Constructivist explanations of international reality, the identity phenomenon of actors cannot be separated from the internal and external perceptions of this phenomenon. From this point of view it is expected to develop studies in this direction, which could possibly also improve the debate about the identity of the European Union and its definition in international relations.

Thomas Diez is of the opinion that the concept of a normative power has become an important subject of discussion in the field of European Studies. However, a number of important questions related thereto give rise to controversies, among which he lists:

1 issue of dichotomy: the particular interests of the member states versus collective European norms in external relations. This particular issue has seemed quite visible, for example, in relation to the attitude adopted by the EU towards the democratic movements in the Arab states (referred to as 'the Arab Spring'). On one hand, the European Union declared that it would take an active part in building democracy in the region; while on the other, it has supported authoritarian regimes in order to stop the wave of migrants crossing the Mediterranean Sea and in order to secure petroleum supplies coming to Europe;[33]
2 issue of establishing whether the EU as a normative power constitutes an effective actor in international relations; that is, whether the European norms truly influence the behavior of third states: when researched, this question

presents a number of difficulties, as the EU is usually merely one of the actors in the process. It is equally difficult to provide a conclusive and unambiguous proof that, at a given moment, it was the European norms that most influenced the course of events;

3 issue of the level of analysis of the normative power of the EU: in view of the fact that the supranational integration model for external affairs has not yet been established, research into this matter must encompass a number of actors taking part in the process; this concerns both the member states and private actors, such as European companies involved in weapons trade.[34]

Kalypso Nicolaïdis and Robert Howse state that the image of the EU's role in international relations is created by the EU itself and does not reflect its actual role but constitutes a reflection of an ideal that Europe wishes to attain.[35] This means that the European Union does not truly export its normative offer, but rather a certain representation of what the EU wishes to be. The authors of this concept refer to it as 'EUtopia', i.e. a utopia that the European Union has created about itself. Hence the international activity of the EU constitutes a form of a projection or a presentation of the myth that Europe is a community of norms and values. This particular strategy is based on the assumption that the EU is indeed a role model for the rest of the world and that it sets an example to be followed. This attitude can be seen, for instance, in the European support for regional forms of integration in various parts of the world, such as, for example, the African Union. However, as pointed out by Nicolaïdis and Howse, the true identity of the EU and the image that it wishes to create in international relations are not consistent, which, in turn, decreases its credibility in the eyes of the international public.

Notes

1 More on this subject: H. Larsen, 'The EU as a Normative Power and the Research on External Perceptions: The Missing Link', *Journal of Common Market Studies*, vol. 52, no. 4, 2014, pp. 896–910.
2 I. Manners, 'Normative Power Europe: A Contradiction In Terms?', *Journal of Common Market Studies*, vol. 40, no. 2, 2002, pp. 235–258.
3 F. Duchêne, 'Europe's Role in World Peace', in R.J. Mayne (ed.), *Europe Tomorrow: Sixteen Europeans Look Ahead*, London, HarperCollins Distribution Services, 1972, pp. 32–47; K.E. Smith, 'Still "Civilian Power EU"?', Paper presented at the CIDEL Workshop, *From Civilian to Military Power: The European Union at a Crossroads?*, Oslo, 2004, www.arena.uio.no/cidel/WorkshopOsloSecurity/Smith.pdf, (accessed 25 June 2018).
4 E. Tulmets, 'The European Union: A Soft Power with Civilian Means?', *Kultura i Polityka,* vol. 2/3, 2008, pp. 60–74; B. Piskorska, *Soft Power w Polityce Unii Europejskiej Wobec Państw Partnerstwa Wschodniego*, Lublin, Wydawnictwo KUL, 2017.
5 E.g. the works of: N. Chaban, O. Elgström, and M. Holland, 'The European Union as Others See It', *European Foreign Affairs Review*, vol. 11, 2004, pp. 245–262.
6 Duchêne, Europe's Role in World Peace'.
7 K. Twitchet (ed.), *Europe and the World: The External Relations of the Common Market*, New York, St. Martin's Press, 1976, pp. 1–2.

8 I. Manners, 'The Concept of Normative Power in World Politics', *DIIS Brief*, May 2009, http://pure.diis.dk/ws/files/68745/B09_maj_Concept_Normative_Power_World_Politics.pdf, (accessed 25 June 2018).
9 I. Manners, 'Normative Power Europe: The International Role of the EU', *Archive of European Integration,* 2001, http://aei.pitt.edu/7263/, (accessed 25 June 2018), p. 13.
10 N. Tocci, 'Profiling Normative Foreign Policy: The European Union and its Global Partners', *CEPS Working Document*, vol. 279, 2007, p. 7.
11 H. Larsen, 'The EU as a Normative Power and the Research on External Perceptions', pp. 896–910.
12 Manners, 'Normative Power Europe: A Contradiction', pp. 235–258.
13 Manners, 'Normative Power Europe: A Contradiction', pp. 235–258.
14 F. Schimmelfennig, 'Europeanization Beyond the Member States', Paper for: Zeitschrift für Staats- und Europawissenschaften, 2010, www.ethz.ch/content/dam/ethz/special-interest/gess/cis/european-politics-dam/documents/People/Publications/Europeanization/Member_.pdf, (accessed 25 June 2018), p. 9; J. Kamińska, 'Europeizacja Polskiej Polityki Zagranicznej', *Studia Europejskie*, vol. 3, 2008, pp. 23–38.
15 Ch. Bretherton and J. Vogler, *The European Union as a Global Actor*, New York, Routledge, 2006.
16 Bretherton and Vogler, *The European Union as a Global Actor*, p. 24.
17 Bretherton and Vogler, *The European Union as a Global Actor*, pp. 25–29.
18 A. Skolimowska, 'Teoretyczne i Empiryczne Zastosowanie Konstruktywizmu do Analizy Zewnętrznych Relacji Unii Europejskiej', in J. Czaputowicz (ed.), *Zastosowanie Konstruktywizmu w Studiach Europejskich*, Warsaw, Wydawnictwo Uniwersytetu Warszawskiego, 2015, pp. 109–135.
19 K.E. Jørgensen, 'PoCo: The Diplomatic Republic of Europe', in K.E. Jørgensen (ed.), *Reflective Approaches to European Governance*, Basingstoke, Palgrave Macmillan, 1997, pp. 167–180.
20 B. Tonra, 'Conceptualizing the European Union's Global Role', in M. Cini and A.K. Bourne (eds.), *Palgrave advances in European Union studies*, New York, Palgrave Macmillan, 2006, p. 117.
21 Tonra, 'Conceptualizing the European Union's Global Role', p. 117.
22 M. Holland et al., 'EU in the Views of Asia-Pacific Elites: Australia, New Zealand and Thailand', *NCRE Research Series*, no. 5, Canterbury, National Centre for Research on Europe, 2005, http://aei.pitt.edu/10938/1/appp_elites_publication.pdf, (accessed 25 June 2018).
23 Holland et al., 'EU in the Views of Asia-Pacific Elites', pp. 1–22.
24 Holland et al., 'EU in the Views of Asia-Pacific Elites', pp. 14–16.
25 S. Lucarelli and L. Fioramonti, *External Perceptions of the European Union as a Global Actor*, London, Routledge, 2010.
26 Lucarelli and Fioramonti, *External Perceptions of the European Union*, p. 18.
27 E. Johansson-Nogués, 'Is the EU's Foreign Policy Identity an Obstacle? The European Union, the Northern Dimension and the Union for the Mediterranean', *European Political Economy Review*, vol. 9, 2009, p. 27.
28 R. Whitman, 'The International Identity of the European Union', paper presented to 22nd ECPR Joint Sessions of Workshops, Madrid, April 1994; R. Whitman, 'The International Identity of the EU: Instruments as Identity' in A. Landau and R. Whitman (eds.), *Rethinking the European Union: Institutions, Interests and Identities*, Basingstoke, Palgrave Macmillan, 1997, pp. 54–71; R. Whitman, *From Civilian Power to Superpower? The International Identity of the European Union*, Basingstoke, Palgrave Macmillan, 1998; I. Manners, 'The International Identity of the European Union: Its Internal Construction' paper presented to panel on 'Explaining the International Identity of the European Union', convenors: Richard Whitman and Ian Manners, UACES Annual Research Conference, Loughborough University, September 1997; I. Manners

and J. Raux, 'L'identité Internationale de l'Union Européene', paper presented to group on 'Federalisation of the Union: Myths and Realities?', Contributions for the meeting of the 6–7 July 2000, Intergovernmental Conference 2000.

29 J. Checkel, 'Constructivist Approaches to European Integration', *Arena Working Paper*, vol. 6, 2006, p. 5.

30 The changes introduced by the Lisbon Treaty in the institutional structure under the CFSP are: strengthening the European Council by granting it the status of an EU institution and equipping it with the possibility of issuing binding acts (decisions); separation and creation of two separate configurations within the Council of the European Union: General Affairs Council and Foreign Affairs Council. This exercise was aimed at distinguishing foreign issues from the current issues of European integration; establishment of the institution of the High Representative of the Union for Foreign Affairs and Security Policy (Article 18 TEU). It is appointed to this position by the European Council (acting by a qualified majority) with the consent of the President of the Commission. The High Representative leads the CFSP (the new office combined the tasks of the former two institutions: the High Representative for the Common Foreign and Security Policy and the Commissioner for external relations). He contributes, through his proposals, to the development of CFSP and implements it, acting on the authority of the Council. This also applies to the Common Security and Defense Policy. The High Representative is also the Vice-President of the European Commission (she is responsible for her responsibilities in the field of external relations and coordinates its policies in this matter) and presides over the Foreign Affairs Council (ensures coherence and continuity of work in the field of EU foreign policy). It is also the creation of the European External Action Service, which supports the work of the High Representative. The service cooperates with the diplomatic services of the member states and consists of officials from the relevant services of the General Secretariat of the Council and the Commission, as well as personnel seconded by national diplomatic services. It started functioning on January 1, 2011. The office of the permanent President of the European Council was also appointed and equipped with the competence to conduct external activities. He is responsible for the preparation and continuity of the work of the European Council, in cooperation with the President of the Commission and on the basis of the work of the General Affairs Council. The activities of EU bodies in the field of external activities are supported by such institutions as: COREPER, the Political and Security Committee, the European Defense Agency or the European Union Satellite Center. The role of the European Commission in the field of the CFSP is defined by the Treaties. The Court of Justice of the European Union is not competent in this matter, with the exception of jurisdiction to control compliance with the legality of certain decisions. The role of the European Parliament in the field of external relations has been strengthened by, inter alia, the ability to address questions or formulate recommendations to the Council and the High Representative. Twice a year it conducts a debate on the progress of the CFSP, including a common security and defense policy.

31 C. Hay and B. Rosamond, 'Globalisation, European Integration and the Discursive Construction of Economic Imperatives', *Journal of European Public Policy*, vol. 9, no. 2, 2002, p. 151.

32 T. Diez, Speaking Europe, Drawing Boundaries: Reflections on the Role of Discourse in EU Foreign Policy and Identity, in C. Carta and J-F. Morin (eds.), *EU Foreign Policy Through the Lens of Discourse Analysis Making Sense of Diversity*, London, Ashgate Publishing Limited, 2014, pp. 27–41.

33 T. Diez, 'Constructing the Self and Changing Others: Reconsidering Normative Power Europe', *Millennium: Journal of International Studies*, vol. 33, no. 3, 2015, p. 635.

34 T. Diez, *Normative Power as Hegemony*, Paper for presentation at the 2011 EUSA Biennial International Conference, Boston, MA, 3–5 March 2011, http://euce.org/eusa/2011/papers/7l_thomas.pdf, (accessed 25 June 2018), p. 2.

35 K. Nicolaïdis and R. Howse, 'This Is My EUtopia. . .: Narrative as Power', *Journal of Common Market Studies*, vol. 40, no. 4, 2002, p. 768.

Bibliography

Bretherton, Ch. and J. Vogler, *The European Union as a Global Actor*, New York, Routledge, 2006.

Brubaker, R., and F. Cooper, 'Beyond "Identity" ', *Theory and Society*, vol. 29, 2000, pp. 1–47.

Busekist, von A., 'Uses and Misuses of the Concept of Identity', *Security Dialogue*, vol. 35, no. 1, 2004, pp. 81–98.

Chaban, N., O. Elgström and M. Holland, 'The European Union as Others See It', *European Foreign Affairs Review*, vol. 11, 2004, pp. 245–262.

Checkel, J., 'Constructivist Approaches to European Integration', *Arena Working Paper*, vol. 6, 2006.

Checkel, J. and P. Katzenstein, *European Identity*, New York, Cambridge University Press, 2009.

Diez, T., 'Constructing the Self and Changing Others: Reconsidering Normative Power Europe', *Millennium: Journal of International Studies*, vol. 33, no. 3, 2015, pp. 613–636.

Diez, T., *Normative Power as Hegemony*, Paper presented at the 2011 EUSA Biennial International Conference, Boston, MA, 3–5 March 2011, http://euce.org/eusa/2011/papers/7l_thomas.pdf, (accessed 25 June 2018).

Diez, T., *Speaking Europe, Drawing Boundaries: Reflections on the Role of Discourse in EU Foreign Policy and Identity*, in C. Carta and J-F. Morin (eds.), *EU Foreign Policy Through the Lens of Discourse Analysis Making Sense of Diversity*, London, Ashgate Publishing Limited, 2014, pp. 27–41.

Duchêne, F., 'Europe's Role in World Peace', in R.J. Mayne (ed.), *Europe Tomorrow: Sixteen Europeans Look Ahead*, London, HarperCollins Distribution Services, 1972, pp. 32–47.

Erikson, E., *Identity: Youth and Crisis*, New York, W.W. Norton Company, 1968.

Hay, C. and B. Rosamond, 'Globalisation, European Integration and the Discursive Construction of Economic Imperatives', *Journal of European Public Policy*, vol. 9, no. 2, 2002, pp. 147–167.

Holland, M. et al., 'EU in the Views of Asia-Pacific Elites: Australia, New Zealand and Thailand', *NCRE Research Series*, no 5, 2005, http://aei.pitt.edu/10938/1/appp_elites_publication.pdf, (accessed 25 June 2018).

Hopf, T., 'The Promise of Constructivism in International Relations Theory', *International Security*, vol. 23, no. 1, 1998, pp. 171–200.

Jørgensen, K.E., 'PoCo: The Diplomatic Republic of Europe', in K.E. Jørgensen (ed.), *Reflective Approaches to European Governance*, Basingstoke, Palgrave Macmillan, 1997, pp. 167–180.

Kamińska, J., 'Europeizacja Polskiej Polityki Zagranicznej', *Studia Europejskie*, vol. 3, 2008, pp. 23–38.

Larsen, H., 'The EU as a Normative Power and the Research on External Perceptions: The Missing Link', *Journal of Common Market Studies*, vol. 52, no. 4, 2014, pp. 896–910.

Lucarelli, S. and L. Fioramonti, *External Perceptions of the European Union as a Global Actor*, London, Routledge, 2010.

Manners, I., 'Normative Power Europe: A Contradiction in Terms?', *Journal of Common Market Studies*, vol. 40, no. 2, 2002, pp. 235–258.

Manners, I., 'Normative Power Europe: The International Role of the EU', *Archive of European Integration*, 2001, http://aei.pitt.edu/7263/, (accessed 25 June 2018).

Manners, I., 'The Concept of Normative Power in World Politics', *DIIS Brief*, May, 2009, http://pure.diis.dk/ws/files/68745/B09_maj_Concept_Normative_Power_World_Politics.pdf, (accessed 25 June 2018).

Manners, I., 'The International Identity of the European Union: Its Internal Construction' paper presented to panel on 'Explaining the International Identity of the European Union', convenors: Richard Whitman and Ian Manners, UACES Annual Research Conference, Loughborough University, September 1997.

Manners, I. and J. Raux, 'L'identité Internationale de l'Union Européene', Paper Presented to Group on 'Federalisation of the Union: Myths and Realities?', Contributions for the Meeting of the 6–7 July 2000, Intergovernmental Conference.

Manners, I. and R. Whitman, *The 'Difference Engine' Constructing and Representing the International Identity of the European Union*, Copenhagen, Copenhagen Peace Research Institute, 2001, https://rucforsk.ruc.dk/ws/portalfiles/portal/38395747, (accessed 25 June 2018).

Marcusen, M., et al., 'Constructing Europe? The Evolution of Nation-State Identities', in T. Christiansen, K.E. Jørgensen and A. Wiener (eds.), *The Social Construction of Europe*, London, Sage Publications, 2001, pp. 101–120.

Nicolaïdis, K. and R. Howse, 'This is my Eutopia. . . .: Narrative as Power', *Journal of Common Market Studies*, vol. 40, no. 4, 2002, pp. 767–792.

Piskorska, B., *Soft Power w Polityce Unii Europejskiej Wobec Państw Partnerstwa Wschodniego*, Lublin, Wydawnictwo KUL, 2017.

Reus-Smit, Ch., 'Konstruktywizm', in S. Burchill, et al. (eds.), *Teorie Stosunków Międzynarodowych*, Warsaw, Wydawnictwo Naukowe UW, 2006, pp. 269–296.

Smith, K.E., 'Still 'Civilian Power EU'?', Paper Presented at the CIDEL Workshop, *From Civilian to Military Power: The European Union at a Crossroads?*, Oslo, 2004, www.arena.uio.no/cidel/WorkshopOsloSecurity/Smith.pdf, (accessed 25 June 2018).

Schimmelfennig, F., 'Europeanization Beyond the Member States', Paper for: Zeitschrift für Staats- und Europawissenschaften, 2010, www.ethz.ch/content/dam/ethz/special-interest/gess/cis/european-politics-dam/documents/People/Publications/Europeanization/Member_.pdf, (accessed 25 June 2018).

Skolimowska, A., 'Teoretyczne i Empiryczne Zastosowanie Konstruktywizmu do Analizy Zewnętrznych Relacji Unii Europejskiej', in J. Czaputowicz (ed.), *Zastosowanie Konstruktywizmu w Studiach Europejskich*, Warsaw, Wydawnictwo Uniwersytetu Warszawskiego, 2015, pp. 109–135.

Tocci, N., 'Profiling Normative Foreign Policy: The European Union and Its Global Partners', *CEPS Working Document*, vol. 279, 2007, pp. 1–18.

Tonra, B., 'Conceptualizing the European Union's Global Role', in M. Cini and A.K. Bourne (eds.), *Palgrave advances in European Union studies*, New York, Palgrave Macmillan, 2006, pp. 117–130.

Tulmets, E., 'The European Union: A Soft Power with Civilian Means?', *Kultura i Polityka*, vol. 2/3, 2008, pp. 60–74.

Twitchet, K. (ed.), *Europe and the World: The External Relations of the Common Market*, New York, St. Martin's Press, 1976.

Wendt, A., 'Anarchy Is What States Make of It: The Social Construction of Power Politics', *International Organization*, vol. 46, no. 2, 1992, pp. 391–425.

Wendt, A., 'Collective Identity Formation and the International State', *The American Political Science Review*, vol. 88, no. 2, 1994, pp. 384–396.

Wendt, A., 'Identity and Structural Change in International Politics', in Y. Lapid and F. Kratochwil (eds.), *The Return of Culture and Identity in IR Theory*, Boulder-London, Lynne Rienner Publisher, 1996, pp. 47–64.

Wendt, A., *Social Theory of International Politics*, Cambridge, Cambridge University Press, 1999.

Wendt, A., *Społeczna Teoria Stosunków Międzynarodowych*, Warsaw, Wydawnictwo Naukowe Scholar, 2008.

Whitman, R., *From Civilian Power to Superpower? The International Identity of the European Union*, Basingstoke, Palgrave Macmillan, 1998.

Whitman, R., 'The International Identity of the EU: Instruments as Identity' in A. Landau and R. Whitman (eds.), *Rethinking the European Union: Institutions, Interests and Identities*, Basingstoke, Palgrave Macmillan, 1997, pp. 54–71.

Whitman, R., 'The International Identity of the European Union', Paper Presented to 22nd ECPR Joint Sessions of Workshops, Madrid, April 1994.

Wight, M., 'The Balance of Power', in H. Butterfield, M. Wight and H. Bull (eds.), *Diplomatic Investigations: Essays in the Theory of International Politics*, London, Allen & Unwin, 1966, pp. 149–175.

Wight, M., 'Western Values in International Relations', in H. Butterfield, M. Wight and H. Bull (eds.), *Diplomatic Investigations: Essays in the Theory of International Politics*, London, Allen & Unwin, 1966, pp. 89–131.

Wight, M., 'Why Is There no International Theory?', in H. Butterfield, M. Wight and H. Bull (eds.), *Diplomatic Investigations: Essays in the Theory of International Politics*, London, Allen & Unwin, 1966, pp. 17–34.

Zehfuss, M., 'Constructivism and Identity: A Dangerous Liaison', *European Journal of International Relations*, vol. 7, no. 3, 2001, pp. 315–348.

4 The social construction of identity and belonging

Perceptions of EU in the Western Balkans

Laura Maria Herţa and Adrian Corpădean

Introduction and research design

The main objective of the chapter is to explore identity construction and reconstruction in countries currently associated with the Western Balkans, previously parts of Yugoslavia. The methodological approach is a social-constructivist one. Therefore, concepts such as identity, perceptions, social facts and social world, discourse, structures and agency will be pivotal in this endeavour. Since this chapter focuses on EU's relations with countries from the Western Balkans and investigates their enlargement conditionality and future prospects for membership, Croatia will be excluded from this analysis. Also, because one goal here is to explore identity, belonging and perceptions on the *self* and the *other*, from Yugoslavia to Western Balkans, hence focusing on former republics and provinces of Former Yugoslavia, Albania will also be excluded from this analysis. This chapter is structured in three main parts. The first will analyse the construction of identity in communist Yugoslavia and will focus on the meanings associated with the Yugoslav civic identity. Also, external perception of the wars occurring during the break-up of Yugoslavia will be presented and analysed. The second section of this chapter will provide an overview of EU's relations with each country from the region (except from Croatia and Albania for reasons mentioned previously). The last part of this research will present perception on EU from the Western Balkan countries.

From Yugoslavia to Western Balkans: discursive practices and the social construction of identity and belonging

Yugoslavism as identity construction

The second Yugoslav state (often referred to as "Tito's Yugoslavia") was born in 1943 at Jajce, when the Partisan congress voted to reconstruct the old state as a new federal one comprising of six republics (Serbia, Croatia, Slovenia, Montenegro, Macedonia, and Bosnia-Herzegovina) and two autonomous provinces within Serbia (Vojvodina and Kosovo-Metohija). As indicated by scholars, the ethnic identities of constituent peoples were represented in two ways. On one hand, *narodi* signified the status of Slovenes, Croats, Serbs, Macedonians and

Montenegrins as nationality groups that enjoyed equal constitutional status. They were acknowledged as the "constitutive nations". Later, in 1974, the Muslims, including the Bosnian Muslims, were added to this category. On the other hand, *narodnosti* referred to nationalities that existed in Yugoslavia as protected minorities (Albanians, Hungarians, Slovaks etc.).[1] In territorial terms, the republics comprising post-Second World War federal Yugoslavia were created based on national and historical principles and were defined as "sovereign homelands of sovereign nations".[2] The minorities within the republics, while enjoying the same rights as the majority, "were defined as part of their own nation" (such as the Serbs living in Eastern Croatia or Bosnia-Herzegovina).[3]

The Yugoslav Federation was based on the structure of political power which roughly corresponded to ethnic identities and historical experiences. Nevertheless, as Franke Wilmer indicated, "certain discontinuities were as deeply rooted in historical experiences as the continuities": for instance, many Serbs living for centuries in Eastern Slavonia, which according to the boundaries constructed by Tito was "in" Croatia, did not identify themselves as "Croatians", but thought of themselves "as members of the Serbian *narodi*, who just happened to live in Croatia".[4] Except for Bosnia Herzegovina, the republics were considered national states, in the sense that they were more or less tantamount to the homeland of the dominant nationality living within the frontiers of each republic. But, at the same time, as Paul Shoup observed, they were meant to act as counterforce for national emotions, without diminishing the power of the communist party.[5] The recurrent theme of Tito's partisans was the need to conceive a political organization capable of annihilating the divisive forces of nationalism and capable of remedying the flaws of the interwar Kingdom of Serbs, Croats and Slovenes. The slogan *Brotherhood and Unity* (*Bratstvo i jedinstvo*) was meant to support such ambitions. During the Second World War the Yugoslav Communist Party had tried to unite all the "patriotic", "antifascist" forces in an all-Yugoslav "national liberation struggle". According to Aleksa Djilas, this policy was efficient enough, so that different political parties joined the Partisan movement.[6]

According to Dennis Rusinow, in the immediate aftermath of the war, the recognition of separate national cultures and identities, the creation of republics treated as self-standing national states, and the presence of a multinational leading apparatus (replacing the old Serb-dominated one) had an enormous psychological impact and managed to reconcile, temporarily, inter-communal strife and tensions.[7] The memory of violence and suffering experienced during the Second World War was somehow alleviated by prospects accompanying the new structure of the state. As George Schőpflin emphasized, the traumatizing and horrid recollection of fratricidal war and disunity led many people to believe that their ethnic identities were no longer such a powerful source of meaning (as they were during the interwar period), even though 'people continued to identify themselves with their ethnic affiliation'.[8] Thus, ethnic identities coexisted with an all-encompassing Yugoslav identity.

The underlying unifying value in the new political structure was centred on equality,[9] which was formalized on several levels in the 1946 constitution. First of all, Yugoslav citizens enjoyed "equal rights and duties, regardless of nationality or religion", according to the constitution. This form of equality emerged from the Partisan conception of the liberation struggle, embedded in the wartime slogan *Brotherhood and Unity*, which had promised that members of different nations of Yugoslavia would fight, work and live together with equal rights and duties. Second of all, not only citizens, but also all nations of Yugoslavia were considered equal. Federal Yugoslavia was defined as "a community of peoples with equal rights", according to Article 1 of the constitution. The equality of nations was synonymous to the absence of one "leading nation". Another form of equality was actually a derivative of Yugoslav communist discourse, which emphasized the contribution of all nations of Yugoslavia to the struggle for national liberation, but this "equality applied only to the South Slav nations of Yugoslavia" whereas non-South Slav minorities, such as Germans, Italians, Hungarians and Albanians were excluded.[10] Therefore, the Federal Socialist State was firmly rooted within the narrative of partisan struggle against fascists during the Second World War.

Mirko Tepavać, former foreign minister in ex-Yugoslavia, expressed amazement to the fact that in just two years after the Second World War, Tito and his partisan followers managed to establish a peaceful coexistence, however coercive. Immediate Titoist actions included the trial and punishment of pro-Axis war criminals, as well as the anathemization of all expressions of nationalism, while the slogan of "brotherhood and unity" sealed any chances to (re)discuss the horrors of the war.[11] According to Tepavać, "Tito's slogan 'Brotherhood and Unity', which today is frequently an object of scorn, was not empty demagoguery in a country where one million seven hundred thousand men, women, and children had lost their lives, many because of ethnic hatred. The slogan reflected new hope in a population that had undergone a catharsis."[12] But, as Dubravka Ugrešić has underlined, "terror by remembering is a parallel process to terror by forgetting and both processes have the function of building a new state and a new truth".[13] The following questions were often raised: did Titoist or partisan narrative on the Second World War really reconcile multiple Croatian, Serbian, Montenegrin, Muslim historical narratives? Or did it just extract the common goal aiming at liberating the country while, at the same time, neglecting unhealed grievances?

While certain collective war wounds remained unaddressed or suppressed and the national problem became a frozen issue, unifying efforts did not include attempts "to integrate the sectional national feelings into an overall Yugoslav consciousness" because communists associated such practices with *l'ancien regime*. According to Stevan Pavlowitch, the slogan *brotherhood and unity* did contain "a large dose of genuine optimism based on the belief that communism would make the matter redundant anyway".[14]

Yugoslavism and its meanings: a social-constructivist interpretation

Constructivist claims in international politics focus on the role of ideational factors, alongside with material ones, which shape identities and interests of states, communities and groups. Structures and agents constitute each other. They are in a co-determinant relation, in which structures impact on agents' behaviour (because of regulative effects, but also constitutive ones, because the agents define and redefine their identities and interests through interactions), but also agents reproduce, perpetuate, alter or (re)construct the very same structures in which they interact. The social life entails a structure governed by norms, ideas, and intersubjective knowledge; therefore, material facts play a role insofar as agents assign meanings to them. The basic contention is that individuals, groups, communities or states (understood as social entities) do not simply respond to the reality around them, but to the way in which such reality is perceived.[15] Perceptions, therefore, are crucial for the way in which groups identify and define themselves, relate to *and* respond to events and phenomena around them (by contextualizing them and by assigning meanings to them), and the way in which the others are represented and dealt with.

Constructivist approaches on identity formation rest on certain basic assumptions: "identity is not stable or fixed, it is rather fluid and contextual"; it is "multifaceted, perhaps even consisting of layered, intersecting identities"; "identity is referential", in the sense that it exists only in reference to the *other* or multiple *others*.[16] Franke Wilmer explains that the *self* is not understood only as a position from which individuals experience life, but it is also an "agent engaging in interpretive acts", which in turn contain the meanings through which social order is constructed, perpetuated or altered; therefore, "identity is constituted by referring the bounded self to something else, something with which the self is either *identified* (as the same) or from which the self is *different*."[17] A social-constructivist approach emphasizes that it is not the "fact" of difference *per se* that matters, but the *meaning* assigned to difference. Social-constructivist interpretations indicate that, even though differences are "real", what really counts is the significance they have to social action and the way in which they are constructed within social processes. According to Wilmer, "the ways in which people are different" (be it language, religion, cultural affinity or how each identifies himself or herself within a historical narrative) "are not as important as *how those differences structure their social relations*".[18] Herbert Blumer's symbolic interactionism[19] is revealing in this sense: individuals react to objects around them on the basis of meanings assigned to them; also, meanings assigned to objects or to others are the result of social interaction which includes the individual's relation with the others and his/her relation with the society; meanings are modified through a process of interpretation to which individuals resort while they are confronted with *and* deal with those objects (or the others).

The overall Yugoslav identity was based on narratives of collective identity which were provided by the victorious partisan forces and the legitimate unifying political figure of Tito. Even though there was genuine enthusiasm for such an identity among all Yugoslav nations, seen as panacea for previous horrid ethnic rivalries and war atrocities, wartime suffering inflicted by other groups was never addressed or healed. Narratives of collective identity were "officially" decided upon, constructed, and conveyed. Given the bloody break-up of Yugoslavia in the 1990s, legitimate questions were posed: was Yugoslavia an artificial state created and maintained by communist authorities? To what extent did individuals appropriate Yugsolavism (alongside with *or* instead of ethnic identification)? Was Yugoslavism a precarious, fragile identity construction, never able to replace ethnic identities or to surmount ethnic cleavages?

Some explanations offered a link between the international structure and Yugoslavia as agent, having to react to a threatening *other*. As such, the willingness or propensity to embrace Yugoslav identity should be contextualized, in the sense that it was strongly linked to the reference of the collective *Yugoslav self* to the *other*; more precisely, to the *existence of threats of the other*. Throughout the entire existence of Yugoslavia the menacing *other* took on different forms or "faces", from the fascist forces invading the country, to the "imperialist" threatening forces constructed by communist propaganda, to the Soviet *enemy/Other* after the Tito-Stalin rift in 1948. The more menacing the external threats were, the more solid the rallying around Yugoslav identity tended to be. For example, according to William Zimmerman, the persistence of exogenous threats shaped the Yugoslav state's behaviour within the system of international relations or within the structure of the Cold War. But, already in the 1970's some voices indicated the worryingly co-dependent relation between internal Yugoslav unity and external threats. For instance, Stane Dolanć (prominent figure of the League of Communist of Yugoslavia) stated that Yugoslavia would hold together if threatened by outside, but, he continued, "what will happen to Yugoslavia if it is not threatened?".[20]

A social-constructivist approach looks at the multitude of meanings assigned to Yugoslavism and investigates how such meanings were constituted. For the Yugoslav communists, Yugoslavism meant "the eradication of political loyalties to particular nations in Yugoslavia and their transformation into a Yugoslav national consciousness".[21] As underlined by Aleksa Djilas, the communists conceived Yugoslavism in three major ways: Yugoslavism as antinationalism, "meaning opposition to all the nationalisms of the nations that constituted Yugoslavia"; Yugoslavism as patriotism, associated with "the struggle for the liberation of Yugoslavia from the Germans, Italians and others that occupied it"; and Yugoslavism as internationalism, which designated "the unity of the working people who would disregard nationality in the struggle for a social revolution".[22] Such narrative of collective identity was almost ubiquitous: it was present in party documents, in books, articles. According to Tito, Yugoslav communists were supposed to treat any type of opposition to Yugoslavism as a form of "reactionary" nationalism. As emphasized by Franke Wilmer, "Tito articulated Yugoslav identity as his own version of communist ideology", attempting "both to provide a normative basis for the development of a Yugoslav civic identity while constituting the counterforce to antagonistic nationalisms".[23] This Titoist *meaning* of Yugoslavism represented what Sabrina Ramet called "patriotic communism" or "Yugoslav socialist patriotism".[24]

But what other meanings did Yugoslavism have for people in socialist and post-socialist Yugoslavia? According to interviews taken by Franke Wilmer,

Yugoslavism had multiple paralleling meanings, reflecting "intersecting, and sometimes, overlapping identities". For certain citizens of Former Yugoslavia, there was a layer of this identity that referred both to "the Yugoslav position in the world" (associated to the non-aligned movement) and to a "special status in Eastern Europe" (associated to freedoms such as that of crossing borders, in contrast to neighbouring communist regimes);[25] for one Croat respondent, Yugoslavism was synonymous to a Serb identity, because some interpreted it as a "reward" for the Serbian readiness and firmness to fight in the two world wars; such perceptions were centred on the fact that Yugoslavia's government was dominated by Serbs and also the capital city was in Belgrade.[26] In contrast, for some Serbs, Yugoslavism was the equivalent of reward-giving to other non-deserving nationalities; according to this perception, the Serbian nationality was actually fractured and dispersed in different republics (in Croatia, Bosnia Herzegovina) and Serbia was in a way punished by the creation of two autonomous provinces only in Serbia. Most Bosnian Muslims displayed a strong predisposition to identify themselves as Yugoslavs in a civic and multicultural sense; the primary explanation for this rests on the fact that prior to 1971 census, "Muslim" (used by Bosnian Muslims) was not listed as nationality. For others, Yugoslavism was associated to a class identity, rather than a civic one and the slogan "brotherhood and unity" gradually became an empty vessel.[27]

However, many respondents did internalize the *Yugoslav* identity. For some people, usually those from mixed marriages, Yugoslavism meant the inclusive identity comprising all members of the family and relatives living in different republics. Yugoslavism as reality, as incorporated sense of belonging (and not artificial, superimposed rhetoric) is reflected in such responses: "I was a Yugoslav before the war and nothing else. We were all Yugoslavs in my family"; or "I always say when asked 'What is your identity?' that I am a Yugoslav. Why? I explain that because I was born in the Yugoslav state, and also the fact that both of my parents and grandparents are Serbs, although my father is from Bosnia"; other perceptions on Yugoslavism are conveyed like this: "Not only was I educated to believe that the whole territory of ex-Yugoslavia was my homeland, but because we could freely travel abroad (while people of the Eastern bloc countries couldn't), I almost believed that borders, as well as nationalities, existed only in people's heads"; or "I belong to that way of thinking, of being a Yugoslav and living my whole life in Yugoslavia. [. . .] For me Yugoslavia and my Yugoslav identity was reality, that was my life [. . .]".[28]

Given all this, what went wrong in Yugoslavia? One needs to undermine certain fissures in Yugoslav social construction, but also the ambivalence of Tito's project. First of all, wartime narratives were never addressed and grievances remained unhealed and supressed. Constant recollections of historical enemies would have never been the solution, but also erasing the memory of wartime events was not an answer. It only allowed for some people to dwell on victimization in their personal life while never addressing such issues in public life. A true process of healing never occurred and some psychological wounds remained open. Second of all, the absence of a real Yugoslav-based civil society also played a role. In the words of Slavenka Drakuli,

> the communist state [. . .] oppressed ethnic, national and religious beliefs, permitting only class identification; and in the end, communist leaders manipulated these beliefs, playing one nationality against another to keep themselves in power for as long as they could.[29]

The ambivalence of Tito's project rested upon the following: trying to surmount ethnic identification, while, at the same time, organizing party politics, institutional life, and political representation along ethnic lines and ethnic belonging. The expectation was that the state, together with ethnic nationalism, would "wither away". Instead, the state collapsed and violence broke out.

According to Mary Kaldor, the Yugoslav regime consistently attempted to make sure that no ethnic group became dominant (by introducing a system of check and balances) while in effect institutionalizing ethnic differences.[30] Also, Franke Wilmer showed that "solidarity within the Yugoslav state depended on the creation of a Yugoslav civic identity, but the structure of multi-ethnic federalism only punished people for declaring 'Yugoslav' as their identity by diminishing their capacity for political participation".[31] Since political representation went through the nationalities, individuals could not be represented as citizen members of civil society. This means that the civic identity was downsized because it was necessary for individuals to have representation through a national group at the federal level. Therefore, according to Wilmer, there was a perennial contradiction which was never properly addressed or resolved: the "institutionalization of link between ethnic identities and political participation".[32]

The dissolution of Yugoslavia and the Western perceptions on the "ethnic wars in the Balkans"

Constructivist claims on ethnicity focus on the fact that ethnic identity is neither pre-given nor natural; also, it is not merely a tool which is "invoked and manipulated by ethnic entrepreneurs for individual or collective political ends".[33] In other words, ethnic identity is socially constructed and is internalized by individuals (but the degree of internalization varies). One main assumption pertaining to constructivist theorizing is that the social construction of phenomena which comprise international politics plays a major role in understanding how threats, enemies and crises are construed, perceived and dealt with. Social-constructivist literature emphasizes the role of ideas (which are treated as complementary to material factors or to elements that belong to the so-called "hard politics") and argues that meanings assigned to facts or associated with decisions represent key elements in decision-making processes. Social-constructivist literature focuses on ideational or social phenomena, on the issue of need (dis)satisfaction and the resulting emotions, and on the mechanisms and conditions under which norms play an influential role in world politics. For instance, Alexander Wendt emphasized the social construction of fear and anxiety and explained how people experience the emotion of satisfaction when needs are met, and how they experience anxiety, fear or frustration when such needs are not met.[34]

When analysing ethnic conflict, constructivists reject the idea that ethnic identity is biologically given or a natural phenomenon and contend that "ethnic identities are enduring social constructions" and they are "products of human actions and choices" rather than biologically given.[35] According to Cristoph Zürcher, "ethnicity *per se* is never an explanation for conflict; rather, the way ethnicity is institutionalized and how this institutionalization becomes contested in periods of rapid social change explains conflict".[36] Valery Tishkov argued against oversimplified typologies and claimed that "the basic methodological weakness of such theories of conflict analysis lies in their vision of groups as collective bodies with needs and universal motivation – not as situations, feelings, or acts of speech".[37] If we adopt such an approach, we then focus on single-factor understandings of the nature and dynamic of conflict. But, when we reject this reductionist typology (which is in fact quantitative), we focus on ethnic boundaries or ethnic divisions whose content, linguistic utterance and narrative are not immutable, but rather altered, interpreted and embedded in (political) speech acts. The convincing and coherent argument developed by Zürcher is that

> ethnic boundaries, while not a *cause* of conflict *per se*, become reinforced or even reinvented *during* conflict. The salience of ethnicity can therefore be the result of the 'ethnicization' of conflict. Cultural difference becomes important in the course of conflicts, for it is the material from which the barriers between groups are built.[38]

In the case of Yugoslavia, the tendency was to immediately associate violence with enduring and irreconcilable ethnic identities. As such, the conflicts in Yugoslavia were perceived as part of "Balkan-ridden" nationalism and violence. Such perceptions on the nature of violence not only exacerbated the ethnic dimension, but also presented a reductionist outlook at causes of conflict while also de-politicizing them. The ethnic identities of individuals were not enough to trigger inter-communal war; the causes were political mobilization, the (re)construction of enemies by recourse to historical grievances and narratives, propaganda, inflammatory speeches, and social construction of threat, all these occurring in the context of economic crisis and federal institutional break-down.

An analysis on the mixed reactions of the international community with respect to the dissolution of Yugoslavia (and the outburst of violent conflict in Bosnia-Herzegovina) reveals the vacillations of the West between perceptions of the Bosnian conflict as endemic to the Balkans, on the one hand, and a plight of innocent civilians generated by genocide-type actions of extremists, on the other hand.[39] On the one hand, one major construction on the break-up of Yugoslavia was intimately intertwined with the ideas of bloody, inevitable Balkan wars, of an inescapable inter-ethnic age-long hatred (which is such a strong specificity to the Balkans that no solution from outside could put an end to it). Such a construction was shaped through political discourses and media portrayals of a "Bosnian/ Balkan war"[40] waged among three equally intransigent ethnic groups. The latter replaced the more accurate description of the violence as one perpetrated by local extremist groups against the civilian population.[41] On the other hand, another construction of the war in Bosnia indicated the nature and dynamic of the violence as the plight of innocent civilians caught among brutal nationalisms (which required clear-cut actions from the West). The second portrayal of the armed conflict and humanitarian crisis in Bosnia was also shaped by certain media accounts and certain political speeches.

The prevailing discursive construction was based upon the perception that the violence in Bosnia is inherently framed within the historical Balkan predisposition to ethnic strife and therefore cannot easily be solved from outside.

Basically, the international community's perceptions of the war in Bosnia indicated an archetypal example of ethnic violence, characterized by rivalries among three ethnic groups fighting against each other, and not as deliberate ethnic cleansing or genocide committed against civilians belonging to specific communities. Mary Kaldor emphasized the misunderstanding of the nature of violence within the international community, which "fell into the nationalist trap" and explained that all peace plans for Bosnia-Herzegovina were centred on the partition along ethnic lines (as if the three groups could no longer live together), which had in fact been the chief aim of the nationalists and the outcome of ethnic cleansing.[42] Negotiating peace for Bosnia meant separating the three communities according to some sort of fait accompli in 1992, but in fact, as underlined by Lene Hansen, "most of the Serbs' territorial gains were made within the first months of the war".[43] This meant on-going de facto partition with the use of ethnic cleansing and atrocities against civilians, and engagement in peace negotiations based on this fait accompli. Therefore, from that point on, the external solutions for ending the conflict accommodated the new status quo which was brought about by force.

The reaction of the international community to the outburst of violence in Bosnia-Herzegovina was intertwined with the portrayal of the nature of the conflict. One major perception regarding the type of conflict was linked to what could be called "the inescapable ancient hatred", meaning that the conflict was seen as merely a continuation of previous bloody episodes in the history of the Balkans and, more specifically, in the history of Bosnia. Hence, this perception was centred on the idea that the three communities were predestined to confrontation and cannot escape self-perpetuating ethnic rivalries.[44]

This interpretation of the Bosnian war was included in political discourses and in media accounts. American president George H. Bush argued that "the collapse of communism has thrown open a Pandora's Box of ancient ethnic hatreds, resentment, and even revenge" while senator John McCain described Bosnian violence in terms of "a conflict which has been going on in the Balkans for hundreds of years".[45] According to Lene Hansen, these explanations amounted to a "Balkan discourse" which articulated the nature and dynamic of the conflict in Bosnia as "a 'Balkan war' driven by violence, barbarism, and ancient intra-Balkan hatred stretching back hundreds of years".[46]

Therefore, the proclivity towards violence was considered a local, Balkan feature and was attributed to all three parties of the conflict equally, as if they were inherently and irreversibly consumed by nationalism. Tom Gallagher coined this "the equivalence of the guilt" and proved that "on both sides of the Atlantic, there were often frantic searches for corroborating evidence to suggest that the doctrine of equivalence was the most useful approach to the Bosnian problem".[47] According to Gallagher, this was illustrated in Lord Carrington's statement in 1992 when referring to the three communities in Bosnia as "all impossible people . . . all as bad as each other".[48] Also, Senator McCain mentioned that the primary American responsibility targets US troops whose lives would be jeopardized in such an area of violence, hence the nature of the "Balkan warfare" was linked with previous traumatic episodes that resulted in bloodshed on the American side, like Vietnam, Beirut and Mogadishu. Therefore, as Hansen showed, by articulating the "ancient roots" of the conflict, this discourse tried to prove that there was not much that the "West" could do.[49]

Alongside this portrayal of an exclusively ethnic (and difficult to solve) armed conflict in the Balkans, another discourse was shaped indicating the Bosnian Serbs as responsible for the plight of Muslim civilians, for the concentration camps and the siege of Sarajevo. Therefore, this construction of violence in Bosnia argued in favour of the West's responsibility to stop atrocities. This interventionist discourse was constituted by media representations of the nature of violence in Bosnia and was congruent to certain political speeches.[50] It was chiefly built on the critique of the so-called "ancient hatred explanation" for the war. For instance, *The Independent* indicated a "deep sense of collective shame that is building up among the people of this country as they watch the atrocities in Bosnia unfold".[51] Another journalist critique of the "ancient ethnic hatred" idea came from Paul Harris who, in a Scottish newspaper in 1992, pointed to the fact that "just as in Bosnia, Scotland [. . .] could be consumed with violence in just a few weeks. All this would happen not because the Scots actually hate the English but because the situation had been engineered by a relatively small group of people with access to media and weapons".[52]

The reaction to violence in Kosovo (and the ensuing Albanian refugee crisis) a few years later was not at all reluctant (albeit controversial) and reflected attempts of overcoming failure in Bosnia and compensating with decisive intervention in Kosovo.[53] One major explanation for the use of force against Milošević and immediate military reaction in the Kosovo war (in contrast to delayed and hesitant reaction to the Bosnian war) was the need to right the wrongs and shortcomings in Bosnia, and to prevent another failure to stop violence (which in Bosnia was achieved only after three years of human suffering). Therefore, in contrast to the hesitant and inconsistent reaction to the plight of Bosnian civilians, one could identify a transatlantic consensus over the following ideas, in the case of Kosovo: first of all, the international community (represented by USA, Great Britain, Germany, and France) was adamant to not by-stand another genocidal episode in the Balkans, to not tolerate another humanitarian crisis, and to undertake immediate and unwavering action. Second of all, in contrast to the reaction towards the Bosnian war, in the case of Kosovo there was another point of transatlantic convergence: neutrality was no longer the adequate attitude, and pinpointing the aggressors (Milošević and the Serb Security Forces) and separating them from the victims were needed in order to not repeat past mistakes.

According to Mark Smith, the term "ethnic cleansing" was used to reflect the type of violence occurring in Bosnia in 1992–1995 and, in 1999, it "provided the lens through which Western viewers interpreted the images of renewed Serb barbarism in Kosovo".[54] Apart from rational decision-making in world politics, states (theorized as social actors by constructivist literature) often reflect the interplay of emotions in designing foreign policy. For example, many scholars analysed German involvement in the Kosovo war in terms of "German shame, German guilt"[55] or in terms of "Balkan wars as German trauma"[56] (Weber, 2011, 16). According to Brent Steele, German involvement in the Kosovo war should be understood in terms of "shame" (which is produced by "actions which contradict self-identity of states"), because it was an "encompassing force in the German decision, although, [. . .] the 'decision' by Germany to deploy forces in Kosovo looked more like a process rather than a simple 'event', as Gerhard Schroeder [. . .] and fellow Cabinet members had to make the case that Germany had a responsibility to act".[57] Reconciling with the German traumatic past entailed full commitment to ending human suffering in Kosovo; also, it triggered Germany's immediate and active participation in NATO's efforts towards this goal.

Perceptions related to the "Balkan-ness" of Former Yugoslavia prevailed at the beginning of the wars. The international community reacted in different ways to the Bosnian war and the Kosovo war. In the following section we will discuss the "Western Balkans" in geopolitical terms, but we also want to investigate the social construction and representation of this area in the EU labelling and in its approach on the region.

A new (social) construction, a new discursive representation: the Western Balkans

The term *Western Balkans* was coined in 2003 at the EU–Western Balkan Summit in Thessaloniki. In geopolitical terms, the phrase reflected a group of states which emerged after the dissolution of Yugoslavia (except for Slovenia) plus Albania. In constructivist terms, Western Balkans is both a geographic reference and a social construction; it is the representation of a region via EU discourse and practices.

Janusz Bugajski defined it as follows:

> The term Western Balkan is both geographic and political. It was initially employed by US and European policymakers to describe the part of the Balkan Peninsula that remained outside of both the North Atlantic Treaty Organization (NATO) and the European Union (EU) since the early 1990s. It included all seven states that were formed during the collapse of Yugoslavia (Bosnia-Herzegovina, Croatia, Kosovo, Macedonia, Montenegro, Serbia, and Slovenia) together with Albania, which was emerging from international

isolation. [. . .] Following the EU's Thessaloniki Summit in June 2003, commitments were made to include all the Western Balkan states in the European Union [. . .].[58]

The EU–Western Balkans Summit in Thessaloniki issued a declaration which reflected at least two important things. On the one hand, commitment for future EU integration was expressed: "the EU reiterates its unequivocal support to the European perspective of the Western Balkan countries. The future of the Balkans is within the European Union".[59] On the other hand, what has been emanating from EU declarations ever since then is a process of norm transference to the region. The European Union has been acting out its roles of norm-setting and norm-diffusion and envisions the incorporation of such norms by non-member countries through socialization processes. The social-constructivist concept of *socialization* is based on ideational factors, meaning the capacity of agents to gradually internalize norms, patterns of behaviour and rules and become elements of certain structures (such as the EU). Literature on EU normativity[60] is linked to the way in which European institutions are able to establish norms, diffuse them and act upon reactions to such normativity. Analysing European preferences and norms, Zaki Laïdi explained that "norms are standards aiming at codifying the behaviour of actors sharing common principles" and they are meant to generate collective disciplines and to dissuade undesired conduct.[61] An extended work on "the socializing potential of international institutions" was provided by Jeffrey T. Checkel who examined "the conditions under which, and mechanisms through which, institutions in Europe socialize states and state agents, leading them to internalize new roles or group-community norms".[62]

It has often been said that "Western Balkans" is a term born in Brussels and, hence, it is assigned to a region that finds itself in a position of just filling in the label. For example, Igor Štiks noticed that "the geopolitical landscape in the Western Balkans is not as uniform or homogenous as the umbrella term might suggest" and that "the region christened 'the Western Balkans' by Brussels is basically a space squeezed between EU member states, supposedly destined to join them but without a clear accession timetable".[63] Also, others emphasized that the "gaps in understanding the regional approach(es) for the Western Balkans", because it "did not reflect any bottom-up idea pushed for by the local actors".[64] It should be noted that identification to this label or geographic representation was not indigenous; instead, it was assigned by external actors.

According to Kristijan Fidanovski, the label triggered certain negative effects:

it has perpetuated the ever-present stereotype of Balkan backwardness; restored the old stereotype of 'Balkan-ness' as 'Western-ness' in waiting; pitted (Western) Balkan nations against each other; and, most importantly, delayed the region's European integration that it was allegedly created to accelerate.[65]

Consequently, the term Western Balkans incorporates pejorative recollections of previous perceptions on the Balkan wars, but also retains the "Balkan" enduring character of the region (often presented as opposed to the developed and civilized Europe).

The precursor of the Western Balkans can be identified in the Stability Pact for South-Eastern Europe, launched in 1999, aiming at bringing "stability and economic development to South East Europe (SEE), a region where too often ethnic hatred, bad governance and economic backwardness have spawned conflicts that have at times spilled over into wider European wars".[66] At the time, the region comprised Albania, Bosnia-Herzegovina, Bulgaria, Croatia, the Federal Republic of Yugoslavia, the Former Yugoslav Republic of Macedonia and Romania. Later, in 2003, at the Thessaloniki Summit, the EU goal was reaffirmed in terms of integration into European structures and, ultimately, membership into the European Union. The new umbrella term Western Balkans excluded Bulgaria and Romania. Later, Montenegro emerged as component of Western Balkans (after 2006), as well as Kosovo (after 2008). Formally and institutionally, however, the Stability Pact was replaced by the Regional Cooperation Council in 2008.[67]

However, as indicated previously, the countries have been "placed" in the Western Balkans region through discourses and practices of the European Union. Their belonging to this social and geographic representation was exogenous to their agency. People in countries associated with the Western Balkans thought a lot about their former Yugoslav identity (some believing it was frail or imposed, but many strongly identifying to it), but one could easily expect them not to self-identify in "Balkan" terms. The historical narrative and representation of the Balkans as ridden by barbarity and backwardness, especially the break-up of Yugoslavia which was tackled by the media and political discourses in the West in terms of "Balkan wars", leads to the idea that their "features" and "belonging" is decided by outsiders.

According to commentators, "the Balkan-ness" of wars occurring in the 1990s seems to be replaced by the term Western Balkans, the word Western indicating "EU's faith in its candidate members to reconcile their actual Balkan-ness with their wannabe Western-ness".[68] According to Fidanovski, this reflects "an incomplete self" and shows that "the 'Western Balkan' variant is, in fact, merely a modern articulation of the old Balkan stereotype: a faceless entity whose only goal is to catch up with the West as a mark of civilization".[69] Practices that reproduce the "Balkan stereotype" are rejected by people in the region. For example, a 14-year-old from Zagreb says: "No one wants to be part of the Balkans – for Croatians, the Balkans begin in Bosnia; in Bosnia, the Balkans begin in Serbia; and in Serbia, they begin in Romania – because of the prejudices of the Western countries".[70]

From the EU's (pragmatic and bureaucratic) perspective, the Western Balkans are undergoing a process of enlargement conditionality. In his State of the Union Address of 13 September 2017, Jean-Claude Juncker, president of the European Commission, acknowledged the strategic importance of further enlargement when the candidate countries meet the accession criteria.[71]

The following sections will present and analyse EU's relations with Serbia, Montenegro, Former Yugoslav Republic of Macedonia, Bosnia and Herzegovina and Kosovo, and perceptions on EU in these countries.

EU's relations with countries from the Western Balkans

EU's relations with Serbia

One can only speak of Serbia's progress on the path to European integration after the dissolution of Slobodan Milošević's government, with the famous admission of defeat in the Yugoslav presidential elections of September 2000, to Vojislav Koštunica.[72] In the light of the Feira and Thessaloniki European Councils and the EU's openness exhibited towards the Western Balkans, Serbia expressed interest in joining the Stabilization and Association Agreement, which became an option in 2007, as the country formally agreed to fully cooperate with the International Criminal Tribunal for the former Yugoslavia, as the successor to that country. The first major accomplishment in this respect was the apprehension of Radovan Karadžić and his extradition to the Hague, to stand trial for genocide, war crimes and crimes against humanity.

Progress was steady after that moment, as Serbia saw the adoption of the 2008 European Partnership and the signing of the SAA, an event that led to the first notable change in perception of the integration file by the Serbian Government. While then-President Boris Tadić voiced his support for the signing of the SAA, Prime Minister Vojislav Koštunica, a stark critic of the West and a vehement detractor of the state of Kosovo, took a radically opposed stance. In April 2008, as the internal political debate on the adoption of the Agreement was under way, Koštunica uttered a series of public statements that connected the document with the break-up of Serbia, manifesting hostility towards its so-called artisans, Olli Rehn and Javier Solana, and accusing any Serbian politician that would sanction it of acting against national interest. In Koštunica's own words: "Olli Rehn's statement, and those from other EU officials, show that the real goal of signing the Solana agreement is only one, and that is to tomorrow claim that Serbia has recognized the fake state of Kosovo".[73]

Following the snap elections called amid this political turmoil and the advent of a pro-European Government, led by Mirko Cvetković, the official line of the country towards this priority began to normalize itself. EU visa requirements were lifted on 19 December 2009, a much-expected development, followed three days later by Serbia's official application for EU membership. As the SAA was undergoing its ratification process by the member states, Serbia prepared the answers to the Commission's questionnaire, which it was able to provide in January 2011, prompting a positive opinion on the part of first the European Commission and then the European Council. The arrests of Ratko Mladić and Goran Hadžić, and the fact that they were handed over to the ICC,[74] mark an important step for the improvement of Serbia's international image and gradual detachment from the thorny Yugoslav file. Acquiring official candidate status on 1 March 2013, Serbia got the green light from the European Council that very year to start accession negotiations, an event set against the background of the coming into force of the SAA, on 1 September 2013.[75]

There were no formal objections to the opening of negotiation chapters, albeit Romania had hinted at possible opposition as of 2008, if the rights of its minority group – the Vlachs on the Timok River – to benefit from education and religious service in Romanian, were not guaranteed. This prompted a hasty initial reaction on the part of President Boris Tadić,[76] and then the normalization of bilateral relations, in spite of the somewhat uncertain resolution of the matter.[77] Croatia also raised concerns over judicial reforms in Serbia, in 2016. Regardless, the process of opening the 35 chapters of the acquis (starting with Chapter 32, financial control, and Chapter 35, other issues) began in December 2015 and has met with a rather slow-paced, but mostly unhindered progress, to the extent that at present, 12 chapters have been subjected to scrutiny, two of which being provisionally closed.[78] It becomes apparent that, from the standpoint of policy compliance, the most difficult chapters include financial and budgetary provisions, judiciary and fundamental rights, justice, freedom and security, as well as agriculture and rural development.[79] The funding received from the Commission in order to assist the preparation of the country for the adoption of the acquis consisted, during the 2007–2013 period, of the sum of 1.2 billion euros,[80] while for the current multiannual framework (2014–2020), the country has been allocated 1.5 billion under the IPA II.[81]

Nevertheless, the course of action and, to some degree, changes of attitude on the part of the Serbian Government towards the country's EU integration bid have been intrinsically linked to the intricate Kosovo file. While we do not aim to provide a comprehensive insight into the conflict, notably into its historical unfolding and outcome, including the creation of the partly recognized state of Kosovo, we shall extract perceptions of the latter that have been inherently connected to the EU accession endeavour. Since 23 out of the 28 member states of the EU recognize Kosovo as a country and given the activity of the EULEX mission there,[82] there has been quite a lot of pressure on Serbia on the part of Brussels to normalize relations with Kosovo. An important aspect in this regard, nevertheless, is the extent to which Serbia's future EU membership will be conditioned by a formal recognition of Kosovo, which would be extremely contentious for the Serbian nation and, possibly, a deal breaker. In June 2011, Serbian President Tomislav Nikolić stated that his meetings with European Council President Herman Van Rompuy and European Commission President José Manuel Barroso had led him to understand that the recognition of Kosovo was not a prerequisite for accession talks to go ahead. In his own words: "I have received the assurance that the EU will not demand we recognize Kosovo", which appears to contradict Barroso's previous statement on this topic: "normalization of Serbian relations with Kosovo remains an absolutely central condition for the Commission to be able to recommend the start of accession talks to member states".[83] Perhaps the most meaningful step to date in the normalization of relations between Serbia and Kosovo has been the Brussels Agreement of 19 April 2013, signed by Serbian Prime Minister Ivica Dačić and Kosovo Prime Minister Hashim Thaçi, with EU High Representative Catherine Ashton as a mediator, establishing a series of administrative, police and logistical principles, but falling short of political recognition.[84]

EU enlargement commissioner Johannes Hahn, in a recent statement, hypothesized that Serbia's potential accession to the EU in 2025 was conditioned by the resolution of the Kosovo file: "The EU cannot and will not import bilateral problems (. . .) Serbia must conclude and irreversibly implement a legally binding agreement with Kosovo".[85] On the other hand, in October 2017, amid the turmoil in Catalonia, Serbian PM Ana Brnabić accused the European Commission of having a double standard given the way it refers to Kosovo, further fuelling the tensions around the complicated topic: "We completely agree with the EU Commission on everything that has been said with regards to Spain and respecting the Spanish Constitution, respecting the international law and sovereignty of the kingdom of Spain".[86]

As for the leading political party in Serbia, the Serbian Progressive Party, in spite of its nationalist drive, it has embraced a pro-EU agenda, whilst attempting to maintain a rather unnatural balance between the former and the traditional closeness to Russia, as it becomes apparent from President Aleksandar Vučić's rhetoric. The country's neutral status sets it apart from its ex-Yugoslav neighbours in matters of NATO integration, while serving as an auspicious argument for Russia's traditional interests in and influence on Belgrade. According to PM Ana Brnabić, this alleged balance in foreign affairs does not prevent Serbia from fulfilling its pre-accession duties – which is doubtful, given the country's refusal to implement the EU's sanction regime against Russia, for instance. According to Brnabić: "We are not a kind of Trojan horse for Russia in the EU. Russia is our important trading partner and our friend, but this, in any way, does not basically limit our strategic EU integration".[87]

What about popular support for EU integration? Over the years, polls have shown some fluctuations in this regard, although the favourable voices have always been more numerous. According to Euractiv, a 2018 survey yielded a majority of Serbs (52%) willing to vote in favour of EU accession, compared to 24% who would reject it.[88] Nevertheless, if asked to pick between a package deal consisting of EU integration plus the recognition of Kosovo, and no EU membership and no recognition of Kosovo, no fewer than 81% of Serbs would opt for the latter, according to a survey conducted in March 2018.[89] This is clearly indicative of the exceptionally strong feelings surrounding the file and the nationalist tendencies in Serbian society that take precedence over more pragmatic priorities.

Somewhat half-way to the completion of its EU integration bid, Serbia is still marred by the remnants of the twists and turns of the former Yugoslav file, which add to the already complicated economic, environmental and social chapters that need to be mended prior to the completion of accession negotiations. Less prepared than its neighbour, Montenegro, but without facing long-standing opposition from EU member states, as it is the case of FYROM, Serbia's stance on Kosovo remains one of the most spectacular topics in the history of EU enlargement. Surrounded by hypotheses such as a partition of Kosovo, a simultaneous membership decision, and outright recognition, the path to be taken for this file to meet with success appears to echo a statement made by German Foreign Minister Sigmar Gabriel in Pristina, on 14 February 2018: "If Serbia wants to move toward the European Union, the building of the rule of law is a primary condition, but naturally also the acceptance of Kosovo's independence".[90]

EU's relations with Montenegro

In the debate on future EU enlargement in the Western Balkans, the case of Montenegro[91] is not necessarily indicative of the situation of the entire region, but it may be regarded as the closest file we have at present to eventual membership. The size of the country creates a deceptive feeling of simplicity around the subject, but there are various factors that render Montenegro's EU file interesting – a country that recently achieved independence, with an unusually strong desire to seek both NATO and EU integration, reminiscent of other countries in East-Central Europe in the mid-1990s, and with economic peculiarities without precedent in the negotiation process.[92]

The country matches a certain regional profile from the viewpoint of its recent history, even prior to the notable South-Slavic forms of organization of the 20th century – a monarchic period followed by a declaration of independence tied to the events of 1877–1878.[93] The communist experience of the province, within the Socialist Federal Republic of Yugoslavia, has already been amply discussed in recent literature,[94] but Montenegro's stance amid the dismantlement of the Socialist Federal Republic of Yugoslavia remains of interest. Indeed, the referendum of 1 March 1992 revealed the support of the Montenegrin people for a continuation of political liaisons with Serbia, in the form of a federation. The public consultation enabled then-Prime-Minister Milo Đukanović to drape himself in the success of a plebiscite yielding an overwhelming 95% of the votes in support for a form of administrative union with the Serbs, with a turnout of two-thirds of all eligible voters.[95] At the time, Montenegro also began ridding itself of communist symbols, including the renaming of its capital to Podgorica and the adoption of a separate (albeit similar) flag from those of Serbia.[96]

The road to Montenegrin independence was chiefly paved amid the popular discontent with the wars in Bosnia and Croatia, where the involvement of Montenegro prompted the need to reassess the initial closeness between Milo Đukanović and Slobodan Milošević. The Montenegrin leadership began parting from the latter as of 1996, through economic and political reforms, like the adoption of the Deutsche Mark, already largely in use across the deficit-ridden province.[97]

After becoming president of Montenegro in 1998 in the place of Momir Bulatović, an ally of Milošević, Đukanović proceeded to a clearer separation from Serbia, notably in the aftermath of the 1999 Kosovo campaign, as described in his reform strategy, "Platforma za redefiniciju odnosa Crne Gore i Srbije". As Milošević's grasp on power in Serbia started dwindling in late 2000, the process met with several steps towards full independence, such as the Belgrade Agreement of 2002, witnessed by EU High Representative Javier Solana, transforming the tainted Federal Republic of Yugoslavia into a loose union of Serbia and Montenegro. The deal had been brokered by the EU, which acknowledged the differences between the two, but favoured an attempt to seek integration in a common endeavour. Nevertheless, given the initial reluctance of Serbia to cooperate with the International Criminal Tribunal for the former Yugoslavia, any prospects of a Stabilization and Association Agreement were postponed in 2004.[98]

The Constitutional Charter of Serbia and Montenegro adopted on 4 February 2003 did little more than to prolong the already complicated federal entente, because it enabled either to opt for eventual independence.[99] The institutional setup provided for a president as head of state, elected by a common parliamentary body composed of 126 members, and an undersized five-member Council of Ministers, with most economic and administrative policies becoming separate.[100]

The tensions within the union were augmented by the assassination of Serbian PM Zoran Đinđić, in March 2003. This, combined with the pro-independence feelings reflected by a significant share of the political parties, prompted the decision by Montenegro to trigger its constitutional prerogative to hold an independence referendum[101] in 2006. The public consultation of 21 May 2006 yielded a narrow result, as the 55% threshold agreed by PM Milo Đukanović with the EU needed for validation was barely attained (55.5%), amid an 86.5% turnout. The legitimacy of the process was acknowledged by the European Union, as well as by the OSCE, leading to swift international recognition, including from Serbia. Hence, the formal declaration of independence was uttered on 2 June 2006.[102]

Montenegro's EU accession bid, unlike its successful NATO integration (in 2017), has proved to be a tortuous endeavour, despite the fact that Montenegro has a small, somewhat manageable economy, which should render the negotiations on at least some of the accession chapters less time-consuming. The initial Feira European Council impetus of 19–20 June 2000, which stamped countries in the Western Balkans as potential candidates, was furthered by the conclusions of the Thessaloniki Council of 19–20 June 2003, which concocted an agenda for the integration of the countries in the region.[103] Furthermore, on 22 January 2007, the Council of the EU concluded the European partnership with Montenegro, setting the conditions for the reforms and priority areas to be tackled, with the help of pre-accession funds.[104] The Stabilisation and Association Agreement was signed on 15 October 2007 and entered into force on 1 May 2010,[105] gathering considerable support from national parties. Furthermore, during the Sarajevo EU–Western Balkans ministerial meeting on 2 June 2010, the Union reaffirmed its commitment to the integration of countries in the area.[106] Montenegro's application for membership was submitted on 15 December 2008 and accepted at the Brussels European Council of 18–19 June 2009.[107] As a consequence, Enlargement Commissioner Olli Rehn presented Podgorica with the customary questionnaire, in December that year. The visa exemption agreement between Montenegro and the EU came into force on 19 December 2009, as a reward for the progress attained in matters ranging from border protection to justice and security reforms.[108]

In December 2010, the Commission awarded Montenegro official candidate status, followed by the opening of negotiations, on 29 June 2012. The Juncker doctrine and the relatively slow progress of negotiations during the mandates of Štefan Füle and Johannes Hahn as Commissioners for Enlargement have not prevented Montenegro from opening 30 out of the 35 chapters, prompting Juncker to hint at a potential accession date in 2025.[109] An analysis of the chapters reveals some optimistic prospects, stemming from the opening of sensitive ones, covering agriculture, justice and human rights, while no veto appears to be looming on the part of any of the member states, unlike in the case of other candidates from the former Yugoslav space. So far, it appears that the most challenging topics have been financial and budgetary matters, as well as fisheries, while economic and monetary policy poses an unprecedented problem (notwithstanding Kosovo),[110] with the unilateral adoption of the euro by Montenegro.

The annual progress report of the country drafted by the European Commission on 9 November 2016[111] paints both a positive and a negative picture of compliance with Community requirements. The former includes the positive outcome of the 2016 general elections, defined by transparency and endowing the newly elected bodies of the state with the necessary legitimacy to further the negotiation process, along with the reduction of bureaucracy and the more uniform approach to salaries in the public sector (the law of March 2016 made public careers more appealing, amid a very low minimum wage – 288,1 euros, which has remained unaltered for several years).[112] The report also emphasizes the need to step up the pace of administrative reform and provide more political independence to the somewhat oversized public service apparatus.

The Commission report dwells on some of the thorniest negotiation chapters, pointing out the need for further reforms in the justice system, still marred by corruption and the rather slow pace of court procedures. Although corruption in the public sector and organized crime remain of some concern, the country did manage to endow itself with an anti-corruption agency in 2016. Some of the other worrying points in the report pertain to the marginalized Roma community in the country, accounting for 0.8% of the population, as per the 2011 census, along with gender equality and freedom of mass media.[113]

From the standpoint of political culture, the mostly centre-left-dominated stage of Montenegro has come a long way from the worrying context of the mid-1990s, but the path to EU integration remains winding, not only because of the reluctance of the current European Commission to pick up the pace of the process, but also given the severity of some of the problems lingering in the negotiation chapters. Podgorica has been the artisan of an in-depth reform endeavour and has attempted to render it perceptible and transparent, including through the publication of significant policy documents in English, the involvement of its emerging NGO sector in the modernization process and the adoption of EU-fashioned e-governance and decentralization administrative patterns, relying on simplification and meritocracy. This is set against the background of a starkly pro-EU feeling of the population – more than 80%, according to a recent survey.[114]

A mostly stable political life has provided EU negotiations with some steadiness and predictability, which enables us to forecast that Montenegro is bound to be the next country to break through the Juncker barrier and replenish – at least – the numerical gap that will once again make the EU a 28-strong construct. Whether the unprecedented euro currency file can be resolved, with a probable melange between the Maastricht criteria and the well-known convergence criteria, and whether the justice and fundamental rights chapters will be regarded as fitting in the next Commission report, it remains to be seen. Nevertheless, the message than the integration of a new country into the EU would convey (chiefly from the West Balkans region) is sure to become a powerful signal of rejuvenation amid the crisis the Union has been struggling with – that it remains an appealing, frequentable and dynamic entity, one that has been capable of overcoming the unfortunate fortress-Europe label and of presenting countries in the region with a solid pro-western and democratic option, at a time when other temptations lurk in the diametrically – and geographically – opposite corners.

EU's relations with former Yugoslav Republic of Macedonia

During the time of the Cold War, the People's (later to be called Socialist) Republic of Macedonia was merely one of the six entities comprising the Federal Republic of Yugoslavia. Led by the principles of Titoism and the claim to be part of the Non-Aligned Movement, the Republic of Macedonia experienced the same one-party system that became the mainstay of the communist bloc, with the League of Communists of Macedonia grasping firmly to the reins of power. This remained valid until 1990, when, set against the background of the wind of political change sweeping across the continent, the constituent country held its first democratic elections in November 1990, thus setting in motion a series of changes that would begin the protracted process of shedding its totalitarian past. The election of experienced politician Kiro Gligorov as President, who assumed office in January 1991,[115] would mark the tendency to engage in a slow-paced detachment from the old regime, as further exhibited by the adoption of the name Republic of Macedonia later that year, prior to the referendum on independence, yielding a landslide positive result of 95.09% on 8 September 1991.[116]

The country's relations with the European Community were initiated as the first representative in Brussels was appointed by the Macedonian administration, in October 1992, whilst on 22 December 1995, official diplomatic relations were set in place, for the purpose of preparing the Cooperation Agreement between the two parties. Four years into the implementation of this Agreement, in 2000, FYROM and the European Commission engaged in surprisingly swift discussions on the nature of the Stabilisation and Association Agreement, signed on 9 April 2001, in Luxembourg, and entered into force in 2004.

One cannot help but wonder about the context that allowed FYROM to attain such progress in relation with the European Union, amid a particularly thorny regional context. In effect, mostly exempt from the hardships of the Kosovo War, the country did suffer from the advent of a very large number of Albanian refugees, whose actions would lead to destabilization on account of the hostile stance of the Albanians' National Liberation Army, acting on Macedonian soil. The peak of the conflict, spanning across the first half of 2001, prompted the intervention of a NATO task force and led to the signing of the Ohrid Agreement, with concessions on both sides and several political and identity-related gains on the part of the Albanian minority within the Republic. The adoption of a new constitution partly defused the tension, allowing the EU to take over the peacekeeping mission from NATO.

On 22 March 2004, FYROM formally submitted the application to become a member of the European Union, doubled by internal preparation endeavours, which eventually took the guise of a National Strategy for European Integration, later that year. The answers to the customary European Commission questionnaire addressed to the Government in Skopje came in February 2005 and enabled both the Commission and the European Council to grant FYROM the status of candidate in the latter months of 2005.[117]

Having already benefitted from the PHARE programme for a decade, in 2007, the country was rendered eligible for the Instrument for Pre-accession Assistance, upon the conclusion of the Framework Agreement with the EU. The continuous implementation of this financial mechanism has been a considerable asset for the modernization of the country and its progress in terms of compliance with the Copenhagen Criteria. In fact, in the period 2007–2013, 622 million euros were allocated to FYROM by the EU, while during the current multiannual framework (2014–2020), the country is eligible for a total of 664.2 million euros under the aforementioned instrument, with such priority areas as democracy and governance, rule of law and fundamental rights, environment and climate action, transport, competitiveness and innovation, social development, agriculture and rural development, as well as regional and territorial cooperation.

Along with visa liberalization, as of December 2009, FYROM received a green light from the Commission with regard to the opening of negotiations, later backed by a resolution of the European Parliament and the start of a High-Level Accession Dialogue between the EC and Skopje, in 2012.[118] Nevertheless, two prominent obstacles had been identified by that time on the way to the country's accession bid – one is the ongoing name and identity dispute with Greece, which will be briefly explained in the following, whereas the other pertained to the clash between then-Prime-Minister Nikola Gruevski, of the Internal Macedonian Revolutionary Organization–Democratic Party for Macedonian National Unity, and opposition leader Zoran Zaev, representing the Social Democratic Union. The principal reasons for the feud lay in alleged wiretapping and the obstruction of a murder investigation by the Government and led to massive street protests and high-level resignations, in May 2005. In response to the crisis, the EU brokered a deal within the country, in the form of the Pržino Agreement, signed in July 2015 by the main political parties of FYROM, calling for elections and the independent investigation of the alleged wrongdoing. Albeit the implementation of the deal has been somewhat unsteady and despite the fact that the December 2016 early elections failed to produce an outright winning party, the EC's progress report on FYROM for 2018[119] acknowledges the end to the political crisis, after the election of Zoran Zaev as PM, on a pro-EU and pro-NATO agenda. The country's so-called urgent reform priorities lie at the core of furthering its integration prospects, and may be defined as follows: "rule of law and judiciary, de-politicisation of public administration, electoral reform, recommendations of the committee of inquiry into the events of 24 December 2012 and media: freedom of expression".[120]

It remains evident that one of the main impediments to FYROM's EU negotiation bid and the sole major obstacle that has so far led to the postponement of a NATO invitation has been the infamous name dispute with Greece, with extraordinary sensitivities on both parts. While it is not our intent at this time to provide a complete historical and symbolic account of the latter,[121] it suffices to say that Athens has maintained opposition to the use of the name Macedonia, citing concerns over potential territorial and cultural disputes owing to the eponymous region located in northern Greece. Furthermore, the pursuit of a so-called antiquisation policy by the Internal Macedonian Revolutionary Organization–Democratic Party for Macedonian National Unity, as of 2006, engendered an adoption of symbols (most commonly revolving around the image of such ancient figures as Alexander the Great and Philip II) that prompted a wave of protests on the part of the Greek government and society.[122] Meanwhile, Bulgaria – itself on the doorstep of the EU at the time – voiced concerns over ethnic tensions with FYROM, thus hinting at the possibility of there arising more than one veto to its EU membership.[123]

The most recent developments and EU/UN mediation on the name dispute appear to have engendered a positive outlook, with a somewhat clearer prospect of a solution that would unclog FYROM's path to NATO and the EU. As stated by Zaev in a February 2018 interview with Reuters, four solutions have presented themselves, based on geographical denominators: "The suggestions are Republic of North Macedonia, Republic of Upper Macedonia, Republic of Vardar Macedonia and Republic of Macedonia (Skopje)".[124] The progress was recently confirmed by Greek Foreign Minister Nikos Kotzias, who, in a news conference held in Skopje, on 23 March 2008, stated: "Today, we made steps to solve the problems we inherited" and "We have agreed in great degree what we want for the future", in a series of positive developments in the relations between FYROM and its EU neighbours.[125]

Amid these favourable prospects, it remains to be added that both major parties in Macedonian politics have traditionally been inclined to have a positive perception of the European Union. While the Internal Macedonian Revolutionary Organization–Democratic Party for Macedonian National Unity has been an associate member of the European People's Party since 2007,[126] the Social Democratic Union of Macedonia is an associate of the Party of European Socialists,[127] both groups taking a pro-European stance and essentially driving the integration and policy-making process. Moreover, the largest Albanian party in FYROM, the Democratic Union for Integration, campaigns under a pro-EU agenda and logo.[128]

As for the public opinion, a survey[129] published on 17 February 2017 by the Macedonian Information Agency and conducted by the Institute for Democracy "Societas Civilis", in cooperation with the Konrad Adenauer Foundation, revealed that 77% of FYROM citizens favoured European integration, with IfD representative Ivan Damjanovski claiming that the figure would stand as high as 90% but for the name dispute. Furthermore, the study indicated that 26% of citizens perceived the EU as the country's strongest foreign ally, followed by Russia (25%) and the USA (17.5%), with a steady pro-Russian ascending trend, partly explicable through the apparent stagnation in the process of reaching closeness to both the EU and NATO. It is also apparent that the roughly 25% of FYROM's population composed of Albanians[130] are more likely to voice affinity towards the west than towards Moscow.

To conclude, FYROM remains in a "stuck" position in the current enlargement framework, being, along with Albania, the only officially accepted candidate that has failed to open any negotiation chapters to date. That said, in the light of the institutional, economic and political progress attained and duly reported in the European Commission's annual country report, as well as the relative openness in FYROM's dialogue with Greece and Sofia, PM Zaev's hint at the possibility that the country will be presented with a potential accession date very soon[131] may not be so easily frowned upon.

EU's relations with Bosnia and Herzegovina

European and American intervention in Bosnia was evident during the bloody war, but also the post-war development of Bosnia and Herzegovina was marked by international involvement. The NATO-led military operation (IFOR, Implementation Force) was authorized to monitor the signing of the Dayton Peace Agreement, which had been brokered by the United States. The Dayton Peace Agreement reflected what was soon to become obvious, namely the separation of military matters (undertaken by the United States) from the civilian aspects (taken over by the Europeans).[132] Tensions were soon revealed, because cooperation between the military and civilian components were limited, hence "undermining the implementation of important clauses of the agreement" (such as the return of displaced people).[133] This led to a situation in which the US military authorities pointed to slow progress on civilian issues while the Europeans blamed the US for failing to provide a secure environment, but also reconstruction funds.[134]

Post-Dayton Bosnia-Herzegovina (BiH) was composed of two entities, Republika Srpska and the Croat-Bosniak Federation, separated by an Inter-Entity Boundary Line (IEBL). The allocation of territory was consistent with the proposals of international negotiators (the Serbs were given 49% of the territory, the Bosniaks 33.3% and the Croats 17.7%),[135] but also spurred more grievances because of recent memory of bloody ethnic cleansing campaigns which had aimed at conquering land by terror. The provisions of the Dayton Peace Agreement were meant to offer reconciliation and future integration, but, at the same time, they designed a structure of political representation based on ethnic belonging and participation and on physical separation among members of the three communities. The complex institutional and political system in Bosnia is centred on self-governing powers assigned to the entities and reflects Arend Lijphart's consociational model of power-sharing. Bosnia represents a "triple power-sharing system, with power-sharing in the entities and cantons, as well as at the state level".[136] The limited prerogatives of central institutions and central government would ideally "facilitate agreement and compromise among Bosnia's political leaders, who hold veto power in all institutions".[137] However, as the case of BiH reveals, it has counter-productive consequences, maintaining the previous form of institutionalized political representation based on ethnic affiliation. As emphasized by Roberto Belloni, the Dayton Peace Agreement

> provides for the direct election of a three-member collective state presidency composed of one Bosniak, one Croat, and one Serb. Crucially, the Bosniak

> and Croat members are elected in the Federation, while the Serb is elected in the RS. This method of election discourages officials from identifying themselves as representatives of the entire Bosnian body politic, and instead encourages ethnic over civic identity.[138]

Apart from hampering a sense of belonging to a strong civic form of identification, the system allows for procedural paralysis, slow decision-making processes, institutional deadlock, weak and fragmented civil society and poor economic performance.

Bosnia and Herzegovina is a semi-protectorate of the international community. Post-war reconstruction and peace building efforts exhibit the international involvement, starting with the Office of the High Representative of the International Community, the Organisation for Security and Cooperation in Europe (OSCE), the Peace Implementation Council (PIC), the Stabilization Force (SFOR, which replaced IFOR in 1996), the Delegation of the European Union to Bosnia and Herzegovina and the European Union Special Representative (EUSR), and various international NGOs, agencies and think tanks.

EU's relations with Bosnia-Herzegovina (BiH) started in 1998, within the framework of assistance in the field of administration, regulatory framework and policies, as conceived by the EU/BiH Consultative Task Force (CTF). An important stage in EU–BiH interaction is the Stabilisation and Association Process, launched in May 1999, which aimed at offering "a clear EU accession perspective for Bosnia and Herzegovina and other five West Balkans countries".[139] BiH became a potential candidate for EU membership during the Thessaloniki European Council summit in June 2003. By 2004–2005, the evolution of Bosnia and Herzegovina was associated to Europeanization and it was often suggested that "its integration in European institutions is the long-term solution for the Bosnian conundrum".[140] Already in 2003, Romano Prodi, then President of the European Commission, said that "the unification of Europe [. . .] cannot be regarded as complete until the Balkan countries are members too. All countries in the Balkans must be offered the prospect of membership".[141] What Belloni dubs "the transition from Dayton to Brussels" entails a series of developments indicative for the EU's increasing focus on the Western Balkans, and more specifically, on Bosnia: Bosnia joined the Council of Europe in 2002, the EU Police Mission (EUPM) became operational in 2003, the US and the EU jointly announced the replacement of SFOR with a European force (EUFOR) in 2003, the latter launching the peacekeeping operation Althea in 2004, and the responsibility for Southeastern Europe (Bosnia, FYROM, Serbia, Montenegro and Kosovo) was assigned to the new EU enlargement Commissioner, Olli Rehn, in 2004.[142] In March 2004, the Council of the European Union adopted the first European Partnership with Bosnia and Herzegovina and a year later negotiations on the Stabilisation and Association Agreement were officially launched. The latter was signed in June 2008.

In 2010 the visa-free regime for Schengen area was introduced for all citizens of Bosnia-Herzegovina. This was meant as a tool for introducing a citizenship regime, as part of the Europeanization of the Western Balkans. However, the process triggered unintended consequences and mirrored the "EU's bureaucratic insensitivity", by deepening divisions in Bosnia and by creating a sense of isolation.[143] Giving visa-free travel to holders of Macedonian, Serbian and Montenegrin biometric passports in 2009, but not to Bosnian citizens, who were delayed until December 2010, created complications for the multi-ethnic Bosnian citizenship landscape. Many citizens of Bosnia possessed the citizenship of one of the neighbouring countries (Croatia or Serbia), hence benefiting from the visa liberalization process while the Bosniaks felt left outside. However, the EU's strategy had an overall effectiveness by prompting local administrative reforms.[144] Even delayed, the granting of free travel was expected to provide Bosnian citizens with a sense of belonging to Europe and to encourage "young people especially to think beyond narrow-minded ethnic divisions and internal segregation".[145]

The EU presence in Bosnia was somehow bicephalous, because the Delegation of the European Union to Bosnia and Herzegovina and the EU Special Representative (EUSR) coexisted. In July 2011 the Council of the European Union decided that the authorities of both the EUSR and the Head of the European Union Delegation Office be vested in the same person, rendering a "one voice" EU presence on the ground.[146]

In June 2012 the EU and BiH launched the High Level Dialogue on the Accession Process and in 2015 the Stabilisation and Association Agreement (SAA) with Bosnia and Herzegovina entered into force. At the same time, the EUFOR/Althea mission was reconfigured in 2012, "focusing on capacity-building and training, while also retaining the means to contribute to the country's deterrence capacity".[147] In 2016 BiH submitted its application to join the EU.

Bosnia and Herzegovina remains divided insofar as domestic (identity) politics governs political, institutional and social life. Physical separation among the three groups (Bosnian Muslims/Bosniaks, Bosnian Croats and Bosnian Serbs) and strong relations with neighbouring countries were enshrined in the Dayton Peace Agreement. The consociational power-sharing system, intended to prevent the domination of one ethnic group over the others, has a counter-productive effect: it favours and perpetuates self-identification with ethnicity and weakens central political institutions. Many Bosnians perceived the Dayton Peace Agreement as necessary to end violence, but also as a temporary solution for the country; the ethnic nature of Bosnian institutions and the ethnically defined entities[148] and citizens is a hurdle for cohesiveness and for transcending ethnic politics. According to a European Parliament Report in 2017, "leaders on all sides [are urged] to refrain from divisive, nationalist and secessionist rhetoric that polarizes society as well as from actions that represent a challenge to the cohesion, sovereignty and integrity of the country".[149] Also, the report suggested serious engagement "in reforms that will improve the socio-economic situation of all BiH citizens, create a democratic, inclusive and functioning state and move the country closer towards the EU".[150]

The European Commission issued its latest report in April 2018 and indicated that BiH's alignment with EU Common Foreign and Security Policy needs to be improved while an analysis on economic development and competitiveness shows an "an early stage of establishing a functioning market economy".[151] With respect to rule of law and fundamental rights, the report mentions that "Bosnia and Herzegovina has some level of preparation to implement the acquis and European Standards in this area", but also expresses concern about widespread corruption. Referring to implementation of human rights, the report emphasizes some progress (especially an action plan for employment for the Roma), but signals that improvements are still needed.[152]

EU's relations with Kosovo

Official relations between the European Union and Kosovo were initiated in 1999, in the aftermath of one of the darkest episodes in modern European history, the Kosovo War. The European Union Rule of Law Mission in Kosovo, also known as EULEX, came as a consequence of UN Security Council Resolution 1244 and has served the purpose of consolidating security and justice on the territory. A unique construct with special mentoring and monitoring powers, EULEX is also endowed with limited executive functions. Together with the Special Representative of the European Union (EUSR), it has provided Brussels with a foothold in Kosovo, having a significant impact on its reform process and policy-making.[153]

It is in this context that in November 2002, a Stabilisation Tracking Mechanism was set in place by the EU, which initially fell short of the expectations of a Stabilisation and Association Agreement, given the uncertain international situation of the territory. This would somewhat change after the Thessaloniki Summit of June 2003, which placed Kosovo within the Stabilisation and Association Process, in line with its neighbouring countries from the West Balkans. Considerable support was received from the European Commission and the Council of the EU, which provided ample backing to Pristina even prior to the formal Declaration of Independence, for instance through the European Partnership, whose implementation in the region began in August 2006 and enabled the EU and the provisional administration of Kosovo to engage in cooperation projects.[154] After the Declaration of Independence adopted by the Kosovar Assembly on 17 February 2008, the thorniest chapter in the country's (a term we shall use for simplification) EU closeness bid inevitably opened, with five EU countries refusing to grant recognition to Kosovo: Cyprus, Greece, Romania, Slovakia and Spain.[155] While this was based on inherently domestic reasons, with an ethnic and a historical substrate, it did engender an unprecedented situation in the enlargement policy, with Kosovo being considered a potential candidate for membership and undergoing considerable interventions on the part of the EU, through the Stabilisation Tracking Mechanism and in keeping with Brussels' approach to the reform process sponsored and championed in the West Balkans.[156]

The course of reform prompted by the EU in Kosovo, entailing such priorities as the rule of law, rights of national minorities, and administrative and economic reforms, led to discussions on the possibility to sign a Stabilisation and Association Agreement, following a recommendation by the Commission, in 2012. Monitored by then-Commissioner for Enlargement Štefan Füle, the progress in this endeavour required some sort of normalization of relations between Belgrade and Pristina, which was also brokered by the EU, with the Brussels Agreement of April 2013. The peculiar understanding, bearing no signature on behalf of the two states, did provide a platform for dialogue and enabled the two parties to attain some progress, at least in the area of local administration and security.[157] It also prompted the Commission to give the go ahead to Pristina for the start of SAA negotiations, while Serbia's membership negotiations also met with a green light, as a sign of good faith.

SAA talks between the Commission and Kosovo were formally initiated in October 2013 and led to the signing of the Agreement in October 2015, under special conditions, enabling the document to come into force without being ratified by all 28 member states, which would have been impossible at the time. Under these circumstances, the SAA became applicable as of 1 April 2016. It promotes "peace, stability, freedom, security and justice, prosperity and quality of life (. . .) stabilisation and the transition to a market economy, regional cooperation and preparation for EU accession",[158] not unlike the priorities announced by the EU in the other, more advanced integration cases within the broader region. The technical progress is chiefly attained by means of the so-called sectoral meetings, conducted annually in such priority fields as "justice, freedom and security; innovation, information society and social policy; agriculture, fisheries, forestry and food safety; internal market, competition and consumer/health protection; trade, industry, customs and taxation; transport, energy, environment and regional development; and economic and fiscal matters" – following the guidelines of some of the most important chapters of the acquis.[159]

One of the complicated files in Kosovo's integration endeavours is the visa liberalization process, which, despite being on the table as of 2012, has so far failed to yield the desired result. This is due to multiple reasons, including the country's limited progress in the fight against organized crime and corruption and the particularly large number of asylum applications registered by Kosovar citizens with the EU.[160] On a positive note, however, the recent border agreement with neighbour Montenegro is regarded as a positive step in Kosovo's EU bid.

Another complicated, albeit not unprecedented, aspect posed by Kosovo's integration effort is the unilateral adoption of the euro as the country's currency, in spite of not meeting the convergence criteria. Much like Montenegro, this assertion of independence was deemed necessary once the Deutsche Mark fell out of use, in 2002, and prompted the country to adopt a currency over which it has no control and which it is unable to mint, but which does create a low-inflation environment.[161] It remains to be seen how this challenge will be overcome in the eventual negotiation process, similarly to the Montenegrin case, although economic convergence is still a remote reality in the Kosovar file.

On a positive note, the EU's financial assistance directed towards Kosovo has turned the Union into the largest donor for the country and has enabled Pristina to benefit from 2.3 billion euros in non-reimbursable assistance since the funding began, in 1999. The application of the Instrument for Pre-Accession Assistance Programme into the country, along with other sources of funding such as Community Assistance for Reconstruction, Development and Stabilisation (CARDS),

TAIEX and Twinning projects, Erasmus+ and the European Instrument for Democracy and Human Rights, has enabled beneficiaries to conduct successful projects, from agriculture to urban development, from human resources to business and infrastructure.[162]

The latest report on Kosovo issued by the European Commission, in April 2018, is a blunt review of the country's recent setbacks in terms of political stability, but does underline some progress achieved in such matters as public administration reform, justice laws and freedom of expression (despite funding problems for the public broadcaster). The on-going fight against organized crime and corruption is seen by the report as manifesting itself in an early stage, with issues like terrorism and money laundering being given as worrying examples. Economically, the country has met with moderate progress in terms of freedom of movement, the fight against tax evasion and the promotion of customs security, but falls short of EU expectations in environmental protection and energy.[163]

While this picture is somewhat bleak, it is to be noted that from the standpoint of Kosovo's political spectrum, the three most prominent parties, the Democratic League of Kosovo (EPP observer), the Democratic Party of Kosovo and the Self-Determination Movement (PES member) all share an agenda of Euro-Atlantic integration, with various degrees of nationalism and pan-Albanian commitments. As for the citizens, a survey recently released by Euractiv shows that no fewer than 90% of Kosovars consider the EU to be a good thing, whilst exhibiting great optimism for the future.[164] President Hashim Thaçi, in a statement from October 2017 for the same news agency, stated:

> Enlargement is undoubtedly good for each of the countries of the region individually and as a group and would be good for the EU itself, as it would create stability and economic opportunity in a region ravaged by war less than 20 years ago. I still believe in the core values of the EU, I believe that the will of the people for a united and integrated continent will prevail. Kosovars are overwhelmingly in favour of EU membership and are fully and completely dedicated to European values.[165]

This declaration came after the uncertainty hovering over the Kosovar file and amid the recurrent idea that if West Balkans countries are to join the Union, perhaps due 2025, it is advisable they join in bulk, for fear of subsequent vetoes.

To conclude, although the EU has been a notable presence in Kosovo ever since the end of the war and has succeeded in watching over a slow-paced reform process, the doubtful international status of the country, combined with the justice-related, political and economic setbacks the Commission has not ceased to emphasize in its reports, make the country's accession bid a thorny one, with unprecedented sensitivities.

Perceptions of the EU in the Western Balkans

The previous sections tackled the way in which the Balkan region was perceived by external agents and the way in which Balkan stereotypes created a gap between what is discursively constructed as Western/EU *and* Eastern (even though labelled Western) Balkans. This last section presents perceptions from the opposite side trying to investigate how the EU is perceived in countries from the Western Balkans.

A 2009 Gallup Balkan Monitor report indicated that a strong identification with Europe was visible in Kosovo (72% of respondents) and Macedonia (49% Albanian respondents and 28% nationals) while, at the opposing pole, low percentages in this respect came from regions with Serb populations (Serbia – 23%, Serbs from Kosovo – 15%, Serbs from BiH – 10%). The report mentioned the connection between "a close identification with Europe and strong support for EU integration" while noticing the Bosnian Federation as an exception in this respect, because there "support for EU integration was high despite rather low identification with Europe".[166] In both 2009 and 2010, surveys revealed that majorities of respondents would vote in favour of their country joining the EU in Serbia, BiH, Kosovo, Montenegro, and Macedonia. Reports indicate, however, that granting visa-free travel to Montenegrins, Macedonians and Serbs did not trigger higher levels of EU support in all the countries: "while in Montenegro the proportion of respondents saying that the EU was a good thing increased by six percentage points to 73%, in Macedonia and Serbia the respective shares fell from 62% to 60% and from 50% to 44%".[167] Figures from 2015 indicated that 89% in Kosovo believed that the EU is a good thing while percentages in the other countries showed lower scores: 41% in FYROM, 35% in Montenegro, 30% in Bosnia and Herzegovina, and 24 in Serbia.[168] In 2017 the figures indicated an increase in each of the countries: Kosovo – 90%, FYROM – 54%, Montenegro 44%, BiH – 31%, Serbia – 26%. The observation of the report is that the youngest respondents (58%), those with higher education (60%) and individuals who rate their social status as above average (60%) are significantly in favour of EU membership.[169] Consequently, figures are expected to rise.

Bosnia and Herzegovina is marked by different perceptions on the EU, indicating another level of division in the country. Surveys show that, when asked whether future membership would be a good thing or a bad thing, there are major disparities: in 2006, 70% of respondents in the Croat-Muslim Federation believed it was a good thing, then in 2008 the percentage went down to 59%, then up again to 77% in 2009 and to 75% in 2010. In contrast, there are different perceptions in the Serb Republic: 60% associated the EU membership with something good in 2006, only 31% in 2008, 48% in 2009 and 59% in 2010.[170] As emphasized previously, the power-sharing system in BiH is fraught with slow pace and institutional deadlock. When asked about constitutional reforms (in order to surmount such obstacles) and harmonization with EU legislation, only 10% of Serbs said they would support constitutional change in order to strengthen central government, in contrast to 44% of Bosniaks and Croats.[171] It was clear for many years that Serbs preferred seceding from Bosnia than favouring a centralized Bosnian state. In 2006, after Montenegro separated from Serbia, claims for a similar referendum in Republika Srpska were also voiced. However, throughout the post-war period, "the number of those who support the Bosnian state has increased fourfold", even though in 2002 more than 50% of Bosnian Serbs wanted to be part of an independent state.[172] In 2017 Milorad Dodik, President of Bosnia-Herzegovina's Serb Republic, announced that no referendum on secession will be organized in 2018, but he also signalled that the idea is still contemplated for the future and criticized the European Union for "fading away" from the region.[173]

Public opinion polls conducted in 2012 in Serbia showed that half of the citizens were still in favour of EU membership, although the number of euro sceptics has increased by 10% compared to 2011. When asked to mention consequences of EU membership, most respondents said they would expect to increase Serbia's security (44%) or to contribute to combating corruption (44%) while 41% of respondents believed that joining the EU would lessen the possibility of Serbian citizens for deciding their own fate.[174] What also resulted from such opinion polls is that citizens in Serbia feel more secured by Russia (18%) than by EU (16%) or NATO (4%) while the majority of respondents favour military neutrality (44%).[175]

Regarding prospects of future EU integration, the surveys indicate optimism in Kosovo and pessimism in Serbia: 37% of people believe Kosovo will join the EU by 2020 and 25% by 2025 while only 6% said it would never join it. As opposed to this, in Serbia 9% expect the accession to EU to happen by 2020, 18% by 2025 and 38% expect this to never happen. In Montenegro 28% estimate 2020 as date of accession, 28% say it will happen in 2025 and 17% do not believe this would happen. In FYROM the EU accession is expected by 2020 (25%) or 2025 (24%), but 28% do not see this happening. Bosnia and Herzegovina displays two halves, an optimistic one anchored in the belief that BiH would join the EU either in 2020 (15%) or in 2025 (23%) and a pessimistic one, 33%, never expecting this.[176]

Surveys conducted in Kosovo in November 2017 reflect a strong association (33.5%) between the EU and "an entity that avoids conflicts between countries that are members of the Union and promotes peace and good relations among neighbouring countries", but also a perception that the EU embodies the most developed Western democracies (25.9%); yet, 29.6% of respondents correlate the EU with "an integration of Kosovar society in a union that consists of values completely different from our traditional values".[177]

The region is not as homogenous as the label and geographic representation tries to show. Perceptions of EU vary across countries from the Western Balkans. However, European integration is on the agenda of each of these countries and support of EU is not dropping dramatically, even though their integration is always postponed. The countries included in the Western Balkans region seem to be victims of the so-called "enlargement fatigue" and EU accession sometimes seems to be elusive, even though, as shown previously, there is a growing support for the EU. Norm transference and norm internalization are processes that take time. For Europeanization of the Western Balkans to function, the EU should stay closer to countries from the region and consistently act on its commitments.

The countries from the region labelled as Western Balkans have been going through difficult post-socialist and post-war reconstruction. As discussed in previous sections, the identities in the region have always been multiple and intersecting. As a whole, the identity of the region is decided by outside actors and seems to be exogenous to the countries' agency. The term Western Balkans incorporates both prospects for future European integration, but also recollections of Balkanness, as opposed to the rest of Europe. Such identity (with all its historical burden and innate stereotypes) has been attributed to region. There are rejections of both this "given" identity and forms of incorporation, as if one cannot escape it.

Notes

1 F. Wilmer, *The Social Construction Man, the State, and War. Identity, Conflict, and Violence in Former Yugoslavia*, New York-London, Routledge, 2002, p. 41.
2 A. Djilas, *The Contested Country. Yugoslav Unity and Communist Revolution (1919–1953)*, Cambridge, MA, Harvard University Press, 1991, pp. 161–162.
3 Djilas, *The Contested Country*, pp. 161–162.
4 Wilmer, *The Social Construction Man*, p. 41.
5 P. Shoup, *Communism and the Yugoslav National Question*, New York, Columbia University Press, 1968. See also, P. Shoup 'Yugoslavia's National Minorities Under Communism', *Slavic Review. American Quarterly of Soviet and East-European Studies*, vol. XXII, no. 1, 1963, pp. 64–81.
6 Djilas, *The Contested Country*, pp. 150–151.
7 D. Rusinow, 'Popoarele Iugoslave', in P.F. Sugar, *Naționalismul Est-European în Secolul al XX-lea (East-European Nationalism During the XXth century)*, București, Curtea Veche, 2002, p. 322.
8 G. Schőpflin, *Nations, Identity, Power: The New Politics of Europe*, London, Hurst and Company, 2000, p. 339
9 Djilas, *The Contested Country*, pp. 160–164.
10 Djilas, *The Contested Country*, pp. 160–164.
11 M. Tepavać, 'Tito, 1945–1980', in J. Udovički and J. Ridgeway (eds.), *Burn This House. The Making and Unmaking of Yugoslavia*, Durham-London, Duke University Press, 1997, p. 65.
12 Tepavać, 'Tito, 1945–1980', p. 65.
13 D. Ugrešić, *The Culture of Lies*, London, Phoenix House, 1998; Wilmer, *The Social Construction Man, the State, and War*, p. 128.
14 S.K. Pavlowitch, *Yugoslavia*, London, Ernest Benn Limited, 1971, p. 187.
15 See, *inter alia*, A. Wendt, *Social Theory of International Politics*, Cambridge, Cambridge University Press, 1999; V. Kubálková; N. Onuf and P. Kowert (eds.), *International Relations in a Constructed World*, Armonk, M.E. Sharpe, 1998; N. Onuf, *World of Our Making. Rules and Rule in Social Theory and International Relations*, Columbia, University of South Carolina Press, 1989; M. Barnett, 'Social Constructivism', in J. Baylis and S. Smith (eds.), *The Globalization of World Politics. An Introduction to International Relations*, Oxford, Oxford University Press, 2005; F. Kratochwil, 'Constructing a New Orthodoxy? Wendt's Social Theory of International Politics and the Constructivist Challenge', in S. Guzzini and A. Leander (eds.), *Constructivism and International Relations*, London-New York, Routledge, 2006, pp. 21–47; M. Zehfuss, *Constructivism in International Relations. The Politics of Reality*, Cambridge, Cambridge University Press, 2002; A. Wendt, 'The Agent-Structure Problem in International Relations Theory', *International Organization*, vol. 41, no. 3, 1987, pp. 335–354.
16 Wilmer, *The Social Construction Man*, p. 66.
17 Wilmer, *The Social Construction Man*, p. 67.
18 Wilmer, *The Social Construction Man*, p. 75.
19 H. Blumer, *Symbolic Interactionism: Perspective and Method*, Englewood Cliffs, Prentice Hall, 1969.

20 W. Zimmerman, 'Yugoslav Strategies of Survival: 1948–1980', in W.S. Vucinich (ed.), *War and Society in East Central Europe. At the Brink of War and Peace: The Tito-Stalin Split in a Historic Perspective*, New York, Brooklyn College Studies, 1982, p. 12.
21 A. Djilas, *The Contested Country*, p. 165.
22 Djilas, *The Contested Country*, p. 165.
23 Wilmer, *The Social Construction Man*, p. 43.
24 S. Ramet, *Nationalism and Federalism in Yugoslavia, 1962–1991*, Bloomington, Indiana University Press, 1992.
25 Wilmer, *The Social Construction Man*, p. 87.
26 Wilmer, *The Social Construction Man*, p. 89.
27 Wilmer, *The Social Construction Man*, pp. 87–92.
28 Wilmer, *The Social Construction Man*, pp. 88–89, 91.
29 S. Drakuli, *The Balkan Express: Fragments from the Other Side of the War*, New York-London, W.W. Norton & Company, 1993; Wilmer, *The Social Construction Man, the State, and War*, p. 92.
30 M. Kaldor, 'Bosnia-Herzegovina: A Case Study of a New War', in M. Kaldor (ed.), *New and Old Wars*, Stanford, Stanford University Press, 2001, p. 36.
31 Wilmer, *The Social Construction Man*, p. 93.
32 Wilmer, *The Social Construction Man*, p. 93.
33 R.C. Taras and R. Ganguly, *Understanding Ethnic Conflict. The International Dimension*, third edition, New York-London, Longman, 2008, p. 12.
34 Wendt, *Social Theory of International Politics*, p. 132.
35 Taras and Ganguly, *Understanding Ethnic Conflict*, p. 12.
36 C. Zürcher, *The Post-Soviet Wars. Rebellion, Ethnic Conflict, and Nationhood in the Caucasus*, New York-London, New York University Press, 2007, p. 54.
37 V. Tishkov, 'Ethnic Conflict in the Former USSR: The Use and Misuse of Typologies and Data', *Journal of Peace Research*, vol. 36, no. 5, 1999, p. 572.
38 Zürcher, *The Post-Soviet Wars*, p. 55.
39 L.M. Herţa, 'The Violent Conflicts in Former Yugoslavia and the Vacillations of The West: Transatlantic Discourse Constructions of the Yugoslav Wars', *On-line Journal Modelling the New Europe*, vol. 17, 2015, pp. 164–185.
40 L. Hansen, *Security as Practice: Discourse Analysis and the Bosnian War*, London-New York, Routledge, 2006, pp. 5, 27, 94, 96.
41 Kaldor, 'Bosnia-Herzegovina', pp. 58–59.
42 Kaldor, 'Bosnia-Herzegovina', pp. 58–59.
43 Hansen, *Security as Practice*, p. 104.
44 L.M. Herţa, 'Intra-State Violence in Bosnia-Herzegovina and the Mixed Reactions from the International Community. An Analysis of the Ambivalence of the Transatlantic World', *Romanian Review of International Studies*, vol. VI, 2, no. 2014, pp. 23–38.
45 Quoted in Hansen, *Security as Practice*, p. 94.
46 Hansen, *Security as Practice*, p. 94.
47 T. Gallagher, *The Balkans After the Cold War. From Tyranny to Tragedy*, London-New York, Routledge, 2003, pp. 93–94.
48 Gallagher, *The Balkans After the Cold War*, pp. 93–94.
49 Hansen, *Security as Practice*, pp. 96–97.
50 Hansen, *Security as Practice*, pp. 114–116.
51 Hansen, *Security as Practice*, p. 114.
52 Quoted in Gallagher, *The Balkans after the Cold War*, p. 97.
53 Herţa, 'The Violent Conflicts in Former Yugoslavia and the Vacillations of the West', pp. 178–182.
54 M. Smith, 'The Kosovo Conflict. U.S. Diplomacy and Western Public Opinion', *CPD Perspectives on Public Diplomacy*, Paper 3, 2009, p. 21.
55 B. Steele, *Ontological Security in International Relations. Self-Identity and the IR State*, London-New York, Routledge, 2008, p. 135.

56 B. Weber, 'Germany's Shift on Bosnia Policy', *Democracy and Security in Southeastern Europe*, May 2011, www.democratizationpolicy.org/pdf/Bodo_Weber-Germanys_shift_on_Bosnia_policy.pdf, (accessed 25 June 2018), p. 16.

57 Steele, *Ontological Security in International Relations*, p. 136.

58 J. Bugajski, 'The Western Balkans', *Oxford Bibliographies*, 27 September 2017, www.oxfordbibliographies.com/view/document/obo-9780199743292/obo-9780199743292-0094.xml, (accessed 25 June 2018).

59 *EU-Western Balkans Summit Declaration*, Thessaloniki, 21 June 2003, 10229/03 (Presse 163), www.consilium.europa.eu/ueDocs/cms_Data/docs/pressdata/en/misc/76291.pdf, (accessed 25 June 2018).

60 See: I. Manners, 'Normative Power Europe: A Contradiction in Terms?', *Journal of Common Market Studies*, vol. 40. No. 2, 2002, pp. 235–258; S. Lucarelli and I. Manners (eds.), *Values and Principles in European Union Foreign Policy*, London-New York, Routledge, 2006.

61 Z. Laïdi (ed.), *EU Foreign Policy in a Globalized World. Normative Power and Social Preferences*, London-New York, Routledge, 2008, p. 4.

62 J.T. Checkel, 'International Institutions and Socialization in Europe: Introduction and Framework', in J.T. Checkel (ed.), *International Institutions and Socialization in Europe*, Cambridge, Cambridge University Press, 2007, p. 4.

63 I. Štiks, 'The European Union and Citizenship Regimes in the Western Balkans', in J. Rupnik (ed.), *The Western Balkans and the EU: 'the Hour of Europe'*, Paris, Institute for Security Studies European Union, 2011, p. 123.

64 C. Marazopoulos, 'Constructing the Western Balkans: Understanding the European Commission's Regional Approach from a Constructivist Perspective', PhD Thesis, University of Bath, 2013, http://opus.bath.ac.uk/44950/1/MARAZOPOULOS_Christos_PhD_Thesis_final.pdf, (accessed 25 June 2018).

65 K. Fidanovski, 'Why I Don't Like the Term "Western Balkans". A Comment', *Osservatorio Balcani e Caucaso*, 29 May 2018, www.balcanicaucaso.org/eng/Areas/Balcani-notizie/Why-I-don-t-like-the-term-Western-Balkans-187621, (accessed 25 June 2018).

66 European Commission, *Stability Pact for South-Eastern Europe*, 1999, https://ec.europa.eu/neighbourhood-enlargement/policy/glossary/terms/stability-pact_en, (accessed 25 June 2018).

67 Following the meeting of Foreign Ministers of South-East European Cooperation Process (SEECP), in February 2008, when the RCC was officially launched.

68 Fidanovski, 'Why I Don't Like the Term "Western Balkans"'.

69 Fidanovski, 'Why I Don't Like the Term "Western Balkans"'.

70 'Croatian Pupils Voice Mixed Views on "Balkan" Identity', *Balkan Insight*, January 2018, www.balkaninsight.com/en/article/croatian-pupils-split-between-europe-and-balkans-01-11-2018, (accessed 25 June 2018).

71 J.C. Juncker, 'President Jean-Claude Juncker's State of the Union Address', speech, Brussels, 13 September 2017, http://europa.eu/rapid/press-release_SPEECH-17-3165_en.htm, (accessed 25 June 2018).

72 C. Stephen, *Judgement Day: The Trial of Slobodan Milošević*, New York, Atlantic Monthly Press, 2005, p. 159.

73 'Koštunica on SAA: Who Dares to Become Accomplice', *B92*, 26 April 2008, www.b92.net/eng/news/politics.php?yyyy=2008&mm=04&dd=26&nav_id=49765, (accessed 25 June 2018).

74 Ph. Webb, *International Judicial Integration and Fragmentation*, Croydon, Oxford University Press, 2013, p. 167.

75 The Delegation of the European Union to the Republic of Serbia, *Milestones in EU-Serbia Relations*, http://europa.rs/serbia-and-the-eu/milestones/?lang=en, (accessed 25 June 2018).

76 P. Tomic and E. Moroiu, 'Istoria nu începe cu aderarea Serbiei la UE! Cine sunt de fapt vlahii din Serbia', *RFI*, 29 February 2012, www.rfi.ro/articol/stiri/politica/istoria-nu-incepe-aderarea-serbiei-ue-cine-sunt-fapt-vlahii-serbia, (accesses 25 June 2018).

77 S. Ghica, 'România îşi reafirmă sprijinul pentru integrarea Serbiei în UE, chiar dacă românii timoceni rămân lipsiţi de drepturi', *Adevărul*, 8 March 2018, http://adevarul.ro/news/eveniment/romania-isi-reafirma-sprijinul-integrarea-serbiei-ue-romanii-timoceni-raman-lipsiti-drepturi-1_5aa12675df52022f7556505c/index.html, (accessed 25 June 2018).

78 The Delegation of the European Union to the Republic of Serbia, *Milestones in EU-Serbia Relations*.

79 European Commission, *Serbia 2018 Report. Accompanying the Document. Communication from the Commission to the European Parliament, the Council, the European Economic and Social Committee and the Committee of the Regions. 2018 Communication on EU Enlargement Policy*, 17 April 2018 SWD(2018) 152 final.

80 E. Casinge, 'Commission could spend EU funds better in Serbia, auditors say', *Euractiv*, 13 January 2015, www.euractiv.com/section/enlargement/news/commission-could-spend-eu-funds-better-in-serbia-auditors-say, (accessed 25 June 2018).

81 European Neighbourhood Policy and Enlargement Negotiations, European Commission, *Serbia – Financial Assistance Under IPA II*, https://ec.europa.eu/neighbourhood-enlargement/instruments/funding-by-country/serbia_en, (accessed 25 June 2018).

82 E. Dijxhoorn, *Quasi-state Entities and International Criminal Justice: Legitimising Narratives and Counter-Narratives*, New York, Taylor & Francis, 2017, p. 91.

83 C. Hasselbach, 'Kosovo question still divides EU', *Deutsche Welle*, 8 September 2012, www.dw.com/en/kosovo-question-still-divides-eu/a-16226802, (accessed 25 June 2018).

84 M. Milanovic and M. Wood (eds.), *The Law and Politics of the Kosovo Advisory Opinion*, Oxford, Oxford University Press, 2015, pp. 264–265.

85 A. Vasovic, 'Serbia Must Reach Agreement with Kosovo to Join EU by 2025', *Reuters*, 7 February 2018, www.reuters.com/article/us-serbia-eu-enlargement/serbia-must-reach-agreement-with-kosovo-to-join-eu-by-2025-idUSKBN1FR2JP, (accessed 25 June 2018).

86 S. Grobe, 'Serbian PM: Kosovo Major Obstacle in EU Talks', *Euronews*, 11 October 2017, www.euronews.com/2017/10/11/serbian-pm-kosovo-major-obstacle-in-eu-talks, (accessed 25 June 2018).

87 Grobe, 'Serbian PM'.

88 J. Simić, 'Most Serbs Support EU Membership, Cite Job Opportunities, in New Poll', *Euractiv*, 25 January 2018, www.euractiv.com/section/enlargement/news/most-serbs-support-eu-membership-cite-job-opportunities-in-new-poll, (accessed 25 June 2018).

89 S. Bjelotomic, 'Forced to Pick Between Kosovo and EU, Serbs Would Pick Kosovo', *Serbian Monitor*, 29 March 2018, http://serbianmonitor.com/en/forced-to-pick-between-kosovo-and-eu-serbs-would-pick-kosovo/, (accessed 25 June 2018).

90 F. Bytyci, 'Serbia Must Accept Kosovo Independence to join EU: German Foreign Minister', *Reuters*, 14 February 2018, www.reuters.com/article/us-kosovo-germany-serbia/serbia-must-accept-kosovo-independence-to-join-eu-german-foreign-minister-idUSKCN1FY329, (accessed 25 June 2018).

91 For an analysis of institutional reform in Montenegro, see: A. Corpădean, 'Les Fondements de la Bonne Gouvernance au Monténégro Dans le Contexte de Son Intégration Euro-Atlantique', in S. Mişcoiu (ed.), *La «bonne gouvernance», peut-elle freiner le recul démocratique contemporain?*, Larcier-Bruylant (publication pending). Also, for a comparative view of Montenegro's NATO and EU integration bids, see: A. Corpădean, 'Assessments and Prospects for the Integration of the West Balkans. The Case of Montenegro', *On-line Journal Modelling the New Europe*, vol. 25, 2018, pp. 87–105 – recurrently quoted in the present text.

92 See, for instance: O. Alger, *Montenegro History and Culture: Early History, Montenegro and Serbia Period, Separation Process and History, Self-Sovereignty, People, and Environment, Tourism*, Create Space Independent Publishing Platform, 2016; K. Morrison, *Montenegro: A Modern History*, London, I.B. Tauris, 2008.

93 D. Högger, *The Recognition of States: A Study on the Historical Development in Doctrine and Practice with a Special Focus on the Requirements*, Zurich, LIT Verlag, 2015, p. 168.

94 See: L.M. Herța, *De la Relațiile Româno-Sârbe la Relațiile Româno-Iugoslave. Interpretări Constructiviste*, Cluj-Napoca, EFES, 2012, pp. 66–71, 89, 137, 158–159.

95 R. Bideleux and I. Jeffries, *The Balkans: A Post-Communist History*, New York, Routledge, 2007, pp. 477–478.

96 Morrison, *Montenegro*, p. 68.

97 K. Liebscher et al. (eds.), *European Economic Integration and South-East Europe: Challenges and Prospects*, Northampton, Edward Elgar Publishing, 2005, p. 165.

98 J. Kim, 'Serbia and Montenegro Union: Prospects and Policy Implications', *Report for US Congress*, 2 February 2005, https://fas.org/sgp/crs/row/RS21568.pdf, (accessed 25 June 2018).

99 M. Braniff, *Integrating the Balkans: Conflict Resolution and the Impact of EU Expansion*, London, I.B. Tauris, 2011, pp. 141–142.

100 Bideleux and Jeffries, *The Balkans*, pp. 500–501.

101 See: OSCE, ODIHR, *Republic of Montenegro Referendum on State-Status 21 May 2006, OSCE/ODIHR Referendum Observation Mission Final Report*, Warsaw, 4 August 2006, www.osce.org/odihr/elections/montenegro/20099?download=true, (accessed 25 June 2018).

102 A. Fruhstorfer and M. Hein, *Constitutional Politics in Central and Eastern Europe: From Post-Socialist Transition to the Reform of Political Systems*, Berlin, Springer, 2016, p. 295.

103 M. Cini and N. Nieves Pérez-Solórzano Borragán, *European Union Politics*, Oxford University Press, 2016, p. 233.

104 *Council Decision of 22 January 2007 on the Principles, Priorities and Conditions Contained in the European Partnership with Montenegro (2007/49/EC)*, Official Journal of the European Union L 20/16, 27 January 2007, https://eur-lex.europa.eu/legal-content/EN/TXT/HTML/?uri=CELEX:32007D0049&from=EN, (accessed 25 June 2018).

105 Council of the European Union, *Stabilisation and Association Agreement Between the European Communities and Their Member States of the One Part, and the Republic of Montenegro, of the Other Part*, Brussels, 21 September 2007, 2007/0123(AVC), http://register.consilium.europa.eu/doc/srv?l=EN&f=ST%2011566%202007%20INIT, (accessed 25 June 2018).

106 European Commission, *Analytical Report. Communication from the Commission to the European Parliament and the Council. Commission Opinion on Serbia's Application for Membership of the European Union*, Brussels, 12 October 2011, COM (2011) 668, www.europa.rs/upload/Report%202011.pdf, (accessed 25 June 2018).

107 European Council, *Delegations Will Find Attached the Revised Version of the Presidency Conclusions of the Brussels European Council*, Presidency Conclusions, Brussels, 17 July 2008, 11018/1/08, www.consilium.europa.eu/ueDocs/cms_Data/docs/pressData/en/ec/101346.pdf, (accessed 25 June 2018).

108 European Commission, *Visa Free Travel for Citizens of the Former Yugoslav Republic of Macedonia, Montenegro and Serbia Before Christmas*, 30 November 2009, IP/09/1852, http://europa.eu/rapid/press-release_IP-09-1852_en.htm, (accessed 25 June 2018).

109 'EU Advances Membership Talks for Montenegro, Serbia', *Euractiv*, 12 December 2017, www.euractiv.com/section/enlargement/news/eu-advances-membership-talks-for-serbia-montenegro, (accessed 25 June 2018).

110 A. Ilirjani, *The Euro Before the EU?: An Estimate of the Economic Effects of Euroization in the Western Balkans*, Chapel Hill, Globic Press, 2006, p. 103.
111 European Commission, *Montenegro 2016 Report. Accompanying the Document Communication from the Commission to the European Parliament, the Council, the European Economic and Social Committee and the Committee of the Regions. 2016 Communication on EU Enlargement Policy*, Commission Staff Working Document, COM (2016) 715 final, Brussels, 9 November 2016, https://ec.europa.eu/neighbourhood-enlargement/sites/near/files/pdf/key_documents/2016/20161109_report_montenegro.pdf, (accessed 25 June 2018).
112 'National Minimum Wage – Montenegro', *Country Economy*, 2017, http://countryeconomy.com/national-minimum-wage/Montenegro, (accessed 25 June 2018).
113 Statistical Office of Montenegro, *Census 2011 Data*, www.monstat.org/eng/page.php?id=393&pageid=57, (accessed 25 June 2018).
114 Delegation of the European Union to Montenegro, *Positive Attitude Towards the European Union Grows*, 18 January 2018, www.delmne.ec.europa.eu/code/navigate.php?Id=3973, (accessed 25 June 2018).
115 J. Bugajski, *Ethnic Politics in Eastern Europe: A Guide to Nationality Policies, Organizations, and Parties*, Armonk, M.E. Sharpe, 1995, pp. 102–104.
116 M. Klemenčič and M. Žagar, *The Former Yugoslavia's Diverse Peoples: A Reference Sourcebook*, Santa Barbara, ABC-CLIO, 2004, p. 358.
117 Government of the Republic of Macedonia, Secretariat for European Affairs, *Timeline of the Relations with EU*, www.sep.gov.mk/en/content/?id=8#.WuZLKYhuaUl, (accessed 25 June 2018). See also: Delegation of the European Union to the Former Yugoslav Republic of Macedonia *Chronology of Bilateral Relations*, http://eeas.europa.eu/archives/delegations/the_former_yugoslav_republic_of_macedonia/eu_the_former_yugoslav_republic_of_macedonia/chronology/index_en.htm, (accessed 25 June 2018).
118 European Commission, *Start of the High Level Accession Dialogue with the Government of the Former Yugoslav Republic of Macedonia*, MEMO/12/187, Skopje, 15 March 2012, http://europa.eu/rapid/press-release_MEMO-12-187_en.htm?locale=en, (accessed 25 June 2018).
119 European Commission, *The Former Yugoslav Republic of Macedonia 2018 Report. Communication from the Commission to the European Parliament, the Council, the European Economic and Social Committee and the Committee of the Regions 2018 Communication on EU Enlargement Policy*, Commission Staff Working Document, Strasbourg, 17.4.2018 SWD(2018) 154 final, https://ec.europa.eu/neighbourhood-enlargement/sites/near/files/20180417-the-former-yugoslav-republic-of-macedonia-report.pdf, (accessed 25 June 2018).
120 European Commission, *The Former Yugoslav Republic of Macedonia 2018 Report*, p. 5.
121 For such an outlook, see: J. Shea, *Macedonia and Greece: The Struggle to Define a New Balkan Nation*, Jefferson, McFarland, 2008.
122 See: A. Vangeli, 'Nation-Building Ancient Macedonian Style: The Origins and the Effects of the So-called Antiquisation in Macedonia', *Nationalities Papers*, vol. 39, January 2011, pp. 13–32.
123 S.J. Marusic, 'Bulgaria and Greece Block Macedonia's EU Talks', *Balkan Insight*, 12 December 2012, www.balkaninsight.com/en/article/bulgaria-joins-greece-in-blocking-macedonia-s-eu-bid, (accessed 25 June 2018).
124 M. Jones, 'Macedonia Has Four Options to Resolve Name Dispute with Greece: PM', *Reuters*, 27 February 2018, www.reuters.com/article/us-macedonia-greece/macedonia-has-four-options-to-resolve-name-dispute-with-greece-pm-idUSKCN1GB1WA, (accessed 25 June 2018).
125 'Greek, Macedonian Officials See Progress in Name Dispute', *Radio Free Europe/Radio Liberty*, 23 March 2018, www.rferl.org/a/greece-macedonia-name-dispute-skopje-negotiations/29120384.html, (accessed 25 June 2018).

126 T. Jansen and S. Van Hecke, *At Europe's Service: The Origins and Evolution of the European People's Party*, London-New York, Springer, 2011, p. 79.
127 The pro-EU agenda of the Party also emerges from the strategic documents published on its official platform: www.sdsm.org.mk.
128 Same observation as the preceding. See: http://bdi.mk/en/index.php.
129 'Public Support for EU Membership in Macedonia Drops to 77%: Poll', *Macedonian Information Agency*, 17 February 2017, www.mia.mk/en/Inside/RenderSingleNews/289/133575238, (accessed 25 June 2018.
130 J.E. Cole, *Ethnic Groups of Europe: An Encyclopaedia*, Santa Barbara, ABC-CLIO, 2011, p. 8.
131 'Zaev: Real Possibilities for Macedonia to Receive Date for EU Accession Negotiations', *European Western Balkans*, 8 September 2017, https://europeanwesternbalkans.com/2017/09/08/zaev-real-possibilities-macedonia-recieve-date-eu-accession-negotiations, (accessed 25 June 2018).
132 R. Belloni, *State Building and International Intervention in Bosnia*, London-New York, Routledge, 2007, p. 21.
133 Belloni, *State Building and International Intervention in Bosnia*, p. 21.
134 F. Friedman, *Bosnia and Herzegovina. A Polity on the Brink*, London-New York, Routledge, 2005, p. 116.
135 Belloni, *State Building and International Intervention in Bosnia*, p. 16.
136 F. Bieber, *Post-War Bosnia. Ethnicity, Inequality and Public Sector Governance*, Basingstoke, Palgrave Macmillan, 2006, p. 44.
137 Belloni, *State Building and International Intervention in Bosnia*, p. 46.
138 Belloni, *State Building and International Intervention in Bosnia*, p. 46.
139 Directorate for European Integration Bosnia and Herzegovina, *Chronology of Relations Between BiH and the EU*, www.dei.gov.ba/dei/bih_eu/default.aspx?id=9808&langTag=en-US, (accessed 25 June 2018).
140 Belloni, *State Building and International Intervention in Bosnia*, p. 152.
141 R. Prodi, 'The State of the Union in 2003', Speech, Plenary Session of the European Parliament, Strasbourg, 11 March 2003, http://europa.eu/rapid/press-release_SPEECH-03-120_en.htm, (accessed 25 June 2018).
142 Belloni, *State Building and International Intervention in Bosnia*, p. 154.
143 I. Štiks, 'The European Union and Citizenship Regimes in the Western Balkans', in J. Rupnik (ed.), *The Western Balkans and the EU: 'the Hour of Europe'*, Paris, Institute for Security Studies European Union, 2011, June 2011, p. 130.
144 Štiks, 'The European Union and Citizenship Regimes in the Western Balkans', pp. 127–130.
145 D. Sarajlić-Maglić, 'BiH After the Elections – A Tale of Disillusioned Iptimism', in J. Rupnik (ed.), *The Western Balkans and the EU: 'the Hour of Europe'*, Paris, Institute for Security Studies European Union, 2011, p. 54.
146 European Union in Bosnia and Herzegovina, *EUD/EUSR – Delegation of the European Union to Bosnia and Herzegovina and European Union Special Representative*, www.eubih.eu/eu-delegation-eu-special-representative-in-bih, (accessed 25 June 2018).
147 European Neighbourhood Policy and Enlargement Negotiations, European Commission, *Bosnia and Herzegovina*, https://ec.europa.eu/neighbourhood-enlargement/countries/detailed-country-information/bosnia-herzegovina_en, (accessed 25 June 2018).
148 Belloni, *State Building and International Intervention in Bosnia*, p. 161.
149 European Parliament, *Report on the 2016 Commission Report on Bosnia and Herzegovina*, (2016/2313(INI)), 6 February 2017, www.europarl.europa.eu/sides/getDoc.do?pubRef=-//EP//NONSGML+REPORT+A8-2017-0026+0+DOC+PDF+V0//EN, (accessed 25 June 2018).

150 European Parliament, *Report on the 2016 Commission Report on Bosnia and Herzegovina.*
151 European Commission, *Bosnia and Herzegovina 2018 Report. Accompanying the Document Communication from the Commission to the European Parliament, the Council, the European Economic and Social Committee and the Committee of the Regions 2018 Communication on EU Enlargement Policy*, Commission Staff Working Document, Strasbourg, 17 April 2018, https://eur-lex.europa.eu/legal-content/EN/TXT/PDF/?uri=CELEX:52018SC0155&from=EN, (accessed 25 June 2018).
152 European Commission, *Bosnia and Herzegovina 2018 Report.*
153 See: B.J. Gippert, *Local Legitimacy in Peacebuilding: Pathways to Local Compliance with International Police Reform*, New York, Routledge, 2017.
154 A. Fagan, *Europe's Balkan Dilemma: Paths to Civil Society or State-Building?*, London, I.B. Tauris, 2012, pp. 35–38.
155 A. Kartsonaki, *Breaking Away: Kosovo's Unilateral Secession*, Lanham, Lexington Books, 2018, p. 76.
156 See: M. Kmezic, *EU Rule of Law Promotion: Judiciary Reform in the Western Balkans*, New York, Routledge, 2016.
157 M. Spernbauer, *EU Peacebuilding in Kosovo and Afghanistan: Legality and Accountability*, Boston, Martinus Nijhoff Publishers, 2014, pp. 168–171.
158 European Union Office in Kosovo, *An Overview of Relations Between the EU and Kosovo*, 12 May 2016, https://eeas.europa.eu/delegations/kosovo/1387/kosovo-and-eu_en, (accessed 25 June 2018).
159 European Union Office in Kosovo, *An Overview of Relations between the EU and Kosovo.*
160 Kartsonaki, *Breaking Away*, p. 84.
161 E. Schleicher, *Positive Peace in Kosovo: A Dream Unfulfilled*, Frankfurt am Main, Peter Lang, 2012, p. 66.
162 European Union Office in Kosovo, *An Overview of Relations Between the EU and Kosovo.*
163 European Commission, *Kosovo 2018 Report. Accompanying the Document Communication from the Commission to the European Parliament, the Council, the European Economic and Social Committee and the Committee of the Regions 2018 Communication on EU Enlargement Policy*, Commission Staff Working Document, Strasbourg, 14 April 2018, SWD (2018) 156 final, https://ec.europa.eu/neighbourhood-enlargement/sites/near/files/20180417-kosovo-report.pdf, (accessed 25 June 2018).
164 J. Simić, 'Balkan Citizens Doubt They Will Ever Join EU', *Euractiv*, 12 October 2017, www.euractiv.com/section/enlargement/news/balkan-citizens-doubt-they-will-ever-join-eu, (accessed 25 June 2018).
165 H. Thaçi, 'EU Enlargement: Tear Down Mental Walls in the Balkans', *Euractiv*, 5 October 2017, www.euractiv.com/section/enlargement/opinion/eu-enlargement-tear-down-mental-walls-in-the-balkans, (accessed 2 June 2018).
166 Gallup Balkan Monitor, *Perceptions of the EU in the Western Balkans*, 2009, www.esiweb.org/enlargement/wp-content/uploads/2009/02/2009-Focus-on-perceptions-of-the-EU-in-the-Western-Balkans.pdf, (accessed 25 June 2018).
167 Gallup Balkan Monitor, *Insights and Perceptions: Voices of the Balkans, Summary of Finding 2010*, http://reforma.bezbednost.org/wp-content/uploads/downloads/2012/09/2010-Balkan-Monitor-Insights-and-Perceptions-Voices-of-the-Balkans-GALLUP-i-European-Fund-for-the-Balkans1.pdf, (accessed 25 June 2018), p. 7; R. Manchin, 'Balkan Public Opinion and EU Accession', in J. Rupnik (ed.), *The Western Balkans and the EU: 'the Hour of Europe'*, Paris, Institute for Security Studies European Union, 2011, pp. 163–172.
168 E. Turbedar, 'Balkan Barometer 2015. Public Opinion Survey. Analytical Report', *Regional Cooperation Council*, vol. 1, Sarajevo, 2015, www.rcc.int/seeds/files/

RCC_BalkanBarometer2015_PublicOpinion_FIN_forWeb.pdf, (accessed 25 June 2018).

169 M. Handjiska-Trendafilova, 'Public Opinion Survey. Balkan Barometer 2017', *Regional Cooperation Council*, vol. 3, Sarajevo, 2017, www.rcc.int/seeds/files/RCC_BalkanBarometer_PublicOpinion_2017.pdf, (accessed 25 June 2018), pp. 54–55.

170 Gallup Balkan Monitor, *Insights and Perceptions*, p. 22.

171 Gallup Balkan Monitor, *Insights and Perceptions*, p. 22; See also Sarajlić-Maglić, 'BiH After the Elections', p. 55.

172 UNDP, *Early Warning System: Annual Report*, Sarajevo, 2002, in: R. Belloni, *State Building and International Intervention in Bosnia*, Routledge, 2007, p. 163.

173 A. Macdowall, 'Bosnia's Serb Republic Leader: No Breakaway Vote Next Year', *Politico*, June 2017, www.politico.eu/article/milorad-dodik-bosnia-serb-republic-serbia-leader-no-breakaway-vote-next-year/, (accessed 25 June 2018).

174 Belgrade Centre for Security Policy, *Citizens of Serbia Between EU, NATO and Russia. Public Opinion Survey Findings*, 17 October 2012, www.bezbednost.org/upload/document/citizens_of_serbia_between_eu_nato_and_russia_bcsp.pdf, (accessed 25 June 2018).

175 Belgrade Centre for Security Policy, *Citizens of Serbia Between EU, NATO and Russia*.

176 Handjiska-Trendafilova, 'Public Opinion Survey. Balkan Barometer 2017', p. 54.

177 U. Cucchi, 'Kosovo, European Integration and the SAA: An Analysis of Citizens' Perceptions', *Group for Legal and Political Studies*, vol. 03, 2017, www.legalpoliticalstudies.org/wp-content/uploads/2017/11/GLPS-Kosovo-European-Integration-and-the-SAA-An-analysis-on-citizens%E2%80%99-perceptions.pdf, (accessed 25 June 2018), p. 6.

Bibliography

Alger, O., *Montenegro History and Culture: Early History, Montenegro and Serbia Period, Separation Process and History, Self- Sovereignty, People, and Environment, Tourism*, Create Space Independent Publishing Platform, 2016.

Barnett, M., 'Social Constructivism', in J. Baylis and S. Smith, *The Globalization of World Politics. An Introduction to International Relations*, Oxford, Oxford University Press, 2005, pp. 148–165.

Belgrade Centre for Security Policy, *Citizens of Serbia between EU, NATO and Russia. Public Opinion Survey Findings*, 17 October 2012, www.bezbednost.org/upload/document/citizens_of_serbia_between_eu_nato_and_russia_bcsp.pdf, (accessed 25 June 2018).

Belloni, R., *State Building and International Intervention in Bosnia*, London-New York, Routledge, 2007.

Bideleux, R. and I. Jeffries, *The Balkans: A Post-Communist History*, New York, Routledge, 2007.

Bieber, F., *Post-War Bosnia. Ethnicity, Inequality and Public Sector Governance*, Basingstoke, Palgrave Macmillan, 2006.

Bjelotomic, S., 'Forced to pick between Kosovo and EU, Serbs would pick Kosovo', *Serbian Monitor*, 29 March 2018, http://serbianmonitor.com/en/forced-to-pick-between-kosovo-and-eu-serbs-would-pick-kosovo/, (accessed 25 June 2018).

Blumer, H., *Symbolic Interactionism: Perspective and Method*, Englewood Cliffs, Prentice Hall, 1969.

Braniff, M., *Integrating the Balkans: Conflict Resolution and the Impact of EU Expansion*, London, I.B. Tauris, 2011.

Bugajski, J., *Ethnic Politics in Eastern Europe: A Guide to Nationality Policies, Organizations, and Parties*, Armonk, M.E. Sharpe, 1995.

Bugajski, J., 'The Western Balkans', *Oxford Bibliographies*, 27 September 2017, www.oxfordbibliographies.com/view/document/obo-9780199743292/obo-9780199743292-0094.xml, (accessed 25 June 2018).

Bytyci, F., 'Serbia Must Accept Kosovo Independence to Join EU: German Foreign Minister', *Reuters*, 14 February 2018, www.reuters.com/article/us-kosovo-germany-serbia/serbia-must-accept-kosovo-independence-to-join-eu-german-foreign-minister-idUSKCN1FY329, (accessed 25 June 2018).

Casinge, E., 'Commission Could Spend EU Funds Better in Serbia, Auditors Say', *Euractiv*, 13 January 2015, www.euractiv.com/section/enlargement/news/commission-could-spend-eu-funds-better-in-serbia-auditors-say, (accessed 25 June 2018).

Checkel, J.T., 'International Institutions and Socialization in Europe: Introduction and Framework', in J.T. Checkel (ed.), *International Institutions and Socialization in Europe*, Cambridge, Cambridge University Press, 2007, pp. 3–28.

Cini, M. and N. Nieves Pérez-Solórzano Borragán, *European Union Politics*, New York, Oxford University Press, 2016.

Cole, J.E., *Ethnic Groups of Europe: An Encyclopaedia*, Santa Barbara, ABC-CLIO, 2011.

Corpădean, A., 'Assessments and Prospects for the Integration of the West Balkans. The Case of Montenegro', *On-line Journal Modelling the New Europe*, vol. 25, 2018, pp. 87–105.

Corpădean, A., 'Les Fondements de la Bonne Gouvernance au Monténégro Dans le Contexte de Son Intégration Euro-Atlantique', in S. Mişcoiu (ed.), *La " bonne gouvernance ", peut-elle freiner le recul démocratique contemporain ?*, Larcier-Bruylant (publication pending).

Council Decision of 22 January 2007 on the Principles, Priorities and Conditions Contained in the European Partnership with Montenegro (2007/49/EC), Official Journal of the European Union L 20/16, 27 January 2007, https://eur-lex.europa.eu/legal-content/EN/TXT/HTML/?uri=CELEX:32007D0049&from=EN, (accessed 25 June 2018).

Council of the European Union, *Stabilisation and Association Agreement Between the European Communities and Their Member States of the One Part, and the Republic of Montenegro, of the Other Part*, Brussels, 21 September 2007, 2007/0123(AVC), http://register.consilium.europa.eu/doc/srv?l=EN&f=ST%2011566%202007%20INIT, (accessed 25 June 2018).

'Croatian Pupils Voice Mixed Views on 'Balkan' Identity, *Balkan Insight*, January 2018, www.balkaninsight.com/en/article/croatian-pupils-split-between-europe-and-balkans-01-11-2018, (accessed 25 June 2018).

Cucchi, U., 'Kosovo, European Integration and the SAA: An Analysis of Citizens' Perceptions', *Group for Legal and Political Studies*, vol. 03, 2017, www.legalpoliticalstudies.org/wp-content/uploads/2017/11/GLPS-Kosovo-European-Integration-and-the-SAA-An-analysis-on-citizens%E2%80%99-perceptions.pdf, (accessed 25 June 2018).

Delegation of the European Union to Montenegro, *Positive Attitude Towards the European Union Grows*, 18 January 2018, www.delmne.ec.europa.eu/code/navigate.php?Id=3973, (accessed 25 June 2018).

Delegation of the European Union to the Former Yugoslav Republic of Macedonia *Chronology of Bilateral Relations*, http://eeas.europa.eu/archives/delegations/the_former_yugoslav_republic_of_macedonia/eu_the_former_yugoslav_republic_of_macedonia/chronology/index_en.htm, (accessed 25 June 2018).

Delegation of the European Union to the Former Yugoslav Republic of Macedonia, *The Former Yugoslav Republic of Macedonia and the EU*, 12 May 2016, https://eeas.europa.eu/delegations/former-yugoslav-republic-macedonia/1457/former-yugoslav-republic-macedonia-and-eu_en, (accessed 25 June 2018).

The Delegation of the European Union to the Republic of Serbia, *Milestones in EU-Serbia relations*, http://europa.rs/serbia-and-the-eu/milestones/?lang=en, (accessed 25 June 2018).

Dijxhoorn, E., *Quasi-state Entities and International Criminal Justice: Legitimising Narratives and Counter-Narratives*, New York, Taylor & Francis, 2017.

Directorate for European Integration Bosnia and Herzegovina, *Chronology of Relations Between BiH and the EU*, www.dei.gov.ba/dei/bih_eu/default.aspx?id=9808&langTag=en-US, (accessed 25 June 2018).

Djilas, A., *The Contested Country. Yugoslav Unity and Communist Revolution (1919–1953)*, Cambridge, MA, Harvard University Press, 1991.

Drakuli, S., *The Balkan Express: Fragments from the Other Side of the War*, New York-London, W.W. Norton & Company, 1993.

'EU Advances Membership Talks for Montenegro, Serbia', *Euractiv*, 12 December 2017, www.euractiv.com/section/enlargement/news/eu-advances-membership-talks-for-serbia-montenegro, (accessed 25 June 2018).

EU-Western Balkans Summit Declaration, Thessaloniki, 21 June 2003, 10229/03 (Presse 163),www.consilium.europa.eu/ueDocs/cms_Data/docs/pressdata/en/misc/76291.pdf, (accessed 25 June 2018).

European Commission, *Analytical Report. Communication from the Commission to the European Parliament and the Council. Commission Opinion on Serbia's Application for Membership of the European Union*, Brussels, 12 October 2011, COM (2011) 668, www.europa.rs/upload/Report%202011.pdf, (accessed 25 June 2018).

European Commission, *Bosnia and Herzegovina 2018 Report. Accompanying the Document Communication from the Commission to the European Parliament, the Council, the European Economic and Social Committee and the Committee of the Regions 2018 Communication on EU Enlargement Policy*, Commission Staff Working Document, Strasbourg, 17 April 2018, https://eur-lex.europa.eu/legal-content/EN/TXT/PDF/?uri=CELEX:52018SC0155&from=EN, (accessed 25 June 2018).

European Commission, *The Former Yugoslav Republic of Macedonia 2018 Report. Communication from the Commission to the European Parliament, the Council, the European Economic and Social Committee and the Committee of the Regions 2018 Communication on EU Enlargement Policy*, Commission Staff Working Document, Strasbourg, 17.4.2018 SWD(2018) 154 final, https://ec.europa.eu/neighbourhood-enlargement/sites/near/files/20180417-the-former-yugoslav-republic-of-macedonia-report.pdf, (accessed 25 June 2018).

European Commission, *Kosovo 2018 Report. Accompanying the document Communication from the Commission to the European Parliament, the Council, the European Economic and Social Committee and the Committee of the Regions 2018 Communication on EU Enlargement Policy*, Commission Staff Working Document, Strasbourg, 14 April 2018, SWD (2018) 156 final, https://ec.europa.eu/neighbourhood-enlargement/sites/near/files/20180417-kosovo-report.pdf, (accessed 25 June 2018).

European Commission, *Montenegro 2016 Report. Accompanying the Document Communication from the Commission to the European Parliament, the Council, the European Economic and Social Committee and the Committee of the Regions. 2016 Communication on EU Enlargement Policy*, Commission Staff Working Document, COM (2016)

715 final, Brussels, 9 November 2016, https://ec.europa.eu/neighbourhood-enlargement/sites/near/files/pdf/key_documents/2016/20161109_report_montenegro.pdf, (accessed 25 June 2018).

European Commission, *Serbia 2018 Report. Accompanying the Document. Communication from the Commission to the European Parliament, the Council, the European Economic and Social Committee and the Committee of the Regions. 2018 Communication on EU Enlargement Policy*, 17 April 2018 SWD(2018) 152 final.

European Commission, *Stability Pact for South-Eastern Europe*, 1999, https://ec.europa.eu/neighbourhood-enlargement/policy/glossary/terms/stability-pact_en, (accessed 25 June 2018).

European Commission, *Start of the High Level Accession Dialogue with the Government of the Former Yugoslav Republic of Macedonia*, MEMO/12/187, Skopje, 15 March 2012, http://europa.eu/rapid/press-release_MEMO-12-187_en.htm?locale=en, (accessed 25 June 2018).

European Commission, *Visa Free Travel for Citizens of the Former Yugoslav Republic of Macedonia, Montenegro and Serbia Before Christmas*, 30 November 2009, IP/09/1852, http://europa.eu/rapid/press-release_IP-09-1852_en.htm, (accessed 25 June 2018).

European Council, *Delegations Will Find Attached the Revised Version of the Presidency Conclusions of the Brussels European Council*, Presidency Conclusions, Brussels, 17 July 2008, 11018/1/08, www.consilium.europa.eu/ueDocs/cms_Data/docs/pressData/en/ec/101346.pdf, (accessed 25 June 2018).

European Neighbourhood Policy and Enlargement Negotiations, European Commission, *Bosnia and Herzegovina*, https://ec.europa.eu/neighbourhood-enlargement/countries/detailed-country-information/bosnia-herzegovina_en, (accessed 25 June 2018).

European Neighbourhood Policy and Enlargement Negotiations, European Commission, *Serbia – financial assistance under IPA II*, https://ec.europa.eu/neighbourhood-enlargement/instruments/funding-by-country/serbia_en, (accessed 25 June 2018).

European Parliament, *Report on the 2016 Commission Report on Bosnia and Herzegovina*, (2016/2313(INI)), 6 February 2017, www.europarl.europa.eu/sides/getDoc.do?pubRef=-//EP//NONSGML+REPORT+A8-2017-0026+0+DOC+PDF+V0//EN, (accessed 25 June 2018).

European Union in Bosnia and Herzegovina, *EUD/EUSR – Delegation of the European Union to Bosnia and Herzegovina and European Union Special Representative*, www.eubih.eu/eu-delegation-eu-special-representative-in-bih, (accessed 25 June 2018).

European Union Office in Kosovo, *An Overview of Relations Between the EU and Kosovo*, 12 May 2016, https://eeas.europa.eu/delegations/kosovo/1387/kosovo-and-eu_en, (accessed 25 June 2018).

Fagan, A., *Europe's Balkan Dilemma: Paths to Civil Society or State-Building?*, London, I.B. Tauris, 2012.

Fidanovski, K., 'Why I Don't Like the Term "Western Balkans". A Comment', 29 May 2018, *Osservatorio Balcani e Caucaso*, www.balcanicaucaso.org/eng/Areas/Balcani-notizie/Why-I-don-t-like-the-term-Western-Balkans-187621, (accessed 25 June 2018).

Friedman, F., *Bosnia and Herzegovina. A Polity on the Brink*, London-New York, Routledge, 2005.

Fruhstorfer, A. and M. Hein, *Constitutional Politics in Central and Eastern Europe: From Post-Socialist Transition to the Reform of Political Systems*, Berlin, Springer, 2016.

Gallagher, T., *The Balkans After the Cold War. From Tyranny to Tragedy*, London-New York, Routledge, 2003.

Gallup Balkan Monitor, *Insights and Perceptions: Voices of the Balkans, Summary of Finding 2010*, http://reforma.bezbednost.org/wp-content/uploads/downloads/2012/09/

2010-Balkan-Monitor-Insights-and-Perceptions-Voices-of-the-Balkans-GALLUP-i-European-Fund-for-the-Balkans1.pdf, (accessed 25 June 2018).

Gallup Balkan Monitor, *Perceptions of the EU in the Western Balkans*, 2009, www.esiweb.org/enlargement/wp-content/uploads/2009/02/2009-Focus-on-perceptions-of-the-EU-in-the-Western-Balkans.pdf, (accessed 25 June 2018).

Ghica, S., 'România îşi reafirmă sprijinul pentru integrarea Serbiei în UE, chiar dacă românii timoceni rămân lipsiţi de drepturi', *Adevărul*, 8 March 2018, http://adevarul.ro/news/eveniment/romania-isi-reafirma-sprijinul-integrarea-serbiei-ue-romanii-timoceni-raman-lipsiti-drepturi-1_5aa12675df52022f7556505c/index.html, (accessed 25 June 2018).

Gippert, B.J., *Local Legitimacy in Peacebuilding: Pathways to Local Compliance with International Police Reform*, New York, Routledge, 2017.

'Greek, Macedonian Officials See Progress in Name Dispute', *Radio Free Europe/Radio Liberty*, 23 March 2018, www.rferl.org/a/greece-macedonia-name-dispute-skopje-negotiations/29120384.html, (accessed 25 June 2018).

Government of the Republic of Macedonia, Secretariat for European Affairs, *Timeline of the Relations with EU*, www.sep.gov.mk/en/content/?id=8#.WuZLKYhuaUl, (accessed 25 June 2018).

Grobe, S., 'Serbian PM: Kosovo Major Obstacle in EU Talks', *Euronews*, 11 October 2017, www.euronews.com/2017/10/11/serbian-pm-kosovo-major-obstacle-in-eu-talks, (accessed 25 June 2018).

Handjiska-Trendafilova, M., 'Public Opinion Survey. Balkan Barometer 2017', *Regional Cooperation Council*, vol. 3, Sarajevo, 2017, www.rcc.int/seeds/files/RCC_BalkanBarometer_PublicOpinion_2017.pdf, (accessed 25 June 2018).

Hansen, L., *Security as Practice: Discourse Analysis and the Bosnian War*, London-New York, Routledge, 2006.

Hasselbach, C., 'Kosovo Question Still Divides EU', *Deutsche Welle*, 8 September 2012, www.dw.com/en/kosovo-question-still-divides-eu/a-16226802, (accessed 25 June 2018).

Herţa, L.M., *De la Relaţiile Româno-Sârbe la Relaţiile Româno-Iugoslave. Interpretări Constructiviste*, Cluj-Napoca, EFES, 2012.

Herţa, L.M., 'Intra-State Violence in Bosnia-Herzegovina and the Mixed Reactions from the International Community. An Analysis of the Ambivalence of the Transatlantic World', *Romanian Review of International Studies*, vol. VI, no. 2, 2014, pp. 23–38.

Herţa, L.M., 'The Violent Conflicts in Former Yugoslavia and the Vacillations of The West: Transatlantic Discourse Constructions of the Yugoslav Wars', *Online Journal Modelling the New Europe*, vol. 17, 2015, pp. 164–185.

Högger, D., *The Recognition of States: A Study on the Historical Development in Doctrine and Practice with a Special Focus on the Requirements*, Zurich, LIT Verlag, 2015.

Ilirjani, A., *The Euro Before the EU?: An Estimate of the Economic Effects of Euroization in the Western Balkans*, Chapel Hill, Globic Press, 2006.

Jansen, T. and S. Van Hecke, *At Europe's Service: The Origins and Evolution of the European People's Party*, London-New York, Springer, 2011.

Jones, M., 'Macedonia Has Four Options to Resolve Name Dispute with Greece: PM', *Reuters*, 27 February 2018, www.reuters.com/article/us-macedonia-greece/macedonia-has-four-options-to-resolve-name-dispute-with-greece-pm-idUSKCN1GB1WA, (accessed 25 June 2018).

Juncker, J.C., 'President Jean-Claude Juncker's State of the Union Address', speech, Brussels, 13 September 2017, http://europa.eu/rapid/press-release_SPEECH-17-3165_en.htm, (accessed 25 June 2018).

Kaldor, M., 'Bosnia-Herzegovina: A Case Study of a New War', in M. Kaldor (ed.), *New and Old Wars*, Stanford, Stanford University Press, 2001, pp. 31–68.

Kartsonaki, A., *Breaking Away: Kosovo's Unilateral Secession*, Lanham, Lexington Books, 2018.

Kim, J., 'Serbia and Montenegro Union: Prospects and Policy Implications', *Report for US Congress*, 2 February 2005, https://fas.org/sgp/crs/row/RS21568.pdf, (accessed 25 June 2018).

Klemenčič, M. and M. Žagar, *The Former Yugoslavia's Diverse Peoples: A Reference Sourcebook*, Santa Barbara, ABC-CLIO, 2004.

Kmezic, M., *EU Rule of Law Promotion: Judiciary Reform in the Western Balkans*, New York, Routledge, 2016.

'Koštunica on SAA: Who Dares to Become Accomplice', *B92*, 26 April 2008, www.b92.net/eng/news/politics.php?yyyy=2008&mm=04&dd=26&nav_id=49765, (accessed 25 June 2018).

Kratochwil, F., 'Constructing a New Orthodoxy? Wendt's Social Theory of International Politics and the Constructivist Challenge', in S. Guzzini and A. Leander (eds.), *Constructivism and International Relations*, London-New York, Routledge, 2006, pp. 21–47.

Kubálková, V., Onuf, N. and P. Kowert (eds.), *International Relations in a Constructed World*, Armonk, M.E. Sharpe, 1998.

Laïdi, Z. (ed.), *EU Foreign Policy in a Globalized World. Normative Power and Social Preferences*, London-New York, Routledge, 2008.

Liebscher, K. et al. (eds.), *European Economic Integration and South-East Europe: Challenges and Prospects*, Northampton, Edward Elgar Publishing, 2005.

Lucarelli, S. and I. Manners (eds.), *Values and Principles in European Union Foreign Policy*, London-New York, Routledge, 2006.

Macdowall, A., 'Bosnia's Serb Republic Leader: No Breakaway Vote Next Year', *Politico*, June 2017, www.politico.eu/article/milorad-dodik-bosnia-serb-republic-serbia-leader-no-breakaway-vote-next-year/, (accessed 25 June 2018).

Manchin, R., 'Balkan Public Opinion and EU Accession', in J. Rupnik (ed.), *The Western Balkans and the EU: 'the Hour of Europe'*, Paris, Institute for Security Studies European Union, 2011, pp. 163–172.

Manners, I., 'Normative Power Europe: A Contradiction in Terms?', *Journal of Common Market Studies*, vol. 40, no. 2, 2002, pp. 235–258.

Marazopoulos, C., 'Constructing the Western Balkans: Understanding The European Commission's Regional Approach from a Constructivist Perspective', PhD Thesis, University of Bath, 2013, http://opus.bath.ac.uk/44950/1/MARAZOPOULOS_Christos_PhD_Thesis_final.pdf, (accessed 25 June 2018).

Marusic, S.J., 'Bulgaria and Greece Block Macedonia's EU Talks', *Balkan Insight*, 12 December 2012, www.balkaninsight.com/en/article/bulgaria-joins-greece-in-blocking-macedonia-s-eu-bid, (accessed 25 June 2018).

Milanovic, M. and M. Wood (eds.), *The Law and Politics of the Kosovo Advisory Opinion*, Oxford, Oxford University Press, 2015.

Morrison, K., *Montenegro: A Modern History*, London, I.B. Tauris, 2008.

'National Minimum Wage – Montenegro', *Country Economy*, 2017, http://countryeconomy.com/national-minimum-wage/Montenegro, (accessed 25 June 2018).

Onuf, N., *World of Our Making. Rules and Rule in Social Theory and International Relations*, Columbia, University of South Carolina Press, 1989.

Ordanoski, S., 'The Story of Macedonian Populism: "All We Want Is Everything!"', in J. Rupnik (ed.), *The Western Balkans and the EU: 'the Hour of Europe'*, Paris, Institute for Security Studies European Union, 2011, pp. 95–110.

OSCE, ODIHR, *Republic of Montenegro Referendum on State-Status 21 May 2006, OSCE/ODIHR Referendum Observation Mission Final Report*, Warsaw, 4 August 2006, www.osce.org/odihr/elections/montenegro/20099?download=true, (accessed 25 June 2018).

Pavlowitch, S.K., *Yugoslavia*, London, Ernest Benn Limited, 1971.

Prodi, R., 'The State of the Union in 2003', Speech, Plenary Session of the European Parliament, Strasbourg, 11 March 2003, http://europa.eu/rapid/press-release_SPEECH-03-120_en.htm, (accessed 25 June 2018).

'Public Support for EU Membership in Macedonia Drops to 77%: Poll', *Macedonian Information Agency*, 17 February 2017, www.mia.mk/en/Inside/RenderSingleNews/289/133575238, (accessed 25 June 2018.

Radulović, M., 'Montenegro's Journey Towards EU Accession', in J. Rupnik (ed.), *The Western Balkans and the EU: 'the Hour of Europe'*, Paris, Institute for Security Studies European Union, 2011, pp. 79–94.

Ramet, S., *Nationalism and Federalism in Yugoslavia*, 1962–1991, Bloomington, Indiana University Press, 1992.

Rupnik, J., 'The Balkans as a European Question', in J. Rupnik (ed.), *The Western Balkans and the EU: 'the Hour of Europe'*, Paris, Institute for Security Studies European Union, 2011, pp. 17–30.

Rusinow, D., 'Popoarele Iugoslave', in P.F. Sugar, *Naţionalismul Est-European în Secolul al XX-lea (East-European Nationalism during the XXth Century)*, Bucureşti, Curtea Veche, 2002.

Sarajlić-Maglić, D., 'BiH After the Elections – A Tale of Disillusioned Optimism', in J. Rupnik (ed.), *The Western Balkans and the EU: 'the Hour of Europe'*, Paris, Institute for Security Studies European Union, 2011, pp. 47–58.

Schleicher, E., *Positive Peace in Kosovo: A Dream Unfulfilled*, Frankfurt am Main, Peter Lang, 2012.

Schőpflin, G., *Nations, Identity, Power: The New Politics of Europe*, London, Hurst and Company, 2000.

Shea, J., *Macedonia and Greece: The Struggle to Define a New Balkan Nation*, Jefferson, McFarland, 2008.

Shoup, P., *Communism and the Yugoslav National Question*, New York, Columbia University Press, 1968.

Shoup, P., 'Yugoslavia's National Minorities under Communism', *Slavic Review. American Quarterly of Soviet and East-European Studies*, vol. XXII, no. 1, 1963, pp. 64–81.

Simić, J., 'Balkan Citizens Doubt They Will Ever Join EU', *Euractiv*, 12 October 2017, www.euractiv.com/section/enlargement/news/balkan-citizens-doubt-they-will-ever-join-eu, (accessed 25 June 2018).

Simić, J., 'Most Serbs Support EU Membership, Cite Job Opportunities, in New Poll', *Euractiv*, 25 January 2018, www.euractiv.com/section/enlargement/news/most-serbs-support-eu-membership-cite-job-opportunities-in-new-poll, (accessed 25 June 2018).

Smith, M., 'The Kosovo Conflict. U.S. Diplomacy and Western Public Opinion', *CPD Perspectives on Public Diplomacy*, Paper 3, 2009.

Spernbauer, M., *EU Peacebuilding in Kosovo and Afghanistan: Legality and Accountability*, Boston, Martinus Nijhoff Publishers, 2014.

Statistical Office of Montenegro, *Census 2011 data*, www.monstat.org/eng/page.php?id=393&pageid=57, (accessed 25 June 2018).

Steele, B., *Ontological Security in International Relations. Self-Identity and the IR State*, London-New York, Routledge, 2008.

Stephen, C., *Judgement Day: The Trial of Slobodan Milošević*, New York, Atlantic Monthly Press, 2005.

Štiks, I., 'The European Union and Citizenship Regimes in the Western Balkans', in J. Rupnik (ed.), *The Western Balkans and the EU: 'the Hour of Europe'*, Paris, Institute for Security Studies European Union, 2011, pp. 123–134.

Surroi, V., 'The Unfinished State(s) in the Balkans and the EU: The Next Wave', in J. Rupnik (ed.), *The Western Balkans and the EU: 'the Hour of Europe'*, Paris, Institute for Security Studies European Union, 2011, pp. 111–120.

Taras, R.C. and R. Ganguly, *Understanding Ethnic Conflict. The International Dimension*, third edition, New York- London, Longman, 2008.

Teokarevic, J., 'Ten Years of post-Milosevic Transition in Serbia: Problems and Prospects', in J. Rupnik (ed.), *The Western Balkans and the EU: 'the Hour of Europe'*, Paris, Institute for Security Studies European Union, 2011, pp. 59–78.

Tepavać, M., 'Tito, 1945–1980', in J. Udovički and J. Ridgeway (eds.), *Burn this House. The Making and Unmaking of Yugoslavia*, Durham-London, Duke University Press, 1997, pp. 64–79.

Thaçi, H., 'EU Enlargement: Tear Down Mental Walls in the Balkans', *Euractiv*, 5 October 2017, www.euractiv.com/section/enlargement/opinion/eu-enlargement-tear-down-mental-walls-in-the-balkans, (accessed 25 June 2018).

Tishkov, V., 'Ethnic Conflict in the Former USSR: The Use and Misuse of Typologies and Data', *Journal of Peace Research*, vol. 36, no. 5, 1999, pp. 571–591.

Tomic, P. and E. Moroiu, 'Istoria nu începe cu aderarea Serbiei la UE! Cine sunt de fapt vlahii din Serbia', *RFI*, 29 February 2012, www.rfi.ro/articol/stiri/politica/istoria-nu-incepe-aderarea-serbiei-ue-cine-sunt-fapt-vlahii-serbia, (accesses 25 June 2018).

Turbedar, E., 'Balkan Barometer 2015. Public Opinion Survey. Analytical Report', *Regional Cooperation Council*, vol. 1, Sarajevo, 2015, www.rcc.int/seeds/files/RCC_BalkanBarometer2015_PublicOpinion_FIN_forWeb.pdf, (accessed 25 June 2018).

Ugrešić, D., *The Culture of Lies*, London, Phoenix House, 1998.

UNDP, *Early Warning System: Annual Report*, Sarajevo, 2002, in R. Belloni (ed.), *State Building and International Intervention in Bosnia*, London, Routledge, 2007.

Vangeli, A., 'Nation-Building Ancient Macedonian Style: The Origins and the Effects of the So-called Antiquisation in Macedonia', *Nationalities Papers*, vol. 39, January 2011, pp. 13–32.

Vasovic, A., 'Serbia Must Reach Agreement with Kosovo to Join EU by 2025', *Reuters*, 7 February 2018, www.reuters.com/article/us-serbia-eu-enlargement/serbia-must-reach-agreement-with-kosovo-to-join-eu-by-2025-idUSKBN1FR2JP, (accessed 25 June 2018).

Webb, Ph., *International Judicial Integration and Fragmentation*, Croydon, Oxford University Press, 2013.

Weber, B., 'Germany's Shift on Bosnia Policy', *Democracy and Security in Southeastern Europe*, May 2011, www.democratizationpolicy.org/pdf/Bodo_Weber-Germanys_shift_on_Bosnia_policy.pdf, (accessed 25 June 2018).

Weller, M., 'Negotiating the Final Status of Kosovo', *Chaillot Papers*, vol. 114, 2008.

Wendt, A., 'The Agent-Structure Problem in International Relations Theory', *International Organization*, vol. 41, no. 3, 1987, pp. 335–354.

Wendt, A., *Social Theory of International Politics*, Cambridge: Cambridge University Press, 1999.

Wilmer, F., *The Social Construction Man, the State, and War. Identity, Conflict, and Violence in Former Yugoslavia*, New York-London, Routledge, 2002.

'Zaev: Real Possibilities for Macedonia to Receive Date for EU Accession Negotiations', *European Western Balkans*, 8 September 2017, https://europeanwesternbalkans.com/2017/09/08/zaev-real-possibilities-macedonia-recieve-date-eu-accession-negotiations, (accessed 25 June 2018).

Zehfuss, M., *Constructivism in International Relations. The Politics of Reality*, Cambridge, Cambridge University Press, 2002.

Zimmerman, W., 'Yugoslav Strategies of Survival: 1948–1980', in W.S. Vucinich (ed.), *War and Society in East Central Europe. At the Brink of War and Peace: The Tito-Stalin Split in a Historic Perspective*, New York, Brooklyn College Studies, 1982.

Zürcher, C., *The Post-Soviet Wars. Rebellion, Ethnic Conflict, and Nationhood in the Caucasus*, New York-London, New York University Press, 2007.

5 The European Union and the countries of Eastern Partnership – the type of cooperation and neighbours' perception

Beata Piskorska

The European Union's significance in the international arena is not determined only by the EU itself. It is also influenced by external actors' perception of the EU role and by their reaction to the EU initiatives. Outsiders' perceptions of the EU is a key to the Union's impact on the final outcome. The EU's economic and financial crisis, the Brexit and the growing populism and scepticism of the selected EU countries add to the uncertainty surrounding the influence exerted by the EU. It is particularly visible in the area of eastern neighbours that the EU's power is threatened by Russian policy in the region.

The research on Eastern Partnership countries has mostly concentrated on their domestic development as an object of EU policies.[1] Rarely are the questions posed on how the EU and its initiatives are viewed in these countries. Yet, in order to be able to make meaningful conclusions concerning the effectiveness and aptness of the EU policies for the EaP states, it is essential first to understand the perceptions and expectations of stakeholders within these states vis-à-vis the EU and its initiatives. It is assumed that the main reason for the lack of interest regarding the EaP countries' perceptions of the EU is rooted in the assumption that they are not influential enough in policy-making and have little impact on political developments in the EaP countries.[2]

The purpose of this chapter is to analyse the main type of cooperation between the EU and its eastern neighbourhood through the prism of the main approach used to examine the external policy of this organization, namely normative power. It is also the conceptual foundation for the study of external perception of the EU by Eastern Europe countries. The EU roles are based on both an actor's own role perception and other actors' expectations (role prescriptions) and shaped in continuous interactions with other actors. The effect of the EU's actions is influenced by its perception as normative, civilian or soft power. But it is difficult to lead if the EU's promises are not credibly backed up. It is impossible for the EU to be a normative power if the outsiders (Eastern partners in this case) do not perceive its ideas as legitimate. In particular, the perceived incoherence between words and acts, but also across the EU institutions – may create obstacles to the EU effective action towards the East.[3] An analysis of the outsider's views of the EU is essential because it contributes to better understanding of the EU self-identification and the roles the EU plays in international politics, and it provides insight into how this role shapes the impact that the EU policies have on external actors.

Therefore the objective of the chapter is to examine how the EU is viewed in the region at the centre of the EU geopolitical interest – the Eastern Partnership countries (situated in Eastern Europe – Ukraine, Belarus and Moldova). The main assumption of the chapter is that perception of the EU by authorities, official representatives and society of these countries depends on their willingness to integrate, possibilities of systems' transformation and the nature and intensity of relations with the EU. It is assumed that a wide difference exists in the attitude to the EU between the authoritarian regime of Belarus, which does not want to integrate with the EU on one hand, and Ukraine and Moldova that want to be close to it on the other hand. Additionally, we can observe a source of serious misunderstanding concerning the EU's role in the region and international relations. Moreover the EU's declared role in the region is to act as a normative actor by creating the main rules, imposing values and principles, which is not accepted by some selected countries in the area, for example by Belarus.

The main research questions are:

- What is the EU theoretical discussion of the EU's role in international relations?
- What is the type of cooperation used by the EU with the region?
- What are the achievements and shortcomings of the relations between the EU–Eastern Partnership states?
- What is the perception of the European Union and its role by Eastern Partnership countries?
- What is public opinion on the role of the EU in the region?

Furthermore, the research needs to take into account additional questions: whether the EU should continue building its identity as a soft, normative, civilian power to manage problems in this area or whether it needs strong, even military measures in order to influence Russia's policy in the region. Focusing on Eastern Europe, which has close and often problematic historical and geographical ties with Europe, the chapter provides an assessment of how external perceptions from this region relate to the EU policy towards them.

The problem calls for an analysis of a few issues. Firstly, we need to hold a theoretical discussion of the EU's role in the world. Secondly, the main forms of previous and current cooperation between the EU and Eastern Europe neighbours and the assessment of its results should be analysed. Thirdly, the EU's external image and expectations articulated in the region and finally, the perception of the EU by the Eastern Partnership countries and their societies should be scrutinized.

A central question in debate about European foreign policy, mainly of the EU international actorness in or outside the EU is the issue of research methods that can be used in analysing this policy. Most theory-informed research on the Common Foreign and Security Policy employs the deductive method and a large number of theories or framework of analysis have been applied in research on the CFSP. Both the EU and the process of European integration in foreign policy matters are contested discursive fields. By now, every imaginable theory has been applied: realism, neo-liberal institutionalism, regime theory, world systems theory and so on.[4] Institutionalist analyses of European foreign policy in particular are limited by a set of weaknesses, the most serious being the absence of a developed view of state/actor behaviour, a simplified view of policy-making processes and a restrictive definition of foreign policy in a European context. On the other hand, the possibility of Foreign Policy Analysis (FPA) providing an approach that fills those gaps is dependent upon the adaptability of traditional FPA. If FPA remains tied to state-centric realism, its value is clearly limited, though this should not be taken to imply that states are not important actors in European foreign policy. The argument here is that FPA is not necessarily tied to state-centricity nor is it dependent upon a realist paradigm. To summarize the rest of the argument, the essence of FPA is that it offers an actor rather than a state perspective and, equally important, it provides a policy focus at the international level.

Since the early 1990s, social constructivist discourse analysis has become increasingly popular across the social sciences, including international relations. Constructivism focuses on the norms, conventions and rules which make up international and European politics. It is not material capabilities that matter as much as how 'we' view our place in the world. As such, constructivists focus on how identities are formed and their role in foreign policy-making. In the context of the EU perception in the world, the national interests of Eastern European societies should be take into account in order to shape the role they think the EU should pursue in the world. For constructivists, the understanding of the EU external perception will require an explanation of the way in which the Eastern Partnership states construct its identity.

Hence the possibilities of using discourse analysis in the study of European foreign policy appeared, locating it within the wider field of social constructivism. In other words, Europe's foreign policy appears to be an ideal case for showing the potential and limits of social constructivism. Scholars familiar with social constructivist perspectives recognize many of the features well known from the rich toolbox provided by that approach. That is why it is argued that discourse analysis should be used as the main research methodology in the chapter (both as a theory and a method) based on the assumption that language constitutes meaning.

A central issue to approach from a discourse perspective is the representation of EU actorness. If there is no joint representation of the EU as a foreign policy actor of some kind at the EU level among the central EU actors or outside the EU, it may not make sense to inquire further into the issue of EU foreign policy from a discourse perspective focusing on the EU level (although it might be interesting to inquire into the discursive dimension of various national European foreign policies and how these make sense of and shape the European foreign policy).[5] In this case the basic realistic approach to EU foreign policy would seem to be confirmed as the policy stances taken by the EU in its relations with the outside world.

The theoretical discussion of the EU's role in the world

We can find many studies on the EU's creation of foreign policy, especially in terms of the EU's 'actorness' and 'role' in its direct neighbourhood. In order to establish whether the EU is still a model for emulation in neighbouring countries or whether it is losing the battle for influence to Russia, we need to define the type of power and influence the EU is expected to yield. The most influential analyses of the EU's role in its neighbourhood and further afield have developed the concepts of soft, normative, civilian and transformative power (J.S. Nye, I. Manners, F. Duchêne, M. Leonard, H. Grabbe). Comparing the scope and elements of these concepts, we suggest that transformative power approaches a broad spectrum of reform targeting future members, while soft and normative power addresses any third states, especially in the East. For states which wanted to join the EU, the Union did not only promote international norms but encouraged a wide range of reforms related to democracy, market economy and good governance, earning it the name of 'transformative power'. To some extent, the transformative power of the EU identified during the enlargement also applies to the ENP and other foreign policies, despite the absent perspective of accession.[6]

On the other hand, soft power includes aspects contributing to the EU's attractiveness derived from political values, culture and foreign policy based on these values.[7] In a well-known definition of soft power, J.S. Nye stated that: 'The EU appeared to yield the power to get neighbouring European states to want what it wanted'. In his seminal article about soft power J.S. Nye argued that soft or 'co-optive' power means 'getting others to want what you want' and that whoever possessed it would be able to influence other countries' preferences by means of 'intangible factors such as ideology, culture and institutions'. Being able to establish international norms close to their own norms, he claimed, would make states able to co-opt others. Soft power, in his definition, would also entail having attractive culture or ideology and creating institutions attractive to other states and capable of constraining their actions. Following J.S. Nye's assertion that developing norms that will be accepted by other states as universal is an instrument of soft power, we can claim that when the EU spread norms related to democracy and human rights which were accepted by many states in eastern Europe, through the enlargement process in the late 1990s and early 2000, the Union was exercising its soft power.[8]

Two major lines of reasoning dominate the theoretical approaches towards the study of the EU impact on domestic changes in non-member states. The first one builds on rationalist accounts and argues that the power of European influence derives from its direct pressure through material and political benefits provided by the EU. In this context, the Europeanization literature on candidate states argues that the combination of EU membership perspective with intermediary rewards was the central element of EU leverage in successful implementation of democratic and market economy reforms in Central Eastern Europe candidate countries.[9] EU incentives provided technical and financial support to domestic reformers and political legitimacy for like-minded national actors. The lack of full membership promise, the major instrument of EU external leverage, decreases substantially EU bargaining power and the acceptance of EU requirements by domestic utility-maximizing actors, as it is the case of European Neighbourhood Policy.[10]

An alternative reasoning builds on constructivist understanding of the normative power of the European Union. So, EU constitutive liberal-democratic values and 'ways of doing things' can be 'exported' outside the EU official boundaries through mechanisms of socialization and persuasion, depending on their attractiveness to domestic political and societal actors and their historical and cultural heritage.[11]

One central argument in this approach is that the precondition for the EU to be a special normative power is that the outside world attributes a distinct role to the Union. However, literature on Normative Power Europe has not been engaged with empirical studies on how the outside world looks at the EU.[12] The starting point of these attitudes is that studies of external perceptions of the EU offer some findings that are helpful for the debate about whether the EU can be considered a normative power.

Consequently, the concept of Normative Power Europe attracted much interest within the study of the EU and many authors continue to describe the EU in some 'adjectival prefixes'.[13] Many researchers have examined how the EU projects its internal solutions externally and under what conditions EU modes of governance can be effective in the neighbourhood.[14] Initially, the discussion of the Union as a normative power appeared to be an answer to critics focusing on the weakness of the EU in military terms, but it quickly developed into something more, generating research into the EU's normative identity and how it defined its actions in the international arena.

The concept of the EU's normative power focuses primarily on norms in its relations with third states.[15] The idea of Normative Power Europe also has roots in a long tradition of theorizing the EU concept. Most notably, it builds upon the work of F. Duchêne in his notion of *idée force* or civilian power[16] and J. Galtung's ideological power.[17] Defining the EU's foreign policy in normative terms means that the EU's power cannot be reduced to either military or purely economic means; rather, it 'works through ideas, opinions and conscience'.[18]

I. Manners argued that norms, especially legal norms, have been part of the EU's constitutive foundations and are more important for the Union than for any nation state. The combination of the historical context within which the EU arose, its hybrid character and legal constitution ensure, according to Manners, that the EU places universal principles and norms (such as human rights or rule of law) at the centre of its relations with the member states and third states. The key norms the EU stands for are defined by Manners as peace, liberty, including economic aspects, rule of law and human rights, supplemented by social solidarity, anti-discrimination, sustainable development and good governance.[19]

As the European Union (EU) evolved as an international actor in the 1990s, it placed a commitment to promote certain values at the core of its foreign policy. These values include democracy, respect for human rights and the rule of law, which led to the branding of the EU by some scholars as a 'normative power'. Democracy, however, is but one of many values promoted by the EU, and may not necessarily represent the most important value in its relationship with other countries.[20] These days the European Union is treated as community of values and seeks to promote those values both inside and outside its borders. In order to establish the area stability, security and well-being in its neighbourhood, the Union encourages third countries to adopt its political and economic model.

What type of cooperation with the region does the EU use?

After the collapse of the Soviet Union and the Berlin Wall (the disintegration of the communist Eastern Bloc), the western world's norms and values such as democracy, liberty, human rights, the rule of law, and market economy seemed to have become European aspirations. The preceding events created an opportunity for Europe without dividing lines. The European Union considered its enlargement by entering into the former communist territory and building a reunified Europe. The enlargement procedure resulted in widened democratic Europe and was seen to be the most successful foreign policy strategy in EU history.[21] After the enlargement process in 2004, the European Neighbourhood Policy (ENP) was developed as an alternative strategy to enlargement, building good relationships with new neighbouring states.[22] The ENP was then addressed to all bordering countries from the Commonwealth of Independent States (CIS), as well as to those participating in the Barcelona process (Mediterranean countries).[23] However, although the Neighbourhood Policy is now being implemented, the nature of the relations between the EU and its neighbours is still not clearly defined. In the EU discourse, the offer remains 'more than partnership and less than membership'.[24] The ENP aimed to build a 'ring of friends' around the EU.[25]

These aims were often criticized because there was an internal clash between the mentioned goals and the latter subjugated to the EU's economic or security interests.[26] The role of the EU in the accomplishment of these goals is undermined by the Ukrainian–Russian conflict and the destabilized situation of the region outside the EU in the South (conflict in Syria). It made the EU vision of creating a ring of friends through the ENP fail, which questions the idea of a contemporary normative power in Europe. The EU policy is currently accused of creating a 'ring of fire' instead of a 'ring of friends' around it.

The European Neighbourhood Policy (ENP) as a general approach towards all direct neighbours of the EU has been accused of numerous sins: ineffectiveness, incoherence, double standards.[27] However, the policy has recently undergone three reviews, in May 2011 and in November 2015 but, according to its critics, it has done little to address the problems. The basic narrative of ENP from 2003 to 2010 was dominated by the discourse of stability, good governance and prosperity, in 2011 a shift towards 'healthy' and 'deep and sustainable' democracy took place. But in 2015 it was replaced by a discourse of (in)stability and security, where stabilizing the neighbourhood became a top priority that preceded the objective of fostering 'good governance, democracy, rule of law and human rights'. The 2015 communication proposed the following priorities for cooperation (the order is not incidental): 1) economic development for stabilization; 2) security dimension; 3) migration and mobility; 4) regional cooperation.[28]

As a response to new challenges of the evolving neighbourhood the EU adopted on 18 May 2017 Joint Report on the implementation of the European Neighbourhood Policy, which demonstrates that the new policy approach ensures stronger joint ownership and more flexibility by recognizing different aspirations and diversity of each partner.[29] The revised ENP reinvigorated the relations between the European Union and its neighbours to the East and South, with a greater focus on stabilization, resilience and security.[30]

Following the discussion on the necessity of reforming the EU policy, the Eastern Partnership (EaP) was launched in spring 2009 after years of policy development towards non-member states and as a specific eastern dimension and supplement of the ENP.[31] The EaP specifically focused on six Eastern European states: Armenia, Azerbaijan, Belarus, Georgia, Moldova, and Ukraine. The new initiative was to advance the cause of democracy in these states, which would have a positive effect on the EU.[32] The main goal of the EaP is to accelerate political association and further economic integration between the EU and interested partner countries by means of bilateral and multilateral cooperation. On the basis of this collaboration, the EU wants to offer more incentives, in short, more 'partnership' to the six former Soviet states, but without offering them the main reward, namely a membership perspective.[33]

The Commission's proposals are to embed the Eastern Partnership within the wider ENP. They are also to give the Eastern Partnership a multilateral framework but with the bulk of its implementation pursued bilaterally with the participating states. The multilateral framework constitutes four 'policy platforms' of democracy, good governance and stability, economic integration and convergence with EU policies; energy security and contacts between people.

This initiative also combined normative concerns: issues of rights, human rights or rights of minorities or groups and the death penalty are included within the first criterion of Copenhagen but also in the EU's agreements with third states which do not aim to join the Union. When engaging with candidates, the range of political integration issues the EU raises is broader, for example democratic principles and procedures, elections, balance of power between different branches of the executive and so on. Last but not least, for countries seeking closer integration with the EU, for example through *Deep and Comprehensive Free Trade Agreements* (DCFTA's),[34] there are a number of categories relating to harmonization of standards and rules.

Bilaterally, each of the participants is offered the prospect of an Association Agreement with the EU but with no commitment that these agreements hold out any prospect of future full membership of the Union. The Association Agreements would provide for the creation of individual deep and comprehensive free trade areas (DCFTA) with each partnership country, which, in turn, could be joined together to form a Neighbourhood Economic Community. Mobility and Security Pacts are also envisioned to ease cross-border movement and as part of a 'phased approach' via visa facilitation negotiations with partners and, 'in the longer term', full visa liberalization meaning visa-free travel to the EU, membership of the Energy Community created in 2006 for the Western Balkan countries, to incorporate them into the EU gas and electricity markets.[35]

In the ENP and the EaP, democracy plays a significant role, both as a prerequisite for the EU goals of stability and economic development in the neighbourhood and as a goal of reforms in the partner countries to be supported by the EU.[36] The fact that Belarus was initially excluded from the ENP (and was only included in the multilateral aspect of the EaP) due to its inadequate record on democracy and human rights also sends a signal about the importance attributed to democracy in the ENP context.

Apart from the bilateral track, the EaP also envisaged a multilateral dimension, i.e. cooperation between the six countries covered by the EaP as well as between them as a group and the EU. This type of cooperation is implemented by four common thematic platforms and six flagship initiatives in various areas. It was governed by the same principles as the European Neighbourhood Policy, that is differentiation, conditionality and more for more principles.

The ENP and now EaP and its instruments such as Association Agreements (AAs) and Deep Comprehensive Free Trade Agreements (DCFTA) have mainly been used as case studies to illustrate conceptual approaches to the EU as an international actor. The first grid of analysis applied to the ENP is based upon Manner's concept of the EU as a normative actor. The ENP is frequently used as a case to illustrate the discrepancies between a policy discourse mainly developed around the notion of the EU as a normative power and implementation reflecting the various tensions inherent to a policy which, at the image of the EU, still encounters difficulties to define itself.[37] The approach relies on a similar content as the accession conditionality, first developed for the candidate countries from Eastern and Central Europe, found in the policy discourse of the ENP, as neighbouring countries have to respect the

> commitment to shared values, that is respect for human rights, including minority rights, the rule of law, good governance, the promotion of good neighbourly relations, and the principles of a market economy and sustainable development as well as to certain key foreign policy goals.[38]

However, because the ENP does not pursue the aim of EU accession, it serves as a real capability test for the EU to define itself as an international actor, even more so as the neighbourhood has been identified as a key area for European security.[39]

But nowadays it seems that the EU influence on its neighbours seems to be waning and its main policy instruments aiming to achieve stability and prosperity in its neighbourhood ENP, appear to have fallen short of their objectives. Whether defined as a 'soft', 'normative' or 'transformative' power, the EU's influence is founded on a complex mix of economic attractiveness, interdependence, the promotion of international norms and the potential promise for closer integration as attractive for some of its Eastern neighbours. Ultimately the EU's influence also depends on its actual policies and its ability to communicate them effectively.[40]

The discussion of the necessity to reform the EU policy was particularly important in the light of launching the process of reviewing the ENP with a consultation paper in March 2015 and a strategic debate on the adoption of new Global Strategy of the EU in 2016.[41] As it was stressed earlier, the first document called for greater differentiation in the EU's relations with its partner countries (particularly division between two different regions such as Eastern and Southern neighbours) and a more pragmatic approach to the varying levels of ambition for cooperation or integration of neighbouring countries. The second one promotes pragmatism and resilience as principles of bilateral relations.[42]

Achievements and shortcomings of the relations between the EU–Eastern Partnership states

From its very beginning the EaP has been criticized for its ineffectiveness. It is partly true, but since the initiative was launched in 2009, we have observed much turbulence and many challenges troubling the region. About 8 years after this policy was created, the environment around these countries has profoundly changed. It started from the revolution on Maidan in Ukraine at the end of 2013, the peaceful change of power in Georgia in 2012 as a result of parliamentary elections and the massive protests in Moldova against corrupt authorities in 2015. The next breakthrough event was the Russian aggression in Ukraine with the annexation of Crimea in spring 2014 and the military intervention in Donbas and Lugansk. Finally, the continued aggression of Russia has altered the political landscape and the original concept of the Eastern Partnership. For that reasons this project is no longer able to meet the challenges of 2016 and beyond. Also Eastern Europe is trying to find its place in this more unstable international environment.

In addition to the recent challenges faced by the region, we can still list three extremely important achievements after almost eight years of the EaP's existence. These are, however, limited to three countries: Ukraine, Republic of Moldova, and Georgia. They are as follows:

Firstly, the signing of Association Agreements, including DCFTAs, between the EU and these three countries in 2014, promoting comprehensive reforms in key sectors. This is the principal achievement. The agreements were preceded by difficult negotiations, especially in the case of Ukraine. However, the signing of the documents is only an initial step. The implementation of the agreements will be the next huge challenge. Agreements embrace many new areas of cooperation and are intended to help create strong political ties, but they are also the basis for the implementation of legislation and the EU standards in this country in the future. Making progress in the area of democracy, the rule of law and respecting human rights are the main conditions to start negotiations and the same ensure the privileged position in the EU. It means in practice the biggest restrictiveness of the conditions for the associated countries obliged to achieve deeper harmonization than it was assumed in the Partnership and Cooperation Agreements.

Secondly, the establishment of a visa-free regime firstly with Republic of Moldova set an extremely important precedent in EU relations with the countries of the Eastern neighbourhood in 2014. We can also see some visible progress in the case of both Ukraine and Georgia after fulfilling the second part of the VLAPs. Following to the European Union decision granting visa liberalization for Ukraine in May 2017, visa-free regime entered into force on 11 June 2017.[43] Visa-free travel for Georgian citizens for a period of 90 days in any 180-day period to 26 countries of the Schengen area was adopted by the Council of the European Union on 27 February 2017.[44] These are probably the most important issues for the citizens of EaP countries, especially in the case of the countries directly bordering the EU.

Thirdly, membership in the Energy Community for Republic of Moldova in 2010, Ukraine in 2011 and Georgia in October 2016.[45] This is a step towards integration of the EaP countries with EU energy markets. The main aim is: to support energy sector reforms, investments in infrastructure modernization and harmonization of regulations in this area.

Summing up, the results are unexpectedly good, bearing in mind all the problems and challenges analysed previously, including Russian pressure, the frequently weak performance of EaP countries, and the EU's initial reluctance to become deeply engaged in the Eastern neighbourhood. However, these achievements are only the beginning of a painful process of integration with the EU for three partners, because a successful implementation of the new contractual framework, the DCFTA especially, remains an extremely difficult challenge. These three countries will have to implement deep reforms of their institutions and economies.

The other three countries covered by the EaP – Azerbaijan, Armenia and Belarus – chose a different path and it seems that they are not interested in gradual integration with the EU. Belarus and later Armenia decided to join the Eurasian Economic Union (members of the union also include Kazakhstan, Kyrgyzstan) led by Russia on 2nd January 2015. As a result they are clearly divided into two groups: one group comprising three of the afore-mentioned states which have signed AAs with the EU, and the second one which will not sign it in the coming future.

However, currently Armenia is returning to negotiations over a new treaty. A new legally binding and overarching agreement with Armenia was proposed by the Foreign Affairs Council on 12 October 2015 and adopted the corresponding negotiation mandate. The official launch of negotiations on the Comprehensive and Enhanced Partnership Agreement took place on 7 December 2015. The negotiations were successfully concluded on 26 February 2017 and will be followed by the necessary procedural steps meant to enable the initialling and signature of the agreement. The new agreement will replace the current EU–Armenia Partnership and Cooperation Agreement.[46] It is based on the European Neighbourhood Policy Review[47] guidance and the new agreement and consultations with Armenia on a new, more focused, country-specific framework for bilateral cooperation in the form of joint Partnership Priorities, aimed at replacing the ENP Action Plan, have been launched.[48]

Similar talks on a new agreement with Azerbaijan were launched in February 2017. Currently the DCFTA is not possible as Azerbaijan is not a member of the WTO, therefore the EU proposed in May 2013 to negotiate a Strategic Modernisation Partnership (SMP) with this country to avoid an impasse as a process complementary to the AA talks. Unfortunately, there is no progress in reforms concerning respect for human rights by regime.

High-level relations between the EU and Belarus are semi-frozen as the country does not respect human rights, release all political prisoners or improve the rule of law and democratic principles.Nonetheless, an informal Coordination Group, formed by the EU and Belarus senior officials, was set up at the beginning of 2016 to better reflect the state of bilateral relations. Tangible steps taken by Belarus to respect universal fundamental freedoms, rule of law and human rights, including the application of the death penalty, will be of key significance for the shaping of the EU's future policy towards that country.[49]

The movement to the multilateral dimension of the EaP in general brought modest achievements. Neither six thematic platforms nor flagship initiatives helped much to introduce reforms in EaP countries, the same as the activities of the Euronest Parliamentary Assembly (EPA). Maybe only the Platform on Economic Integration visibly helped in the process of DCFTA negotiations and contributed to a better understanding of EU requirements. Also the EaP Civil Society Forum can be considered, partially at least, as an achievement, due to its comprehensive work and facilitation of good contacts between participants from all six partner countries and the EU.

The main reason for the slow progress to date has been the lack of political will and institutional capacity on the part of the partner countries to implement reforms. Reform of public administration remains one of the key obstacles to the creation of a well-governed state in all the EaP countries.

A crucial factor in the case of the Eastern neighbourhood, one which should be seriously taken into account in the EU policy towards its neighbours, is the Russian factor. Russia is putting pressure on these countries in order to prevent the closer cooperation and integration of EaP countries with the EU and the West (it remains a factor in Putin's policies). Russia's policy was proven during the war with Ukraine in 2013. It used several means against Ukraine, including: soft power (talk of a shared Orthodox heritage), carrots (cheap gas and access to markets) and sticks (trade sanctions). Russia conducted a similar campaign with the Republic of Moldova.

Perception of the European Union and its role by Eastern Partnership countries

Most studies on the EU leadership present a one-dimensional picture of EU activities where the Union is either seen as a great power or not. Nevertheless, perceptual patterns are actually more nuanced and complex, and images of the EU vary depending on the issue at hand and across regions. In one area the Union may be considered a great power or leader, whereas in another region it is seen quite differently.[50] When it comes to eastern neighbours of the EU covered by the Eastern Partnership we should stress that at least three of them, that is Ukraine, Moldova, and Georgia, have declared European integration a national strategic objective. The selected three states have so far made a clear pro-European choice by signing Association Agreements with the EU and have more viable civil society landscapes compared to the other countries addressed by the EaP (Belarus, Armenia and Azerbaijan).

Additionally, certain civil society groups, for instance think tanks, are by all means important opinion-makers, who seek to impact decision-making processes and policy choices in their countries, including vis-à-vis the EU. Depending on more or less positive perceptions of the EU, its initiatives and expectations of what they can (or cannot) offer, civil society actors would be more or less eager to be involved with the EU and to promote a pro-European choice in the foreign policy of their country. A study of civil society's perceptions of the EU would thus be the first step towards understanding to what extent Brussels is on the right track in its approach to non-state actors in EaP countries. At the same time, an analysis of the civil society's views on Europe would contribute to the study of the capability-expectation gap in the EU's foreign policy vis-à-vis its immediate neighbourhood. However, the question is how the EU is perceived by these countries and whether the EU as a normative power is still attractive for them.

It was evident that the EU for a long time had been a source of legitimization for political forces, businessmen and reformers and civil society in the whole region. However, its image was very often undermined by anti-reforming/democratic political forces in some member states. That is why it is essential to strengthen its image in the perception of neighbour states' society. Moreover, of particular interest are perceptions to the civil society actors of the EU, whose role is recognized by the EU, although it has been underestimated (at least in the selected EaP countries). It derives from the assumption that they are not influential enough in policy-making and have little impact on political developments in the EaP countries.

Perception is the notion which derives from the images belonging to the 'psychological milieu' of decision makers – the world as the actor sees it.[51] They can be conceptualized as mental pictures composed of our cumulated experienced-based knowledge about the surrounding world and beliefs about the desirable behaviour.[52] There is also often an affective component, as one can expect a consistent set of affective responses to cognitive images.[53] Perception is also defined as the 'result of the subjective and psychological cognition of the observer rather than the objective reflection of the object that is being observed'.[54] Applied to international actors, the perceptions are 'complex constellations of meanings shaped by a number of interacting factors', including by the perceived developments both within an international actor (the EU) and outside it, e.g. within the countries in question, especially in this case Ukraine, Georgia and Moldova.[55]

N. Chaban stresses the importance of an actor's image, linking influence to how an international actor, in this case the EU, is perceived.[56] Some scientists have shown that EU norms are perceived by other states as potentially contested, sometimes converging, but sometimes diverging with domestic norms.[57] The literature points to a limited perception of the EU as a normative power depending on the geographical area. By comparison, the image of a powerful economic actor is predominant. The main research of external perception of the EU was conducted by N. Chaban,[58] S. Lucarelli and L. Fioramonti within the Garnet Project.[59] In both papers there is an agreement that in the most frequently surveyed regions the EU is not viewed as a normative power (Brazil, China, India, Russia or South Africa).[60]

However, there are some important geographical exceptions to the conclusion that the EU is not predominantly seen as a normative power. Such perceptions are much more prominent just in the EU's eastern and southern neighbourhoods.[61] But the EU is not widely or predominantly seen as a 'normative power' with a special role and legitimacy in exporting the norms mentioned by I. Manners.

According to R. Bengtson and O. Elgström,[62] Ukraine, Georgia, Armenia, Azerbaijan and Moldova (but not Belarus) 'readily recognize both the great power status of the EU and the attractiveness of its normative agenda. [. . .] the civilizing mission of the EU is perceived in positive [. . .] terms as a contribution to desirable transformation'.[63] Among the general public in these countries, values such as human rights, democracy and freedom of speech are frequently associated with Brussels. The EU is seen as having contributed to developing democracy in these countries and human rights are viewed as an important area of co-operation; however, in line with the general picture, trade and economic development remain the areas where the most important role for the EU is envisaged.[64]

According to research carried out by V. Axyonova and S. Gerasymchuk on a selected group of leading think tanks publications[65] in the three countries, integration with the EU is narrated as a chance to put an end to economic and political hardships and improve almost all aspects of life, mainly in Ukraine. In this context, the European Union is often portrayed as a transformative power, which through its insistence on political and economic reforms could trigger a positive change in the country. The authors argue that EU membership prospects would speed up transformation processes in the country and highlight Ukraine's European identity. At the same time, they stress that a successful transformation would be only possible if the Ukrainian government fulfilled its own commitments with regard to political reforms. The authors further agree that visa-free regime should be used by the EU as a leverage to enhance the fight against corruption in Ukraine.

Apart from that, the EU is framed as a key provider of economic assistance (a *donor* frame), whose role is essential in overcoming the present crisis in Ukraine. In this context, some authors call for creating a European 'Marshall Plan for Ukraine', whereas others argue for a 'more-for-more' approach to be used by the EU, i.e. for making the provision of economic support dependent on the Ukrainian government's commitment to reforms.[66] A number of publications assess the Eastern Partnership initiative rather negatively, as an amorphous and ineffective approach, needing reconsideration.

Although the EU is often discussed in the context of the current security situation in the eastern neighbourhood, particularly in Ukraine and the ongoing conflict there, it is hardly ever framed as strong. Instead, the EU is presented as an actor 'with limited military potential'. Its role in the process of conflict resolution processes in the east of Ukraine is often questioned due to the EU's reactive (rather than proactive) policy, hesitation, and lack of unity in approaching 'the Russian aggression'.[67] Nevertheless, the EU is viewed as Ukraine's ally and a counterpole to Russia. Moreover, there is an understanding that the '*conflict cannot be resolved without mediation and the most likely mediator is the EU*'.[68]

In summary, an image of the EU as a normative power can be found in its neighbourhood and in individual countries around the world, but, in general terms, the perception of the EU as an economic power is the dominant image. Quite importantly, the general absence of images of the EU as a normative power takes three very different forms. The first presents the EU as a partner with no special normative status. The second sees the EU as a self-declared promoter of legitimate norms, but views this as an attempt by the EU and its former colonial powers to reintroduce neo-colonial control. The third one sees the EU as a power that attempts to further its own norms rather than universal norms.[69]

The sustainable growth element of normative power also clashes with what is seen as the EU's *de facto* actions in the economic field. Issues such as free trade, non-tariff barriers and agricultural subsidies produce an image of the EU as an actor that perpetuates neo-colonial domination.[70] The EU does not have a special status through its norms which might give it influence. To the extent that there is a component of EU normative power connotations that is widely accepted, it is the 'peace' element. The EU's status as a mediator or reconciler is viewed in less ambivalent and more positive terms than the rest of Manners' nine norms.[71]

Public opinion on the role of the European Union in the region

Analysing the actual public opinion trends, the EU's attractiveness and position in the region are experiencing some decline. In three countries (Ukraine, Moldova and Belarus), the Eurasian Economic Union is seen as a possible and viable alternative to the EU, with this trend most pronounced in Belarus.[72] We can also find statements that the EU has been losing the 'soft power' contest to Russia in the Eastern Partnership countries.[73]

Public opinion trends from Moldova show the changing dynamics of support for regional powers, suggesting there is some cause for concern regarding perceptions of the EU. Based on the Institute for Public Policy (IPP) public opinion barometer presented in April 2016, support for European integration has dropped: from 76% in November 2007 to 63% in 2010 to 41% in April 2016. Meanwhile, support for the Russian integration projects (Customs Union/EEU) has grown from 45% in November 2014 to 53% in April 2016.[74]

At the same time, the EU's attractiveness is still considerable and based on the potential of free movement of people and education. As it is presented in the EU-STRAT Project '*The EU and Eastern Partnership Countries – An Inside-Out Analysis and Strategic Assessment*' (EU-STRAT)[75] in Ukraine, where the most positive attitudes can be observed, 50% of citizens support European integration, as shown in a survey conducted in the autumn of 2015.[76] There is, however, considerable regional variation subsumed in these averages. In West and Central Ukraine, the view that Ukraine would benefit from European integration is shared by 77% and 57.5% respectively. Other regions have a majority of respondents that believe Ukraine has more to lose than to gain from (potential) EU accession. The main advantages of (potential) EU membership are considered to be free movement of people (39%), welfare improvements (37%) and free access for youth to study in the EU (34%). Importantly, every fourth Ukrainian believes EU membership will facilitate domestic reforms in Ukraine (24%).[77]

A cross-temporal public opinion analysis drawing on public opinion polls in Belarus in 2009, 2013 and 2016 also shows the Economic Eurasian Union and the European Union are considered rival integration models in the region. While recognition for the EU is rising, the majority of Belarus citizens would still prefer integration with the EEU.[78] Awareness of the Eastern Partnership has increased threefold since 2009 (60%), but respondents also believe there should be a new, stronger framework for relations between the EU and Belarus and that its most important goal should consist in strengthening economic and trade relations (48%).[79] Two thirds of the respondents believe that Belarus should develop a new framework for relations with the EU, which would prioritize economic and trade relations (48%), as well as visa liberalization and financial aid (20%). Only 8% share an opinion that Belarus could benefit from the EU's experience of democracy and good governance (a more than twofold decrease since 2009).

The Belarus survey also distinguishes two different models perceived by Belarus citizens. The EU model is associated with liberal democracy, market economy, economic prosperity, human rights and individual freedoms.[80] The EEU, on the other hand, is associated with a model seen as closer to Belarus' own and containing elements of 'social democracy', albeit comprising 'a curious mix of qualities'.[81]

There is a perceivable overlap in the benefits that the EU and the EEU could offer, which exacerbates a sense of rivalry between the two powers, in the eyes of the respondents. Trade and economic development are prioritized in the relationship with both, but more opportunities for cooperation are seen with the EEU. While the attitudes towards the EU are becoming more positive and affirmative, the same cannot be said about the normative underpinnings of these relations. On the one hand, the Belarus–EU relations are progressively driven by more common interest and positive perceptions of each other.

At the same time, there are persistent normative differences in public perceptions of their greater neighbours: while the EU continues to associate with a model of liberal democracy; the EEU presents a hybrid case of 'social democracy', with a mix of liberal and socialist (egalitarian) values – which is closer to 'the hearts and minds' of the Belarusians.

Interestingly, in relation to the EEU or Belarus respondents do not seem to refer to 'democracy' as a value, but instead prioritize stability, security and cultural traditions, which is broadly reflective of the survey findings in 2009 and 2013. The preceding thus indicate a profound normative gap in the associative models of democracy which the respondents continue to distinguish all three cases by.

The perception of the nature of this relationship demonstrates a significant substantive change: 50% (+16 since 2009) believe the EU–Belarus relations are now founded on common (rather than the EU's) values and interests; among which joint economic (47%; +13), security (and 45%; +10) and legal international (52%; +9) interests explicitly prevail. Moreover, a quarter of respondents contend that the relations are of reciprocal and equal nature (+4 since 2009), which once again comes in stark contrast with the previous findings.[82]

For the first time however, market economy, a prevalent feature in both models, is seen as a ground for closer convergence between the two normative models.

These results suggest that the elements which characterize the EU's model and mode of integration are fairly well known and stable: on the one hand, political ones such as liberal democracy, rights, freedoms and rule of law, on the other, economic integration including trade, support for market economy, economic cooperation.[83]

Given the complex mix of incentives and norms contained in EU policies towards its Eastern neighbours and the amalgamated image of liberal democracy and economic cooperation in citizens' perceptions, we believe that the broad definition and operationalization of soft power adopted here, including economic and democracy concept clusters, serves best as a tool to analyse the EU communications. It is, however, possible that the EU communications would emphasize mostly norms and rights in which case it would be communicating as a normative power.

By contrast, if the EU employs a broad range of tools at its disposal for integration, from communication to assistance, targeting a broad area of reforms, we can speak of communicating as a transformative power. We must note, however, that the leverage of the Union as a transformative power depends on much more than communications: the credibility of its promises and threats which are influenced by a host of domestic political dynamic and EU level factors.

The best idea is to pay attention to the level of political support for European integration presented by citizens of EaP countries. According to the latest *EU Neighbourhood Barometer – Eastern Partnership, Autumn 2014*, the European Union appears in a mostly positive light in the Eastern Partnership countries: 40% of respondents now see the image of the EU as positive, while 32% of respondents see the EU in a neutral light.[84] Around a fifth of respondents (21%) have a negative stance towards the EU. However, perceptions of the EU have clearly worsened since spring 2013. This is, however, unsurprising given the recent events and conflict with Ukraine.

Respondents who have the most positive image reside in Ukraine (45%) and Moldova (42%), but the lowest support was given by respondents particularly in the case of Azerbaijan and Belarus. The majority of respondents agree with three statements:

1 that the EU is an important partner to their respective countries (58%), the most likely to agree are the respondents in Georgia 69%, Armenia 67% and Ukraine 63%,

Table 5.1 Does the European Union conjure up for you a very positive, fairly positive, neutral, fairly negative or very negative image?

	Total 'Negative'	*Diff. Aut 2014–Sp. 2014*	*Total 'Positive'*	*Diff. Aut. 2014–Sp. 2014*	*Neutral*	*Diff. Aut 2014–Sp. 2014*	*Don't know*	*Diff. Aut 2014–Sp. 2014*
ENPI East	17%	−4	44%	+4	33%	+1	5%	−1
ARMENIA	19%	−6	48%	+8	31%	−1	2%	−1
AZERBAIJAN	17%	+4	34%	−1	33%	+5	16%	−8
BELARUS	20%	−4	28%	+6	46%	−2	5%	−1
GEORGIA	7%	−2	40%	=	49%	+1	4%	=
UKRAINE	17%	−6	50%	+5	29%	+1	4%	=
MOLDOVA	21%	−4	45%	+3	31%	+3	3%	−2
RUSSIA	46%	+10	13%	−4	36%	−7	5%	+1

Source: On the basis of the TNS, *EU Neighbourhood Barometer Eastern Partnership. Autumn 2014 – Wave 6*, 2014, https://library.euneighbours.eu/sites/default/files/attachments/ENPI%20Wave%206%20-%20Report%20East_EN.pdf, (accessed 25 June 2018), p. 40.

Table 5.2 Could you tell me to what extent you agree or disagree with each of the following statements concerning the European Union?

	(OUR COUNTRY) and the European Union have sufficient common values to be able to cooperate		*The European Union brings peace and stability in the region surrounding (OUR COUNTRY)*		*The European Union has the appropriate level of involvement in (OUR COUNTRY)*		*The European Union is an important partner of (OUR COUNTRY)*		*The European Union is an important partner of (OUR COUNTRY)*	
	Total 'Agree'	*Diff. Aut. 2014–Sp. 2014*	*Total 'Agree'*	*Diff. Aut. 2014–Sp. 2014*	*Total 'Agree'*	*Diff. Aut. 2014–Sp. 2014*	*Total 'Agree'*	*Diff. Aut. 2014–Sp. 2014*	*Total 'Agree'*	*Diff. Aut. 2014–Sp. 2014*
ENPI East	59%	+3	52%	+4	61%	+3	47%	+3	47%	−4
ARMENIA	62%	+10	62%	+12	75%	+8	65%	+7	59%	+6
AZERBAIJAN	47%	−1	38%	−4	42%	=	37%	−2	40%	−7
BELARUS	51%	=	30%	+3	42%	=	22%	=	25%	+1
GEORGIA	56%	=	58%	+2	68%	−1	55%	−3	39%	−6
UKRAINE	63%	+5	58%	+6	67%	+4	51%	+5	52%	−5
MOLDOVA	54%	=	48%	−2	60%	+1	60%	+2	58%	−3
RUSSIA	58%	−1	19%	−6	52%	−2	25%	−7	50%	+1

Source: On the basis of the TNS, *EU Neighbourhood Barometer Eastern Partnership. Autumn 2014 – Wave 6*, 2014, https://library.euneighbours.eu/sites/default/files/attachments/ENPI%20Wave%206%20-%20Report%20East_EN.pdf, (accessed 25 June 2018), p. 44.

2 that their country and the EU have sufficient common values to be able to cooperate (56%), 58% Ukraine,
3 that the EU has the appropriate level of involvement in their country (51%), the most likely in Moldova 61%.

The most important areas of cooperation – those mentioned by the largest proportion of respondents – are peace and security; next, tackling poverty; and the EU development aid that should focus more on peace and security.

Assessing the role of the EU, the EaP states consider that the EU should play in the region the roles of the supporter of economic development and respecting human rights, mostly areas which correspond well to the goals of the ENP. As far as the image of the EU is concerned, relations between the Eastern Partnership countries and the European Union continue to be perceived in a predominantly positive light. Of respondents, 53% describe relations between their country and the EU as good whereas 16% believe these relations to be bad.

Conclusions

To sum it up, the analysis of the type of relations between the EU and neighbouring states and the perception of the EU in the EaP countries allows us to state that the European Union was firstly perceived as a transformative power and as a donor or rarely a security provider. Integration with the EU (what Euromaidan demonstration revealed in 2013) is perceived mostly as an opportunity for Ukraine rather than possible risks. We can assume that Ukraine is a representative example for all countries of Eastern Europe. In other words, the EU offered to all the EaP partners the policy tools that have been tested on and in some ways shaped by Ukraine.[85]

The EU was seen as a chance to put an end to economic and political hardships and improve almost all aspects of life in Ukraine. In this context, the European Union is often portrayed as a transformative power, which through its insistence on political and economic reforms could trigger a positive change in these countries. Mostly the visa-free regime should be used by the EU as a leverage to enhance the fight against corruption in Ukraine and Moldova.

Finally, there are two factors which influence most of all Eastern Europe countries perception of the EU: firstly, according to rationalist perception, geographical proximity to (short distance from) the EU borders – the further these states move away from the EU borders, the harder it is to measure the scope and scale of the EU impact on domestic changes – the rationalists argue that geographic proximity and the economic interdependence represent two of the explanatory factors that contribute towards the support from EU members for further European enlargement – operationalized as economic and security dimensions.

Secondly, an idealist perception – the nature and degree of impact of European integration on party politics and party systems (historical and cultural variables) – operationalized as historical-cultural and liberal-democratic dimensions.

Thirdly, acknowledgement that the EU's attractiveness might be challenged by the rising Russian influence and its alternative regional project (Eurasian Union).

Fourthly, several major findings are worth mentioning: a) in the case of Ukraine and Moldova, bordering the EU provides the political parties in the EaP states with the opportunity to talk more realistically about the European integration than in countries further away from the EU border, such as Georgia. Apart from the rationalist arguments, such as economic cooperation or movement of people, the ideational arguments of feeling European, based on the sharing of common historical past, are weaker in Georgia as compared with Ukraine and Moldova; b) opposition parties shared a similar perception of the EU and European integration; c) it is worth stressing that the cost-benefit calculations (economic dimension) were the dominant element of the EaP European discourse; d) from the security point of view, the EU and the European integration are described as the only alternative to Russian influence in the region and the protection of national sovereignty.

Notes

1 E. Korosteleva, 'Change or Continuity: Is the Eastern Partnership an Adequate Tool for the European Neighbourhood?', *Sage Journals: International Relations*, vol. 2, no. 25, 2011, pp. 243–262.

2 S. Gänzle, 'EU Governance and the European Neighbourhood Policy: A Framework for Analysis', *Europe-Asia Studies*, vol. 10, no. 61, 2009, pp. 1715–1734; V. Axyonova and S. Gerasymchuk, *The European Union as a Transformative Power, a Donor or a Security Provider? A View from the Eastern Partnership Countries*, Concept paper presented at the ECPR General Conference 2016 Section S20: EU Global Perceptions, Prague, 7–10 September 2016, p. 1; K. Zarembo, 'Perception of CSDP Effectiveness in Ukraine: A Host State Perspective', *European Security*, vol. 26, no. 2, 2017, p. 4.

3 O. Elgström and N. Chaban, 'Studying External Perceptions of the EU: Conceptual and Methodological Approaches', in V. Bachmann and M. Muller (eds.), *Perceptions of the EU in Perceptions of the EU in Eastern Europe and Sub-Saharan Africa Looking in from the Outside*, London, Palgrave Macmillan, 2015, pp. 17–18.

4 B. Tonra and T. Christiansen (eds.), *Rethinking European Union Foreign Policy*, Manchester-New York, Manchester University Press, 2004, p. 14.

5 H. Larsen, 'British Discourses on Europe: Sovereignty of Parliament, Instrumentality and the Non-mythical Europe', in K.E. Jřrgensen (ed.), *Reflective Approaches to European Governance*, Basingstoke, Palgrave Macmillan, 1997.

6 H. Grabbe, *The EU's Transformative Power. Europeanization Through Conditionality in Central and Eastern Europe*, New York, Palgrave Macmilan, 2006, pp. 39–40.

7 J.S. Nye, *Soft Power: The Means to Success in World Politics*, New York, PublicAffairs, 2004, pp. 166–167.

8 B. Piskorska, *Soft Power w polityce Unii Europejskiej wobec państw Partnerstwa Wschodniego*, Lublin, Wydawnictwo KUL, 2017, pp. 193–210.

9 J. Kelly, 'New Wine in Old Wineskins: Promoting Political Reforms Through the New European Neighbourhood Policy', *Journal of Market Studies*, vol. 44, no. 1, 2006, pp. 29–55.

10 Kelly, 'New Wine in Old Wineskins', pp. 29–55.

11 F. Schimmelfennig and U. Sedelmeier, *Europeanization of Central and Eastern Europe*, New York, Cornell University Press, 2005, pp. 29–51.

12 H. Larsen, 'The EU as a Normative Power and the Research on External Perceptions: The Missing Link', *Journal of Common Market Studies*, vol. 52, no. 4, 2014, pp. 896–910.

13 Ch. Bickerton, *European Union Foreign Policy: From Effectiveness to Functionality*, London, Palgrave Macmilan, 2011. Specialists have affixed various concepts to

the 'power' that the EU possesses in order to define its characteristics. These include civilizing or civilizational power (F. Duchêne, 'Europe's Role in World Peace', in R. Mayne (ed.), *Europe Tomorrow: Sixteen Europeans Look Ahead*, Fontana-London, Palgrave Macmillan, 1972; H. Sjursen, 'The EU as a "Normative" Power: How Can This Be?', *Journal of European Public Policy*, vol. 13, no. 2, 2006), quiet superpower (A. Moravcsik, 'Europe: A Quiet Superpower', *French Politics*, vol. 7, no. 3/4, 2002), ethical power (L. Aggestam, 'Ethical Power Europe?', *International Affairs*, vol. 84, no. 1, 2008), postmodern superpower (J. McCormick, *The European Superpower*, London, Palgrave Macmillan, 2006), responsible power (H. Mayer and H. Vogt (eds.), *A Responsible Europe? Ethical Foundations of EU External Affairs,* London-New York, Palgrave Macmillan, 2006), pragmatic power (S. Wood, 'Pragmatic Power Europe', *Cooperation and Conflict*, vol. 2, no. 46, 2010), vanishing mediator (K. Nicolaïdis, The Power of the Powerless, in T. Lindberg (ed.), *Beyond Paradise and Power: Europe, America, and the Future of the Troubled Relationship*, London, Routledge, 2004) and gentle power (T. Padoa-Schioppa, *Europe's Gentle Power*, Bologna, il Mulino, 2001).

14 S. Lavenex, 'EU External Governance in "Wider Europe"', *Journal of European Public Policy*, vol. 4, no. 11, 2004; Grabbe, *The EU's Transformative Power*; U. Sedelmeier, 'The European Neighbourhood Policy: A Comment on Theory and Policy', in K. Weber et al. (eds.), *Governing Europe's Neighbourhood: Partners or Periphery? Europe in change*, Manchester, Manchester University Press, 2007; S. Lavenex and H. Schimmelfennig, 'EU Rules Beyond EU Borders: Theorizing External Governance in European Politics', *Journal of European Public Policy*, vol. 16, 2009.

15 I. Manners, 'Normative Power Europe: A Contradiction in Terms?', *Journal of Common Market Studies*, vol. 40, no. 2, 2002, pp. 235–258.

16 F. Duchêne, 'The European Community and the Uncertainties of Interdependence', in M. Kohnstamm and W. Hager (eds.), *A Nation Writ Large? Foreign-Policy Problems before the European Community*, London, Palgrave Macmillan, 1973, pp. 1–21.

17 J. Galtung, *The European Community: A Superpower in the Making*, London, Universitetsforlaget, 1973.

18 I. Manners, T. Diez, 'Reflecting on Normative Power Europe', in F. Berenskoetter and M.J. Williams (eds.), *Power in World Politics*, New York, Routledge, 2007, p. 175.

19 I. Manners, 'Normative Power Europe: A Contradiction in Terms?', pp. 242–243.

20 B.T. Powel, 'A Clash of Norms: Normative Power and EU Democracy Promotion in Tunisia', *Democratization*, vol. 16, no. 1, 2009, pp. 193–214.

21 R. Dannreuther, 'Developing the Alternative to Enlargement: The European Neighboorhood Policy', *European Foreign Affairs Review*, vol. 11, no. 2, 2006, p. 183–201; G. Bosse, 'Challenges for EU Governance through Neighbourhood Policy and Eastern Partnership: The Values/Security Nexus in EU-Belarus Relations', *Contemporary Politics*, vol. 15, no. 2, 2009, p. 215.

22 H. Haukkala, 'The European Union as a Regional Normative Hegemon: The Case of European Neighbourhood Policy', *Europe-Asia Studies*, vol. 60, no. 9, 2008, pp. 1601–1622.

23 The ENP is thus addressed to the following countries: Ukraine, Moldova, Belarus, Georgia, Armenia, Azerbaijan, Algeria, Morocco, Tunisia, Libya, Egypt, Jordan, Lebanon, Israel, the Palestinian Authority and Syria.

24 R. Prodi, *A Wider Europe. A Proximity Policy as the Key to Stability*, Speech/02/619, Brussels, December 2002.

25 European Commission, *European Neighbourhood Policy Strategy Paper*, Brussels, 12 May 2004, COM(2004) 373 final.

26 S. Poli, 'Introduction', in S. Poli (ed.), *The European Neighbourhood Policy – Values and Principles*, New York, Routledge, 2016, pp. 1–3.

27 E.A. Korosteleva, M. Natorski and L. Simão (eds.), *EU Policies in the Eastern Neighbourhood. The Practices Perspective,* London, Routledge, 2014, pp. 5–12.

28 European Commission, High Representative of the Union for Foreign Affairs and Security Policy, *Joint Communication to the European Parliament, the Council, the European Economic and Social Committee and the Committee of the Regions: Review of the European Neighbourhood Policy*, Brussels, 18 November 2015, JOIN(2015) 50 final.
29 European Commission, High Representative of the Union for Foreign Affairs and Security Policy, *Joint Communication to the European Parliament, the Council, the European Economic and Social Committee and the Committee: Report on the Implementation of the European Neighbourhood Policy Review*, Brussels, 18 May 2017, JOIN (2017) 18 final.
30 European Commission – Press Release, *Revised European Neighbourhood Policy: Supporting Stabilisation, Resilience, Security*, 18 May 2017, http://europa.eu/rapid/press-release_IP-17-1334_en.htm, (accessed 25 June 2018).
31 Commission of the European Communities, *Communication from the Commission to the European Parliament and the Council: Eastern Partnership*, Brussels, 3 December 2008, COM (2008) 823 final.
32 Manners, 'Normative Power Europe: A Contradiction in Terms?', pp. 235–258.
33 E. Korosteleva (ed.), *Eastern Partnership: A New Opportunity for the Neighbours?*, London-New York, Routledge, 2012, pp. 6–8.
34 European Commission, *EU-Ukraine Deep and Comprehensive Free Trade Area*, https://eeas.europa.eu/sites/eeas/files/tradoc_150981.pdf, (accessed 25 June 2018).
35 R.G. Whitman and S. Wolff, 'Much Ado about Nothing? The European Neighbourhood Policy in Context', in R.G. Whitman and S. Wolff (eds.), *The European Neighbourhood Policy in Perspective. Context, Implementation and Impact*, London, Palgrave Macmillan, 2010, pp. 12–13.
36 S. Stewart, 'EU Democracy Promotion in the Eastern Neighbourhood: One Template, Multiple Approaches', *European Foreign Affairs Review*, vol. 16, no. 5, 2011, p. 610. It should be added, however, that the continued inclusion of Azerbaijan in the European Neighbourhood Policy and Eastern Partnership, despite its clearly authoritarian government, weakens this signal somewhat and points to contradictions in the EU approach.
37 L. Delcour and E. Tulmets, 'Pioneer Europe? The ENP as a Test Case for EU's Foreign Policy', *European Foreign Affairs Review*, vol. 14, no. 4, 2009, pp. 501–523.
38 European Commission, European Neighbourhood Policy Strategy Paper.
39 J. Solana, *A Secure Europe in a Better World, European Security Strategy,* Council of the European Union, Publication Office, Brussels 2009.
40 A. Dimitrova et al., 'Soft, Normative or Transformative Power: What Do the EU's Communications with Eastern Partners Reveal About Its Influence?', EU-STRAT Working Paper, vol. 01, 2016, p. 6.
41 European Commission, High Representative of the Union for Foreign Affairs and Security Policy, *Joint Communication to the European Parliament, the Council, the European Economic and Social Committee and the Committee of the Regions: Review of the European Neighbourhood Policy*.
42 European External Action Service, *Shared Vision, Common Action: A Stronger Europe. A Global Strategy for the European Union's Foreign and Security Policy*, Brussels, 2016, http://eeas.europa.eu/archives/docs/top_stories/pdf/eugs_review_web.pdf, (accessed 25 June 2018).
43 Ukrainian citizens who have biometric passports will be able to enter all EU member states other than Ireland and the United Kingdom without a visa and stay for up to 90 days during any 180-day period. European Commission – Statement, *European Commission Welcomes the Council Adoption of Visa Liberalisation for the Citizens of Ukraine*, 11 May 2017, http://europa.eu/rapid/press-release_STATEMENT-17-1270_en.htm, (accessed 25 June 2018).

44 *Visas: Council Adopts Regulation on Visa Liberalisation for Georgians*, Press Release 88/17, 27 February 2017, www.consilium.europa.eu/en/press/press-releases/2017/02/27/visa-liberalisation-georgia/, (accessed 25 June 2018).
45 European Commission, High Representative of the Union for Foreign Affairs and Security Policy, *Joint Communication to the European Parliament, the Council, the European Economic and Social Committee and the Committee: Report on the Implementation of the European Neighbourhood Policy Review*, p. 7.
46 Delegation of the European Union to Armenia, *EU-Armenia Relations*, 27 February 2017, https://eeas.europa.eu/delegations/armenia/4080/eu-armenia-relations_en, (accessed 25 June 2018).
47 European Commission, High Representative of the Union for Foreign Affairs and Security Policy, *Joint Communication to the European Parliament, the Council, the European Economic and Social Committee and the Committee of the Regions: Review of the European Neighbourhood Policy*.
48 Delegation of the European Union to Armenia, *Remarks by President Donald Tusk After His Meeting with President of Armenia Serzh Sargsyan*, Brussels, 28 February 2017, https://eeas.europa.eu/delegations/armenia/21597/remarks-president-donald-tusk-after-his-meeting-president-armenia-serzh-sargsyan_en, (accessed 25 June 2018).
49 European Commission, High Representative of the Union for Foreign Affairs and Security Policy, *Joint Communication to the European Parliament, the Council, the European Economic and Social Committee and the Committee: Report on the Implementation of the European Neighbourhood Policy Review*, p. 8.
50 N. Chaban et al., 'Images of the EU Beyond its Borders: Issue-Specific and Regional Perceptions of European Union Power and Leadership', *Journal of Common Market Studies*, vol. 51, no. 3, 2013, p. 433.
51 R. Jervis, *Perception and Misperception in International Politics*, Princeton, Princeton University Press, 1976, p. 13.
52 N. Chaban, O. Elgström and M. Holland, 'The European Union as Others See It', *European Foreign Affairs Review*, vol. 11, 2006, pp. 245–262.
53 Chaban, Elgström and Holland, 'The European Union as Others See It', pp. 245–262.
54 F. Shiming, 'Chinese Public Perceptions of Japan and the United States in the Post-Cold War Era', in G.L. Curtis, R. Kokuburn and J. Wang (eds.), *Getting Triangle Straight: Managing China-U.S. Relations*, Tokyo, Japan Center For International Exchange, 2010, p. 269.
55 N. Chaban, M. Holland and S. Kelly, 'Perceptions of 'Normative Power Europe' in the Shadow of the Eurozone Debt Crisis. Public Perspectives on European Integration from the Asia Pacific', in A. Björkdahl (ed.), *Importing EU Norms. Conceptual Framework and Empirical Findings*, New York, Springer International Publishing, 2015, p. 59.
56 N. Chaban and O. Elgström, 'The Role of the EU in an Emerging New World Order: In the Eyes of Chinese, Indian and Russian Media', *Journal of European Integration*, vol. 36, no. 2, 2014, pp. 170–188; N. Chaban and M. Holland, 'Theorising and Framing 'Normative Power Europe': Asian Journalists' Perspectives', *Asia-Europe Journal*, vol. 13, no. 3, 2015, pp. 285–296.
57 Chaban et al., 'Images of the EU Beyond Its Borders', pp. 433–451.
58 A. Björkdahl, N. Chaban and J.L. Annick Masselot (eds.), *Importing EU Norms: Conceptual Framework and Empirical Findings*, London, Springer International Publishing, 2013, pp. 57–78. N. Chaban summarized some of the Elgström/NCRE findings on elites and concluded that the EU is a political and sometimes normative leader through promoting human rights (South Asia), supporting democracy through conditionality (Pacific, Kenya) and crisis prevention (Africa). The EU was seldom viewed as a leader in security or environmental issues.
59 S. Lucarelli and L. Fioramonti, 'Research Report on the Project: The External Image of the European Union – Phase Two', *GARNET Working Paper*, vol. 62, 2009, GARNET – Jointly Executed Research Project 5.2.1, http://warwick.ac.uk, (accessed 25 June 2018).

60 In these studies the European Union is not perceived as a normative power in the United States, where it is often viewed in terms of its member states rather than as a unit. In Australia the image of the EU as a normative power does not feature clearly. The image of an economic power is also dominant in New Zealand and Canada. Lucarelli and Fioramonti, 'Research Report on the Project'; J. Sperling, 'American Elite Perceptions of Italy as a Foreign Policy Actor: Does Italy Figure into American Foreign Policy Calculations?', *Modern Italy*, vol. 15, no. 3, 2010, pp. 259–276; Larsen, 'The EU as a Normative Power', pp. 896–910.

61 TNS, *EU Neighbourhood Barometer, Autumn 2012 – Wave 2*, http://euneighbourhood.eu/wp%20content/uploads/2013/03/Presentation6009ENPIwave2_event20march1.pd, (accessed 25 June 2018).

62 R. Bengtson and O. Elgström, 'Conflicting Role Conceptions? The European Union in Global Politics', *Foreign Policy Analysis*, vol. 8, no. 1, 2012, p. 99.

63 Larsen, 'The EU as a Normative Power', p. 904.

64 TNS, *EU Neighbourhood Barometer*, pp. 16, 18–22.

65 The exact number of interviews cannot yet be specified. The timeframe for the interviews is March 2015 – November 2016. See more: Axyonova and Gerasymchuk, *The European Union as a Transformative Power*, pp. 1–11.

66 Axyonova and Gerasymchuk, *The European Union as a Transformative Power*, p. 8.

67 Axyonova and Gerasymchuk, *The European Union as a Transformative Power*, p. 8.

68 Axyonova and Gerasymchuk, *The European Union as a Transformative Power*, pp. 8–9.

69 Larsen, 'The EU as a Normative Power', pp. 904–906.

70 Larsen, 'The EU as a Normative Power', p. 905.

71 Larsen, 'The EU as a Normative Power', p. 905.

72 E. Korosteleva, 'The EU, Russia and the Eastern Region: The Analytics of Government for Sustainable Cohabitation', *Cooperation and Conflict*, vol. 51, no. 3, 2016, pp. 365–383.

73 K.L. Nielsen and M. Vilson, 'The Eastern Partnership: Soft Power Strategy or Policy Failure?', *European Foreign Affairs Review*, vol. 19, no. 2, 2014, pp. 243–262.

74 Institute for Public Policy (IPP), *Barometer of Public Opinion*, April 2016, http://ipp.md/old/public/files/Barometru/BOP_04.2016_prima_parte_finale-r.pdf, (accessed 25 June 2018).

75 Dimitrova et al., 'Soft, Normative or Transformative Power', p. 6.

76 Dimitrova et al., 'Soft, Normative or Transformative Power', p. 13.

77 Dimitrova et al., 'Soft, Normative or Transformative Power', p. 13.

78 E. Korosteleva, *Belarus Between the European Union and the Eurasian Economic Union: A National Values Survey 2016*, ODB and Global Europe Centre, Brussels, 2016, https://odb-office.eu/expertise_/research/belarus-between-eu-and-eeu-perceptions-preferences-values, (accessed 25 June 2018).

79 Korosteleva, *Belarus Between the European Union and the Eurasian Economic Union*, p. 6.

80 M. Kurki, 'Democracy and Conceptual Contestability: Reconsidering Conceptions of Democracy in Democracy Promotion', *International Studies Review*, vol. 12, no. 3, 2010, pp. 362–386.

81 Korosteleva, *Belarus Between the European Union and the Eurasian Economic Union*, p. 8.

82 Korosteleva, *Belarus Between the European Union and the Eurasian Economic Union*, pp. 6–7.

83 Dimitrova et al., 'Soft, Normative or Transformative Power', p. 14.

84 TNS, *EU Neighbourhood Barometer Eastern Partnership. Autumn 2014 – Wave 6*, 2014, https://library.euneighbours.eu/sites/default/files/attachments/ENPI%20Wave%206%20-%20Report%20East_EN.pdf, (accessed 25 June 2018), p. 40.

85 I. Solonenko, 'Added Value? Eastern Partnership and EU – Ukraine Bilateral Relations', *Internationale Politik und Gesellschaft*, vol. 3, 2011, p. 120.

Bibliography

Aggestam, L., 'Ethical Power Europe', *International Affairs*, vol. 84, no. 1, 2008, pp. 1–11.

Axyonova, V. and S. Gerasymchuk, *The European Union as a Transformative Power, a Donor or a Security Provider? A View from the Eastern Partnership Countries*, Concept paper presented at the ECPR General Conference 2016 Section S20: EU Global Perceptions, Prague, 7–10 September 2016.

Bengtson, R. and O. Elgström, 'Conflicting Role Conceptions? The European Union in Global Politics', *Foreign Policy Analysis*, vol. 8, no. 1, 2012, pp. 93–108.

Bickerton, Ch., *European Union Foreign Policy: From Effectiveness to Functionality*, London, Palgrave Macmillan, 2011.

Björkdahl, A., N. Chaban and J.L. Annick Masselot (eds.), *Importing EU Norms: Conceptual Framework and Empirical Findings*, London, Springer International Publishing, 2013.

Bosse, G., 'Challenges for EU Governance Through Neighbourhood Policy and Eastern Partnership: The Values/Security Nexus in EU-Belarus Relations', *Contemporary Politics*, vol. 15, no. 2, 2009, pp. 215–227.

Bickerton, Ch., *European Union Foreign Policy: From Effectiveness to Functionality*, London, Palgrave Macmillan, 2011.

Chaban, N. and O. Elgström, 'The Role of the EU in an Emerging New World Order: In the Eyes of Chinese, Indian and Russian Media', *Journal of European Integration*, vol. 36, no. 2, 2014, pp. 170–188.

Chaban, N., O. Elgström and H. Holland, 'The European Union as Others See It', *European Foreign Affairs Review*, vol. 11, 2006, pp. 245–262.

Chaban, N. et al, 'Images of the EU Beyond Its Borders: Issue-Specific and Regional Perceptions of European Union Power and Leadership', *Journal of Common Market Studies*, vol. 51, no. 3, 2013, pp. 433–451.

Chaban, N. and M. Holland, 'Theorising and Framing 'Normative Power Europe': Asian Journalists' Perspectives', *Asia-Europe Journal*, vol. 13, no. 3, 2015, pp. 285–296.

Chaban, N., M. Holland and S. Kelly, 'Perceptions of 'Normative Power Europe' in the Shadow of the Eurozone Debt Crisis. Public Perspectives on European Integration from the Asia Pacific', in A. Björkdahl (ed.), *Importing EU Norms. Conceptual Framework and Empirical Findings*, New York, Springer International Publishing, 2015, pp. 57–77.

Commission of the European Communities, *Communication from the Commission to the European Parliament and the Council: Eastern Partnership*, Brussels, 3 December 2008, COM(2008) 823 final.

Dannreuther, R., 'Developing the Alternative to Enlargement: The European Neighborhood Policy', *European Foreign Affairs Review*, vol. 11, no. 2, 2006, pp. 183–201.

Delcour, L. and E. Tulmets, 'Pioneer Europe? The ENP as a Test Case for EU's Foreign Policy', *European Foreign Affairs Review*, vol. 14, no. 4, 2009, pp. 501–523.

Delegation of the European Union to Armenia, *EU-Armenia Relations*, 27 February 2017, https://eeas.europa.eu/delegations/armenia/4080/eu-armenia-relations_en, (accessed 25 June 2018).

Delegation of the European Union to Armenia, *Remarks by President Donald Tusk After His Meeting with President of Armenia Serzh Sargsyan*, Brussels, 28 February 2017, https://eeas.europa.eu/delegations/armenia/21597/remarks-president-donald-tusk-after-his-meeting-president-armenia-serzh-sargsyan_en, (accessed 25 June 2018).

Dimitrova, A. et al., 'Soft, Normative or Transformative Power: What Do the EU's Communications with Eastern Partners Reveal About Its Influence?', *EU-STRAT Working Paper*, vol. 01, 2016.

Duchêne, F., 'The European Community and the Uncertainties of Interdependence', in M. Kohnstamm and W. Hager (eds.), *A Nation Writ Large? Foreign-Policy Problems Before the European Community*, Paris, Palgrave Macmillan, 1973, pp. 1–21.
Duchêne, F., 'Europe's Role in World Peace', in R. Mayne (ed.), *Europe Tomorrow: Sixteen Europeans Look Ahead*, London, Fontana, 1972, pp. 32–47.
Elgström, O. and N. Chaban, 'Studying External Perceptions of the EU: Conceptual and Methodological Approaches', in V. Bachmann and M. Muller (eds.), *Perceptions of the EU in Perceptions of the EU in Eastern Europe and Sub-Saharan Africa Looking in from the Outside*, London, Palgrave Macmillan, 2015, pp. 17–33.
European Commission, *EU-Ukraine Deep and Comprehensive Free Trade Area*, https://eeas.europa.eu/sites/eeas/files/tradoc_150981.pdf, (accessed 25 June 2018).
European Commission, *European Neighbourhood Policy Strategy Paper*, Brussels, 12 May 2004, COM(2004) 373 final.
European Commission – Press Release, *Revised European Neighbourhood Policy: Supporting Stabilisation, Resilience, Security*, 18 May 2017, http://europa.eu/rapid/press-release_IP-17-1334_en.htm, (accessed 25 June 2018).
European Commission, High Representative of the Union for Foreign Affairs and Security Policy, *Joint Communication to the European Parliament, the Council, the European Economic and Social Committee and the Committee: Report on the Implementation of the European Neighbourhood Policy Review*, Brussels, 18 May 2017, JOIN(2017) 18 final.
European Commission, High Representative of the Union for Foreign Affairs and Security Policy, *Joint Communication to the European Parliament, the Council, the European Economic and Social Committee and the Committee of the Regions: Review of the European Neighbourhood Policy*, Brussels, 18 November 2015, JOIN(2015) 50 final.
European Commission – Statement, *European Commission Welcomes the Council Adoption of Visa Liberalisation for the Citizens of Ukraine*, 11 May 2017, http://europa.eu/rapid/press-release_STATEMENT-17-1270_en.htm, (accessed 25 June 2018).
European External Action Service, *Shared Vision, Common Action: A Stronger Europe. A Global Strategy for the European Union's Foreign and Security Policy*, Brussels, 2016, http://eeas.europa.eu/archives/docs/top_stories/pdf/eugs_review_web.pdf, (accessed 25 June 2018).
Galtung, J., *The European Community: A Superpower in the Making*, London, Universitetsforlaget, 1973.
Gänzle, S., 'EU Governance and the European Neighbourhood Policy: A Framework for Analysis', *Europe-Asia Studies*, vol. 10, no. 61, 2009, pp. 1715–1734.
Grabbe, H., *The EU's Transformative Power. Europeanization Through Conditionality in Central and Eastern Europe*, New York, Palgrave Macmillan, 2006.
Haukkala, H., 'The European Union as a Regional Normative Hegemon: The Case of European Neighbourhood Policy', *Europe-Asia Studies*, vol. 60, no. 9, 2008, pp. 1601–1622.
Institute for Public Policy (IPP), *Barometer of Public Opinion*, April 2016, http://ipp.md/old/public/files/Barometru/BOP_04.2016_prima_parte_finale-r.pdf, (accessed 25 June 2018).
Jervis, R., *Perception and Misperception in International Politics*, Princeton, Princeton University Press, 1976.
Joint Report to the European Parliament, the Council, the European Economic and Social Committee and the Committee of the Regions, *Report on the Implementation of the European Neighbourhood Policy Review*, Brussels, 18 May 2017, JOIN(2017) 18 final.
Kelly, J., 'New Wine in Old Wineskins: Promoting Political Reforms Through the New European Neighbourhood Policy', *Journal of Market Studies*, vol. 44, no.1, 2006, pp. 29–55.

Korosteleva, E., *Belarus Between the European Union and the Eurasian Economic Union: A National Values Survey 2016*, ODB and Global Europe Centre, Brussels, 2016, https://odb-office.eu/expertise_/research/belarus-between-eu-and-eeu-perceptions-preferences-values, (accessed 25 June 2018).

Korosteleva, E., 'Change or Continuity: Is the Eastern Partnership an Adequate Tool for the European Neighbourhood', *Sage Journals: International Relations*, vol. 2, no. 25, 2011, pp. 243–262.

Korosteleva, E. (ed.), *Eastern Partnership: A New Opportunity for the Neighbours?*, London-New York, Routledge, 2012.

Korosteleva, E., 'The EU, Russia and the Eastern Region: The Analytics of Government for Sustainable Cohabitation', *Cooperation and Conflict*, vol. 51, no. 3, 2016, pp. 365–383.

Korosteleva, E.A., M. Natorski and L. Simão (eds.), *EU Policies in the Eastern Neighbourhood. The Practices Perspective*, London, Routledge, 2014.

Kurki, M., 'Democracy and Conceptual Contestability: Reconsidering Conceptions of Democracy in Democracy Promotion', *International Studies Review*, vol. 12, no. 3, 2010, pp. 362–386.

Larsen, H., 'British Discourses on Europe: Sovereignty of Parliament, Instrumentality and the Non-mythical Europe', in K.E. Jørgensen (ed.), *Reflective Approaches to European Governance*, Basingstoke, Palgrave Macmillan, 1997.

Larsen, H., 'The EU as a Normative Power and the Research on External Perceptions: The Missing Link', *Journal of Common Market Studies*, vol. 52, no. 4, 2014, pp. 896–910.

Lavenex, S., 'EU External Governance in "Wider Europe" ', *Journal of European Public Policy*, vol. 4, no. 11, 2004, pp. 680–700.

Lavenex, S. and H. Schimmelfennig, 'EU Rules Beyond EU Borders: Theorizing External Governance in European Politics', *Journal of European Public Policy*, 2009, vol. 16, pp. 791–812.

Lucarelli, S. and L. Fioramonti, 'Research Report on the Project: The External Image of the European Union – Phase Two', *GARNET Working Paper*, vol. 62, 2009, GARNET – Jointly Executed Research Project 5.2.1, http://warwick.ac.uk, (accessed 25 June 2018).

Manners, I., 'Normative Power Europe: A Contradiction in Terms?', *Journal of Common Market Studies*, vol. 40, no. 2, 2002, pp. 235–258.

Manners, I. and T. Diez, 'Reflecting on Normative Power Europe', in F. Berenskoetter and M.J. Williams (eds.), *Power in World Politics*, New York, Routledge, 2007, p. 173–188.

Mayer, H. and H. Vogt (eds.), *A Responsible Europe? Ethical Foundations of EU External Affairs*, London-New York, Palgrave Macmillan, 2006.

McCormick, J., *The European Superpower*, London, Palgrave Macmillan, 2006.

Nicolaïdis, K., 'The Power of the Powerless', in T. Lindberg (ed.), *Beyond Paradise and Power: Europe, America, and the Future of the Troubled Relationship*, London, Routledge, 2004, pp. 93–120.

Nye, J.S., *Soft Power: The Means to Success in World Politics*, New York, Public Affairs, 2004, pp. 166–167.

Nielsen, K.L. and M. Vilson, 'The Eastern Partnership: Soft Power Strategy or Policy Failure?', *European Foreign Affairs Review*, 2014, vol. 19, no. 2, p. 243–262.

Padoa-Schioppa, T., *Europe's Gentle Power*, Bologna, il Mulino, 2001.

Piskorska, B., *Soft Power wpPolityce Unii Europejskiej wobec państw Partnerstwa Wschodniego*, Lublin, Wydawnictwo KUL, 2017.

Poli, S., 'Introduction', in S. Poli (ed.), *The European Neighbourhood Policy – Values and Principles*, New York, Routledge, 2016, pp. 1–8.

Powel, B.T., 'A clash of Norms: Normative Power and EU Democracy Promotion in Tunisia', *Democratization*, vol. 16, no. 1, 2009, pp. 193–214.

Prodi, R., *A Wider Europe. A Proximity Policy as the Key to Stability*, Speech/02/619, Brussels, December 2002.

Schimmelfennig, F. and U. Sedelmeier, *Europeanization of Central and Eastern Europe*, New York, Cornell University Press, 2005.

Sedelmeier, U., 'The European Neighbourhood Policy: A Comment on Theory and Policy', in K. Weber et al. (eds.), *Governing Europe's Neighbourhood: Partners or Periphery? Europe in Change*, Manchester, Manchester University Press, 2007.

Shiming, F., 'Chinese Public Perceptions of Japan and the United States in the Post-Cold War Era', in G.L. Curtis, R. Kokuburn and J. Wang (eds.), *Getting the Triangle Straight: Managing China-U.S. Relations*, Tokyo, Japan Center For International Exchange, 2010.

Sjursen, H., 'The EU as a "Normative" Power: How Can This Be?', *Journal of European Public Policy*, vol. 13, no. 2, 2006, pp. 235–251.

Stewart, S., 'EU Democracy Promotion in the Eastern Neighbourhood: One Template, Multiple Approaches', *European Foreign Affairs Review*, vol. 16, no. 5, 2011, pp. 607–621.

Solana, J., *A Secure Europe in a Better World, European Security Strategy*, Brussels, Council of the European Union, Publication Office, 2009.

Solonenko, I., 'Added Value? Eastern Partnership and EU – Ukraine Bilateral Relations', *Internationale Politik und Gesellschaft*, vol. 3, 2011, pp. 120–133.

Sperling, J., 'American Elite Perceptions of Italy as a Foreign Policy Actor: Does Italy Figure Into American Foreign Policy Calculations?', *Modern Italy*, vol. 15, no. 3, 2010, pp. 259–276.

TNS, *EU Neighbourhood Barometer, Autumn 2012 – Wave 2*, http://euneighbourhood.eu/wp%20content/uploads/2013/03/Presentation6009ENPIwave2_event20march1.pd, (accessed 25 June 2018).

TNS, *EU Neighbourhood Barometer Eastern Partnership. Autumn 2014 – Wave 6*, 2014, https://library.euneighbours.eu/sites/default/files/attachments/ENPI%20Wave%206%20-%20Report%20East_EN.pdf, (accessed 25 June 2018).

Tonra, B. and T. Chrostiansen (eds.), *Rethinking European Union Foreign Policy*, Manchester-New York University Press, 2004.

Visas: Council Adopts Regulation on Visa Liberalisation for Georgians, Press Release 88/17, 27 February 2017, www.consilium.europa.eu/en/press/press-releases/2017/02/27/visa-liberalisation-georgia/, (accessed 25 June 2018).

Whitman, R.G. and S. Wolff, 'Much Ado About Nothing? The European Neighbourhood Policy in Context', in R.G. Whitman and S. Wolff (ed.), *The European Neighbourhood Policy in Perspective. Context, Implementation and Impact*, London, Palgrave Macmillan, 2010, pp. 3–26.

Wood, S., 'Pragmatic Power Europe', *Cooperation and Conflict*, vol. 2, no. 46, 2010, pp. 242–261.

Zarembo, K., 'Perception of CSDP Effectiveness in Ukraine: A Host State Perspective', *European Security*, vol. 26, issue 2, 2017, pp. 190–206.

6 Russia's perceptions of the European identity

Olga Barburska

Introduction

Russia occupies a special place among the many actors in the international arena whose attitude towards European identity is studied in this publication. There are many obvious reasons for this, such as Russia's historical ties with Europe, the role of Russia as a nuclear power, its current significance in the EU foreign and commercial policy, etc. In the context of the main research problem of this work, however, what is most important is Russia's specific approach to the notion of identity.

Taking this specificity into account, we can formulate the main research hypothesis that Russia perceives Europe (which can justifiably be equated with the European Union) and its identity mainly from the perception angle of its own, Russian identity, by establishing a direct opposition between European identity and Russian identity. In other words, Russians perceive the traits that characterise Europeans as mirroring their own traits, which is the consequence of the fact that in general terms the Russian world view is developed as the antithesis of the paradigms developed by the West, including Europe. By doing so Russian élites and people – and this is another research hypothesis of this chapter – reject vigorously the idea of the European Union as a normative power, considering this very notion as a direct threat to their own identity, as well as to Russia's vital national interests.

Those two hypotheses are consistent with the main research questions of the book, first of all concerning the content of public discourse on the EU's identity in the third countries, in this particular case in Russia. Another research question: whether such a discourse is reflected among Russian political élites, public opinion and civil society is also dealt with, because that discourse does exist (as it is proved in this study). Moreover, it changes in time under specific political, ideological and socio-economic circumstances which are presented in the chapter.

For conducting the analysis based on such assumptions it is necessary to put some auxiliary research questions. The first one is whether it is possible to separate mechanically what is Western from what is European in this study – and the answer is that it would be difficult and groundless to do so; although due to geographical and cultural proximity, for Russians Europe (or presently the EU) has undeniably been the best-known representative of the entire Western world.

Another important research question is how we should understand the very notion of identity as well as its perception. The issue is examined in more detail in other chapters of this book, so here it is sufficient to note that this chapter is based on the Constructivist approach, which emphasises the importance of norms.[1] According to this approach 'norms define awareness', which means that what is fundamental is the value system adopted by the given actor.[2] This includes ideology, political views, culture, historical tradition, religion, language issues, customs, etc., and concerns individuals and societies as well as states and international organisations such as the European Union. As far as the notion of perception is concerned, an approach adopted here is based on another research question of this book. It defines perception as the discursive shaping of the EU's image presented in statements made by representatives of political élites, academic community, civil society and other social actors in Russia. They articulate expectations of the EU's international role in the region (in this case in Eastern Europe), especially in the context of recognising the European Union's identity as a normative power – although at the same time they in general reject the EU's geopolitical posture and condemn its normative influence.

As for the research methods used in this study, the focus, as we have already mentioned, is on the achievements of Constructivism, which emphasise the necessity of the normative approach. At the same time the systemic method is used, which treats the European Union and the Russian Federation as political entities that, although internally very diverse, each form a self-contained whole. The issue under study also required the application of the comparative method in order to make the necessary comparisons between these entities. The specificity of the issue further required the use of primarily academic literature on the subject comprising analytical material and source texts, but also official documents and statements, as well as data on the results of public opinion polls.

The chapter begins with a discussion of the conceptual basis making it possible to understand the genesis, sources and nature of Russians' specific approach to the notion of identity, including a description of the main currents in Russian political and ideological thought. Further, it discusses Russians' approach to the West and to Europe, manifested in the achievements of these main currents, as well as in political and social discourse. The chapter is concluded by an attempt to present the axiological nature of the differences between Russia and Europe (the European Union).

The main currents in Russian political and ideological thought

Russia's attitude towards the West – and especially towards Europe – is reflected on the conceptual level in the rich output of Russian researchers, analysts and politicians representing various views and diverse political and ideological options.[3] The main research problem here is the lack of uniform criteria for identifying ideological and programme orientations. In the opinion of Stanislaw Bieleń, among the political camps that emerged after the collapse of the Soviet Union we can distinguish, for example, the following groups: Atlanticists, Eurasianists, proponents of a strong state and pragmatists.[4]

Generally speaking, from the historical and contemporary point of view we can distinguish two main currents in Russian political thought. Stanislaw Bieleń calls the first one Westernisation, meaning 'opening up to Western ideas and values', and the second one is 'escaping towards autarky and isolation'. The latter involves the search for some mythical third way of development that would make it possible to emphasise and preserve the specificity and uniqueness of the Russian civilisation.[5] On the basis of this distinction, we can further distinguish two main currents present in science (especially in geopolitics), as well as reflected in political discourse and practice. The first one is (1) Atlanticism, also referred to as Occidentalism (Rus. *atlantizm, zapadnichestvo*), and the second one is (2) Eurasianism (Rus. *evrazijstvo*) and its modernised version: Neo-Eurasianism.[6]

Atlanticism

Atlanticism advocates establishing closer cooperation between Russia and all of the West, especially with the United States and with Europe. This would involve the adoption of the Western system of values and even accession to the main Western organisations (including the EU and NATO), while abandoning imperial superpower aspirations. This concept draws on the tradition of liberalism and Occidentalism, which have been present in the Russian state thought at least since the time of Peter the Great and which assumed the need to maintain close ties with more developed European countries. Among contemporary politicians who support Atlanticism one can name, for example: Yegor Gaidar and Andrei Kozyrev, and among researchers and analysts, Vladimir Baranovsky, Oleg Bogomolov, Dmitri Trenin and Sergey Karaganov.

Sergey Karaganov formulated the concept of a strategic alliance between the Russian Federation and the European Union, which could replace the current balance of power in the world. He believes that we are witnessing the emergence of a bipolar order with the United States and China at the top. This order would, however, be much more stable if it had a third element: a Union of Europe. This new grouping would be composed of the EU, Russia and a number of other states (e.g.: Turkey and Ukraine) and would work in a similar way to how *de facto* the EU functions, that is ensuring a relatively close integration in the spheres of politics and economy.

Dmitri Trenin, on the other hand, advocates a departure from the traditional division into the East and the West and, above all, stresses the need for Russia to abandon its superpower perspective. In his opinion, we are currently witnessing the emergence of a 'third West' (after the one from the age of European colonial expansion and the one dominated by the US in the Cold War era), one with worldwide extent. Trenin perceives it in terms of a system of values, norms and technologies, constituting a synonym for 'international society'. Russia should become a full member of this 'society', by both strengthening its relations with the world leader, the United States, and adopting the political and socio-economic principles of the European Union. This, however, should take place without formal membership in the EU as it would be unnecessary – as Leszek Sykulski puts it: 'Russian analyst proposes not so much that Russia integrates with the West but that it simply becomes the West'.[7] This means that in Trenin's opinion, there will be some spontaneous unification, an integration of Eurasia, through its evolutionary inclusion in the ranks of the West.

According to the views of contemporary Atlanticists, the new Russia should find its place in the changing, pluralist world taking advantage of the achievements of the West and especially Europe, considered a symbol of universalism and a place for dialogue between different cultures. Thus Atlanticists assumed that Russia needs the West, but the West also needs Russia.[8] However, after Vladimir Putin came to power, the current that represents these views has been marginalised and it does not seem to have any significant impact on scientific research, not to mention political practice at present.

Eurasianism

The second main current in Russian political thought and the one that clearly prevails is Eurasianism, referred to as Neo-Eurasianism in its modernised version. It is based on the key principle that Russia, as a unique state, is the embodiment of a separate civilisation, combining the historical, political and cultural traditions of two continents: Europe and Asia but at the same time not belonging to either one. It is therefore a singular entity, one whose main characteristics include being predestined to play the role of both a huge empire of global magnitude and a messiah in world history – in line with the concept of 'Russia as the Third Rome'.

Contemporary Neo-Eurasianism draws inspiration from classical Eurasianism, which has developed vigorously since the first half of the 20th century. The most eminent representatives of this current included Peter Savitsky, Nikolai Trubetzkoy and George Vernadsky. They drew inspiration from various historical sources, for example: the tradition of tsarist imperialism, the idea of Orthodox Messianism, Slavophile and Pan-Slavic concepts, and the works of authors who propagated national ideas, such as Leo Tolstoy and Fyodor Dostoyevsky. What played the most important role here, however, were the concepts put forward by the earlier thinkers of the nationalist current, especially Nikolay Danilevsky, who published the monumental *Russia and Europe* in 1871. The work quickly became known as the catechism of Russian nationalism, and its theses were further developed by many followers, including Ivan Dusinsky, who focused on geopolitics. According to Piotr Eberhardt, the two authors 'dreamt of a great Russia that would dominate both Europe and the world', but at the same time they perceived it not only as imperial power but also as magnificent civilisation.[9]

In the contemporary times, the notion of Eurasianism was intensively developed by, among others, the late Aleksandr Solzhenitsyn, Elgiz Pozdniakov, Igor Panarin and Lev Gumilyov. Gumilyov, for example, in his works points at the uniqueness of the phenomenon of Russia as a specific civilisation whose geographical location, history and supranational culture predestine it to play the leading role in the world. At the same time, he stresses the importance of the idea of Eurasianism, declaring outright that Russia can only survive as a Eurasian power and only through Eurasianism.[10] This notion is clearly based on Russian nationalism, a telling sign of which is, among others, the fact that Russian Eurasianists have always combated other, non-Russian Eurasian ideologies, such as Pan-Turkism and Kazakh Eurasianism.[11] To Russians, they are not only a competition but in fact a threat to the implementation of what Andrzej Szabaciuk refers to as President Putin's Eurasian integration project.[12]

Igor Panarin, in turn, refers to the concept of 'Russia as Third Rome' and believes that Russia's main goal should be to become a global power centre. This would make it possible to create a geopolitical entity called Eurasian Rus which resembles the European Union in its organisational principles. This new entity would include not only Russia and other countries of the former Soviet Union but also the former Soviet satellite countries, including Poland. Eurasian Rus' allies would include the major countries of Western Europe, India, the Islamic world and – above all – China, which is very important in the context of Panarin's forecasts of the inevitable clash between China and the new empire emerging due to a closer alliance between the United States and the United Kingdom.

Presently, however, the best-known and most influential representative of Russian Eurasianism is Aleksandr Dugin.[13] He presented his views in numerous publications, including the extensive book *The Foundations of Geopolitics: The Geopolitical Future of Russia*, published in 1999. Being both a researcher and a *de facto* politician, he gained considerable influence, acting as advisor to President Putin and working with other major politicians, such as Vladimir Zhirinovsky and Gennady Zyuganov; he also plays an important role in academic and analytical communities.

Aleksandr Dugin's concepts are based to a large extent on ideas put forward by one of the founding fathers of geopolitics, Halford J. Mackinder, primarily on his main thesis of the existence of a World Island, composed of Asia, Europe and Africa, and its north-eastern part: the Heartland. According to this thesis: he who rules the Heartland commands the World Island; he who rules the World Island commands the world.[14] Dugin naturally equates the Heartland with the Russian state, once existing as the Russian Empire, then the Soviet Union, and presently as the Russian Federation.[15] He supplements Mackinder's concepts, however, with the theory presented by Carl Schmitt in his 1959 work under the telling title: *The Planetary Tension Between Orient and Occident and the Opposition Between Land and Sea*. Schmitt contrasted there two mega-civilisations: one based on maritime power and the other based on land power ('Sea' versus 'Land'). Thus, according to Dugin, the Eurasian Russia should rule the Heartland and, at the same time, develop great land power, which would enable it to realise its fundamental geopolitical goal: overcome the Atlantic world, based on maritime power of first the United Kingdom and now the United States.

In Aleksandr Dugin's opinion, the conflict between Russia and the West is unavoidable in the long run, which makes it absolutely necessary to rebuild the Russian empire; as he noted: 'Russia will either be great, or will not be at all'.[16] Proper preparation for the future clash will require first eliminating NATO, thus breaking the alliance between the United States and Europe, and subsequently weakening the European Union and, if possible, facilitating its dissolution. In order to achieve these goals it is necessary to establish a system of alliances, preferably in the form of three axes: Moscow – Berlin, Moscow – Tokyo and Moscow – Tehran; the most important one obviously being the close geopolitical cooperation between Russia and Germany.

This would give rise to a powerful Eurasian empire, one that could change the current international order. This order is characterised by unipolarity, manifested in the hegemony of the Atlantic world (its centre being the United States), subordination of the so-called Third World and the existence of a certain strategic 'black hole', namely Russia, the last bastion holding out against Western domination. According to Aleksandr Dugin and other Russian Eurasianists, the optimal global order should consist in the development of a multipolar system through the emergence of four zones, including a pan-Eurasian one that would comprise Russia, a part of Eastern Europe and the Balkans, the Middle East as well as Central and South Asia. This would ensure stability of the new international order, which should be developed in accordance with the principles of equality of all actors.

While the views of Dugin and other Russian Eurasianists have not been officially adopted by the authorities in the Kremlin, they do in fact form the conceptual basis for the principles of Russian foreign policy, constituting an example of imperialist and nationalist thinking. It is based on the assumption that Russia is to play the dominant role in the world, being both admired and – and this needs to emphasised – feared (the use of fear as an instrument of foreign and internal policy is a centuries-old tradition of Russian statehood). This is accompanied by the conviction that Russia was created by God to achieve great goals, and it consistently needs to keep fulfilling this purpose.[17] As Roman Bäcker put it, it is a programme of expansive imperialism, which 'mainly comes down to a rather overt programme of conquering at least a large part of the world, if not all of it'.[18]

The need to pursue such goals is explicitly stressed by Aleksandr Dugin and his followers. According to Elgiz Pozdniakov, for example, only complete Russian domination of the Eurasian continent guarantees balance and stability in the world. Dugin himself goes even further, stating outright that: 'We Russians (. . .) think in terms of expansion and will never do otherwise. We are not simply interested in preserving our state and nation. We are interested in delineating our strategic geopolitical borders'.[19] Calling Poland and the other states of Central Europe by the derogatory name of 'sanitary cordon', Aleksandr Dugin believes that it is Eurasia's task to obliterate this 'cordon'.[20] Such views have considerable, even if not absolute, influence on the formation of Russians' attitudes towards the West and Europe.

The attitude towards the West and Europe in Russian political thought

In accordance with the research hypothesis of this chapter, the perception of the West – and especially that of Europe – by both the Russian society and its élites is shaped by sharp criticism of the Western civilisation and by contrasting it with their own paradigms. In other words, as regards the issue of European identity, it can be said that Russians view this identity as the antithesis of their own system of values. The identity of Russia as a state – but ultimately also as a nation and civilisation – is 'defined not in inclusive terms, within the system of membership in the international community, but rather in exclusive terms: "against" other states', which means emphasising differences and contrasts and attachment to one's own specificity. In short, Russians defined themselves rather in opposition to others, especially to Europeans.[21]

As a result, Russian Eurasianists focus on stressing the differences between the European sense of identity and the set of attributes that is to characterise the Russian nation. According to Andrzej Szabaciuk, Eurasianists 'believe Russia plays a unique role of the leader in the struggle against the corruption brought by Western postmodernism, globalisation, ultraliberalism', which undermine 'all the traditional forms of identity, the significance of the state, religion, nation, ethnos, family and the human being itself'. In this view, 'Western civilisation is a civilisation of death with obvious destructive characteristics'. Russia, in turn, having a messianic mission to fulfil, chose 'fraternity of nations based on strong historical, cultural and spiritual foundations' as the cornerstone of the Eurasian civilisation it is building.[22]

The approach that depreciates the West in general and Europe in particular resulted in, among others, the promotion of the concept of the so-called Western project. The concept was formulated outside the Western civilisation and is clearly aimed against it; as Samir Amin puts it, the term signifies an offensive of imperialism of 'the Triad' (the US, Europe and Japan) with the aim of conquering and subjugating the whole world, some supposed contemporary signs of it being the US intervention in Iraq and the NATO armed operation in Afghanistan.[23]

In Russia, the concept of the Western project was developed by, for example, Igor Kefeli in his work *Philosophy of Geopolitics*, published in 2007. It is used to refer to 'a certain programme, system of values, conduct promoted by the West that threatens cultural diversity, thus weakening the sense of belonging to a different, non-Western civilisation and culture'. This is to concern Russia in particular, which means that 'the project creates a threat to the Russian state's position and role in the international arena'.[24] According to Igor Panarin, the civilisation created by Russia has a special right to criticise the Western project because it shares a 'Greek core' with the West. Russia has managed to create solutions alternative to the Western ones in the sphere of religion ('Moscow as Third Rome' in opposition to Catholicism and Protestantism) and politics, first building the tsarist empire, then the Soviet empire, and now the Russian Federation. This is also why it is supposedly especially strongly attacked by the West, and the accusations against the West in this context become close to maniacal – according to Panarin, 'the Russian Orthodox culture had the honour of becoming the main focus of Western Olympic hatred'.[25]

The development of this way of thinking was influenced by a number of diverse factors, including, to a large extent, what is referred to as the Russian Idea.[26] The term was propagated towards the end of the 19th century by Vladimir Solovyov and was later developed by, among others, Nikolai Berdyaev in his book *The Russian Idea*. It comes down to the conviction that Russia has its own, independent culture and tradition, and at the same time that on this basis Russia should develop an ideal model of society, one that would reject egoistic utilitarianism and be based on community identity. Since the fall of the Soviet Union, the idea has been used to consolidate the Russian society, experiencing a huge trauma resulting from the loss of superpower status.

To Russians, the collapse of the Soviet Union was a slap to their national pride and thus an attack against their sense of identity. This confirms Stanislaw Bieleń's opinion that 'the most important element of the contemporary Russian Idea is opposition towards everyone who would humiliate Russia'.[27] Bieleń as well as other researchers cites the sharp reaction to the armed conflict in Chechnya as a good example of such an approach. Russia put down the Chechen liberation movement in a systematic, calculated and ruthless way because by doing this it took revenge for the humiliation it had suffered.[28] However, Russia exhibits a similar way of thinking also regarding other societies and states that do not agree with the Kremlin's imperial aspirations, and this is first of all the West, Europe in particular.

The important thing for the present deliberations is that the concept of Russian Idea is based on contrasting and deeming Russian identity superior to European identity. This is a consequence of the conviction that Russia's own culture and tradition places it right next to the West and ensures future prosperity. What is more, 'while in order to survive Europe needs to discard its unfortunate past, Russia can draw on its rich heritage without limitations'.[29] This heritage includes a specific sense of community, as well as spirituality based on Orthodoxy and remaining in opposition to Western and European individualism and materialism. In other words, Russian identity very early began to develop in opposition to the West and as a kind of antidote to Western remedies.[30]

One of the fullest manifestations of such thinking is the renaissance of yet another idea proclaiming Russian specificity and known under the name Russian World (*Russkiy Mir*).[31] Its beginnings go back to the mid-19th century, and its fathers include the high-ranking imperial officials Count Sergey Uvarov and General Mikhail Chernyayev. As scholars such as Norman Davies pointed out, it was an attempt to create a concept that would demonstrate Russia's ideological and moral high ground over its competitors or enemies and in this sense was one of the precursors of Eurasianism.[32] The concept flourished again, however, only under President Putin, who seems to have deemed it the suitable political and propaganda instrument to pursue his neo-imperial foreign and internal policy.

The concept of *Russkiy Mir* refers to an 'imagined community', that is a community based not only on ethnic criteria but primarily on common culture, tradition, identity and language, all of which can also characterise people from other nations and inhabitants of countries other than Russia. The focus is therefore on a broader category referred to as the 'Russian people', which includes also Ukrainians, Belarusians and other nations that used to be part of the Russian state. The notion of the Russian World can be used both as a new model for the functioning of internal relations within the Russian Federation and at the same time as an instrument in Russian foreign policy.

This is because it is addressed to the large Russian diaspora in the countries of the post-Soviet area and to all other people who feel a connection with the Russian civilisation; it can provide the Kremlin with a handy pretext to interfere with the policies conducted by its neighbours, the countries of what Russia calls the 'close abroad'. The Kremlin receives considerable support in this respect from the Orthodox Church, which is trying to maintain or expand its control over the entire Orthodox post-Soviet space.[33] The apologists for this idea, such as Aleksandr Dugin, go as far in imparting positive aspects to it as to claim – contrary to obvious facts – that 'it is clear to every Russian that the *Russkiy Mir* is not nationalist'; at the same time, however, Dugin nationalistically declares that 'Russia's domination in this world would only serve to ensure its multipolarity'.[34]

Just like the previous concepts, the idea of the Russian World is based primarily on anti-Occidentalism and anti-Europeanism. The two are in fact at its core; as Piotr Kościński puts it, Russian ideologists present this idea as 'radically different from the Western ones: peaceful as opposed to warlike, conservative as opposed to radically liberal, recognising cultural differences as opposed to imposing culture on others'.[35] This aspect was also highlighted by Norman Davies, who pointed out that the Russian Orthodox Church, the Russian authorities and various nationalist forces have always reacted against the more powerful West, producing theories which claim the truth and future for themselves. They have repeatedly maintained that although the West may be well rich and powerful, the East is free from moral and ideological corruption.[36]

President Putin himself presents a similar outlook. In 2014 he stated on television that Russians – and more broadly: the people of the *Russkiy Mir* – believe in man's higher moral destiny; they think about others and are open to them. This is to be the opposite of Western values, which involve only striving to get richer and becoming blinded by one's own egoism.[37] Generally speaking, the idea of the Russian World fits very well within the current of Russian Eurasianism. It is therefore justified, despite the differences between the two concepts, to treat them as ideological variants of Russian neo-imperialism.

Russia's position towards the West and Europe in public discourse

As mentioned previously, although the official goals of Russia's foreign policy towards the West and Europe are not based directly on the principles of Eurasianism, they are in fact closely related to them.[38] The evolution of this policy can be best shown by comparing the changes introduced in important documents, such as the Foreign Policy Concept of the Russian Federation. Compared to a similar document from 2013, the latest Concept, published in November 2016, no longer prioritises the relations and strategic community of goals with the Euroatlantic world. What particularly stands out is that it lacks any reference to a common civilisation identity shared by Russia and the West, which only confirms the conjecture that the authors remained strongly influenced by nationalist thought.[39]

In the sphere of relations with the European Union, which is most interesting to us, we can clearly see a shift of emphasis: the EU is no longer perceived as the 'main' partner but merely an 'important' one, and only in the economic sphere. The new document does not mention many elements of political cooperation, such as the conclusion of another strategic partnership agreement. Moreover, it does not mention the EU as a potential partner in the international arena but instead it focuses on the individual member states. This not only proves that the approach to the relations with the EU has changed, but it also shows the intent to disintegrate it.

The goals of the Russian foreign policy are to be facilitated by the growing importance of the idea of the Russian World, very strongly emphasised in the new Concept. The promotion of this nationalist ideology is in fact a cover for Russian propaganda, being brought to nations and countries that do not belong to the Russian World at all – it is also aimed at the societies of Europe which are close to Russia. In their case, promotion of the Russian way of life serves not only the purpose of raising the acceptance of Russia's global power policy but also weakening their value system. The ultimate goal is to undermine their European identity through, for example, touting the advantages of nationalist views modelled after Russian chauvinism to the individual EU societies. This is evidenced by, among others, intensive development of various Russian media aimed at influencing countries abroad, including the well-known television network Russia Today. They have already played a role in supporting Russia's interference in the political and social life of European states, including the Brexit referendum campaign in 2016 or the 2017 presidential elections in France, and everything seems to indicate that interference of this kind will be continued, possibly even more intensively.

This is to be justified by the fact – strongly emphasised in the Concept – that the relations between Russia and the West are in a deep crisis, supposedly caused by the geopolitical expansion of not only the United States and NATO (which used to be the standard justification) but the European Union as well. Putting pressure on Russia by various means is, however, presented as completely ineffective and leading only to destabilisation of the global order. According to Russians, international relations are currently evolving towards a departure from the global balance of power based on domination of the United States – and, more broadly, the West – towards greater multipolarity. This is supposed to be conducive to Russia's efforts to replace its relations with the Western world with much closer relations with the new Asian powers: China and India, as well as with other non-Western partners.

In a nutshell, the aim of the part of the Concept dedicated to relations with the West is to make the impression that Russia's revisionist policy in Europe is purely defensive and that the Western policy of putting pressure on Russia is doomed to fail because it is at variance with the objective evolution of the shift of power on the global scale. The authors of the document do not hesitate to put political pressure on Western countries, suggesting that maintaining tensions in their relations with Russia will be very harmful to them. Such pressure is intended to complement the aforementioned ideological and propaganda pressure. Their combined effect is meant to soften the Western world, Europe in particular, in terms of both security and the sense of a community of values and interests.

This fits well with the previously mentioned strategy – adopted under President Putin – of weakening or even destroying the unity of the EU, to be achieved through such means as diversification of the policy towards individual EU countries. This strategy has already yielded some success, as proven by the fact that several member states have changed their foreign policy orientation to a more pro-Russian one, namely Hungary, the Czech Republic, Greece, Austria or Italy. In these circumstances it is understandable that Russia is greatly displeased with the EU's undertakings that show the Union's unity and effectiveness; even more so if they are aimed directly or indirectly at Russia.

The most important undertaking is the EU's European Neighbourhood Policy,[40] which the Kremlin believes – according to Anne-Sophie Maass and Hannes Adomeit – threatens Russia's vital interests, hurts its pride and constitutes an attempt to limit Russia's influence in the post-Soviet space.[41] The same is true of the EU's Eastern Policy, especially its flagship initiative, the Eastern Partnership, established in 2008.[42] Russia has always approached the idea of the Partnership with aversion and even hostility: Foreign Minister of Russia Sergey Lavrov, for example, accused the EU of building its own area of influence in the East at the expense of Russian interests.[43] What is more, the attempts of the last two decades to develop a strategic partnership between the EU and Russia have failed as well, the main reason being that the two partners represent fundamentally different, incompatible political and economic systems and rapprochement between them is impossible in the present circumstances, and additionally the parties have expectations of each other that simply cannot be met.[44] The situation is currently further exacerbated by the crisis in Ukraine, which sees both the EU and Russia throwing grave accusations and imposing political and economic sanctions against each other.

Intensive promotion by Russian scientific and opinion-forming circles and by state authorities of certain ideological and political principles towards the West as a whole, but especially towards Europe, has been yielding results not only in the political sphere. This is also true of the shaping of the social consciousness, as exemplified by the far-reaching changes in the attitudes of Russian public opinion. Following a propaganda campaign, conducted on a massive scale, especially strongly after the outbreak of the Ukrainian crisis in 2014, Russian's attitudes towards the United States and the European Union deteriorated drastically. While back in 2010–2012 (during the so-called reset in the US–Russia relations initiated by President Barack Obama) 40–60 per cent of respondents in public opinion polls declared positive sentiments towards America and as many as 70 per cent towards the EU, in 2015 the percentages fell to 13 and 20, respectively, with a tendency to decrease further.[45]

Russian government propaganda, employing various techniques and considered an important element of the so called hybrid warfare against Ukraine,[46] promotes what we might call negative identity. In this propaganda, Russia is defined as the antithesis of the postmodernist West; it is therefore easier to evoke the belief that 'others are at fault'. This makes it possible to convince the Russian society that it is not the country's internal problems that are the most important (as it was in the opinion of 63 per cent of respondents in 2011) but external threats, as was the opinion of 77 per cent of respondents already three years later.[47] These threats supposedly arise especially in the West, including the European Union, and take the form of a direct attack against Russian interests (especially in Ukraine) and an attack on the Russian, Orthodox system of values, being the antithesis of the identity of 'corrupted Europe'.

A dispute over values

In the context of these deliberations, it is vital to notice that one of the most contentious issues or differences between the EU and Russia – apart from differences in the sphere of vital geostrategic interests – are broadly defined axiological issues. At the same time, it needs to be noted that as regards the first of these spheres (i.e. specific issues concerning politics, economy or even security), compromise is possible and Russians are capable of showing far-reaching pragmatism. Even when opting for rivalry or confrontation with the West, including the EU, in the end the Kremlin needs Western partners to secure the country's fundamental interests (as proven by, for instance, the considerable economic and trade exchange between Russia and the EU despite the tensions between the two sides).

The situation is different, however, in the second most important sphere – the value system that forms the basis for the development of identity. In this sphere, there is virtually no room for compromise as it would require both parties to make concessions undermining their ideological and ethical 'backbone'. For Russians, this 'backbone' is based on the aforementioned set of various, more or less nationalistic concepts. For Europeans, it is primarily based on the system of democratic and liberal values most fully expressed in the form of the EU's catalogue of European values, including democracy, protection of human rights and civil freedoms, the rule of law, solidarity, etc.; and in the sphere of relations abroad – solving disputes in a peaceful manner, preference for diplomatic and economic instruments as well as observance of international law.[48]

The fact that the EU is based on such principles makes it, as has already been mentioned, a normative power.[49] Ian Manners, considered the main author of this concept, believes that all material attributes of the power of the EU as a global actor 'are secondary to its ability to shape the ideational constitution of international relations'.[50] This means that, as Anna Skolimowska puts it, the EU's power in the world results not from the fact that it has certain material assets at its disposal but rather from the Union basing its activity 'on the meaning of the core ideas, norms and values of the European integration project'. This power consists therefore 'in the ability to propagate European political and legal norms, ideas, discourses, models of integration and using them to shape the international environment'.[51] As we can see, this is not only about passively presenting one's offer to the world but primarily about actively exerting real influence on it.[52]

It is also this particular aspect of the European Union's international activity that gives rise to discontent and passionate opposition in Russia. The latter now accuses the EU of not only exporting European values but also of forcing them onto the international community. This supposedly takes place without regard for the specificity of the individual members of this community, especially those like Russia – unique and having their own value systems. In the words of Tatiana Romanova, the very concept of the European Union as normative power 'conflicts with some of the Russian Federation's fundamental foreign policy ideas'.[53] This refers to, inter alia, the EU supposedly very obviously failing to treat any of its partners as equals, playing the role of a judge who verifies whether others obey to the standards set up arbitrarily by the EU. What is most important in the context of this chapter, however, is that Russia believes 'the way that the EU defines itself and its normative power to be an attack on its identity'.[54] Consequently, the conditions that Russian authorities want their Western partners to meet before cooperation can be resumed include first and foremost 'recognising Russian "specificity" in the sphere of values and refraining from interfering with Russia's internal affairs'.[55]

The Russian propaganda uses various measures in its efforts to weaken the European sense of shared common identity. For example, it tries to drive a wedge between the European Union and its most important ally, the United States. The arguments Russian nationalists often use include stressing that the present EU is in fact an 'American Europe', one that not only loses its independence but even its own identity. Another method used increasingly often is an attempt to break apart the EU's unity through the promotion of a division into 'true Europe', that is the Russia-friendly countries, and 'false Europe', that is the countries that do not support Russian interests, especially some countries that joined the EU in the last big enlargement, such as Poland and the Baltic states.[56]

This way, 'by drawing these normative and identity lines, Russia tries to put limits on how new EU member states can exploit the EU's normative power'.[57] In the opinion of Aleksandr Dugin, the present European Union has for a long time had real divisions into better and worse citizens, and they can only become stronger: 'The inhabitants of such countries as Spain, Portugal, Italy and Greece are considered second-class citizens in the EU. And what class are Romanians? What class will Moldovans be?' This goes of course hand in hand with calls for the EU to follow the example of the Russian civilisation, which 'means a revival of culture, respect for spirituality, tradition, Christianity' and therefore is the antithesis of the European civilisation.[58]

If we acknowledge one of the main research hypotheses of this chapter that Russians treat European identity as the antithesis of their own identity, in the end it is worth discussing the prospects in this respect. In so doing, we need to take into account the fundamental factor of huge axiological incompatibility between the value systems of Russia and Europe, which inevitably impacts their sense of identity. A thorough analysis of the reasons behind this state of affairs would require a separate study; here we will therefore only point out that this incompatibility is determined by, among others, fundamentally different visions of the world and of the place the European Union and the Russian Federation do and should hold in it.

According to Josef M. Fiszer, 'the EU was formed in response to threats of nationalism and catastrophic rivalry between European nation states', whereas to Russia 'the most important problems are those resulting from the dissolution of the Soviet Union, which Putin and millions of Russians have so far been unable to come to terms with'. For the European Union, the main reason behind the instability in Eurasia is the lack of democracy, which it therefore strives to promote by exporting European values, which at the same time support the emergence of new, more democratic and more liberal identities. For Russia, in turn, the EU's policy of exporting democracy is the main cause of international instability, because this country believes only 'in power, unilateralism and an unbounded ambition to satisfy national interest', and because it understands sovereignty only as economic independence, military power and cultural identity. As a result, 'it was inevitable that sooner or later the two contrasting views of the European order in the 21st century would clash', and 'the European hopes that Russia could become a partner to the European Union (. . .) proved vain'.[59]

On a positive note, it needs to be pointed out that despite all the current turbulence, the European direction must remain one of the priorities of Russia's foreign policy. As a result, regardless of Russia's attempts to find its own path of development, it simply cannot afford to abandon cooperation with the West, in particular with the European Union. A vision of such cooperation was presented by President Putin himself in his early days in office: for example, during an official visit to Germany in 2001, he expressed the belief that 'in the long-term perspective Europe can become a powerful and independent centre of world policy only if it combines its assets (. . .) with the economic, cultural and military potential of Russia'.[60]

At the same time, for the European Union Russia is and will remain one of the key partners in the international arena, one whose economic, political and social stability can, to a great extent, determine the security and development of all of Europe. There is hard political, economic and military evidence for this; there are also studies of the European decision-making élites' views in this regard that confirm this: the results of a 2016 study of the opinions of influential representatives of 20 European countries made by European Leadership Network show that it is possible for the EU to achieve a mutually satisfactory modus vivendi with Russia, but at the same time, the respondents also believed that 'Moscow's current policy towards the region remains the main obstacle to reaching it'.[61]

We should therefore hope that the two partners will at some point be able to work out a model of mutually beneficial cooperation; this will, however, probably be much easier in the political and economic practice than with regard to changes in the social consciousness. The latter evolves much more slowly than the material world, which means that value systems and the resulting identities of individuals and entire societies can persist much longer than the objectively existing determinants that created them. On the other hand, as Alexander Wendt puts it, 'identities may be hard to change, but they are not carved in stone'.[62] It means that in the coming years the European Union needs to develop a model of truly effective strategic partnership with its largest eastern neighbour, which, if possible, should also include calming the controversies concerning the sphere of axiology and identity.

Notes

1 A norm in sociological terms could be understood as being: 'A principle or standard of correctness that reflects people's expectations of behavior', and as regards the international relations 'norm is probably best understood as being a shorthand way of expressing what passes for "normal"' in utilitarian, social, moral, and narrative sense – see: I. Manners, *Normative Power Europe: The International Role of the EU*, Madison ECSA Biennial Conference, 31 May 2001, p. 10.
2 O. Barburska, 'Podstawy Normatywne Funkcjonowania Unii Europejskiej w Stosunkach Międzynarodowych – Ujęcie Teoretyczne', *Stosunki Międzynarodowe*, vol. 4, 2016, p. 68. See also: A. Skolimowska, 'Potęga Norm w Stosunkach Międzynarodowych', in A. Skolimowska (ed.), *Normatywna Potęga Unii Europejskiej w Obliczu Umiędzynarodowionych Konfliktów Wewnętrznych,* Warszawa, Dom Wydawniczy Elipsa, 2015.
3 More in: V. Morozov, *Russia's Postcolonial Identity: A Subaltern Empire in a Eurocentric World*, London, Palgrave Macmillan, 2015; J. Potulski, 'Rosyjskie Koncepcje Geopolityczne jako Wyraz Poszukiwania Formuły Imperialnej?', in S. Bieleń and A. Skrzypek (eds.), *Rosja. Rozważania Imperiologiczne*, Warszawa, Oficyna Wydawnicza Aspra-JR, 2015; I. Neumann, *Russia and the Idea of Europe: A Study in Identity and International Relations*, London-New York, Routledge, 1996.
4 S. Bieleń, *Tożsamość Międzynarodowa Federacji Rosyjskiej*, Warszawa, Oficyna Wydawnicza Aspra-JR, 2006, p. 61.
5 Bieleń, *Tożsamość Międzynarodowa Federacji Rosyjskiej*, p. 44.
6 More in: A.P. Tsygankov, *Russia and the West from Alexander to Putin. Honor in International Relations*, Cambridge, Cambridge University Press, 2014; L. Sykulski, 'Integracja Polityczna Eurazji we Współczesnej Rosyjskiej Myśli Geopolitycznej', in P. Eberhardt (ed.), *Prace Geograficzne, Studia nad Geopolityką XX wieku*, vol. 242, 2013; M. Sawicka, 'Rosyjska Odpowiedź na Zachodni Globalny Projekt', *Przegląd Geopolityczny*, vol. 1, 2009.
7 Sykulski, 'Integracja Polityczna', pp. 351–352; see also: D. Trenin, *Getting Russia Right*, Washington, Carnegie Endowment for International Peace, 2007.
8 Bieleń, *Tożsamość Międzynarodowa*, p. 70.
9 P. Eberhardt, 'Koncepcje Geopolityczne Iwana Dusińskiego', *Studia z Geografii Politycznej i Historycznej*, vol. 1, 2012, p. 41.
10 More in: S. Pomarin (ed.), *Eurasia: People & Myths*, Moscow, Natalis Press, 1993.
11 See: G. Mustafa, 'The Concept of Eurasia: Kazakh Eurasian Policy and Implications', *Journal of Eurasian Studies*, vol. 3, 2013.
12 A. Szabaciuk, 'Eurazjatycki Projekt Integracyjny Władimira Putina: Szanse i Zagrożenia', *Rocznik Instytutu Europy Środkowo-Wschodniej*, vol. 5, 2014.
13 More in: B. Gołąbek, *Lew Gumilow i Aleksander Dugin. O Dwóch Obliczach Eurazjatyzmu w Rosji po 1991 Roku*, Kraków, Wydawnictwo Uniwersytetu Jagiellońskiego, 2012.
14 See: H.J. Mackinder, 'The Geographical Pivot of History' *The Geographical Journal*, vol. 4, 1904.
15 See: G. Robbins, 'The Post-Soviet Heartland: Reconsidering Mackinder', *Eurasian Studies*, vol. 3, 1994, p. 35.
16 See: Szabaciuk, 'Eurazjatycki Projekt', p. 83.

17 Eberhardt, 'Koncepcje Geopolityczne', p. 223.
18 R. Bäcker, 'Współczesny Antyokcydentalizm Rosyjski', in Z. Anculewicz and J. Sobczak (eds.), *Europa a Rosja. Opinie, Konflikty, Współpraca*, Olsztyn, Wydawnictwo UWM, 2003, p. 267.
19 Eberhardt, 'Koncepcje geopolityczne', pp. 224, 235.
20 K. Nieczypor, 'Aleksander Dugin – Eurazjatycki Głos w Twoim Domu', 06 February 2017, www.eastbook.eu/2017/02/06/aleksander-dugin-eurazjatycki-glos-w-twoim-domu/, (accessed 25 June 2018).
21 Bieleń, *Tożsamość Międzynarodowa*, pp. 46, 59.
22 Szabaciuk, 'Eurazjatycki Projekt', pp. 83–84. See also: M. Laruelle, 'Beyond Anti-Westernism. The Kremlin's Narrative about Russia's European Identity and Mission', *PONARS Eurasia Policy Memo*, vol. 326, 2014.
23 S. Amin, *The Liberal Virus: Permanent War and the Americanization of the World*, New York, Monthly Review Press, 2004, pp. 106–116.
24 Sawicka, 'Rosyjska odpowiedź', p. 87.
25 Sawicka, 'Rosyjska odpowiedź', p. 88.
26 More in: Bieleń, *Tożsamość Międzynarodowa*, p. 55.
27 Bieleń, *Tożsamość Międzynarodowa*, p. 57.
28 A. Ananicz, 'Rosja po Dwóch Małych Wojnach', *Sprawy Międzynarodowe*, vol. 1, 2009, p. 15. See also: H. Smith, *Russian Greatpowerness: Foreign policy, the Two Chechen Wars and International Organisations*, Helsinki, University of Helsinki, 2014.
29 Bieleń, *Tożsamość międzynarodowa*, p. 55.
30 Bieleń, *Tożsamość międzynarodowa*, pp. 57, 59.
31 More in: P. Kościński, '"Russij Mir" – Rosyjska Polityka Sąsiedztwa', *Sprawy Międzynarodowe*, vol. 1, 2015; M. Laruelle, *The 'Russian World'. Russia's Soft Power and Geopolitical Imagination*, Washington, DC, CGI Center on Global Interest, 2015.
32 See: N. Davies, *Europe: A History*, Oxford, Harper Perennial, 1996.
33 More in: A. Curanović, 'The Guardians of Traditional Values. Russia and Russian Orthodox Church in the Quest for Status', *Transatlantic Academy Paper Series*, vol. 1, 2015; M. Suslov, 'Holy Rus': The Geopolitical Imagination in the Contemporary Russian Orthodox Church', *Russian Social Science Review*, vol. 3, 2015.
34 See: Kościński, '"Russij mir"', p. 74.
35 Kościński, '"Russij mir"', p. 73.
36 Davies, *Europe: A History*, p. 26.
37 See: Kościński, '"Russij mir"', p. 74.
38 More in: J.M. Fiszer, 'Zadania i Cele Polityki Zagranicznej Władimira Putina', *Myśl Ekonomiczna i Polityczna*, vol. 1, 2016; P. Felgenhauer, 'Russia Prepares for War with the USA and NATO, while Lucking Resources', *European Dialogue*, 14 March 2013, https://jamestown.org/program/russia-prepares-for-war-with-the-us-and-nato-while-lacking-resources/, (accessed 25 June 2018).
39 *The Foreign Policy Concept of the Russian Federation (approved by President of the Russian Federation Vladimir Putin on November 30, 2016)*, www.mid.ru/en/foreign-policy/document/, (accessed 25 June 2018).
40 See more in: S. Poli (ed.), *The European Neighbourhood Policy – Values and Principles*, New York, Routledge, 2016; T. Stępniewski, 'ENP or ENPs? The Curious Web of the European Neighborhood Policy: The Southern and Eastern Dimensions Revisited', *Yearbook of the Institute of East-Central Europe*, vol. 4, 2015; J. Gower and G. Timmins (eds.), *The European Union, Russia and Shared Neighbourhood*, London, Routledge, 2011.
41 A.S. Maass, *EU-Russia Relations, 1999–2015: From Courtship to Confrontation*, London-New York, Routledge, 2017, especially chapter 3; H. Adomeit, 'Russia. ENP Competitor', in E. Lannon (ed.), *The European Neighbourhood Policy's Challenges/*

Les défis de la Politique Européenne de Voisinage, Brussels, Series: College of Europe Studies/Cahiers du Collège d'Europe, vol. 14, 2012, pp. 393–394.

42 See more in: T. Stępniewski, 'The European Union and Eastern Partnership: Crises and Strategic Assessment', *Yearbook of the Institute of East-Central Europe*, vol. 5, 2016; O. Barburska and D. Milczarek, *Polityka Wschodnia Unii Europejskiej: Porażka czy Sukces?*, Warszawa, Oficyna Wydawnicza Aspra-JR, 2014; D. Milczarek, 'More Gains or Losses? Review of the European Union's Eastern Policy', in B. Góralczyk (ed.), *European Union on the Global Scene: United or Irrelevant?*, Warsaw, Centre for Europe, University of Warsaw, 2015, pp. 35–62; I. Gretskiy, E. Treshchenkov, K. Golubiev, 'Russia's Perceptions and Misperceptions of the EU Eastern Partnership', *Communist and Post-Communist Studies*, vol. 3–4, 2014.

43 Barburska and Milczarek, *Polityka Wschodnia*, p. 72.

44 See: O. Barburska, 'Relacje Unia Europejska-Federacja Rosyjska: Kryzys Partnerstwa Strategicznego', *Studia Europejskie*, vol. 4, 2014, p. 28. See also: M. Klatt and T. Stępniewski, *Normative Influence, The European Union, Eastern Europe and Russia*, Lublin-Melbourne, The Catholic University of Lublin, 2012.

45 J. Prus and S. Secrieru, 'Nastroje Antyzachodnie w Rosji', *Biuletyn PISM*, vol. 35, 14 April 2015, pp. 1–2.

46 For more see: R. Sakwa, *Frontline Ukraine: Crisis in the Borderlands*, London-New York, I.B. Tauris, 2015.

47 Prus and Secrieru, 'Nastroje Antyzachodnie', p. 2.

48 More in: Barburska, 'Podstawy Normatywne', pp. 67–89.

49 More in: H. Larsen, 'The EU as a Normative Power and the Research on External Perceptions: The Missing Link', *Journal of Common Market Studies*, vol. 52, no. 4, 2014, pp. 896–910; T. Forsberg, 'Normative Power Europe, Once Again: A Conceptual Analysis of an Ideal Type', *Journal of Common Market Studies*, vol. 6, 2011; Z. Laïdi, *Norms Over Force: The Enigma of European Power*, New York, Palgrave Macmillan, 2008; H. Sjursen, 'The EU as a Normative Power: How Can This Be?', *Journal of European Public Policy*, vol. 2, 2006.

50 Manners, *Normative Power Europe*.

51 Skolimowska, 'Normatywna Potęga Unii Europejskiej', p. 12.

52 The idea of the EU as a normative power is strongly connected with other similar concepts like 'soft power' (see: J.S. Nye, 'Soft power', *Foreign Policy*, vol. 80, 1990; O. Barburska, 'Argument Siły czy Siła Argumentów? Unia Europejska w Stosunkach Międzynarodowych jako "Soft Power"', *Rocznik Integracji Europejskiej*, vol. 10, 2016) or 'civilian power' – see: F. Duchêne, *Europe's Role in World Peace*, in R. Mayne (ed.), *Europe Tomorrow: Sixteen Europeans Look Ahead*, London, Fontana, 1972; D. Milczarek, 'The International Role of the European Union As a "Civilian Power"', *The Polish Foreign Affairs Digest*, vol. 4, 2003.

53 T. Romanova, 'Normative Power Europe: Russian View', in A. Gerrits (ed.), *Normative Power Europe in Changing World: A Discussion*, The Hague, Netherlands Institute of International Relations, 2009, p. 53.

54 Romanova, 'Normative Power Europe', p. 65.

55 M. Fiszer, 'Zadania i Cele', p. 183.

56 See: V. Morozov, 'Europe: Self-Alignment in Time and Space', *Russia in Global Affairs*, vol. 3, 2008.

57 Romanova, 'Normative Power', p. 65.

58 See: Kościński, '"Russij mir"', p. 74.

59 Fiszer, 'Zadania i Cele', pp. 188–189.

60 See: Sykulski, 'Integracja Polityczna', p. 359. For more see: A.P. Tsygankov, 'Vladimir Putin's Vision of Russia as a Normal Great Power', *Post-Soviet Affairs*, vol. 2, 2005.

61 The European Leadership Network, *What is the Future for EU-Russia Relations? A Survey of European Leadership Network Members for the EU's Global Strategy*

on Foreign and Security Policy, May 2016, www.europeanleadershipnetwork.org, (accessed 25 June 2018).

62 A. Wendt, *Social Theory of International Politics*, Cambridge, Cambridge University Press, 1999, p. 70.

Bibliography

Adomeit, H., 'Russia. ENP Competitor', in E. Lannon (ed.), *The European Neighbourhood Policy's Challenges/Les Défis de la Politique Européenne de Voisinage*, Brussels, Series: College of Europe Studies/Cahiers du Collège d'Europe, vol. 14, 2012, pp. 381–397.

Amin, S., *The Liberal Virus: Permanent War and the Americanization of the World*, New York, Monthly Review Press, 2004.

Ananicz, A., 'Rosja po Dwóch Małych Wojnach', *Sprawy Międzynarodowe*, vol. 1, 2009, pp. 13–26.

Barburska, O., 'Argument Siły czy Siła Argumentów? Unia Europejska w Stosunkach Międzynarodowych jako "Soft Power" ', *Rocznik Integracji Europejskiej*, vol. 10, 2016, pp. 335–351.

Barburska, O., 'Podstawy Normatywne Funkcjonowania Unii Europejskiej w Stosunkach Międzynarodowych – Ujęcie Teoretyczne', *Stosunki Międzynarodowe*, vol. 4, 2016, pp. 67–89.

Barburska, O., 'Relacje Unia Europejska-Federacja Rosyjska: Kryzys Partnerstwa Strategicznego', *Studia Europejskie*, vol. 4, 2014, pp. 9–31.

Barburska, O. and D. Milczarek, *Polityka Wschodnia Unii Europejskiej: Porażka czy Sukces?*, Warszawa, Oficyna Wydawnicza Aspra-JR, 2014.

Bäcker, R., 'Współczesny Antyokcydentalizm Rosyjski', in Z. Anculewicz and J. Sobczak (eds.), *Europa a Rosja. Opinie, Konflikty, Współpraca*, Olsztyn, Wydawnictwo UWM, 2003, pp. 263–274.

Bieleń, S., *Tożsamość Międzynarodowa Federacji Rosyjskiej*, Warszawa, Oficyna Wydawnicza Aspra-JR, 2006.

Curanović, A., 'The Guardians of Traditional Values. Russia and Russian Orthodox Church in the Quest for Status', *Transatlantic Academy Paper Series*, vol. 1, 2015.

Davies, N., *Europe: A History*, Oxford, Harper Perennial, 1996.

Duchêne, F., 'Europe's Role in World Peace', in R. Mayne (ed.), *Europe Tomorrow: Sixteen Europeans Look Ahead*, London, Fontana, 1972, pp. 32–47.

Eberhardt, P., 'Koncepcje Geopolityczne Iwana Dusińskiego', *Studia z Geografii Politycznej i Historycznej*, vol. 1, 2012, pp. 39–59.

The European Leadership Network, *What is the Future for EU-Russia Relations? A Survey of European Leadership Network Members for the EU's Global Strategy on Foreign and Security Policy*, May 2016, www.europeanleadershipnetwork.org, (accessed 25 June 2018).

Felgenhauer, P., 'Russia Prepares for War with the USA and NATO, While Lucking Resources', *European Dialogue*, 14 March 2013, https://jamestown.org/program/russia-prepares-for-war-with-the-us-and-nato-while-lacking-resources/, (accessed 25 June 2018).

Fiszer, J.M., 'Zadania i Cele Polityki Zagranicznej Władimira Putina', *Myśl Ekonomiczna i Polityczna*, vol. 1, 2016, pp. 167–201.

The Foreign Policy Concept of the Russian Federation (approved by President of the Russian Federation Vladimir Putin on November 30, 2016), www.mid.ru/en/foreign-policy/document/, (accessed 25 June 2018).

Forsberg, T., 'Normative Power Europe, Once Again: A Conceptual Analysis of an Ideal Type', *Journal of Common Market Studies*, vol. 6, 2011, pp. 1183–1204.

Gołąbek, B., *Lew Gumilow i Aleksander Dugin. O Dwóch Obliczach Eurazjatyzmu w Rosji po 1991 Roku*, Kraków, Wydawnictwo Uniwersytetu Jagiellońskiego, 2012.

Gower, J. and G. Timmins (eds.), *The European Union, Russia and Shared Neighbourhood*, London, Routledge, 2011.

Gretskiy, I., E. Treshchenkov and K. Golubiev, 'Russia's Perceptions and Misperceptions of the EU Eastern Partnership', *Communist and Post-Communist Studies*, vol. 3–4, 2014, pp. 375–383.

Klatt, M. and T. Stępniewski, *Normative Influence, The European Union, Eastern Europe and Russia*, Lublin-Melbourne, The Catholic University of Lublin, 2012.

Kościński, P., '"Russij Mir" – Rosyjska Polityka Sąsiedztwa', *Sprawy Międzynarodowe*, vol. 1, 2015, pp. 71–87.

Laïdi, Z., *Norms Over Force: The Enigma of European Power*, New York, Palgrave Macmillan, 2008.

Larsen, H., 'The EU as a Normative Power and the Research on External Perceptions: The Missing Link', *Journal of Common Market Studies*, vol. 4, 2014, pp. 896–910.

Laruelle, M., 'Beyond Anti-Westernism. The Kremlin's Narrative About Russia's European Identity and Mission', *PONARS Eurasia Policy Memo*, vol. 326, 2014, pp. 1–6.

Laruelle, M., *The 'Russian World'. Russia's Soft Power and Geopolitical Imagination*, Washington, DC, CGI Center on Global Interest, 2015.

Maass, A.S., *EU-Russia Relations, 1999–2015: From Courtship to Confrontation*, London-New York, Routledge, 2017.

Mackinder, H.J., 'The Geographical Pivot of History', *The Geographical Journal*, vol. 4, 1904, pp. 421–436.

Manners, I., *Normative Power Europe: A Contradiction in Terms?*, BISA Conference, Manchester, December 1999.

Manners, I., 'Normative Power Europe: A Contradiction in Terms?', *Journal of Common Market Studies*, vol. 2, 2002, pp. 235–258.

Manners, I., *Normative Power Europe: The International Role of the EU*, Madison, ECSA Biennial Conference, 31 May 2001.

Milczarek, D., 'The International Role of the European Union As a "Civilian Power"', *The Polish Foreign Affairs Digest*, vol. 4, 2003, pp. 137–161.

Milczarek, M., 'More Gains or Losses? Review of the European Union's Eastern Policy', in B. Góralczyk (ed.), *European Union on the Global Scene: United or Irrelevant?*, Warsaw, Centre for Europe, University of Warsaw, 2015, pp. 35–62.

Morozov, V., 'Europe: Self-Alignment in Time and Space', *Russia in Global Affairs*, vol. 3, 2008, pp. 136–148.

Morozov, V., *Russia's Postcolonial Identity: A Subaltern Empire in a Eurocentric World*, London, Palgrave Macmillan, 2015.

Mustafa, G., 'The Concept of Eurasia: Kazakh Eurasian Policy and Implications', *Journal of Eurasian Studies*, vol. 3, 2013, pp. 160–170.

Neumann, I., *Russia and The Idea of Europe: A Study in Identity and International Relations*, London-New York, Routledge, 1996.

Nieczypor, K., *Aleksander Dugin – Eurazjatycki Głos w Twoim Domu*, 6 February 2017, www.eastbook.eu/2017/02/06/aleksander-dugin-eurazjatycki-glos-w-twoim-domu/, (accessed 25 June 2018).

Nye, J.S., 'Soft Power', *Foreign Policy*, vol. 80, 1990, pp. 153–171.

Poli, S. (ed.), *The European Neighbourhood Policy – Values and Principles*, New York, Routledge, 2016.

Pomarin, S. (ed.), *Eurasia: People & Myths*, Moscow, Natalis Press, 1993.

Potulski, J., 'Rosyjskie Koncepcje Geopolityczne Jako Wyraz Poszukiwania Formuły Imperialnej?', in S. Bieleń and A. Skrzypek (eds.), *Rosja. Rozważania Imperiologiczne*, Warszawa, Oficyna Wydawnicza Aspra-JR, 2015, pp. 39–66.

Prus, J. and S. Secrieru, 'Nastroje Antyzachodnie w Rosji', *Biuletyn PISM*, vol. 35, 14 April 2015, www.pism.pl/files/?id_plik=19539, (accessed 25 June 2018).

Robbins, G., 'The Post-Soviet Heartland: Reconsidering Mackinder', *Eurasian Studies*, vol. 3, 1994, pp. 95–108.

Romanova, T., 'Normative Power Europe: Russian View', in A. Gerrits (ed.), *Normative Power Europe in Changing World: A Discussion*, The Hague, Netherlands Institute of International Relations, 2009, pp. 51–66.

Sakwa, R., *Frontline Ukraine: Crisis in the Borderlands*, London-New York, I.B. Tauris, 2015.

Sawicka, M., 'Rosyjska Odpowiedź na Zachodni Globalny Projekt', *Przegląd Geopolityczny*, vol. 1, 2009, pp. 81–90.

Sjursen, H., 'The EU as a "Normative" Power: How Can This Be?', *Journal of European Public Policy*, vol. 2, 2006, pp. 235–251.

Skolimowska, A., 'Normatywna Potęga Unii Europejskiej: Struktura Teoretyczno-Metodologiczna Badania', in A. Skolimowska (ed.), *Normatywna potęga Unii Europejskiej w Obliczu Umiędzynarodowionych Konfliktów Wewnętrznych*, Warszawa, Dom Wydawniczy Elipsa, 2015, pp. 9–21.

Skolimowska, A., 'Potęga Norm w Stosunkach Międzynarodowych', in A. Skolimowska (ed.), *Normatywna Potęga Unii Europejskiej w Obliczu Umiędzynarodowionych Konfliktów Wewnętrznych*, Warszawa, Dom Wydawniczy Elipsa, 2015, pp. 23–40.

Smith, H., *Russian Greatpowerness: Foreign Policy, the Two Chechen Wars and International Organisations*, Helsinki, University of Helsinki, 2014.

Stępniewski, T., 'ENP or ENPs? The Curious Web of the European Neighborhood Policy: The Southern and Eastern Dimensions Revisited', *Yearbook of the Institute of East-Central Europe*, vol. 4, 2015, pp. 29–42.

Stępniewski, T., 'The European Union and Eastern Partnership: Crises and Strategic Assessment', *Yearbook of the Institute of East-Central Europe*, vol. 5, 2016, pp. 337–344.

Suslov, M., 'Holy Rus': The Geopolitical Imagination in the Contemporary Russian Orthodox Church', *Russian Social Science Review*, vol. 3, 2015, pp. 43–62.

Sykulski, L., 'Integracja Polityczna Eurazji we Współczesnej Rosyjskiej Myśli Geopolitycznej', in P. Eberhardt (ed.), *Prace Geograficzne, Studia nad Geopolityką XX Wieku*, vol. 242, 2013, pp. 349–363.

Szabaciuk, A., 'Eurazjatycki Projekt Integracyjny Władimira Putina: Szanse i Zagrożenia', *Rocznik Instytutu Europy Środkowo-Wschodniej*, vol. 5, 2014, pp. 75–96.

Trenin, D., *Getting Russia Right*, Washington, Carnegie Endowment for International Peace, 2007.

Tsygankov, A.P., *Russia and the West from Alexander to Putin. Honor in International Relations*, Cambridge, Cambridge University Press, 2014.

Tsygankov, A.P., 'Vladimir Putin's Vision of Russia as a Normal Great Power', *Post-Soviet Affairs*, vol. 2, 2005, pp. 132–158.

Wendt, A., *Social Theory of International Politics*, Cambridge, Cambridge University Press, 1999.

7 From the hopeless continent towards the rising star

The perceptions of the European Union by African elites

Anna Masłoń-Oracz and Iwona Janczyk

Introduction

In the past decades Africa was seen as a hopeless continent.[1] Due to huge Chinese investment (in 2001 the Forum on China–Africa Cooperation [FOCAC] was established and has so far invested more than $300 billion in different African states, mostly in infrastructure) the Pan-African vision of an integrated, prosperous and peaceful continent guided by its citizens, acting as a dynamic force in the international arena, has shaped a new order in international relations.

Manners binds the idea of the normative power of the EU with its ability to exert an ideological, cultural and symbolic influence on actors in international relations.[2] To underline the importance of the chosen analysis one should draw the reader's attention to the Mozambican president who stated: 'We must help each other to improve our governance on the basis of friendship and mutual trust. It is only in this way that we can dissipate the negative image of our continent as an incapable Africa without a future'.[3] Africa's role and participation in international relations can be traced back to 'The slave trade, the scramble for Africa and the subsequent colonial period; the proxy wars of the Cold War; and the increasing importance of the continent's natural resources'.[4]

This chapter includes parallel and independent examination of the analysis of public discourse, public opinion research and the analysis of think-tank opinions.

The preceding research problem, the defined task and the objectives of this chapter determined the research methodology. The following methods have been used:

1 the analysis of the literature, source materials as well as program documents;
2 the comparative and descriptive analysis.

The completion of the defined research task and objectives was based on foreign literature, mainly including English-speaking economic literature devoted to the role and identity of the European Union in African States. However, due to the lack of empirical data on perceptions and mass opinion, the conclusions can only be tentative. The research questions were:

1 Who are the African elites?
2 What is the perception of the European Union by African elites?

The word 'elite', used in science for about two hundred years, is derived from the Latin word *eligere*, or from Old French *eslite* (or eslit), which is past participle of the verb *eslire*[5] Political African elite as a category is one of the most unexplored phenomena in social science. The lack of quantitative, representative data accounts for the fact that most publications continue to depict the role and character of the African ruling class selectively and vaguely, usually referring to the elite of a particular state, to individuals, or to specific spheres of social life in modern Africa or the historical period. On the other hand, while dealing with Africa's development too much attention was paid to economic issues, overlooking the highly important political dimension of the process.[6]

The gap between the political leaders and the mass

African elites struggle to engender effective leadership and governance in Africa. However, there is a big chasm between the African political class and the masses. This is the consequence of the collision between two Africas, namely: pre-colonial and the new post-colonial one. European residues interfere with traditional Black Land values. Many African people associate the concept of the Western civilisation with a highly organised system of domination that is functioning to coerce the rest of the world into submissiveness within such domains as politics, economics, or culture. As a result, pre-colonial African society based on the rules like equalitarianism and coexistence, was changed by Western capitalism and colonial administration into a class and corporative society. The rising discrepancy, both in quantitative and qualitative terms, between the narrow elites and the rest of the societies, and the alienation process of the former may result in an unforeseeable fallout in the future.[7]

Due to the alienation process, the elitist social groups have a similar approach to the rest of Africans as boomers did have in the past. The position of African elites is polymorphic. It constitutes the symbol of autonomy and power, yet the world perceived it as something worse because from the European point of view elites should be supported by masses, yet, in Africa it is not always the case.[8]

In Africa there is no separation between political and economic dimension of the authority. Therefore, the ruling party is automatically the most important beneficiary of economic power. The border between private incomes and public revenues is vague or as such does not exist. One other problem connected with the African elites is the so-called *psycho-existential complex*, meaning that for instance once Africans gained profound educational background from Western European universities, they succumbed to Occidentalism/westernisation. Due to this process, they disposed of their 'black soul' and were more prone to be like a European race. Thus, African identity somehow gave in to atrophy because a well-educated African is not understood by the majority of representatives of his/her own race. Looking for the alternatives, he/she is more willing to coexist with Europeans and cut off his/her cultural and ethnic roots. F. Fanon, a political activist and psychiatrist of Martinique origin, calls it *ambivalence of fidelity* to African values and ideas. As a result, many African leaders created their own concepts, based on glorification of Negroid race, humanism, or *ujamaa* (meaning 'familyhood' in Swahili) to constrain the ongoing identity degradation. However, African elites were unsuccessful to combat totally the impact of westernisation processes.[9]

Types of African elites

Marek Szczepanski divides African elites into several categories, namely: political and administrative cadre, intellectual elite, officer elite, group of technocrats and managers, trade bourgeoisie (mainly wealthy merchants), and relatively rare industrial and financial bourgeoisie. The first mentioned group constitutes the upper class. They gained control over both political and economic machinery of state. The affiliation to elitist groups is very often associated with not only educational background or wealth but also with participation in the nationalist and independence fights. Even now, many fighters for freedom or decolonisation hold presidential or ministerial offices. Moreover, in some African countries (Nigeria, Ghana or Uganda), endemic rulers, tribal chieftains, ancestral nobilities and dynastic families play a significant role in the ruling process. The so-called *basis of huge prestige* (namely: the state, army, economic institutions) is highly monopolised and personalised, as the same representatives of leading groups move from the military to the government and later from administration to powerful economic/financial institutions.[10]

Half of African countries have undergone various processes of transition from single party and military rule to multiparty forms of politics. In the new geopolitics order this development has, however, tended to prevent scholars from addressing critical questions about the elites that exercise and wield political power on the continent beyond banal generalisations about (neo-) patrimonialism and the post-colony.[11]

African perceptions of the EU

Based on studies of EU foreign policy, such as EU effectiveness[12] and Normative Power Europe,[13] the chapter presents different aspects of African perceptions of the EU:

1. EU as a promoter of democracy and human rights;
2. EU trade policy with Economic Partnership Agreement and its role in transition economies;
3. EU engagement in peace and security matters.

Moreover, this chapter explores the perception of the European Union in some African countries, placing particular emphasis on the themes of European integration and the external policies of the EU. In order to capture the image of the EU in Africa, the perceptions from key elite groups in selected countries are explored.

The EU's external policy, in normative terms, assumes that it is not an expression of particular interests of individual states, but an articulation of the common conviction of the member states about what must be done in the face of this international challenge. For African elites economic nationalism is based on: 'empirically verifiable figures (. . .) which must carry conviction by means of rational arguments' rather than being based upon: 'metaphysical essences or subjective emotions', to quote Carreras.[14]

In Africa, the European Union is perceived both politically as the home of former colonial masters and the promoter of free trade and liberal democracy and economically as a body assisting the African Union in implementing its Agenda 2063 vision.[15]

The colonial and slavish past are deep-rooted reasons for the mutual mistrust still present in the relations between Europeans and Africans. In the eyes of the latter the EU countries are regarded as former colonial powers, and, although the independence was gained by African states decades ago, the colonialism has left a difficult legacy. The famous book written by Guyanese historian Walter Rodney titled 'How Europe Underdeveloped Africa',[16] although a classic of anti-imperialist literature,[17] is still present in the mode of thinking of both African mass and elites, who from time to time are invoking the right to obtain reparations and write off their debts.

As aptly stated by S. Schmidt,[18] African perceptions of the EU and its role in Africa are ambivalent as the perception of the EU depends on the field of cooperation. Generally, the EU is seen as a normative actor fostering values (namely: democratic principles, human rights, and good governance) and a supportive force for African efforts to spread peace and security. As found by the previously mentioned author, various activities and instruments to foster peace and security are also understood by Africans as value driven. There is not much critique in principle against democracy and peace promotion from the African side. However, African elites and intellectuals do not accept conditionality as a policy instrument. The practice by the EU and other donors to withhold funds or to postpone the disbursement of ODA (Official Development Assistance) in cases of human rights violations is criticised by African governments and civil society as selective and inappropriate because it would hit the poor and not the perpetrators. Africans often argue that they should have a say in using the conditionality instrument and that violations of human rights and democratic principles are foremost an African problem which should be addressed by Africans.[19] However, we might find different voices. According to Denis Mukwege[20], a medical doctor and activist from Congo:

> 'Development aid without conditions often rolls out the red carpet for dictators. And we know very well that such people let their citizens starve, cheat in elections, change the constitution and lose all European respect (. . . .) Democracy and good governance are not purely European concepts. They belong to mankind's common heritage, which includes Africa (. . .) The future relations between Africa and Europe must be based on such values (. . .)'. 'If you look at some African countries today, their problems do not come from a lack of human or material resources, but from bad government'.

Moreover, Mukwege believes that Africa must free itself from the role of being the eternal beggar. There is a link between peace, security and development, but this is only possible if there is an established basis of democracy and good governance.[21]

The specific way in which the policies are conducted, however, is often criticised. As pointed out by S. Schmidt,[22] the self-attributed image of the EU as a promoter of values is to a considerable extent shared by Africans. The foreign policy identity of the EU manifested in such roles as civilian power is supported and strengthened by Africans. But the findings in the trade sector are not corresponding to the EU's self-proclaimed foreign policy identity. In trade relations the perception of the EU policy is much more critical. The EU is seen as a protectionist and paternalistic power with limited will for compromise and respect for African interests. Africans argue that in trade negotiations the EU shows a different face: The EU is regarded as a tough negotiator driven by economic interests and using instruments of coercion. Critics come not only from governments, but also from the AU, sub-regional organisations and non-state actors.[23] For instance, AU leaders argue that the EU both overlooks the development demands of its African counterparts and also limits the EU market access for African products, thereby contributing to keeping African economies in a disadvantaged position. Moreover, they underline that notwithstanding the EU pressures for liberalisation agreements, the block itself has not yet dismantled protectionist measures against foreign products.[24] Furthermore, with comparison to China, according to African elites, the EU's trade agreements are by far too conditional. The EU, by including in its trade deals human rights and democracy clauses, is regarded as less attractive or competitive than the Chinese counterpart.[25]

Besides, trade agreements (Economic Partnership Agreements) are regarded by some African officials as simply neo-colonial tools that use a *divide and conquer* tactic with African countries. For instance, the present Tanzanian President John Magufuli stated that 'after studying EPA he had realized that African countries would not benefit from it economically as its architects touted' and that this trade deal is 'bad for our country'.[26] Additionally, EPAs are perceived as a way to threaten the regional integration.[27] According to the former Nigerian Federal Minister of Industry, Trade and Investment, Olusegun Aganga:

> Africa is on the rise. It is a very big and strategic market for any trading partner. That is what the EU wants from us but Africa must jealously protect what it has (. . . .) We should leverage our abundant natural resources and large market to develop our industries; create jobs for our people; increase intra-African trade and achieve regional integration. We must not be in a hurry to give away what we have. We must not sign an agreement without first of all carrying out a robust economic analysis of the overall impact the agreement will have on the region, our children and future generations (. . . .) The population of Africa is growing very rapidly. Statistics shows that more than 50 per cent of our population are between 18 and 30 years. If we sign the

EPA, how do we create the jobs that we require for our growing population; how do we stop the illegal migration of our youths to developed countries?[28]

As observed by S. Schmidt,[29] the main reasons for the ambivalent perceptions are the different roles the EU performs and policy incoherencies between democracy and peace promotion on the one hand and trade policy on the other hand. The EU is neither perceived exclusively as a soft power nor as a neo-colonial power. The limited character of the EU military interventions shows that the EU is risk-averse and clearly not motivated by neo-colonialist or neo-imperialist ambitions. But from a realistic interpretation one could argue that the EU tries to increase its prestige and emphasise its actorness by military operations.

An interesting research was conducted by F. Keuleers on the basis of AfroBarometer data from 19 countries comparing the perceptions of the EU and China by the African public opinion. Firstly, it indicated that the EU is not very well known among sub-Saharan African populations. China has succeeded in achieving a clearer profile in almost all countries in the study, and has done this in a very limited period of time. Despite its longer engagement, the EU is struggling in terms of its visibility. Secondly, both the EU and China enjoy broad-based support as a development partner. Thirdly, African evaluations of the EU versus Chinese support do not at all reflect the antagonistic representations that are dominant in much of the scholarly literature. African populations appear to see engagement by traditional and emerging development partners as complementary rather than mutually exclusive.[30]

Despite the 2008 global financial crisis, in Africa there are the world's fastest-growing economies, such as Mozambique, Tanzania, Ethiopia and Rwanda. Their growth is phenomenal considering the small base from which it comes. The EU, while helping the African countries, appears to be reacting to an engagement in Africa by other global actors: China, Turkey, USA, and Russia.

EU policy in Africa is based on the European experience. The rollback of the state from health care, education and other essential sectors has slowed economic development in many African countries. And privatisation of key services like water and electricity added the next setback to poor African countries which relied on the state for providing their livelihoods.

In November 2017 the fifth African Union (AU)–European Union (EU) summit was held in Abidjan, Ivory Coast,[31] under the central theme: 'Investing in youth for a sustainable future'. The European and African leaders adopted a joint declaration outlining common priorities for the EU–Africa partnership in four strategic areas, namely: economic opportunities for youth; peace and security; mobility and migration; and cooperation on governance. Opinions of the meetings' outcomes are diverse. According to Tighisti Amare and Paul Melly from the Chatham House, the Royal Institute of International Affairs: 'the EU continues to set the agenda, often fails to consult its African partners and remains stuck in a post-colonial mentality' and 'Building a new Africa–EU relationship based on mutual respect and collective decision-making presents a huge challenge'.[32]

According to the Tanzanian Jenerali Ulimwengu, a political analyst and regular contributor to the Deutsche Welle: 'It is all well to have countries and governments abroad who are willing to underwrite your development and other expenditure, but one has to always worry about over-dependency on this kind of funding. It is not only that this kind of support is essentially unsustainable, simply because it flows from the forces that Africa cannot hope to control, and it may dry up just when it is most needed and there is no fallback plan. Past experience has shown this to be true, and it is indeed extraordinary that African leaders have allowed themselves back into this kind of situation'.[33]

It is crucial for African governments, sub-regional and regional organisations to closely work with foreign powers in creating future development plans. African states should decide what they want from the countries investing in their economies and how this policy must be developed.

Western assistance was long conditioned by colonial masters. The early aid strategy focused on rescuing 'backward Africa' from poverty and disease. However, critics rightly point out that aid has prevented African growth by creating its overdependence on aid.

The end of the Cold War in the 1990s brought a resurgence of internationalism which sought to bring trade and aid together into a developmental framework. The 2000 Millennium Development Goals (MDG) became the guide for Africa's future. The MDGs were to be achieved through a consolidated global effort. Indicators were to be periodically revived to measure development. At the heart of MDGs is the notion that the most peaceful and stable democratic governments can register substantial development.

The 2030 Sustainable Development Goals are the successors of the MDGs. There are 17 goals with 169 targets crucial to African states. Generally African countries performed poorly in the MDGs. Only Botswana and Equatorial Guinea met the first goal of halving the number of people living below the poverty line. Experts were of the opinion that to meet some of the goals, African states would have needed to register annual growth rates of 7%. This could be achieved only by acceleration of the African development. That is why EU engagement is essential for the accomplishment of these goals. African underdevelopment has long been a topic of contentious debate at different EU forums. Calls for reparations for colonialism and the scrapping of African debt are often voiced at different levels of the EU–African cooperation.

Conclusions

Agenda 2063 is the African Union's blueprint for the future based on inclusive growth and sustainable development. It calls for an integrated Africa guided by Pan-African ideals: an Africa shaped by good governance, democracy, respect for human rights, justice and rule of law; a peaceful and secure Africa; an Africa with a strong cultural identity, common heritage, shared values and ethics; an Africa whose development is people-driven with a key role for women and the youth; a strong, united Africa that can be an influential global player. These strategies were worked out taking into consideration the EU cooperation and ideals.

Africa needs to strengthen its ties with other global powers, among which the leading EU countries play an important role. Through these relations, African states can benefit from increased investment and cooperation within multilateral organisations like the World Trade Organisation and United Nations Trade and Development Conference.

Notes

1 'Hopeless Africa', *The Economist*, 11 May 2010, www.economist.com/node/333429, (accessed 25 June 2018).
2 I. Manners, 'Normative Power Europe: A Contradiction In Terms?', *Journal of Common Market Studies*, vol. 2, no. 40, 2002, pp. 235–258.
3 Mozambican President Joachim Chissano, *Cape Times*, 11 July 2003.
4 J. Bayart, 'Africa in the World: A History of Extraversion', *African Affairs*, vol. 99, 2000, pp. 217–267; J. Bayart, *The State in Africa: The Politics of the Belly*, Cambridge, Polity Press, 2010.
5 Merriam Webster Dictionary Online: https://www.merriam-webster.com/dictionary/elite. Accessed 25 June 2018.
6 M. Bratton and D. Rothchild, 'The Institutional Bases of Governance in Africa', in G. Hyden and M. Bratton (eds.), *Governance and Politics in Africa*, Boulder-London, Lynne Rienner Publishers, 1992, p. 263.
7 A. Smardz, 'Afrykańskie Elity Polityczne. Problemy Badawcze', *Wrocławskie Studia Politologiczne*, vol. 12, 2011, pp. 143–157.
8 Smardz, 'Afrykańskie Elity Polityczne', p. 147.
9 Smardz, 'Afrykańskie Elity Polityczne', p. 145.
10 Smardz, 'Afrykańskie Elity Polityczne', pp. 147–148.
11 CODESRIA, Council for the Development of Social Science Research in Africa, 2003.
12 D. Torney, 'External Perceptions and EU Foreign Policy Effectiveness: The Case of Climate Change', *Journal of Common Market Studies*, vol. 52, no. 6, 2014.
13 H. Larsen, 'The EU as a Normative Power and the Research on External Perceptions: The Missing Link', *Journal of Common Market Studies*, vol. 52, no. 4, 2014, pp. 896–910.
14 F. de Carreras, 'The Economics of Catalan Independence Don't Add Up', *The Guardian*, 22 November 2012, www.theguardian.com/commentisfree/2012/nov/22/economics-catalan-independence-dont-add-up, (accessed 25 June 2018).
15 It is a strategic framework for the socio-economic transformation of the continent over the next 50 years. It builds on, and seeks to accelerate the implementation of past and existing continental initiatives for growth and sustainable development. Compare: African Union, *Agenda 2063*, https://au.int/agenda2063/about, (accessed 25 June 2018).
16 W. Rodney, *How Europe Underdeveloped Africa*, London, Bogle-L'Ouverture Publications, 1973. The whole book is available at: http://abahlali.org/files/3295358-walter-rodney.pdf, (accessed 25 June 2018).
17 Compare for example: S. Smiley, 'How Europe Underdeveloped Africa (Book Review)', *Mosaic Africa Studies E- Journal,* vol. 1, no. 7, 2010.
18 S. Schmidt, 'Soft Power or Neo-Colonialist Power? – African Perceptions of the EU', *Review of European Studies*, vol. 4, no. 3, 2012, p. 108.
19 Schmidt, 'Soft Power or Neo-Colonialist Power?', p. 105.

20 The Norwegian Nobel Committee decided to award the Nobel Peace Prize for 2018 to Denis Mukwege and Nadia Murad for their efforts to end the use of sexual violence as a weapon of war and armed conflict. The Nobel Prize, https://www.nobelprize.org/prizes/peace/2018/press-release/, (accessed 10 October 2018).
21 B. Wesel, *EU and Africa: Partners with Different Interests*, 29 November 2017, www.dw.com/en/eu-and-africa-partners-with-different-interests/a-41579977, (accessed 25 June 2018).
22 Schmidt, 'Soft Power or Neo-Colonialist Power?', p. 108.
23 Schmidt, 'Soft Power or Neo-Colonialist Power?', p. 108.
24 S. Lucarelliand and L. Fioramonti, *External Perceptions of the European Union as a Global Actor*, New York, Routledge, 2010.
25 L. Fioramonti, *African Perceptions of the European Union: Assessing the Work of the EU in the Field of Democracy Promotion and Peacekeeping*, International IDEA, Stockholm, 2009, p. 3.
26 D. Kamagi, 'EPA Trade Deal with Europe Is a Form of Colonialism, Says Magufuli', *The EastAfrica*, 27 February 2017, www.theeastafrican.co.ke/news/ea/Signing-EPA-with-Europe-is-bad-declares-Magufuli/4552908-3829308-brbfjxz/index.html, (accessed 25 June 2018).
27 'EPA and diplomatic chess games in EAC', *The Citizen*, 1 March 2017, www.thecitizen.co.tz/magazine/politicalreforms/EPA-and-diplomatic-chess-games-in-EAC/1843776-3832306-ayq8imz/index.html, (accesssed 25 June 2018).
28 P. Oladunjoye, *EPA: African Leaders Align with Nigeria's Position*, 5 May 2014, www.tralac.org/news/article/5600-epa-african-leaders-align-with-nigeria-s-position.html, (accessed 25 June 2018).
29 Schmidt, 'Soft Power or Neo-colonialist Power?', p. 108.
30 F. Keuleers, 'Explaining External Perceptions: The EU and China in African Public Opinion', *Journal of Common Market Studies*, vol. 53. no 4, 2015, p. 818.
31 Relations between Africa and the European Union are governed by partially overlapping policy frameworks. The most important ones are the EU-ACP Cotonou Agreement from 2000 and the Joint Africa–EU Strategy (JAES) agreed to in 2007. Relations with Northern African countries are governed by the Euro-Mediterranean Partnership (EUROMED) launched in 2008 and the European Neighborhood Policy (ENP). Source: M. Grajewski, 'The EU and Africa [What Think Tanks are Thinking]', *European Parliamentary Research Service Blog*, 17 November 2017, https://epthinktank.eu/2017/11/17/the-eu-and-africa-what-think-tanks-are-thinking-2/, (accessed 25 January 2018).
32 T. Amare and P. Melly, 'Can Africa and the EU Forge a Partnership of Equals?', *Chathamhouse*, 5 December 2017, www.chathamhouse.org/expert/comment/can-africa-and-eu-forge-partnership-equals, (accessed 25 June 2018).
33 J. Ulimwengu, *Opinion: Africa Should Not Become Too Dependent on Europe*, 28 November 2017, www.dw.com/en/opinion-africa-should-not-become-too-dependent-on-europe/a-41558697, (accessed 25 June 2018).

Bibliography

Abegunrin, O., *African in Global Politics in Twenty-First Century. A Pan-African Perspective*, London, Palgrave and Macmillan, 2013.

Adekeye, A. and K. Whiteman, *The EU and Africa. From Eurafrique to Afro-Europe*, New York, Columbus University Press, 2012.

Agenda 2063, https://au.int/agenda2063/about, (accessed 25 June 2018).

Amare, T. and P. Melly, 'Can Africa and the EU Forge a Partnership of Equals?', *Chathamhouse*, 5 December 2017, www.chathamhouse.org/expert/comment/can-africa-and-eu-forge-partnership-equals, (accessed 25 June 2018).

Amoah, M., *Nationalism. Globalization and Africa*, London, Palgrave Macmillan, 2011.
Andeva, M., 'The Theories And Practical Implications of Cross-Border Cooperation: The EGTC "EURO-GO" as an Example of an Instrument for Promoting Integration Among Neighbouring Countries', in I. Dodovski et al. (eds.), *The Europe of Tomorrow: Creative, Digital, Integrated*, Skopje, University American College, 2014, pp. 99–112.
Bacon, P. and E. Kato, 'Potential Still Untapped: Japanese Perceptions of the European Union as an Economic and Normative Power', *Baltic Journal of European Studies*, vol. 3, 2013, pp. 59–84.
Bailey, D.J., 'The European Union in the World: Critical Theories', in J-U. Wuderlich and D.J. Bailey (eds.), *The European Union and Global Governance*, London, Routledge, 2011.
Bayart, J. 'Africa in the World: A History of Extraversion', *African Affairs*, vol. 99, 2000, pp. 217–267.
Bayart, J., *The State in Africa: The Politics of the Belly*, Cambridge, Polity Press, 2010.
Bell, D.A., *China's New Confucianism: Politics and Everyday Life in a Changing Society*, New Jersey, Princeton University Press, 2010.
Binnis, T., A. Dixon and D. Nel, *Africa: Diversity and Development*, Abingdon, Routledge, 2012.
Blaauw, L., 'Challenging Realists International Relations Theory: Soft Balancing and Agency in the International Relations of African States', *Afro Asian Journal of Social Sciences*, vol. 5, no. 5.2, 2014, pp. 1–23.
Bratton, M. and D. Rothchild, 'The Institutional Bases of Governance in Africa', in G. Hyden and M. Bratton (eds.), *Governance and Politics in Africa*, Boulder-London, Lynne Rienner Publishers, 1992.
Carreras, de F., 'The Economics of Catalan Independence Don't Add Up', *The Guardian*, 22 November 2012, www.theguardian.com/commentisfree/2012/nov/22/economics-catalan-independence-dont-add-up, (accessed 25 June 2018).
Chabal, P., 'The Quest for Good Government and Development in Africa: Is NEPAD the Answer?', *International Affairs*, vol. 78, no. 3, 2002, pp. 447–462.
Chafer, T. And G. Cumming, *From Rivalry to Partnership: New Approaches to the Challenges of Africa*, London, Ashgate Publishing, 2011.
Cheesemann, N., *Democracy in Africa. Successes, Failures and the Struggle for Political Reforms*, New York, Cambridge University Press, 2015.
'China's African Policy', *Xinhua News Agency*, January 2006, www.china.org.cn/english/features/focac/183721.htm, (accessed 25 June 2018).
'China's Investments in Africa: What's the Real Story', *Knowlage@Wharton*, 16 January 2016, http://knowledge.wharton.upenn.edu/article/chinas-investments-in-africa-whats-the-real-story/, (accessed 25 June 2018).
'Chinese Investment in Africa: Beijing's Testing Ground', *Financial Times*, 13 June 2017, www.ft.com/content/0f534aa4-4549-11e7-8519-9f94ee97d996, (accessed 25 June 2018).
Chun, Z., 'The Sino-Africa Relationship: Toward a New Strategic Partnership', *Emerging Powers in Africa*, Special Report SR016, 2013, www.lse.ac.uk/ideas/Assets/Documents/reports/LSE-IDEAS-Emerging-Powers-in-Africa.pdf, pp. 10–28, (accessed 25 June 2018).
Diakite, T., *50 ans apres, l'Afrique*, Paris, Arlea, 2011.
Eom, J. et al., 'The United States and China in Africa: What Does the Data Say?', *Policy Brief*, China Africa Research Initiative, vol. 18, 2017.

'EPA and Diplomatic Chess Games in EAC', *The Citizen*, 1 March 2017, www.thecitizen.co.tz/magazine/politicalreforms/EPA-and-diplomatic-chess-games-in-EAC/1843776-3832306-ayq8imz/index.html, (accesssed 25 June 2018).

Falola, T. And K. Essien, *Pan-Africanism and the Politics of African Citizenship and Identity*, Abingdon, Routledge, 2013.

Fioramonti, L., *African Perceptions of the European Union: Assessing the Work of the EU in the Field of Democracy Promotion and Peacekeeping*, Stockholm, International IDEA, 2009.

Government Communication, *Sweden and Africa – A Policy to Address. Common Challenges and Opportunities*, Govt Comm. Stockholm, 2007/08:67.

Grajewski, M., 'The EU and Africa [What Think Tanks are thinking]', *European Parliamentary Research Service Blog*, 17 November 2017, https://epthinktank.eu/2017/11/17/the-eu-and-africa-what-think-tanks-are-thinking-2/, (accessed 25 June 2018).

'Here's What Africans Think About China's Influence in Their Countries', *AfroBarometer*, 28 October 2016, http://afrobarometer.org/blogs/heres-what-africans-think-about-chinas-influence-their-countries, (accessed 25 June 2018).

'Hopeless Africa', *The Economist*, 11 May 2010, www.economist.com/node/333429, (accessed 25 June 2018).

Kamagi, D., 'EPA Trade Deal with Europe Is a Form of Colonialism, Says Magufuli', *The EastAfrica*, 27 February 2017, www.theeastafrican.co.ke/news/ea/Signing-EPA-with-Europe-is-bad-declares-Magufuli/4552908-3829308-brbfjxz/index.html, (accessed 25 June 2018).

Keuleers, F., 'Explaining External Perceptions: The EU and China in African Public Opinion', *Journal of Common Market Studies*, vol. 53. no 4, 2015, pp. 803–821.

Kohnert, D., 'EU-African Economic Relations: Continuing Dominance, Traded for Aid?', *GIGA Working Papers*, vol. 82, 2008.

Kotze, H. and C. Steyn, *African Elites Perspectives: AU and NEPAD: A Comparative Study Across Seven African Countries*, Johannesburg, Konrad Adenauer Stiftung, 2003.

Larsen, H., 'The EU as a Normative Power and the Research on External Perceptions: The Missing Link', *Journal of Common Market Studies*, vol. 52, no. 4, 2014, pp. 896–910.

Lucarelli, S. and L. Fioramonti, *External Perceptions of the European Union as a Global Actor*, New York, Routledge, 2010.

Mangala, J., *Africa and the European Union. A Strategic Partnership*, New York, Palgrave Macmillan, 2013.

Manners, I., 'Normative Power Europe: A Contradiction in Terms?', *Journal of Common Market Studies*, vol. 2, no. 40, 2002, pp. 235–258.

Mbeki, T., 'African Union Is the Mother, NEPAD is Her Baby', *New African*, February 2003, pp. 44–45.

Matlosa, K., 'New Regionalist Impulses: Implications of the New Partnership for Africa's Development (NEPAD) for Regional Integration in Southern Africa', paper presented at the 10th General Assembly of CODESRIA on the Theme: *Africa in the New Millennium*, Nile International Conference Centre, Kampala, Uganda, 8–12 December 2002.

Milewski, J.J. and W. Lizak (eds.), *Stosunki Międzynarodowe w Afryce*, Warsaw, Wydawnictwo Naukowe Scholar, 2002.

4th Meeting of the Joint Coordination Committee [JCC] of the Africa Peace Facility, Addis-Ababa, 4 February 2008.

Nafziger, E.W, *Inequality in Africa: Political Elites, Proletariat, Peasants and the Poor*, New York, Cambridge University Press, 1988.

Oladunjoye, P., *EPA: African Leaders Align with Nigeria's Position*, 5 May 2014, www.tralac.org/news/article/5600-epa-african-leaders-align-with-nigeria-s-position.html, (accessed 25 June 2018).

Oliver, G., 'South Africa: The EU South Africa and the Search for Stability in Africa', in M. Ortega (ed.), *Global View on the European Union*, Paris, Institute for Security Studies, 2004, pp. 13–26.

Oshikoya, T., *Monetary and Financial Integration in West Africa*, Abingdon, Routledge, 2010.

Rodney, W., *How Europe Underdeveloped Africa*, London, Bogle-L'Ouverture Publications, 1973.

Schmidt, S., 'Soft Power or Neo-Colonialist Power? – African Perceptions of the EU', *Review of European Studies*, vol. 4, no. 3, 2012, pp. 100–110.

Smardz, A., 'Afrykańskie Elity Polityczne. Problemy Badawcze', *Wrocławskie Studia Politologiczne*, vol. 12, 2011, pp. 143–157.

Smiley, S., 'How Europe Underdeveloped Africa (Book Review)', *Mosaic Africa Studies E- Journal*, vol.1, no.7, 2010.

Sprysak, J., 'Zaangażowanie Chin w Rozwój Afryki', in K.A. Kłosiński (ed.), *Afryka o Godność Życia*, Lubin, Wydawnictwo KUL, 2012, pp. 341–362.

Stevanova, B., 'An Ethnonational Persepective on Territorial Politics in the EU: East-West Comparisons from a Pilot Study', *Nationalities Papers*, vol. 42 no. 3, 2014, pp. 449–468.

Taylor, I. and P. Williams (eds.), *Africa in International Relations: External Involvement on the Continent*, London-New York, Routledge, 2004.

Torney, D., 'External Perceptions and EU Foreign Policy Effectiveness: The Case of Climate Change', *Journal of Common Market Studies*, vol. 52, no. 6, 2014, pp. 1358–1373.

'50 years of ACP-EU Cooperation', *The Courier*, March 2008, Special Issue, www.acp.int/sites/acpsec.waw.be/files/story-pdf/en/TheCourier-2008-X01.pdf, (accessed 25 June 2018).

Ulimwengu, J., *Opinion: Africa Should Not Become Too Dependent on Europe*, 28 November 2017, www.dw.com/en/opinion-africa-should-not-become-too-dependent-on-europe/a-41558697, (accessed 25 June 2018).

UNAIDS and ECA, *AIDS in Africa, Country by Country, African Development Forum 2000*, Geneva, Joint United Nations Programme on HIV/AIDS (UNAIDS) 2000.

Wesel, B., *EU and Africa: Partners with Different Interests*, 29 November 2017, www.dw.com/en/eu-and-africa-partners-with-different-interests/a-41579977, (accessed 25 June 2018).

The World Bank, *Can Africa Claim 21st Century?*, Washington, DC, The International Bank for Reconstruction and Development / The World Bank 2000.

Websites

News24.com
www.au2002.gov.za/doca/key_oau/au_act.htm
www.freedomhouse.org/pfs2003/pfs2003.pdf
www.freedomhouse.org

8 EU–India dialogue and the changing self-representations of the actors

Ana Pantea

Introduction

The Norwegian Nobel Committee decided to award the Peace Prize to the European Union, in 2012. The Committee justified this choice with the following words: "The Union and its forerunners have for over six decades contributed to the advancement of peace and reconciliation, democracy and human rights in Europe".[1] In his address of receiving the prize, José Manuel Barroso started his speech quoting Baruch Spinoza for whom "peace is not mere absence of war, it is a virtue". He then stressed the historical significance of the Union's political project, which "embodies, as a community of values, [a] vision of freedom and justice".[2] In Barroso's words, the cosmopolitan order promoted by the EU within its own borders represents "a powerful inspiration for many around the world".[3]

Such self-representation of EU is based on the assumption that the EU's foreign policy follows principles and values that are fundamentally different from that of the nation states, which define their foreign policy objectives according to the "national interest". This vision, which inspires others, matches to Ian Manners' view of a new conceptual framework known as Normative Power Europe (NPE). Manners argues that the EU should be understood not as a civilian power based upon intergovernmental co-operation but as "a normative power of an ideational nature characterised by common principles".[4] For Manners, "the EU is not what it does or what it says, but what it is". Under this logic, NPE is endowed with several fundamental qualities: first, it "can be conceptualised as a changer of norms in the international system", second, it "acts to change norms", and third, it "should act to extend its norms".[5]

Manners has counseled repeatedly against the militarization of the EU which "does not implicitly increase its power in interstate politics and [. . .] is increasingly risking its normative power".[6] According to him, there are six ways for Normative Power Europe to promote its norms abroad: contagion (the unintentional diffusion of norms), informational diffusion (the diffusion of norms that results from a range of strategic communications), procedural diffusion (the institutionalization of normative behavior); transference (norms are diffused when the EU trades goods, provides financial aid or technical assistance, etc.) overt diffusion (the diffusion of norms that results from the EU's physical presence in third countries), and the cultural filter (the construction of knowledge and ideas, as well as social and political identities).[7]

In terms of foreign policy, the goal of EU is to create the perception of increasing its normative role in international affairs, both in Europe (in the Western Balkans) and outside it (including India). The globalization of trade and the intensification of political, business and cultural contacts between Europe and the rest of the world have led the EU to expand its principles and influence worldwide. However, its external partnerships are marked by hierarchical principles, reflecting the strategic relevance of the regions with which the EU has established formal relations.

> The EU-United States strategic partnership has been historically a dominant theme in the field of European studies on both sides of the Atlantic, although the rise of China and the United States pivot to Southeast Asia are already taking a toll on the popularity of this research area.[8]

In the last 20 years, normative power has become a major foreign affairs topic, increasing the debate over the EU's ability to act effectively on the world stage. EU's self-positioning as Normative Power Europe (NPE) seeks to project values outside of its own borders, utilizing attraction, persuasion and the force of diplomacy to defend its strategic interests. Ian Manner believes that NPE is an appropriate concept for increasing co-operation. His critics,[9] however, show the ineffectiveness of NPE in fields of human rights, energy, security, or limited success in the field of technical assistance, trade and economic co-operation.

Many of these critiques tackle the question of (in)effectiveness of NPE policies, analyzing their roots: complex perception of history; hard postcolonial, nationalistic construction of identity (including Indian one) and post-modern construction of European identity; the perception of EU as not being a political model. The premise of the chapter is the following: because India's complex self-perception as an emerging player can be constructed around its postcolonial experience and recent development, then its perspective should be regarded as important for understanding not only its positioning in international relations, but also for its perception of the European identity.

India–Europe dialogue: historical representation and departures

Trying to sketch the last three hundred years of political, military and diplomatic dialogue, starting from the 16th century, it is evident that there are significant changes in the representation of India in Europe and of Europe in India.[10] Firstly, the 16th century was dominated by Europe, more exactly Portugal, Spain, and Italy (missionary work, spice trade, the birth of the first multinational enterprises, and trade of military equipment), who collected either manuscripts, or artistic and antiquarian objects from India. Secondly, despite the existence of considerable missionary activity in many different parts of India, "there is no evidence currently that manuscripts [. . .] in Sanskrit from any of the Indian traditions made their way to Europe at this time. At best, abridged versions of the doctrines of the 'gentiles' were produced,[11] sometimes by Jesuits in their missions in Goa and southern India".[12] Other objects that were collected included Indian painted textiles, ivories, and elaborately carved wooden objects.

This situation has changed considerably after 1600, due to the entry of other European actors – English, Dutch, Danes, French – into the trade of the Cape Route. The way in which India was perceived by the Dutch and English was less religious centered, and more pragmatic, as the trade epicenter moved geographically towards the Moghul power. Subrahmanym argues:

> [the] emergence of a new orientalism in Western Europe in the closing decades of the sixteenth century, which was in turn partly an offshoot of Biblical scholarship [. . .] The first half of the seventeenth century thus saw a consolidation in Western Europe of a milieu of collectors, who were interested in a variety of objects and cultural products from India: manuscripts, but also paintings and other precious handicrafts made by the expert artisans of the subcontinent. Some of these collectors were clearly royalty and aristocrats.[13]

It can be stated that several conventions regarding the representation of India in Europe had been established, especially in two spheres: politics and religion. The Europeans who arrived in the 1600s found a fragmented political sphere, with many kingdoms in competition; in the second half of the XVIth century, the context changed with the emergence of the Mughals. The seventeenth century was thus essentially a balancing act between the hegemonic Mughals and their smaller rivals, who impeded or at least slowed down their expansion. This meant that the principal preoccupation of the most important European travelers to seventeenth-century India was Mughal rule.[14] When centralized Mughal power fell into decline over the first half of the eighteenth century, the Europeans noticed a great opportunity, intervening in regional politics for its own benefit. "The Mughals were still represented as 'despots', but as weak and ineffective who have betrayed their own traditions and were thus clearly unfit to rule".[15] In addition, in the 1800s, a new shift occurred in the representation of India, as the European artists and engravers produced a canonical version and requested legitimacy over the representation of the whole Indian world.

A similar shift occurred in the discourse on "Indian" religious life. Starting with the seventeen century, the tendency to see Indian religions as polytheistic and *idolâtrique* increased, ending in the nineteenth century English intellectual milieu to produce a detailed iconography of the gods.

> Increasingly in the nineteenth century, the term "Hinduism" – which had never been used as such in the seventeenth and eighteenth centuries – would come to denote the entire complex of beliefs of those denizens of India who were not Muslim, Christian, Jewish, or Zoroastrian. By the mid-1810s, the Bengali intellectual and re-former Raja Rammohan Roy was using the term, as indeed were a number of British administrators. [. . .] The nineteenth

> century view of a single underlying "Hinduism," with different concrete manifestations, would become the basis of a new set of arguments regarding undesirable superstition and necessary reform. This view would be carried through into the twentieth century, and into the self-image of even some key leaders of the Indian nationalist movement.[16]

Following this general trend, over the nineteenth century, a new attitude can be observed, a simultaneous glorification of the distant Indian past and a denigration of their present. The representation created about the Indians was they had once been great, at the moment when they had produced the *Vedas* and the *Upanishads*; however, they had then fallen into the control of religious superstition and the political dominance of Mughals. British rule would thus bring progress and enlightenment.

Mirroring the analysis in the opposite direction, it can be assessed from the beginning that the perception of "Europeans"[17] in the Indian subcontinent was a complex phenomenon. In the first century of cultural encounter, Indians had not a clear understanding of Portuguese and French or other European cultures.

> We can thus legitimately speak of a first moment of perception, when in Indian eyes there are "Europeans without Europe." The beliefs and above all the practices of these Europeans are clear enough. They are seen, especially in the Persian and Arabic chronicles, as a violent lot, who are also given to devious acts and chicanery in order to advance their interests.[18]

Even if historians have identified chronicles that have portrayed the "Europeans" in a more favorable way, the general perception was a mixture between wonder and suspicion. Technical knowledge (military, maritime and medical) and trading skills (e.g. tobacco) were highly appreciated, but nevertheless the religious differences prevailed in the overall perception.

The first Sanskrit representation on "Europeans" appeared in the 1600s, even if the first Indo-Persian eyewitness did not appear until 1750.[19] These have received great attention, as historians remain interested in the problem of Indian identity as defined in a European looking glass. British writers of the colonial period themselves were particularly interested in how they and their civilization were viewed by Indians, a view that was often but not always flattering to the English. In the case of European communities living in India,[20] they lived separately from the Indians, in the Mughal courts, but in a better self-administrated area. Since the first religious missions arrived to the Mughal court in the middle of 16th century, European materials (including maps) had been available to the elite, but usually such materials were received with indifference by the Mughals.

Europeans had been initially considered as remote strangers, as often traditional communities perceive foreigners. It is known that many Indians had traveled to Europe in the 18th century, but no detailed description of Europe emerges from these visits. As the Portuguese, English, Dutch and French increased their presence in India, the opposite side didn't follow the same path. Actually, "images of the Europeans also became available for the first time in Sanskrit, even if these seventeenth-century references tend to be sparse and rather laconic".[21]

Many authors present arguments that the second half of the 18th century marked the consolidation of a sense of European identity, and the birth of the idea of European superiority to "Asiatics" construction of confessional and regional identity. European political hegemony created the conditions for a greater, even self-critical, European engagement with the Indian modes of knowledge and subsequently, Indian engagements with the idea of Europe. The colonial discourse and the emergence of the phenomenon of "colonial knowledge"[22] address the question of the relationship between the establishment of British political dominance and the rise and institutionalization of European attitudes of superiority towards India. There is a noticeable rising consciousness of a shared European identity in contrast to an Indian one despite frequent intra-European warfare, but also the development of the *race*, as a colonial construct having domination purposes. The construction of a true metropolitan "civility" with the consolidation of British rule consolidated and legitimize the English East India Company domination in India.

British rule established a form of political and military power which brought a form of governance in British-ruled India that treated its subjects as strangers and as foreigners in their own country. That style of administration was very different from the way people had been ruled previously, in India or in Britain. If the pre-colonial Mughal rulers had "lived among their people", the British exchanged information with Indian subjects without absorbing Indian ways of life. India's British rulers were preoccupied with the construction of new human typology such as the Indian landholder, the peasant or the Hindu widow.[23]

The consequence of this philosophy was the association of the British rule with conquest, domination and interfering. The domination of strangers and the depersonalization of the Indian population was an "exceptional" measure which was needed by the British power in order to remain in power when the majority of the population was potentially hostile towards British rule.

> "The domination of strangers" [. . .] it denotes governance by modern, impersonal bureaucratic regimes based on abstract categories and positive rules rather than familiar political relationships, the kind of regime that Max Weber analysed and Martin Heidegger and Michel Foucault so vehemently criticised.[24]

This kind of modern socio-political domination means at the same time the domination of foreigners, who will be perceived during and after the colonial period as eternal strangers.

Europe–India relations: the theoretical background

Europe through the lens of the Europeans

India and the European Union are very different actors in the international relations; even they cooperate constantly, since 1963, when India established diplomatic relations with the European Economic Community[25] and deepened their cooperation, and since 2000, organizing annual EU–India summits. Their regional interests and their vision on foreign affairs differ as well: India perceives itself as a modern realist state within which sovereignty is essential, having frozen conflicts and territorial disputes with its neighbors; Europe has embraced the post-sovereign foreign policy, including multilateral arrangement and advocating interregional dialogue. Nevertheless, the strategic partnership between EU and India or China could be seen as an "an attempt to engage these emerging regional and global powers in regional and global governance. After all, the establishment of the strategic partnerships was embraced in the European Security Strategy (ESS) promoting effective multilateralism".[26]

The real interest for India occurred in the early 1990s, when the Indian government reduced import duties and quantitative restrictions, carried out monetary reforms and decreased the regulations on products and services. The EU saluted these reforms, hoping that these will bring economic growth to India and the economical and political elite are going to take further steps to be integrated into the world market.

All the effort and the successes of the last thirty years drove to a new self-representation of the Indian government through which India would like to be perceived as a new emerging political and economic power, backed by nuclear weapons. The same period of time coincides with the self-representation of the EU as an important normative actor. This situation can potentially create dissensions and decrease of the level of cooperation.

> This new [Indian] identity has developed over the past 10–15 years, in which time India has experienced consistent, high growth rates. But the world is not responding to their new identity quickly enough. The explanation for this sluggish reaction can be found buried deep in European history books. Since time immemorial, India was the "other" in Eurocentric world history. In their drawn-out explanations of the caste system, Western philosophers have kept India ancient in European eyes. [. . .] The earlier European writers decided that India was to be studied through religion, and their religion of choice was Hinduism. In the early twentieth century, Indian authors themselves spoke against British utilitarianism and glorified Hinduism, adding to the bulk of the already existing literature on India and Hinduism. For quite some time, European identity was therefore constructed on the basis of a strong superiority complex, regarding Europeans as rational and scientific, and the "others", including Indians, as irrational and imaginative. But this superiority complex also suffered a strong blow in the aftermath of World War II with the horrors of the Holocaust and the barbaric nature of some fellow Europeans. Additionally, World War II heralded a new era in history in which the centre of power and influence shifted from Europe to the US and Soviet Union.[27]

The birth of the European Union and the integration process was followed by the ideological request of the consolidation of a more solid European identity. As a natural consequence of this phenomenon, the political discourse required a new

European identity, based on historical and cultural background. But the EU was not the only one actor with such a strategy; the process of identity-consolidation and transformation occurred in Asia as well, where the new national identities of rising powers, like China or India – which are rivals of EU's – challenges the basic assumption of European identity, which had been formed on a colonial background. Nowadays, we perceive a polarization between different conceptions of European identity.[28] Due to the dichotomy of the present European identity,[29] between the image of a "glorious cultural past" and the present, a new concept has emerged in recent years, exploring the historical relationships between political forms of identity and cultural attitudes in the field of emotions. Some theorists argue[30] that the formation of identity in the European context was linked to the idea of feelings. In the second half of the nineteenth century, the formulation of the emotional "Europeanness" was supported by imperial and colonial experiences, which tried to exclude any influence from Asia or Africa. This led to formulation of a new Eurocentric and racial identity.

The alternative could be the construction of a new cosmopolitan European identity, which takes the form of a post-national, pluralistic, cultural and societal identity, rather than an official EU identity; nevertheless such a construction would be a normative conception, imposing cosmopolitanism, asking for the recognition of different cultures, the integration of minorities, and facing the problems of racism and citizenship.[31] In order to create an operational, functional model of European identity, this model should be stretched beyond the two extreme perceptions mentioned previously, positioning itself within the historical contradictions of European identity and trying to overcome the hegemonic identities of all kinds.

External perception of the EU

The EU as an "unfinished project" and its "unfinished" identity address the issue of how public opinion, civil society, the media and political elites from India view the European Union. G. Oliver and L. Fioramonti analyze the impact of EU in the eyes of "global south", more precisely India, Brazil and South Africa, and how its policies applied abroad challenges to the perception of the its "uniqueness".

In the last twenty years, India has experienced significant economic growth, which makes it one of the most important players in the global economy. At the economic level, its relationship with the EU has mainly been characterized by growing trade volumes (EU is India's first trading partner) and deepening financial relations, in addition to close technological cooperation (for example, the Galileo project). In the same period of time, India suffered a blow after the US turned to Pakistan to seek support for the "war against terrorism".

> While this created a window of opportunity for the EU to expand its political ties with New Delhi, India's continuous refusal to join the Non-Proliferation Treaty (NPT) has reduced the extent of this collaboration. In general, it seems as if the EU has not been able to grasp fully India's security concerns, which span from its relationship with nuclear Pakistan to the growing number of

terrorist groups operating within the country and around its borders as well as its complex relationship with China.[32]

In spite of Europe's advantage in terms of symbolic capital, the EU is perceived in India as a "technocratic" power with few political ambitions, despite being characterized as a great economic power. Foreign relations are generally not a common issue for public opinion[33] and, therefore, the EU is almost unknown in India. There are not even quantitative data available in India on the public's perception of the EU,[34] although the majority of Indian experts acknowledges that a public information deficit exists about the EU. "Indian perceptions of the EU are essentially conditioned by the Anglo-Saxon media, which precludes a more nuanced understanding of the intricacies and complexity of the EU project".[35] Therefore, the Brexit will considerably influence the EU's perception in India.

Since 2005, despite adopting a strategic partnership, India and the EU are still very far from an effective cooperation. For instance, the European political elites describe the EU as a paradoxical power, offering arguments for the ineffectiveness of the cooperation:

> on the one hand, [the EU] is viewed as an important partner for fostering development and economic growth; on the other hand, it is accused of stifling developing economies through its protectionist policies. The first image is mainly due to the fact that the EU is [the] country's largest trading partner. Moreover, the political elites are aware of the magnitude of the European market and see it as a key opportunity to boost their economic growth. Additionally, the EU is also appreciated for being the most significant source of foreign direct investment. By contrast, the second image derives mainly from issues concerning [. . .] non-tariff barriers.[36]

And the paradox stands precisely in the way of future economical potential of the cooperation which is restricted, partly, due to protectionist policies of the EU. Even more, these paradoxical external policies of the EU continue to exist in a globalized world in which international trade is a key priority for India and other developing economies. Indian manufacturers are aware of the EU double standard when it protects its domestic markets; it subsidizes its producers or imposes trade barriers (like environmental standards). "Double standards, inconsistencies and contradictions are at the core of their criticisms of the EU's external policies in the fields of international trade and social development".[37] Many studies have revealed the "self-interested" attitude of the EU in trade negotiations, an opposite image to the one constructed and transmitted through the European public diplomacy. The EU's own trade interests are pragmatically followed in its external policies, regardless of the price paid by its negotiating partners. Since the EU follows simultaneously two contradictory policies, the question arises as to what really defines the EU and what it stands for.[38] And the immediate consequence of the non-tariff barrier policies is the perpetuation of inequalities between developed and developing countries.

EU has often been portrayed as an opportunity for the economic growth of India. Since 2000, the discourse on the India–EU partnership has focused mainly on "common values" and "principles" such as democracy, globalization and tolerance, which make the EU and India allies in areas such as security and world peace. Multilateralism and democratic governance are the common ground for such cooperation, mentioning that India "is not only the biggest democracy in the world, but also the only consolidated democracy in a region dominated by authoritarian regimes".[39]

In addition, Indian civil society has heavily criticized the EU concerning agricultural subsidies, due to the fact that this caused unfair competition in the global market, being perceived in India as a matter of social justice and human rights.[40] The image of the EU as a human rights champion and environmental leader has suffered significant losses, mainly due to EU's incapacity to force European companies to apply the same environmental standards in India as they do in Europe.

In terms of media perception,[41] the main issues associated with the EU – in either negative, positive or neutral way – in the Indian press are: trade, migration, security, agricultural subsidies and cultural cooperation. In many areas, the media emphasizes the technocratic image of the EU and its use of double standards, which overlaps with a more self-conscious India's identity and economical development. In spite of the EU's plans to promote the EU's image in the global arena, it is required to make decisions in regard to trade imbalances if the EU wishes to get rid of the neo-colonial stigma. Moreover, take a real leadership position on critical issues like energy policies and climate change.

Indian public opinion of EU's polices

In the most comprehensive public opinion survey, conducted in 2015 on EU's image in its strategic partner countries (Brazil, Canada, China, India, Japan, Mexico, Russia, South Africa, South Korea, and the USA) the awareness and visibility of EU is the lowest in the US, Canada, Japan and India.[42] In other terms, if the EU is visible at all in India, it is mainly in economic terms and as a source of technology and energy innovation.[43] The analysis of the survey emphasizes the fact that the public opinion reveals a relatively positive evaluation of the EU across the 10 countries. In case of India, such an evaluation is formed by two extremes; first, the media which covers rather negatively the EU's effectiveness in the economic sphere, due to the effects of the economic crisis; and secondly, through interviews which revealed a positive assessment of the EU's capabilities as a trade partner.

> Overall, reporting on the Union's political actorness and effectiveness draws a more positive picture, but is increasingly over-shadowed by the effects of the migration crisis as well as the impending Grexit and Brexit. The EU's handling of the migration crisis is significantly more negatively assessed than the EU's performance in various other fields: protecting the environment, combating climate change or promoting global peace and stability.[44]

In other areas, such as home affairs, foreign policy, social issues, environmental protection and the energy sector, the EU is considered as an active and effective entity in spite of its generally low visibility in the media. Indian public opinion has noticed the role of EU in the Iran negotiations and Ukrainian conflict management, and it is regarded mostly positively, compared to other Strategic Partner countries. The most important indicator for the perception of EU – in the context in which the technocratic power image is still prevailing – occurs in trade and business, which are highly relevant for the partner countries when referring to the EU.

The opposite trend can be noticed regarding the visibility of migration, which is very high in all sample countries including India, and the evaluation of EU politics is largely negative, and assessed as contradicting to the EU's own value system: "[t]he EU is explicitly not seen as a norm setter but rather as not living up to its own standards and betraying its own norms".[45] But migration is a priority for India too (both in terms of brain drain from and migration to the country), as such this topic could open a vivid dialogue.

An important issue for the present study is the perception of NPE within the Indian media. Generally speaking, it is a lack of interest for the construction of such a representation,[46] even though political and cultural elite might express a positive view on the normative construction of the EU.

> [T]he EU is not confronted by a hostile environment in India, although EU officials and others may feel that the EU's place in India's priorities is lower than deserved. As the general public survey demonstrated, the EU was generally viewed positively. [. . .] The EU was most commonly described as modern, strong, efficient and peaceful; and least often described as hypocritical, arrogant or aggressive. This is in line with the positive general view of the EU as well as the positive assessment of India's relationship with the EU.[47]

It must be added that the contemporary private and public Indian discourse try to overcome any focus on the colonial past and transcend the perception of a neo-colonial present.[48] Secondly, India is more aware of the individual European member states, rather than the political construction and the goals of the EU. Multiculturalism is a common topic between the two actors, as the linguistic diversity of EU with its 23 official languages is a familiar topic to India who has 22 official languages and many more dialects. And thirdly, education has always been and continues to be a positive pillar in the perception of EU and for the dialogue between strategic partners. Even the EU is not a top priority of India's foreign policy individual countries and specific topics can play an important role for a better cooperation.

Even if R. K. Jain and M. Holland have shown independently from each other that the Indian elite's perception of the EU is biased by the Anglo-Saxon media, the hard competition between other international relations topics in the media has disadvantaged the EU:

> The EU is simply not "sexy" enough to evoke passion and interest in the Indian print media. [. . .] It remains the appreciation for the Euro as an international

> currency, reservations about the EU as an effective actor in international politics, the comparatively greater importance of the USA in the Indian foreign policy calculus, and greater focus on bilateral relations with key EU Member States rather than the EU as a collectivity. Economic and political aspects of the relationship with the EU generally tended to overshadow social and cultural dimensions.[49]

The EU's role and action on India, and Asia generally, can increase, especially if the EU goes beyond the obtuse profit-oriented external policy perspective, moving toward security concerns of India, developmental issues[50] and cultural cooperation. Any missionary zeal of becoming an exporter of norms for the EU is ineffective, as the EU integration model is probably not helpful in South Asia[51] and the two worldviews remain disconnected.

India–EU strategic partnership: key elements

The *European Security Strategy*[52] was the first EU document to mention "strategic partnerships" as a foreign policy tool to cooperate with Japan, China, Canada, and India, as well as with "all those who share our goals and values, and are prepared to act in their support".[53] After less than one year, following previous ministerial level consultations, the European Commission has launched "An EU-India Strategic Partnership" with four major policy goals: a) cooperation and conflict prevention; b) economic partnership; c) development cooperation; and d) intellectual and cultural exchanges. The official response of Ministry of Foreign Affairs of India was sent a few weeks later, saluting a systematic interaction with the European Union.

In terms of perception, the European Union's strategic partnership with India is one of the ten in the world, and one of four in Asia (with China, Japan, South Korea, and India) and was initiated to replace bilateral diplomacy with new powers. In terms of effectiveness, Jain considers that:

> The EU's strategic partnerships are increasingly perceived as static and disappointing. They are not considered to be truly strategic because not every partner is equally strategic, the Union does not cooperate with its partners on most truly strategic issues, it has no structural or institutional impact on the relationship, and most partners do not regard the EU as a strategic partner at all, in many cases.[54]

On the other hand, India has nearly 25 strategic international partners, including three European ones: France, Germany and UK. India defines such strategy with the EU as an improvement of interactions, primarily in economical sector, but having political, social outcomes as well.

However, EU and India, despite the existing partnership, have not been able to transform shared values into shared interests and priorities, due to different worldviews and agendas, and as they act in different geo-political contexts and have different geographical and geo-political priorities. In addition, both India and the European Union have complex decision-making processes, for example, the consultation mechanisms – an annual summit, Foreign Minister ministerial level dialogue, and 27 sectoral dialogues – which is a long lasting, time consuming process.[55]

EU is often perceived by emerging powers as a conservative and protectionist structure. Contrarily, India is seen as a "premature power"[56] who is making the transition from rule-taker to rule-maker, and as such it has great aspiration to be a more relevant player.

> The Indian strategy in global governance today is to intensively engage leading players and forge issue-based coalitions with like-minded countries. Europe needs to recognize that since the end of the Cold War, India has become more pragmatic and less assertive; it feels it deserves a seat at the high table and should be part of the global management system.[57]

In spite of India's ambitious plans, the normativity of the EU disadvantages the developing countries and, at the same time, safeguards the European interests. The double standards of the Union, as it has been shown in the previous section, make India and other players unwilling to take "ethical lessons" in terms of human rights, democratic consolidation or the energy sector. As such, the goal for India would be to change its position in the international arena, from norm-taker to norm-setter.

In essence, the growing tension on normative level between EU and India creates an acid discourse on EU, the latter being accused of "regulatory imperialism" and being contested even when it acts altruistically.

In terms of security, the European and Indian interpretations on key issues like terrorism, proliferation of weapons of mass destruction, and failed states have differed. Apart from an annual security dialogue, since 2006, there are other security-related dialogues: counter-terrorism; counter-piracy, cyber-security and cyber-crime, and non-proliferation and disarmament. Obviously the security milieu of the Union and India are very different, and India does not even expect a pro-Indian attitude or a firm position regarding Pakistan or China (both non-democratic neighbors of India). The rising military power of China and the increasing cooperation between China and Pakistan (through the Belt and Road Initiative, since 2013) are major concerns for India.

> Europeans do not seem to be overly concerned about the potential security implications of a rising and more assertive China, its military modernization and its rising defense expenditure. This is partly because Asian issues and nations are too distant to directly impinge on its own security, partly because the EU is not militarily present in East Asia, and unlike the United States, does not play the role of an external balancer in Asia. Asian nations continue to have reservations about the European Union's Asian capabilities and credentials.[58]

As such, security remains important only in terms of discourse in the EU–India cooperation, as for neither of them the major security threats can be solved only though the cooperation of the two actors.[59]

Conclusion

The present chapter analyzed the history of the EU–India cooperation and the way in which the two players have seen each other in the last decades. It showed, as well, the causes of EU's unsuccessful effort to develop a really strong, comprehensive, "major power" dialogue with India, and to analyze the permanent responses offered by India to the normative European Union discourse. As the combined economy of the 28 EU countries is the largest in the world, India, with its robust economy, is willing to cooperate with the Union in all respects. Nowadays, trade remains the strongest link between the two actors, even if India and the EU would like to look each other as two well-known friends. In a time when India is more self-confident than ever before, the EU is facing the challenges of Brexit and the Eurozone crisis; and in the meanwhile, the EU is pushing ahead with the normative discourse. Stronger partnership between the two actors would increase wealth, stability and security. But despite shared values, the lack of shared interests on a number of issues are crucial in the present-day dynamic of the partnership. Probably the differences on security priorities cannot be changed, but the rise of mutual confidence regarding shared interests for greater cooperation could move the partnership beyond its present-day status.

Notes

1 The Norwegian Nobel Committee, *The Nobel Peace Prize for 2012: Press Release*, 12 October 2012, www.nobelprize.org/nobel_prizes/peace/laureates/2012/press.html, (accessed 25 June 2018).
2 J.M. Barroso, *From War to Peace: A European Tale. Nobel Peace Prize Lecture on Behalf of the EU*, speech Oslo, 10 December 2012, www.nobelprize.org/nobel_prizes/peace/laureates/2012/eu-lecture_en.html, (accessed 25 June 2018), p. 4.
3 Barroso, *From War to Peace*, p. 5.
4 I. Manners, 'Normative Power Europe: The International Role of the EU', *Archive of European Integration*, 2001, http://aei.pitt.edu/7263/, (accessed 25 June 2018), p. 7.
5 I. Manners, 'Normative Power Europe: A Contradiction in Terms?', *Journal of Common Market Studies*, vol. 40, no. 2, 2002, p. 252.
6 I. Manners, 'Normative Power Europe Reconsidered: Beyond the Crossroads', *Journal of European Public Policy*, vol. 13, no. 2, 2006, p. 194.
7 See G. Voloshin, *The European Union's Normative Power in Central Asia: Promoting Values and Defending Interests*, New York, Palgrave Macmillan, 2014, p. 4.
8 Voloshin, *The European Union's Normative Power in Central Asia*, p. 7.
9 See C. Hill, 'Checks and Balances: The European Union's Soft Power Strategy', in I. Parmar and M. Cox (eds.), *Soft Power and US Foreign Policy: Theoretical, Historical and Contemporary Perspectives*, London, Routledge, 2010, p. 194.
10 S. Subrahmanym, *Europe's India. Words, People, Emprire, 1500–1800*, Harvard, Harvard Univeristy Press, 2017, p. 26.

11 The term Indian "gentiles" or Hindus is a European representation according to which all Indians belonged to a single religion. Similarly, the term "caste" was understood not as an organizing social principle, but as a rigorous and unitary system.
12 Subrahmanym, *Europe's India*, p. 27.
13 Subrahmanym, *Europe's India*, pp. 30–31.
14 See Subrahmanym, *Europe's India*, pp. 36–37.
15 Subrahmanym, *Europe's India*, p. 38.
16 Subrahmanym, *Europe's India*, p. 40.
17 The term "Europeans" designated several ethnic groups, met by the Mughals.
18 Subrahmanym, *Europe's India*, p. 294.
19 See M.H. Fisher, *Counterflows to Colonialism: Indian Travellers and Settlers in Britain, 1600–1857*, Delhi, Permanent Black, 2004.
20 Historical sources speak more about French and English groups.
21 Subrahmanym, *Europe's India*, p. 311.
22 See B.S. Cohn, *Colonialism and Its Forms of Knowledge. The British in India*, Princeton, Princeton University Press, 1996. Cohn conceives the British Empire as an intellectual and cultural phenomenon, in which the British discovery, collection, and codification of information about Indian society contributed to colonial hegemony and political control. The Orientalists' study of India was important to the colonial project of control and command. Their imagination that led to brilliant archaeological finds forays were in fact forms of constructing an India that could be better inferiorized, and ruled.
23 British colonialism can be defined in this context as a form of political dominance in which a group of people actively maintain their strangeness from the population whom they dominate, using in this case the race arguments. See J.E. Wilson, *The Domination of Strangers Modern Governance in Eastern India, 1780–1835*, New York, Palgrave Macmillan, 2008, pp. 4–10, 190–192.
24 Wilson, *The Domination of Strangers Modern Governance in Eastern India*, p. 183.
25 See more on the history of the cooperation S.A. Wülbers, 'EU–India Relations: Debates and Dynamics', in E. Jorgensen et al. (eds.), *The Sage Handbook of European Foreign Policy. Volume 2*, London, Sage, 2015, pp. 634–645.
26 J. Jokela and B. Gaens, 'Introduction', in B. Gaens, J. Jokela and E. Limnell (eds.), *The Role of the European Union in Asia China and India as Strategic Partners*, London, Ashgate, 2009, p. 4.
27 Wülbers, 'EU – India Relations', p. 639.
28 L. Passerini, 'Europe and Its Others: Is There a European Identity?', in D. Stone (ed.), *The Oxford Handbook of Postwar European History*, Oxford, Oxford University Press, 2012, pp. 126.
29 Multiple identity theory refers here to national and supranational, local and global, gender based and religious, professional or any other component of identity. See R. Kastoryano (ed.), *An Identity for Europe: The Relevance of Multiculturalism in the EU Construction,* Hampshire, Palgrave Macmillan, 2009, pp. ix–23.
30 See K. Eder, 'Remembering National Memories Together: The Formation of a Transnational Identity in Europe', in K. Eder and W. Spohn (eds.), *Collective Memory and European Identity: The Effects of Integration and Enlargement*, Ashgate, 2005, pp. 197–220; L. Passerini, *Europe in Love, Love in Europe: Imagination and Politics in Britain Between the Wars*, London-New York, New York University Press, 2000.
31 Passerini, 'Europe and Its Others', p. 133.
32 G. Oliver and L. Fioramonti, 'The Emerging "Global South": The EU in the Eyes of India, Brazil and South Africa', in S. Lucarelli and L. Fioramonti (eds.), *External Perceptions of the European Union as a Global Actor*, New York, Routledge, 2011, p. 106.
33 See also R.K. Jain and S. Pandey, 'The Public Attitudes and Images of the European Union in India', *India Quarterly*, vol. 68, no. 4, 2012, pp. 331–343. Jain emphasizes the fact that Indian newspapers allocate no more than one page for international relations.

34 See *Afrobarometer*, http://afrobarometer.org/data, (accessed 25 June 2018); *Latinobarometro*, www.latinobarometro.org/lat.jsp, (accessed 25 June 2018).
35 Oliver and Fioramonti, 'The Emerging "Global South" ', p. 109.
36 Oliver and Fioramonti, 'The Emerging "Global South" ', p. 110.
37 Oliver and Fioramonti, 'The Emerging "Global South" ', p. 111.
38 G. Oliver, *South Africa and the European Union: Self-Interest, Ideology and Altruism*, Pretoria, Protea Book House, 2006, p. 9.
39 Oliver and Fioramonti, 'The Emerging "Global South" ', p. 112.
40 The opening of the Indian market caused social unrest and poverty, especially for the most vulnerable groups, while the wave of suicides among Indian farmers not able to compete with subsidized produce from Europe and America became a matter of national security. See D. Mahapatra, 'Over 12,000 Farmer Suicides Per Year, Centre Tells Supreme Court', *The Times of India*, 3 May 2017, https://timesofindia.indiatimes.com/india/over-12000-farmer-suicides-per-year-centre-tells-supreme-court/articleshow/58486441.cms, (accessed 25 June 2018).
41 As it is analyzed by R. Jain, G. Oliver or S. Pandey.
42 Public Policy Management Institute, National Research Centre for Europe, Asian Perception of the EU, *Analysis of the Perception of the EU And of the EU's Policies Abroad. Final Report*, 2015, http://ec.europa.eu/dgs/fpi/documents/showcases/eu_perceptions_study_final_report.pdf, (accessed 25 June 2018).
43 See: Public Policy Management Institute, National Research Centre for Europe, Asian Perception of the EU, *Analysis of the Perception of the EU and of the EU's Policies Abroad*, p. 51.
44 Public Policy Management Institute, National Research Centre for Europe, Asian Perception of the EU, p. 21.
45 Public Policy Management Institute, National Research Centre for Europe, Asian Perception of the EU, p. 44.
46 See Public Policy Management Institute, National Research Centre for Europe, Asian Perception of the EU, pp. 129–130.
47 Public Policy Management Institute, National Research Centre for Europe, Asian Perception of the EU, p. 132.
48 See Public Policy Management Institute, National Research Centre for Europe, Asian Perception of the EU, pp. 129–133. Indian newspaper discourse analysis had been conducted by Jain since 2000 up today, reaching the same conclusion.
49 R.K. Jain and S. Pandey, 'The European Union in the Eyes of India', *Asia Europe Journal*, vol. 8, no. 2, 2010, p. 206.
50 See E. Beukel, *ASEAN and ARF in East Asia's Security Architecture: The Role of Norms and Powers*, Copenhagen, Danish Institute for International Studies, 2008.
51 See B. Gaens, J. Jokela, and E. Limnell (eds.), *The Role of the European Union in Asia China and India as Strategic Partners*, London, Ashgate, 2009, pp. 173–188.
52 European Council, *European Security Strategy – A Secure Europe in a Better World*, Brussels, 12 December 2003, https://europa.eu/globalstrategy/en/european-security-strategy-secure-europe-better-world, (accessed 25 June 2018).
53 European Council, *European Security Strategy*, p. 14.
54 R.K. Jain, 'India-EU Strategic Partnership: Perceptions and Perspectives', *NFG Working Paper*, vol. 10, 2014, p. 8.
55 New dialogue formats like the Asia Europe Meeting (ASEM) have emerged.
56 S. Saran, 'The Evolving Role of Emerging Economies in Global Governance – An Indian Perspective', *Research and Information System for Developing Countries*, 7 June 2012, www.ris.org.in/sites/default/files/EmergingEconomiesPaper-final.pdf, (accessed 25 June 2018).
Jain, 'India-EU Strategic Partnership', p. 10.
57 Jain, 'India-EU Strategic Partnership', p. 11.

58 Jain, 'India-EU Strategic Partnership', p. 15.
59 The EU naval operation ATLANTA, in the Gulf of Aden, might change this perception in the near future.

Bibliography

Afrobarometer, http://afrobarometer.org/data, (accessed 25 June 2018).
Ali, M.R., 'European Union South Asia Relation: Defining And Designing New Partnership', *Regional Studies*, vol. 22, nr. 1, 2001, pp. 3–38.
Baroowa, S., 'The Emerging Strategic Partnership Between India And the EU: A Critical Appraisal', *European Law Journal*, vol. 13, no. 6, 2007, pp. 732–749.
Barroso, J.M., *From War to Peace: A European Tale. Nobel Peace Prize Lecture on Behalf of the EU*, speech Oslo, 10 December 2012, www.nobelprize.org/nobel_prizes/peace/laureates/2012/eu-lecture_en.html, (accessed 25 June 2018).
Bava, U.S., 'India–EU Relations: Building a Strategic Partnership', in R. Balme and B. Bridges (eds.), *Europe – Asia Relations: Building Multilateralisms*, Basingstoke, Palgrave Macmillan, 2008, pp. 233–256.
Beukel, E., *ASEAN and ARF in East Asia's Security Architecture: The Role of Norms and Powers*, Copenhagen, Danish Institute for International Studies, 2008.
Bhattacharya, S.K., *India and the European Union: Trade and Non-Tariff Barriers*, New Delhi, Aakar Publications, 2004.
Bretherton, C. and J. Vogler, *The European Union as a Global Actor*, London, Routledge, 2006.
Chaban, N. and M. Holland (eds.), *The European Union and the Asia–Pacific: Media, Public And Elite Perceptions of the EU*, London-New York, Routledge, 2008.
Chaban, N., M. Holland and P. Ryan (eds.), *The EU Through the Eyes of Asia: New Cases, New Findings*, Singapore-London, World Scientific, 2009.
Chaisse, J. and D. Chakraborty, 'The Evolving And Multilayered EU – India Investment Relations: Regulatory Issues And Policy Conjectures', *European Law Journal*, vol. 20, no. 3, 2013, pp. 385–422.
Christiansen, T., E. Kirchner and P. Murray (eds.), *The Palgrave Handbook of EU – Asia Relations*, Basingstoke, Palgrave Macmillan, 2013.
Cohn, B.S., *Colonialism and its Forms of Knowledge. The British in India*, Princeton, Princeton University Press, 1996.
Commission of the European Communities, *Communication from the Commission to the Council, The European Parliament and The European Economic and Social Committee: An EU–India Strategic Partnership*, Brussels, 16 June 2004, COM(2004) 430.
Dixit, J.N., 'Cooperation with Europe: Market and More', *Indian Express*, 10 July, 2000.
Eberhardt, P. and D. Kumar, *Trade Invaders: How Big Business is Driving the EU – India-Free Trade Negotiations*, Brussels, Corporate Europe Observatory, 2010.
Eder, K., 'Remembering National Memories Together: The Formation of a Transnational Identity in Europe', in K. Eder and W. Spohn (eds.), *Collective Memory and European Identity: The Effects of Integration and Enlargement*, Ashgate, Routledge, 2005, pp. 197–220.
European Council, *EU-India Strategic Partnership – Council Conclusions – 11 October 2004*, http://trade.ec.europa.eu/doclib/docs/2004/november/tradoc_119899.pdf, (accessed 25 June 2018).
European Council, *European Security Strategy – A Secure Europe in a Better World*, Brussels, 12 December 2003, https://europa.eu/globalstrategy/en/european-security-strategy-secure-europe-better-world, (accessed 25 June 2018).

Fioramonti, L. and A. Poletti, 'Facing the Giant: Southern Perspectives on the European Union', *Third World Quarterly*, vol. 29, no. 1, 2007, pp. 167–180.

Fisher, M.H., *Counterflows to Colonialism: Indian Travellers and Settlers in Britain, 1600–1857*, Delhi, Permanent Black, 2004.

Gaens, B., J. Jokela and E. Limnell (eds.), *The Role of the European Union in Asia China and India as Strategic Partners*, London, Ashgate, 2009.

Ganguly, S. (ed), *India's Foreign Policy: Retrospect and Prospect*, New Delhi, Oxford University Press, 2012.

Hill, C., 'Checks and Balances: The European Union's Soft Power Strategy', in I. Parmar and M. Cox (eds.), *Soft Power and US Foreign Policy: Theoretical, Historical and Contemporary Perspectives*, London, Routledge, 2010, pp. 182–198.

Holland, M. and N. Chaban (eds.), *Europe and Asia: Perceptions from Afar*, Baden-Baden, Nomos, 2014.

Jain, R.K., 'India-EU Strategic Partnership: Perceptions and Perspectives', *NFG Working Paper*, vol. 10, 2014.

Jain, R.K. and S. Pandey, 'The European Union in the Eyes of India', *Asia Europe Journal*, vol. 8, no. 2, 2010, pp. 193–209.

Jain, R.K. and S. Pandey, 'Indian Elites and the EU as a Normative Power', M. Holland and N. Chaban (eds.), *Europe and Asia: Perceptions from Afar*, Baden-Baden, Nomos-Bloombury, 2015, pp. 252–272.

Jain, R.K. and S. Pandey, 'Perceptions and Misperceptions: Images of the European Union in India', in M. Holland and N. Chaban (eds.), *Europe and Asia: Perceptions from Afar*, Baden-Baden, Nomos, 2014, pp. 143–170.

Jain, R.K. and S. Pandey, 'The Public Attitudes and Images of the European Union in India', *India Quarterly*, vol. 68, no. 4, 2012, pp. 331–343.

Kastoryano, R. (ed.), *An Identity for Europe: The Relevance of Multiculturalism in the EU Construction*, Hampshire, Palgrave Macmillan, 2009.

Keukeleire, S. and B. Hooijmaaijers, 'EU–India Relations And Multilateral Governance: Where Is the "Strategic Partnership"?', *Foreign Policy Research Centre Journal*, vol. 13, 2013, pp. 118–122.

Khandekar, G., 'Building a Sustainable EU – India Partnership', *Policy Brief*, vol. 9, 2012, http://fride.org/download/ESPO_PB9_Building_a_sustainable_EU_India_partnership.pdf, (accessed 25 June 2018).

Khandekar, G., 'EU – India Cooperation On Counter-Terrorism', in L. Peral and V. Sakhuja (eds.), *The EU – India Partnership: Time to Go Strategic?*, Paris, European Union Institute for Security Studies, 2012, pp. 111–124.

Latinobarometro, www.latinobarometro.org/lat.jsp, (accessed 25 June 2018).

Lucarelli, S. and I. Manners (eds.), *Values and Principles in European Union Foreign Policy*, London, Routledge, 2006.

Mahapatra, D., 'Over 12,000 Farmer Suicides Per Year, Centre Tells Supreme Court', *The Times of India*, 03 May 2017, https://timesofindia.indiatimes.com/india/over-12000-farmer-suicides-per-year-centre-tells-supreme-court/articleshow/58486441.cms, (accessed 25 June 2018).

Manners, I., 'Global Europa: Mythology of the European Union in World Politics', *Journal of Common Market Studies*, vol. 48, no. 1, 2010, pp. 67–87.

Manners, I., 'Normative Power Europe: A Contradiction in Terms?', *Journal of Common Market Studies*, vol. 40, no. 2, 2002, pp. 235–258.

Manners, I., 'Normative Power Europe: The International Role of the EU', *Archive of European Integration*, 2001, http://aei.pitt.edu/7263/, (accessed 25 June 2018).

Manners, I. and R. Whitman, 'Towards Identifying the International Identity of the European Union: A Framework for Analysis of the EU's Network of Relationships', *Journal of European Integration*, vol. 21, no. 3, 1998, pp. 231–249.

The Norwegian Nobel Committee, *The Nobel Peace Prize for 2012: Press Release*, 12 October 2012, www.nobelprize.org/nobel_prizes/peace/laureates/2012/press.html, (accessed 25 June 2018).

Oliver, G., *South Africa and the European Union: Self-Interest, Ideology and Altruism*, Pretoria, Protea Book House, 2006.

Oliver, G. and L. Fioramonti, 'The Emerging 'Global South': The EU in the Eyes of India, Brazil and South Africa', in S. Lucarelli and L. Fioramonti (eds.), *External Perceptions of the European Union as a Global Actor*, New York, Routledge, 2011, pp. 105–119.

Passerini, L., 'Europe and Its Others: Is There a European Identity?', in D. Stone (ed.), *The Oxford Handbook of Postwar European History*, Oxford, Oxford University Press, 2012, pp. 120–138.

Passerini, L., *Europe in Love, Love in Europe: Imagination and Politics in Britain Between the Wars*, London-New York, New York University Press, 2000.

Public Policy Management Institute, National Research Centre for Europe, Asian Perception of the EU, *Analysis of the Perception of the EU And of the EU's Policies Abroad. Final Report*, 2015, http://ec.europa.eu/dgs/fpi/documents/showcases/eu_perceptions_study_final_report.pdf, (accessed 25 June 2018).

Roy, A.B., 'India – EU Cooperation on Afghanistan: Context, Constraints And Prospects', in L. Peral and V. Sakhuja (eds.), *The EU–India Partnership: Time to Go Strategic?*, Paris, European Union Institute for Security Studies, 2012, pp. 137–146.

Saran, S., 'The Evolving Role of Emerging Economies in Global Governance – An Indian Perspective', *Research and Information System for Developing Countries*, 7 June 2012, www.ris.org.in/sites/default/files/EmergingEconomiesPaper-final.pdf, (accessed 25 June 2018).

Stephen, M.D., 'India, Emerging Powers and Global Human Rights: Yes, But', in D. Lettinga and van L. Troost (eds.), *Shifting Power and Human Rights Diplomacy: India*, Amsterdam, Amnesty International, 2015, pp. 55–63.

Subrahmanym, S., *Europe's India. Words, People, Emprire, 1500–1800*, Harvard, Harvard University Press, 2017.

Telò, M., *Europe, a Civilian Power? European Union, Global Governance, World Order*, Basingstoke, Palgrave Macmillan, 2006.

Vergeron, K., *Contemporary Indian Views of Europe*, London, Chatham House, 2006.

Voloshin, G., *The European Union's Normative Power in Central Asia: Promoting Values and Defending Interests*, New York, Palgrave Macmillan, 2014.

Youngs, R., *The European Union And the Promotion of Democracy: Europe's Mediterranean and Asian Policies*, Oxford, Oxford University Press, 2002.

Wilson, J.E., *The Domination of Strangers Modern Governance in Eastern India, 1780–1835*, New York, Palgrave Macmillan, 2008.

Wülbers, S.A., 'EU–India Relations: Debates and Dynamics', in E. Jorgensen et al. (eds.), *The Sage Handbook of European Foreign Policy. Volume 2*, London, Sage, 2015, pp. 634–645.

9 East Asia–European Union relations

The case of Japan and South Korea in the last decade

Olga Barbasiewicz

Introduction

Japan and South Korea (Republic of Korea, ROK) are the countries allied with the United States (the US), and their attention is focused mainly on the US, with special emphasis to the security policy. Nevertheless, the European Union (EU) is present in the foreign policy of both Japan and the Republic of Korea because the economic power of these countries makes them cooperate with the European market, especially because the EU as a whole is the largest economy in the world. Nevertheless, such common values as human rights and rules of democracy make both Asian democracies cooperate in the field of moral principles and norms.

During his long awaited visit in Hiroshima in 2016, American president Barack Obama referred to the case of the European Union as a symbol of reconciliation and establishing a peaceful society. He claimed that:

> The nations of Europe built a union that replaced battlefields with bonds of commerce and democracy. Oppressed people and nations won liberation. An international community established institutions and treaties that work to avoid war and aspire to restrict and roll back and ultimately eliminate the existence of nuclear weapons.[1]

This reference shows great importance in the EU's role in the area of freedom, security and justice, being a great example for the Asian states. It can be claimed that the American president assumed the readiness of Japan and Korea[2] to take example from the European countries and to implement in Asia the reconciliation processes which lead to a stable cooperation. This kind of statement, which emphasizes the role of the Union, can be confirmed by Ian Manners' thesis of the EU as the normative power (NPE) in international relations.[3] Manners claims that the normative power refers to the European Union's ability to spread the norms and standards of European integration into the international community, in this case in the Asia-Pacific region. These norms contain respect for human dignity, liberty, democracy, equality, the rule of law, and respect for human rights (TEU, Article 21). They are also similar to the norms promoted by the United States of America (US), especially to those implemented in the Asian states (being contemporary democracies), such as Japan or South Korea, during the postwar democratization processes. While the normative power of the EU lies in exporting the systems of norms, the norms that concern peaceful existence and development are also similar to the 'Western' ones, implemented in Japan and Korea in the postwar period.[4] From the perspective of the democratized Asian states, the American policy brought not only stability but also great economic growth. Therefore, further economic development can be connected with respect for the European norms and values, similarly to respect for American standard accepted by both Asian societies after World War II.

Being a normative actor, however, requires also a certain degree of acceptance for such an identity among third countries. Without such legitimacy the EU's effort to become a normative actor are only an empty and one-side political declaration without international recognition.

It is claimed that despite many cultural differences between European and Asian countries, such Asian democracies as Japan and South Korea share with the EU members democratic and economic values. Therefore, the aim of this chapter is to verify this hypothesis, with certain reference towards the East Asian involvement in the cooperation with the EU in the field of economy, simultaneously assuming that the norms and values represented by the European Union can serve as a common point for cooperation between Europe and East Asian democratic countries. Special attention will be paid not only to the official bilateral agreements, but also to the social moods and political opinions on the issue of their country's relations with the EU. The attitude of the political and social actors representing the Asian states towards the European norms and values will also be an important aspect of this analysis. The last five years will be taken into consideration, when discussing the social moods and political actors' attitude. The range of the dates was decided due to the rule of conservative parties in both countries – Japan and the ROK. In 2017 the conservative government of Liberal Democratic Party was still running the country, while in the South Korea, the Liberal Democratic Party had just came to power. Moreover, the references towards the last two decades in the historical context will also be provided to give a wider view into the Asian democracies–EU negotiation processes. Therefore, the political actors and public opinion reference towards the picture of the EU will be provided in this chapter. The information available for the general audience will be taken into consideration. The very recent period has been marked with vivid negotiations between Japan and the EU. It is also the moment of strong cooperation between the ROK and Europe. Our analysis here focuses mainly on the economic negotiations and partnership, assuming that the norms and values represented by Japan and South Korea, as leading Asian democracies, are largely equal with those on which the EU is based. Japan had to adopt the Western norms during the American occupation period (although its rapid modernization took place in the Meiji period).[5] Immediately after World War II the scientists assumed that even though Japan adopted Western science and technology, it failed in adapting Western civilization and norms.[6] Nonetheless, the surveys in the 1990s revealed that the importance of the life domains was almost the same in Europe and in Japan.[7] Moreover, the values that are defined as Asian, such as honesty, cooperation, manners or obeying the law were also respected by the majority of respondents.[8] Korea, being also connected to the Confucian and Asian standards, has also been under the great influence of Christianity since the 19th century, which is connected with the modernization of the Peninsula.[9]

Therefore, it can be claimed that Europe and Asian democracies share the same values and norms. The reference towards these standards is also used when an Asian country wants to strengthen its position while negotiating with the third party. Gaining the support of a great power such as the EU enforces the negotiating position held by Japan or the ROK.

To verify this thesis, several research questions should be answered. Which bilateral agreements enabled the strengthening of the relations between Japan/Korea and the EU? How do the Asian states cooperate with the European Union in the field of common values and norms? What is the attitude of Asian politicians towards the cooperation with the EU, and how do they refer to this cooperation in their statements and speeches? What is the attitude of the public opinion and society towards the European Union, and how do they use the cooperation for their own purposes? Why do Japanese/Korean leaders refer to the European norms and values in the foreign policy of their countries?

The evaluation of the primary and existing sources is provided in this chapter. While analyzing the contemporary Japanese and Korean policy-makers, their speeches and statements were taken into consideration. In this case, the content analysis will be of crucial importance. Also, for providing a broader analysis, academic papers and newspaper articles were used as well. Because of the deficit of academic analysis of the undertaken issue, the official sources, such as governments' and organizations' websites and newspaper articles will be the main source of information.

In this chapter, the Japanese and English-language sources were used. Due to the author's lack of Korean language knowledge, the chapter relies on the English versions of Korean newspapers, such as 'Korea JoongAng Daily', 'The Korea Herald', and 'The Hankyoreh'. Moreover, the treaties and agreements were also analyzed. This kind of analysis provides a broader view of the use of economic tools to achieve the foreign policy objectives, because strong counties (Japan and South Korea are included in this category because they are leading economies in the region as well as globally) are more likely to initiate economic statecraft as a key foreign policy measure.[10]

The trade agreements between the EU and ROK/Japan: historical background and its influence on the present situation

The leading role in the economic partnership agreement is occupied by the Republic of Korea (ROK). The first agreement between South Korea and the EU was the *Framework Agreement for Trade and Cooperation* between the European Community and its member states on the one hand, and ROK on the other, signed in Luxembourg on 28th October 1996, which came into force on 1st April 2001.

Then, almost ten years later the agreements that have shaped the contemporary European-Korean relations were signed, although the 1996 *Framework Agreement* set an agenda for economic and related fields.[11]

The ROK is the EU's ninth largest export destination for goods, whereas the EU is South Korea's third largest export market with total EU's export to ROK of EUR 47.9 billion. Imports from South Korea totaled EUR 42.3 billion.[12] The EU–South Korea *Free Trade Agreement* (FTA) was signed by both parties on 16th December 2010 and became valid in July 2011. It is the first trade agreement between the EU and an Asian country. The deal eliminates duties for industry and agriculture, addressing non-tariff barriers to trade, specifically on the automotive, pharmaceutical, medical devices and electronics sectors.[13] The FTA was amended only once, to adjust to the situation when Croatia joined the EU and to provide the same possibilities for the new EU member state. Numerous committees and working groups between both parties were established to supervise the implementation of the agreement and its effects. The institution that is responsible for monitoring and ensuring the implementation of the EU–Republic of Korea Free Trade Agreement is the EU Delegation to the Republic of Korea.

South Korea was the first East Asian country that sought to form FTAs not only with its neighboring countries in the region or major trading partners like the US but also with smaller countries in other regions, moreover paying the same attention to European and Latin American countries.[14] This strategy made the ROK the first Asian country with such strong economic relations with the EU.

The foundations of the cooperation between Japan and the European Community (the EC) were determined in the *Japan-EU Joint Declaration*, agreed in 1991. Since then Japan has had to adjust its policy towards the EU together with the changes of the organization's members and status. In 1993, the US was Europe's biggest external market, accounting for approximately 17.5% of its export, and 17.3% of import, while Japan imported 4.7% of the EU's total export, whereas its share in the total EU import was 9.7%.[15] Therefore, the deficit in the economic exchange with Japan was quite noticeable. This accounted for the pressure exerted by the EU on Japan to open its market still further, as it was practiced with the US. This example shows that it was the EU which pushed for closer cooperation with Japan.

The summit meetings between Japan and first the EC, and then the EU were held since 1984. Four of them were held with the EC, and nineteen others with the EU. In 2001 in Brussels, an Action Plan for EU–Japan Cooperation was agreed. It was devoted to the promotion of peace and security, strengthening the economic and trade partnership, coping with global and societal challenges, and cooperation between the citizens of the EU and Japan.

For contemporary Japan the most important agreements that are still under negotiations are the *Japan-EU Economic Partnership Agreement* (EPA) and the *Japan-EU Strategic Partnership Agreement* (SPA).The eighteenth round of negotiations on the *Japan-EU Economic Partnership Agreement* (EPA) was held in Tokyo from April 3 to 5, 2017 and was attended on the Japanese side, by Ambassador Yoichi Suzuki, Representative of the Government of Japan for Free Trade and Economic Partnership Agreements Negotiations (Chief Negotiator) and representatives from other relevant ministries and on the EU side, Mauro Petriccione, Deputy Director-General, Directorate-General for Trade, the European Commission (Chief Negotiator).[16] During the negotiations areas such as trade in services, intellectual property rights, non-tariff measures, government procurement and investment were discussed.[17] The other place for negotiations is the Meeting of Main Ministers on the Japan–EU Economic Partnership Agreement (EPA), which considers 'comprehensive policies toward early conclusion of the negotiation'.[18] The agreement on starting the negotiations of the Japan-EU Strategic Partnership Agreement (SPA) was taken in May 2011, at the 20th Japan–EU Summit. The negotiations are held parallel with the EPA. The agreement provides legal basis for the Japan–EU strategic partnership for the coming decades on the basis of existing cooperation, with a view to achieving peace, stability and prosperity of the world and regions.[19]

The Japanese side is aware of stronger cooperation between South Korea and the EU, as well as between the EU and the US. In his statement on 5th April 2016 during the Plenary Session of Japanese Parliament, Abe claimed that: 'The US and the EU, as well as South Korea were also working on liberalization of trade with each other. In case of Japan I thought that, if it turns inward, there is no possibility for growth as well as for gathering the people of excellent skills'.[20] Therefore, Japan is focusing on both of the preceding agreements in order to strengthen its partnership with the EU.

The European Business Council (EBC) in Japan is an example of a cooperation between the EU and Japan in the field of trade and economy, which has existed since 1972. The EBC represents around 3,000 local European companies and individuals who are members of the EBC through their respective national chamber of commerce or business organization.[21] It is composed of a Board of Governors, an Executive Operating Board, Industry Sector Committees and a Secretariat.[22] At the beginning, the EBC was registered with the Ministry of Economy, Trade and Industry (METI) and in 2008 as the European (EU) Chamber of Commerce in Japan.[23] It cooperates with the Delegation of the European Commission in Japan, embassies of each EU country, on coordination and proposals to Japanese government on the economic and trade cooperation between both sides. This aspect of the cooperation seems to be crucial in giving the directions of future negotiations in achieving full cooperation between the EU and Japan.

Cooperation on major political and global issues between the EU and Japan/Korea

Though arguably it is Japan which shares such fundamental values and principles with the EU as democracy, rule of law and human rights, South Korea does not only focus on the economic ties with the EU, but also on the major political and global issues, namely human rights, non-proliferation of weapons of mass destruction, and counter-terrorism, as well as climate change and energy security.[24] An important aspect of implementing European values and norms, namely human rights, is the case of abolishing the death penalty. In 2007, Ahn Kyung-hwan (An Kyong-hwan), the then-chairman of the National Human Rights Commission, said that South Korea should abolish the death penalty despite public opposition, as was done in most European countries.[25] In Asia governments accept the death penalty, and South Korea is the exception, as it is *de facto*[26] an abolitionist country. This makes the ROK the country which agrees with the European values.

Since 2010 South Korea and the EU have upgraded their relationship to the level of Strategic Partnership. The *Framework Agreement* was signed on the previously mentioned day, but it was implemented four years later. Basing on the agreement the parties, inter alia:

- reaffirmed their attachment to the principles of good governance and the fight against corruption,
- strengthened political dialogue and cooperation, notably on human rights; non-proliferation of weapons of mass destruction; small arms and light weapons; the most serious crimes of concern to the international community; and counter-terrorism,
- strengthen cooperation in the area of sustainable development, notably health; employment and social affairs; environment and natural resources; climate change; agriculture, rural development and forestry; marine and fisheries; and development assistance,
- strengthened cooperation in the field of justice, freedom and security, notably the rule of law; legal cooperation; personal data protection; migration; combating illicit drugs; combating organized crime and corruption; combating money laundering and terrorism financing; combating cybercrime; and law enforcement.[27]

These selected aspects of the *Framework Agreement* show that even though the EU is one of the main external markets to promote the Korean industry, the fact that the country is an East Asian democracy which refers to the European values and norms offers the field for cooperation between the parties. This aspect of the agreement can be defined as a locus of shared values, and identification of the shared values of South Korea and the EU, namely the respect for these values in their actions.[28]

In the case of Japan, the basic slogan used by the Japanese politicians to advocate internal and external policies and to provide justification for cooperation with the EU, is the promotion of global peace and democratic values, being the core of the Japanese postwar policy. These core norms were always emphasized when coming to negotiations and agreements between the EU and Japan. As we mentioned in the previous chapter in the agreements and documents on which Japanese-European partnership is based the major political and global issues are declared. This approach is emphasized in the message from the Ambassador of the Delegation of the European Union to Japan. In his statement, Viorel Isticioaia-Budura states: 'Japan is one of the EU's strategic partners, sharing such values as democracy, the rule of law, open markets and respect for human rights. We cooperate on a wide range of issues ranging from peace-building and anti-piracy missions to science and innovation'.[29]

An important aspect in the cooperation between the EU and Japan are the resolutions on the Situation of Human Rights in the Democratic People's Republic of Korea (DPRK) at the United Nations General Assembly. This Resolution was co-tabled by Japan and the EU, put to vote and adopted on November 19, 2015.[30] In March, 2017 the U.N. Human Rights Council adopted a resolution submitted by Japan and the European Union and, as *Japan Times* reports, backed by the United States on widening 'its investigation into violations in North Korea with a view to documenting alleged crimes against humanity for future prosecution'.[31]

The common norms and values have always been considered as sectors that connect both sides, and H. Mayer claims they 'are qualified to host and sponsor the new global civilian discourse and to contribute to responsible global governance in a fashion that is powerful yet based on soft power'.[32] Japan, assuming the role of the Asian democracy guard, plays this card, searching for the supporters for their activity among Western partners, i.e. the EU, and undertaking bilateral activities to secure its own interests. Frequently, it refers to its own democratic values and asks for help in the international environment that shares the same standards in order to secure a stronger negotiation position in the politically difficult cases that are problematic to Japan.

The common European-Japanese struggle over human rights in North Korea also had its influence on the group of families of Japanese nationals abducted to North Korea, who visited the European Parliament on May 6, 2017 and met ambassadors and members of European Parliament to express their hope to increase pressure on North Korea by European countries, because Japan and the EU are the advocates of human rights in the world.[33]

Another aspect of cooperation between Japan and the EU and its 'soft power' is the EU–Japan Friendship Week, which has been an annual event since 2001, focusing on public diplomacy, academic and cultural activities.[34] This is a great opportunity to make the Japanese familiar with the EU, its tradition and history, so important in the context of relations with Japan.

The perception of the European Union's international role in Japan

The status of the EU as an international organization is well demonstrated on the website of the Ministry of Foreign Affairs of Japan, which places the EU on the list of bilateral partnerships of Japan. The key point for the relations is given in the following statement: 'Japan and the EU share fundamental values and principles such as democracy, rule of law and human rights; common position on a number of global issues'.[35]

The need for deepening economic cooperation mentioned in the introduction to this chapter was noticeable on March 27, 2017, when Ministry of Foreign Affairs of Japan held *Japan–U.S.–Europe Business Seminar*, which was co-organized together with Cabinet Office (CAO), Ministry of Economy, Trade and Industry

(METI), The Japan Institute of International Affairs (JIIA), and Japan External Trade Organization (JETRO). During the event, keynote speeches were delivered mainly on the Japanese side by the representatives of MOFA or METI, and on the European side, by Markus Beyrer, Secretary General Business Europe or Francesco Fini, Deputy Head of the Delegation of the EU to Japan.

Nevertheless, because Japan's postwar political system has strengthened the position of the prime minister, also on foreign policy matters, with particular emphasis on security policy, the analysis of the EU–Japan's PM relations seems to be crucial in this chapter. The postwar changes enabled to play a kind of a 'one-man show' by strong individuals. The case of Abe Shinzō, who is one of the longest serving PMs in Japanese history, can serve as a great example of this kind of leadership, especially while being active for the most of our decade of the 21st century.

The most important year from the perspective of cooperation with the EU with regard to Abe's position was 2014, which will be taken as a case study for the purposes of this analysis.

On May 7, 2014, PM Abe Shinzō met in Brussels for the 22nd Summit between the EU and Japan. During this annual meeting, a joint statement was issued by Abe, Herman Van Rompuy, President of the European Council, and José Manuel Durão Barroso, President of the European Commission. They unanimously confirmed that their relationship is 'founded on the common values of democracy, the rule of law, human rights, and shared principles such as open markets and a rules-based international system'.[36] In the statement, agreement on several crucial issues regarding Japan-EU relations was reached. Among them there were:

1 Strategic Partnership Agreement with a comprehensive coverage as a sound structure for deeper political, global and sectoral cooperation over the coming decades,
2 early conclusion of a Free Trade Agreement (FTA)/ Economic Partnership Agreement (EPA),
3 contribution of the EU–Japan Business Round Table (BRT) to further development of bilateral economic relationship,
4 great value of the Asia-Europe Meeting (ASEM) as a forum for dialogue and cooperation,
5 emphasis of the solid EU–Japan cooperation in a broad range of other sectors and areas, including macroeconomic policies, financial regulation, employment, the environment, and fisheries,
6 enhancing cooperation in the area of disarmament and non-proliferation,
7 EU–Japan cooperation in science, technology and innovation to promote growth, jobs and competitiveness, and to address shared societal challenges,
8 the inaugural meeting of the EU–Japan Space Policy Dialogue in Tokyo,
9 the launch of an EU–Japan Cyber Dialogue, with a view to promoting cooperation on cyberspace through exchanges of our respective extensive experience and knowledge.[37]

These issues agreed by Japan's PM show the significance of the EU–Japan dialogue and the role of Abe in promoting it in Japan. The next common event in which Abe took part was The Asia-Europe Meeting (ASEM) which was held on October 15–18, 2014 in Milan, and it was the 10th meeting of this kind. Japan and the EU common interests were represented by Abe's standpoints on and contributions to the situation in the Middle East, including ISIL and the situation in Ukraine.[38] On the occasion of the ASEM, Abe also held for the second time that year the Summit Meeting with Herman Van Rompuy and José Manuel Barroso. During this meeting the growing rapprochement of Japan–EU relations was emphasized, as well as the need to accelerate of negotiations in order to reach agreement in principle on the Japan–EU Economic Partnership Agreement (EPA) during 2015, and the continuation of cooperation on concluding the Japan–EU Strategic Partnership Agreement (SPA) as rapidly as possible.[39] J. Barroso also mentioned that the EU wants to maintain economic, trade and political dialogue with Japan and that he would like to finalize the EPA by negotiating it at full speed.[40] Abe summarized the meeting in the following way: 'Actively taking on challenges, openness to other countries, and innovation. In line with these keywords that both Asia and Europe have in common, Japan will continue to impart great inspiration and impact so that these regions become a tremendous growth engine that benefits the world'.[41] This leading role of Japan as a promoter of regional stability and peace is also defined as a key dimension for the strategic relations with the EU. Taking these key issues as a starting point for the discussion between both parties, Japan is leading its negotiations in the economic, trade and political rapprochement with Europe.

During the second office of Abe Shinzō in Japanese Parliament, the EU issue was mentioned 927 times.[42] Among this number, 57 were made by Abe Shinzō. He talked about Europe 27 times in the Budget committee, 18 times during the plenary session, and 11 times in the Special Committee on the Trans Pacific Partnership (TPP).

Abe's reference to the EU concerned mostly the economic cooperation and agreement (Jap. *keizai renkei kyōtei*). Among other related issues were: North Korea's issue, both regarding the missile problem[43] and human rights.[44] Moreover, some of the statements concerned the Japanese government aiming at reaching high quality agreements with the EU, The United States Environmental Protection Agency (EPA) and *Regional Comprehensive Economic Partnership* (RCEP),[45] or the energy security.[46] On September 2016 Abe mentioned the economic issues in the context of the Brexit.[47] The EU was also mentioned in the context of Japanese relations with Germany. This analysis shows that the most important aspect of the EU–Japan cooperation is the economic partnership.

The EU's image in the South Korean media (2013–2017)

In this part of the chapter, an analysis of the media picture of the EU in different aspects will be provided. The research focuses mainly on the information from the years 2013–2017 in English-language newspapers, raising the general issue of the EU. The time range was decided, involving the 19th and the beginning of the 20th National Assembly. The English versions of the Korean newspapers will be provided, due to the author's lack of knowledge of Korean language. The focus on general information on the EU is taken because little is written about this institution, and almost all the news refers to the economic partnership. The main research questions provided for this part of the chapter is: What was the main issue raised in Korean newspapers in the period of 2013–2017? Why did Koreans refer mainly to the economic issues?

The following journals were taken into consideration: 'The Korea Herald', a daily English-language newspaper founded in 1953 and published in Seoul, 'The Hankyoreh', established in 1988 as an alternative to existing newspapers, considered as the South Korean media outlet that journalists trust the most for the ninth time in a row,[48] and 'Korea JoongAng Daily', which runs both original English articles by Korean journalists and translations from Korean papers. The recent news analysis will be provided to show the Korean attitude towards European issues in the time of negotiations between Japan and the EU, as well in the time of North Korean missile tests. The analysis will be limited to the selected articles that directly touch the Korean-European relations.

At the beginning of 2013, the main issue raised in the 'Korea JoongAng Daily' was the economic partnership with the EU. The papers concerned cheaper price tags expectations on Europeans cars from July 1 as their tariffs would be sliced 2.4 percentage points to 3.2 percent as a result of the Korea–European Union FTA,[49] the fears of the possibility of the rising trade conflicts between the U.S., EU and China influence on trade conditions of Korean businesses,[50] the EU price-fixing fines and LG Electronics loss.[51] This shows that the main concerns of Korea and the EU relations are related to the economic issues.

In February 2013, Korea considered the negotiations between the US and the EU on Trans Pacific Partnership (TPP) as an opportunity for its own exports, while being a country 'which has free trade pacts with both regions' and 'should welcome the winds of free and fair trade in the global market'.[52] June 2013 brought some concerns regarding the FTA between Korea and the EU, because of the decrease of exports to EU countries during the period from July 2012 through May 2013.[53] The TTP issue was crucial in the Asian states' policy, and hot for the Korean public opinion, because the disputes whether to join to Partnership were heated in Korean politics. Finally, in December 2013 the government of Korea announced the interest in TPP. The European plot in the media debate on the Korean exports at that time could have been helpful for providing the wider perspective to the TPP doubts spreading through the Korean society.

A significant factor in the EU–Korean relations is also the concern for the key challenges of the 21st century, so the 'Korea JoongAng Daily' reported in September 2014 the meeting between selected diplomats of the EU countries, who claimed that: 'United Nations Climate Summit in New York will serve as a "political impetus" for global climate change, top envoys came to Seoul from the European Union, Germany and the United Kingdom'.[54] Nevertheless, the cooperation between Europe and Asia is not on the optimal level; on the occasion of

President Park Geun-hye's state visit to Italy to attend the Asia-Europe Meeting (ASEM) summit, the Korea International Trade Association (KITA) emphasized the need for extended economic cooperation between the European Union and Asian countries.[55] When the first EU Research & Innovation Day hosted by the EU Delegation to Korea and European Chamber of Commerce in Korea (ECCK) in Seoul took place, the role of Korea as the first Asian partner to make such agreements as Horizon 2020, including technology, innovation, science and technology education was pointed out.[56] This leading role among Asian nations is frequently emphasized in Korean media, as well as the political statements on both sides – European and Korean, which is reported by the journalists. As it was stated in the previous section, it is also realized by Japanese political leaders, such as PM Abe.

An important occasion on which the EU–Korea cooperation was emphasized in media was the 60th anniversary of signing of the Rome Treaties. In the article titled *60th anniversary of Rome Treaties* the most important agreements, such as The *EU–Korea Framework Agreement* (2010), which 'amounts to a political declaration to work together on the key challenges of the 21st century, including fighting climate change, securing peace and human rights, countering terrorism, and ensuring energy security amongst many other issues', as well as the EU–Korea FTA (2011), which became a benchmark in negotiating with other partners were discussed.[57]

A very important aspect of Korea–EU cooperation, mentioned in the article is the military cooperation. Korea's Navy participation in the EU's crisis management operation off the coast of Somalia to fight piracy and secure vital shipping lanes is a concrete example of joint cooperation. This kind of partnership started in 2016 under the EU–Korea agreement on crisis management missions.

The newly elected president Moon Jae-in recently sent special envoys to the key partners of ROK, including the EU. Media stressed that: 'From now on the new administration took office through "people power" and that political legitimacy and transparency have now become very important'.[58] This event demonstrated that the new Korean President added the EU to the usual list of four, namely China, Japan, Russia and the US.[59]

The problem of missiles and nuclear tests of North Korea is an important issue in the EU–Korean relations. Three years ago, 'Korea JoongAng Daily' reported Glyn Ford's, who specializes in North Korean affairs and who is a former member of the European Parliament, visit to DPRK, and cited his opinion that the regime is doing quite well and there are not many signs of instability.[60] This report came just before president Park's participation in the 2014 Nuclear Security Summit, held in The Hague. In the same year, 'The Hankyoreh' informed about the EU efforts in passing a human rights resolution on North Korean attempts to pass its own.[61] This newspaper did not pay any attention to the Korea–EU relations, which were covered, for example, in 'Korea JoongAng Daily'. The North Korean missiles tests were mentioned in the context of European values in 'The Korea Herald' in May 2017. The newspaper refers to several analysts who saw the launch as a test for South Korea's new President Moon Jae-In, a liberal who has said he wants to ease tensions with the North.[62]

In recent times, the European Parliament asked for the intergovernmental discussions on Seoul's failure to implement the terms of international labor rights agreements included in the South Korea–EU FTA, which was widely discussed in Korean media.[63] 'The Hankyoreh' reports that: 'Seoul has drawn criticism for its perceived steps backward with freedom of association, as when it revoked the official status of the Korean Teachers and Education Workers' Union'.[64] This example shows that even if the economic ties seem to be strong and innovative from the Asian perspective, the question of labor and environmental issues still needs an improvement.

Conclusion

In this chapter the emphasis was placed on the East Asian involvement in the cooperation with the EU in the field of economic partnership, but also with regard to the norms and values which can be a common point of discussion for Asian democracies and the EU. After the postwar westernization of both countries: Japan and South Korea, it can be claimed that, despite the cultural differences between European and Asian countries which are often emphasized in different analysis, those countries share democratic and economic values with the EU members. While the economic ties are crucial to enforce the leading position of Asian democracies in the region and globally, the European standards are used as a strengthening point of the negotiation position, while involving the third power into a matter crucial for the Asian country.

The role of an Asian innovator in the EU–Asia relations is played by South Korea, which has become a strong partner for Europe. The EU–South Korea Free Trade Agreement (FTA) that was implemented in July 2011 is the first trade agreement between the EU and an Asian country, which is the source of pride for South Korea to have the role of a leader in strengthening the ties between Asia and the European Community. Aware of this state, Japan is still negotiating its partnership with the EU, and the next great step in these negotiations seems to be within reach, as Japan has been looking for new markets and agreements in the recent time of Trump's presidency and his withdrawal from the Trans Pacific Partnership. The economic ties seem to be crucial in both Asian countries' policy toward the EU. For sure, the Korean side represents the main interest in trade partnership with Europe, whereas Japan, whose politicians often raise economic issues concerning the EU policy in the Parliament, frequently refers to the norms and values, which are synonymous to the postwar Japanese attachment to peace and respect for human rights in the negotiations with its European partners. At the same time, the Japanese Prime Minister is perfectly aware of the leading position of Korea in the partnership with the EU, for the time being. As Asian leading economic parties, Japan and Korea's approach to the cooperation with the EU seems to be crucial in achieving political and economic goals. Nevertheless, in the field of norms and values, Japan, pacified by the US in the postwar era, seems to be leading whereas the ROK still needs to focus on improvement, especially taking into consideration labor and environmental issues, as it was recently stated by Korean newspapers.

It seems that one of the future challenges facing the European–South Korean/Japanese relations is economic cooperation and trade. Nevertheless, in order to be treated as equal partners these countries need cooperation in the area of norms and values that are characteristic for the Western democracies as well accepted by Japan and the ROK. The latest visit of the group of families of Japanese nationals abducted to North Korea, who came to the European Parliament, shows the interest of the East Asian society representatives in putting pressure on North Korea, which is also in the sphere of Japanese and South Korean politicians' interests. Moreover, the South Korean society and interest groups see the possibility of European intervention in the national policy in the areas where violations of labor law are common.

In July, 2017 the European Union and Japan reached an agreement in principle on the main elements of the EU–Japan Economic Partnership Agreement, with a Strategic Partnership Agreement still under negotiation.[65] The sudden acceleration of the EU–Japan talks was caused by Donald Trump's withdrawal from the Trans Pacific Partnership, which was one of the major factors for cooperation between PM Abe and President Barack Obama. The results of the EU–Japan agreement will involve more than 600 million people, 30% of the global economy and 40% of total world trade.[66]

Notes

1 'Text of President Obama's Speech in Hiroshima, Japan', *The New York Times*, 26 May 2016, www.nytimes.com/2016/05/28/world/asia/text-of-president-obamas-speech-in-hiroshima-japan.html, (accessed 25 June 2018).
2 In his speech he also referred to the Koreans.
3 I. Manners, 'Normative Power Europe: A Contradiction in Terms?', *Journal of Common Market Studies*, vol. 2, no. 40, 2002, pp. 235–258.
4 For details see: C. Yanaga, 'Japan: Tradition and Democracy', *Far Eastern Survey*, vol. 17, no. 6, 1948, pp. 68–71; J. Williams, 'American Democratization Policy for Occupied Japan: Correcting the Revisionist Version', *Pacific Historical Review*, vol. 57, no. 2, 1988, pp. 179–202; C-N., Kim, 'Changing Northeast Asia and Korea-US Relations', *The Journal of East Asian Affairs*, vol. 14, no. 1, 2000, pp. 1–36.
5 Meiji period – Meiji Restoration (1868–1912).
6 Yanaga, 'Japan: Tradition and Democracy', p. 68.
7 R. Kisala, 'Asian Values Study', *Nanzan Bulletin*, vol. 23, 1999, https://nirc.nanzan-u.ac.jp/nfile/1914, (accessed 25 June 2018), p. 60.
8 Kisala, 'Asian Values Study', p. 61.
9 B-S. Oh, 'Cultural Values and Human Rights: The Korean Perspective', *FOCUS*, vol. 11, 1998, www.hurights.or.jp/archives/focus/section2/1998/03/cultural-values-and-human-rights-the-korean-perspective.html, (accessed 25 June 2018).
10 M. Mastanduno, 'Economic Statecraft', in S. Smith, A. Hadfield and T. Dunne (eds.), *Foreign Policy. Theories, Actors, Cases*, Oxford, Oxford University Press, 2016, pp. 222–223.
11 J. Harrison, 'An Introduction to the Legal Framework for EU–Korea Relations', in J. Harrison (ed.), *European Union and South Korea: The Legal Framework for Strengthening Trade, Economic and Political Relations*, Edinburgh, Edinburgh University Press, 2013, p. 10.
12 European Commission, 'South Korea', http://ec.europa.eu/trade/policy/countries-and regions/countries/south-korea/, (accessed 25 June 2018).

13 European Commission, 'South Korea'.
14 S.H. Park and M.G. Koo, 'Forming a Cross-Regional Partnership: The South Korea-Chile FTA and Its Implications', *Pacific Affairs*, vol. 80, no. 2, 2007, *East Asian Cross-Regionalism*, p. 264.
15 T. Kashioka, 'The EU's New Stance Vis-À-Vis Japan and the US: Is "Ou-Bei" a Valid Expression Today?', *Japan Review*, vol. 9, 1997, p. 199.
16 Ministry of Foreign Affairs of Japan, *Eighteenth Round of Negotiation on the Japan EU Economic Partnership Agreement (EPA)*, February 2016, www.mofa.go.jp/ecm/ie/page24e_000205.html, (accessed 25 June 2018).
17 Ministry of Foreign Affairs of Japan, *Eighteenth Round of Negotiation on the Japan EU Economic Partnership Agreement (EPA)*.
18 Ministry of Foreign Affairs of Japan, *Meeting amongst Main Ministers and Task-force on the Japan-EU Economic Partnership Agreement*, 18 November 2016, www.mofa.go.jp/ecm/ie/page23e_000448.html, (accessed 25 June 2018).
19 Ministry of Foreign Affairs of Japan, *Japan-EU Strategic Partnership Agreement (SPA)*, www.mofa.go.jp/files/000087793.pdf, (accessed 25 June 2018).
20 *The Plenary Session*, 05 April 2016, http://kokkai.ndl.go.jp/cgi-bin/KENSAKU/swk_dispdoc.cgi?SESSION=6678&SAVED_RID=1&PAGE=0&POS=0&TOTAL=0&SRV_ID=10&DOC_ID=6694&DPAGE=2&DTOTAL=57&DPOS=34&SORT_DIR=1&SORT_TYPE=0&MODE=1&DMY=6987, (accessed 25 June 2018).
21 *The European Business Council in Japan*, www.ebc-jp.com/index.php/about-the-ebc/organisation, (accessed 25 June 2018).
22 *The European Business Council in Japan*.
23 Deutsche Inndustrie- und Handelskammer in Japan, *European Business Council*, http://japan.ahk.de/en/membership/membership-benefits/european-business-council/, (accessed 25 June 2018).
24 European Commission, *South Korea*, http://ec.europa.eu/trade/policy/countries-and-regions/countries/south-korea/, (accessed 25 June 2018).
25 S. Ba, 'South Korea's De Facto Abolition of the Death Penalty', *Pacific Affairs*, vol. 82, no. 3, 2009, p. 416.
26 This country carried out its last execution in 1997.
27 *Framework Agreement Between the European Union and Its Member States, on the One Part, and the Republic of Korea, on the Other Part*, OJ L20 of 23/01/2013, https://eeas.europa.eu/sites/eeas/files/framework_agreement_final_en.pdf, (accessed 25 June 2018).
28 J. Harrison, 'Overview of EU-Korea Framework Agreement', in J. Harrison (ed.), *European Union and South Korea: The Legal Framework for Strengthening Trade, Economic and Political Relations*, Edinburgh, Edinburgh University Press, 2013, p. 151.
29 Delegation of the European Union to Japan, *About the EU Delegation to Japan*, 17 January 2017, https://eeas.europa.eu/delegations/japan/18689/node/18689_en, (accessed 25 June 2018).
30 Ministry of Foreign Affairs, *The Adoption of the Resolution on the Situation of Human Rights in the Democratic People's Republic of Korea (DPRK) at the Third Committee of the 70th Session of the United Nations General Assembly (Statement by Foreign Minister Fumio Kishida)*, 20 November 2015, www.mofa.go.jp/press/release/press4e_000945.html, (accessed 25 June 2018).
31 'U.N. Body Adopts Japan-EU Motion to Document North Korea Rights Abuses for Future Prosecution', *The Japan Times*, 25 March 2017, www.japantimes.co.jp/news/2017/03/25/asia-pacific/u-n-document-north-korean-crimes-prosecution-someday/#.WRoMrIVOJYc, (accessed 25 June 2018).
32 H. Mayer, 'Is It Still Called "Chinese Whispers"? The EU's Rhetoric and Action as a Responsible Global Institution', *International Affairs*, vol. 84, no. 1, 2008, *Ethical Power Europe?*, p. 64.

33 *Abductees' kin seek support in EU at film showing*, https://www3.nhk.or.jp/nhkworld/en/news/20170504_09/, (accessed 25 June 2018).
34 Delegation of the European Union to Japan, *EU-Japan Friendship Week*, 2017 https://eeas.europa.eu/delegations/japan/22284/node/22284_en, (accessed 25 June 2018).
35 Ministry of Foreign Affairs of Japan, *Japan-EU relations*, February 2016, www.mofa.go.jp/files/000033265.pdf, (accessed 25 June 2018).
36 European Commission, *22nd EU-Japan Summit Joint Press Statement, The EU and Japan Acting together for Global Peace and Prosperity*, 07 May 2014, http://europa.eu/rapid/press-release_STATEMENT-14-151_en.htm, (accessed 25 June 2018).
37 European Commission, *22nd EU-Japan Summit Joint Press Statement.*
38 Ministry of Foreign Affairs of Japan, *Prime Minister Shinzo Abe's Attendance at the 10th Summit of the Asia-Europe Meeting (ASEM10), (Outline and Outcomes)*, 20 October 2014, www.mofa.go.jp/erp/ep/page23e_000344.html, (accessed 25 June 2018).
39 Ministry of Foreign Affairs of Japan, *Japan-EU Summit Meeting*, 16 October 2014, www.mofa.go.jp/erp/ep/page18e_000111.html, (accessed 25 June 2018).
40 Ministry of Foreign Affairs of Japan, *Japan-EU Summit Meeting.*
41 Ministry of Foreign Affairs of Japan, *Remarks by Prime Minister Shinzo Abe at the Closing Session of the Asia-Europe Business Forum*, 16 October 2014, www.mofa.go.jp/files/000056216.pdf, (accessed 25 June 2018).
42 Data according to the: *Kokkai kaigi-roku kensaku shisutemu* (Search systems for parliamentary records), http://kokkai.ndl.go.jp, (accessed 9 May 2017). The search was conducted basing on the parliamentary minutes from 28 December 2014 until 28 April 2017.
43 *Budget Committee Meeting*, 24 March 2017, http://kokkai.ndl.go.jp/, (accessed 25 June 2018)
44 *Budget Committee Meeting*, 11 November 2015, http://kokkai.ndl.go.jp, (accessed 25 June 2018).
45 *Budget Committee Meeting*, 01 March 2017, http://kokkai.ndl.go.jp, (accessed 25 June 2018).
46 *Budget Committee Meeting*, 12 March 2015, http://kokkai.ndl.go.jp, (accessed 25 June 2018).
47 *The Plenary Session*, 26 September 2016, http://kokkai.ndl.go.jp/cgi-bin/KENSAKU/swk_dispdoc.cgi?SESSION=38354&SAVED_RID=1&PAGE=0&POS=0&TOTAL=0&SRV_ID=10&DOC_ID=7289&DPAGE=2&DTOTAL=57&DPOS=29&SORT_DIR=1&SORT_TYPE=0&MODE=1&DMY=38581, (accessed 25 June 2018).
48 'For ninth consecutive time, journalists name Hankyoreh most trusted news outlet', *The Hankyoreh*, 18 August 2016, http://english.hani.co.kr/arti/english_edition/e_national/757304.html, (accessed 25 June 2018).
49 'New Rules, Prices for Auto Industry', *Korea JoongAng Daily*, 2 January 2013, http://koreajoongangdaily.joins.com/news/article/article.aspx?aid=2964820, (accessed 25 June 2018).
50 'Korea Falling Prey to Growing Protectionism', *Korea JoongAng Daily*, 30 January 2013, http://koreajoongangdaily.joins.com/news/article/article.aspx?aid=2966331, (accessed 25 June 2018).
51 'EU Fines Help Push LG to Post Quarterly Loss', *Korea JoongAng Daily*, 31 January 2013, http://koreajoongangdaily.joins.com/news/article/article.aspx?aid=2966396, (accessed 25 June 2018).
52 'A New Challenge and Opportunity', *Korea JoongAng Daily*, 19 February 2013, http://koreajoongangdaily.joins.com/news/article/article.aspx?aid=2967346, (accessed 25 June 2018).
53 'After FTA, EU Exports Fall', *Korea JoongAng Daily*, 21 June 2013, http://koreajoongangdaily.joins.com/news/article/article.aspx?aid=2973403, (accessed 25 June 2018).

54 'Ambassadors Talk Climate Change', *Korea JoongAng Daily*, 21 September 2014, http://koreajoongangdaily.joins.com/news/article/article.aspx?aid=2995156, (accessed 25 June 2018).

55 'KITA Calls for More Europe-Asia Cooperation', *Korea JoongAng Daily*, 19 October 2014, http://koreajoongangdaily.joins.com/news/article/article.aspx?aid=2996108, (accessed 25 June 2018).

56 'EU, Korean Leaders See Stronger Innovation Ties', *Korea JoongAng Daily*, 26 March 2015, http://koreajoongangdaily.joins.com/news/article/article.aspx?aid=3002359, (accessed 25 June 2018).

57 '60th Anniversary of Rome Treaties', *Korea JoongAng Daily*, 27 March 2017, http://koreajoongangdaily.joins.com/news/article/article.aspx?aid=3031440, (accessed 25 June 2018).

58 'Pres. Moon Asks Special Envoys to Stress Administration's Origins in "people power" ', *The Hankyoreh*, 17 May 2017, http://english.hani.co.kr/arti/english_edition/e_national/795127.html, (accessed 25 June 2018).

59 'Moon Jae-in Names Special Envoys, Adds Europe to List', *The Korea Herald*, 15 May 2017, www.koreaherald.com/view.php?ud=20170515000833, (accessed 25 June 2018).

60 'EU Rep Says North Korea Felt Stable', *Korea JoongAng Daily*, 20 March 2014, http://koreajoongangdaily.joins.com/news/article/article.aspx?aid=2986655, (accessed 25 June 2018).

61 'N. Korea Planning to Submit Its Own Human Rights Resolution at UN', *The Hankyoreh*, 11 October 2014, http://english.hani.co.kr/arti/english_edition/e_northkorea/659319.html, (accessed 25 June 2018).

62 'N. Korea Missile Test a "threat to international peace": EU', *The Korea Herald*, 14 May 2017, www.koreaherald.com/view.php?ud=20170514000339, (accessed 25 June 2018).

63 'European Parliament Requests Talks on S. Korea's Failure to Uphold Labor Rights', *The Hankyoreh*, 28 March 2017, http://english.hani.co.kr/arti/english_edition/e_international/788344.html, (accessed 25 June 2018).

64 'European Parliament Requests Talks on S. Korea's Failure to Uphold Labor Rights'.

65 *In Focus EU-Japan Economic Partnership Agreement*, http://ec.europa.eu/trade/policy/in-focus/eu-japan-economic-partnership-agreement/, (accessed 25 June 2018).

66 I. Kottasova, 'Why Trump May Hate This New Free Trade Deal,' *CNN Money*, 6 July 2017, http://money.cnn.com/2017/07/06/news/economy/japan-eu-trade-deal-trump/index.html, (accessed 25 June 2018).

10 Critical views on the EU's international relations and identity as shaped by Latin American experiences and perspectives

Şerban Văetişi

Latin America–Europe: a difficult connection

Historical approaches and departures

The connections between Latin America and European Union should be reasonably searched in and formed by the historical links established between the two continental regions since the Spanish voyages to the New World at the end of the 15th century and the subsequent colonizations and administration of the American hemisphere by European empires, Spain and Portugal in the first line. Logical though this may sound, it implies, nevertheless, some faults in the apparent linear connection established once in history and supposedly continued till today with modern Latin American states and regional organizations, on one side, and the modern political union which is the EU, on the other side.

One such blunder is given by the fact that the Spanish and Portuguese viceroyalties existing between the 16th and 19th centuries cannot be characterized or reconsidered in retrospect as types of relations within the logic of the contemporary international system. They functioned rather as extensions of the given European powers and not their partnerships abroad.[1] Even if the colonial cultural-political experience nurtured modern theories grouped under the post-colonial paradigm which may be referred to when attempting to capture a Latin American international specificity as post-colonial region, as we will see further, it cannot be seen as a political model of modern cooperation. On the contrary, it brings back the critical histories of asymmetrical relationships of dominance, with the common practices of discrimination, slavery, exploitation and dependency included.

A second insertion in this pre-20th century international history is occasioned, then, by the fact that other European powers, notably the French and the British, started to develop political interest as a strategy to gain some benefits from building up connections with the Southern American subcontinent, precisely when this region started to rebel against the empire and follow the paths towards independence. In the process, the eventual 'Latin' identity was gradually forged, and the conflicts between different parts of this subcontinent became more evident. While France, as far as the Latin identity and name are concerned, played a significant role, with its imperial ambitions in the subcontinent in the name of a Latin 'natural affinity',[2] in the conflicts emerging in the first stages of independence, the British played mediating roles, as for example in the 1820 war between Argentina and Brazil. This is the actual context within which Latin America became part of the international system, in a modern political sense.[3]

As the Spanish and Portuguese colonial pre-modern models were on decline, starting from the beginning of 19th century inter-American relations increasingly pervaded over the distant Latin American–European ones, and the USA became the major involving power (and actor of development) in the region. This became internationally acknowledged with the proclamation of the Monroe Doctrine. As Thomas O'Brien explains:

> In one sense the proclamation hued close to existing US foreign policy – warning of Europeans' attempts to extend their influence in the Western Hemisphere while asserting the right to create an exclusive preserve of US influence in the region. [. . .] Those attempts were driven by Washington's belief in its own genius for effective governance and their ability to spread the virtues of their system to South America. While they believed they could contribute to the creation of democracies, they also viewed their neighbours from a paternalistic perspective. Latin Americans needed their assistance because they were incapable of executing the great liberal project on their own. The triumph of liberal politics and free market economics required US involvement, and if necessary US intrusion.[4]

So, principally, starting with mid-19th century (after the proclamation of Monroe Doctrine) and, more decisively, after 1900 (following the Spanish–American war and the subsequent transfer to the US of the former Spanish possessions Cuba and Puerto Rico), Latin America became more connected to US models of development (meaning modern political values and modernizing policies, and in some cases direct involvement in internal political affairs and military intervention) than European models.

This North American influence and close relationships continued in the whole 20th century with key moments and developments, such as the construction and the control over the Panama Canal, the involvement in local or continental revolutions, massive investments and, at the institutional level, through such organizations as the Organization of the American States or the North American Free Trade Agreement (NAFTA). It is worth noticing that these relationships were not directed only from the US, but were also embraced and even proposed from Latin America. For example, the Organization of the American States was initially proposed by Simón Bolívar in 1826 as a league of republics. Then, in the 20th century, during the Cold War, a vast program of assistance was developed, combining an anticommunist strategy with aid programs based on modernization projects and infusions of US capital, technology and education, which was meant to provide a capitalist path to development,[5] as well as, starting with the 1980s, an economic project supporting export-oriented industrialization, also encouraged by such international organizations as the International Monetary Fund and the World Trade Organization. Thus, economically, politically and strategically, the US played a key role in exporting its neoliberal model, with some successful cases, such as Chile, on one hand; and in exerting its hegemonic control over countries that did not cooperate or opposed its politics, on the other hand, as manifested in the embargo established against Cuba.

Be they admired or condemned, be they seen as beneficial for the economic developments of the subcontinent, or accused for sovereignty violations in many anti-American discourses popular throughout the region (and not only in anti-American leaders such as the Cuban or Venezuelan presidents), it was the USA that played the actual 'neo-imperial role' in the region, not the former European colonial powers. In the more recent global context, however, the neoliberal model was attached to the hegemonic North, the EU included,[6] and thus, the mutations of 'anti-imperialist opposition', long an opposition against the US interferences in the region only, included also an opposition against the EU.

Nevertheless, despite being heavily inspired by the North American model of development, visible for example in the way in which big Latin American cities develop (more similar to North American cities and not to Western European ones), Latin America also forged its own models of development, at least as theoretical contribution, and in some cases as actual genuine solutions in administration, economy, society and regional cooperation.[7] Besides the alternative approaches on development (different from the global-liberal ones) and political participation (privileging disenfranchised rural or indigenous communities) frequently mentioned in international political studies,[8] various Latin American countries developed genuine social movements, such as the indigenous anti-globalization movements and political practices such as community-based decision making, well integrated in national politics, in different countries in the region. This added a Latin American specificity that continued in the 21st century, which was frequently expressed, at the level of political discourse, as a plain rejection of Anglo-European models of development and, at the level of local practices, as conscious alternatives to the same.[9]

Regional evolutions and EU involvements

With the creation of the European Economic Community and later the EU, the Latin American–European relations remained distant, apart from the political declarations and strategies for partnerships. Moreover, even if analysts expected that with the accession of Spain and Portugal in 1985, transcontinental cooperation will be intensified on the basis of historical and linguistic links, the relationship did not improve as anticipated.[10] Spain and Portugal were primarily interested in their integration process, and Latin American counterparts did not start to perceive Europe differently because of the accession of the two former imperial powers. And this may be the stronger representation (and argument) for the idea of a difficult connection, with its historical explanations included. On the one hand, the original and (more influential) EEC state members lacked the cultural-linguistic ties with Latin America; on the other hand, following their accession, Spain and Portugal lacked interest and political motivation to take initiative within the European Community for a stronger European–Latin American relationship. Regarding the EU strategies, it was principally preoccupied with its neighbouring areas, South-Eastern Europe, the Mediterranean Basin and the Middle East, and developed only sporadic involvement in Latin America prior to the 1990s (such as bilateral economic agreements between individual countries during the 1970s or the more consistent engagement in the mediation process and pacification of the Central American area in the context of conflicts occurring there in the 1980s).[11]

A more animated period of inter-regional agenda began in the 1990s, a period when initiatives for sub-regional dialogues and a more sustained interest for economic association and involvement in issues of human rights appeared. This culminated with the European Commission's proposal for the elaboration of its strategy for Latin America and the creation of a framework for permanent partnership based on regular meetings and dialogue.[12] In Rio de Janeiro in 1999, the first biregional Summit of Heads of States and Government was held, which institutionalised the EU–Latin American and Caribbean countries relations (EU-LAC) and facilitated the creation in 2011 of the Community of Latin American and Caribbean States (CELAC). CELAC became the EU's official counterpart for the region-to-region summit process and strategic partnership.[13] Today, the EU's engagement with CELAC is complemented by bilateral relations with individual countries, while deepening cooperation with other sub-regional or regional groups such as Mercosur (The Southern Common Market), CAN (The Andean Community), CARICOM/CARIFORUM (The Caribbean Community), Pacific Alliance, SICA (Central American Integration System) or UNASUR (Union of South American Nations).[14] These (and other smaller or less significant similar regional blocs, doubling and overlapping membership) correspond to various processes of regional integration, reflecting different levels of development and regional, cultural and political diversity, but also enduring Latin American fragmentation. Such cooperation in most cases provides opportunities for signing agreements and developing dialogue on various topics of mutual interests, not actual transfers of models of integration or institutions.

Although Mercosur (a regional unit created by Argentina, Brazil, Uruguay and Paraguay) could be initially seen as the Latin American integrative type closest to the EU, with its focus on democracy and integration,[15] and possibly further emulating the EU model towards incorporating the entire subcontinent, it was eventually CELAC (which is a simple bloc of countries grouped as a forum for political dialogue) that became the actual EU's counterpart in the Latin American region, because it encompasses virtually all countries in the subcontinent. Nevertheless, CELAC does not bear any resemblance to the EU, and the meetings that the two parts have organized regularly since 1999 are not meant to replicate a European political identity model in the region. They make efforts to respond to problems preoccupying many governments represented by two partners, and we may consider that a major outcome is the creation of the Euro-Latin American Parliamentary Assembly (EuroLat), in 2006.[16]

Finally, the difficulty of connecting the two regions at institutional and community level more deeply, beyond the parliamentary and diplomatic agendas, is caused by the fact that the two actors are not unitary players. While Latin American fragmentation is nothing new, the constant trends of Euro-scepticism, culminating in the Brexit, coupled with renewed references to the concentric circle models of integration and the reinforced North-South division in the context of economic crises, implies a similar fragmentation in the EU. Moreover, this EU fragmentation is doubled by many examples of disagreements among members and the lack of coherence regarding its international agenda and external policy.[17] This is what the editors of the previously quoted book portray when referring to EU as an 'incomplete', 'fragmented' and 'impotent' actor.[18] A surprising scenario, after decades of efforts of regional integration in both Europe and Latin America, would be thus the return to national models of cooperation and development, set around the leading countries. As observed in a report published five years ago, "strengthened by their relative economic stability and size, Brazil and Germany are consolidating their leading position in Latin America and the EU, respectively".[19] Maybe, as this report further suggests, in the future they will create a new "dynamic and a different model of cooperation [. . .] replacing outdated formats with an à la carte menu offering bilateral, mini-lateral and inter-regional cooperation, depending on the issues in question, the international weight of the respective partners and common interests".[20] This will, surely, make the EU model even more distant, and the EU identity will appear even less clear and less appealing. Together with the increasingly more active partnership in Asian and Pacific regions, within the South–South cooperation developed by many Latin American countries,[21] the EU political format and influence will presumably remain at the level of a strategic partnership, as recently reassumed,[22] despite the still popular discourses about a European triumphant model worldwide.

A 'triumphant' model? attractiveness, utopia and transatlanticism in crisis

Throughout the second half of the 20th century, and particularly after the Cold War, the European Union was discursively presented and politically built not so much as an alternative but as a triumphant model. This model was offered both to countries from the former communist bloc pursuing European integration, and as an attractive set of values and norms to be embraced by other regions of the world. This can be coupled with the triumphant model of Western-liberal democracy envisaged and theorized, among others, by Francis Fukuyama at the beginning of the 1990s, but also with strategies of the EU's diplomatic influence on the international scene. At a more specific level of EU political characteristics and identity, it was its 'normative power'[23] that epitomized this acclaimed attractiveness, including such powerful norms as liberty, equality, the rule of law and respect for human dignity and rights, stated in its treaties. Beyond their normative characteristics, these principles were, nevertheless, rather perceived as reflecting an ideal to be attained by different countries and regions on the globe, not the actual active role that EU may really have and play internationally. Several countries in the world remained reluctant to embracing liberal democracy or norms put forward by the European Union as a model. Thus, beyond its triumphalism, it can be probably ultimately seen as a myth[24] or a utopian model,[25] created by the EU about itself, within which its identity is constructed, but no substantial influence is exerted. Moreover, as some authors have more recently observed, its 'perfection' may be the cause of its failure.[26]

Starting from another perspective, then, we should maybe interrogate why the already successful model of 'Transatlantic community' failed to be extended over the entire American continent, Latin America included, despite some attempts, including the recent reference to a 'wider Atlantic space' of expanded cooperation and stronger partnerships with Latin America and the Caribbean, made in the 2016 EU Global Strategy.[27] One basic observation here, going beyond the complexity of the Transatlantic community construction,[28] is that values, norms and socio-political practices were embraced, in this case, by both sides; and that the relationship was constantly a relatively balanced one, being more like a partnership between two equally powerful actors, Western Europe, on one side, and the United States on another side. This was not obviously a usual characteristic of the attempts to launch, now or before, international relationships between any European power or today's European Union, on one side, and Latin America as geopolitical region or individual sub-regional unit or country, on the other side. It was rather assumed and expected that one day, in the process of its 'political maturation', Latin America would embrace 'naturally' European (Euroatlantic) values on the basis of the historical connections and the presumed similar political culture and goals. This underlying thought is visible in the way Latin America has constantly been presented by different political voices and different authors. Roberto Domínguez summarizes this position as follows:

> Beyond historical roots, most of the European and Latin American countries share common positions in international organizations and embrace similar political cultures. Despite nuances and differences, the gaps between the European and Latin American worldviews are considerably smaller in comparison to the diplomatic clashes between the European Union and other regions or countries.[29]

Against this observation, the willingness to adopt or replicate European models is rather limited in Latin America. This certainly does not allow one to regard the model as a triumphant one or to see the Transatlanticism as an ideology to be expanded over the Latin American subcontinent soon, especially now, when even the U.S.–European relationships are rather unenthusiastic.

In the following sections I shall investigate some elements of the 'triumphant' European model at the intersection with its normative power, while attempting to understand its weak, critical and failed points in the way in which it is reflected in discourses, opinions and analyses. For that matter I shall firstly refer to some typical aspects of its rhetoric, then to some critical aspects of the EU–Latin America relations, and finally to the way in which Latin American perspectives perceive the EU's image, model and influence.

European Union and Latin America: an unbalanced relationship

Official EU perspectives

In a book edited by Gerhard Wahlers, Konrad Adenauer Foundation expert on Latin America, published in Spanish in 2007, one may find a synthesis of the EU's official vision of its relations with Latin America.[30] Here, key figures of EU politics, including José Manuel Durão Barroso, at that time president of the European Commission, Angela Merkel, then also president of the European Council, Benita Ferrero-Waldner, European Commissioner for External Relations and European Neighbourhood Policy, Hans-Gert Pöttering, president of the European Parliament or Elmar Brok, chair of the European Parliament Foreign Affairs Committee, express the idea of a "successful European model" in relation with Latin America. The purpose of the publication, clearly stated in its prologue is: "to contribute to a better understanding of the EU, its policy, its historical development, its institutions and its great political strength".[31] Together with the informative and normative aspects of these concepts, exposed throughout the book, one can detect the triumphant tone of presenting a model to be expanded through an ideal partnership.

Hans-Gert Pöttering explains the role of the European Parliament in these relations, in the preface to the publication:

> The European Parliament has always been the 'conscience of the EU's foreign policy', by including in the external relations of the EU issues such as human rights, the lack of democracy, the rights of minorities and the protection of the environment. Thus, at the request of the European Parliament, the EU signs cooperation agreements with third countries when, by virtue of a democratic clause, the partner undertakes to protect its democratic institutions and to respect human rights.[32]

In his contribution to the volume, Elmar Brok further clarifies the principles of this collaboration and expectation:

> With Latin America we share many of our values. However, our strengthened partnership should be used to follow promoting democracy, respect for human rights and fundamental freedoms, transparency, good governance, and principles of the rule of law in a context of genuine multilateralism. It should also serve to strengthen our mutual commitment towards a free market economy, the willingness to share the benefits of globalization, promote justice and social equity as well as integrate developing countries into the

global economy. Both the EU and Latin America have a greater political and economic interest in an increasingly solid strategic partnership.[33]

and then refers to some sectors, such the economic, cultural or security sectors that should follow the European model within a partnership of presumed common interest. The Chair of the European Parliament Foreign Affairs Committee concludes:

For the EU, Latin America is an important international partner. We have to advance in this partnership in order to establish many positive examples on how to put together forces optimally to achieve our common goals. The time has come to strengthen our partnership to respond, lead and shape the new global realities. What we need is this kind of solid cooperation between our regions, in order to master the future challenges. We have to share responsibilities for the sake of our common interests.[34]

Beyond the typical political terminology and rhetoric anyone may recognize here, according to these messages, the Latin American participation in accomplishing the common goal basically stands for following the rules of the European Union. Additionally, the language (Spanish) and place of publication (Santiago de Chile) can be seen as aspects of a putatively propagandistic material.

One illustrative example of the policy carried out by the EU to export its model in Latin America is the transfer of know-how, including the development of instruction-parliamentary activities in Mercosur countries with financial or technical support of the European Commission, visits of the European Parliament to Mercosur countries or Mercosur–EU inter-parliamentary meetings.[35] "These seminars and meetings have offered Mercosur civil servants and parliamentarians the opportunity to become familiar with the European experience in terms of history, institutional design, and competences".[36] Nevertheless, the difficulties or reservations concerning the adoption of the EU models demonstrate the limits of their imitation. Mercosur failed to achieve a real enlargement, in spite of developing a program of associate membership; it is marked by instability and recurrent conflicts between members (e.g. between Brazil and Argentina); and has difficulties in implementing common regulations, such as common external tariff or common norms in domestic law.[37] Overall, it lacks a supra-national objective.[38]

These Latin American inabilities to replicate the EU model contrast with the insistence of the EU discourse on universalistic and shared political values. Moreover, discourses and strategies as those exemplified previously express an unbalanced relationship from its very projection. Despite the diplomatic references to 'common goals', 'shared principles', 'cooperation' and 'partnership', it is the EU who is the issuer of these characterizations and the major actor of this international discourse. This already raises the first questions about the true nature of mutual interest and reciprocity. The second type of questions may be related then to the selection of positive, optimistic and, as already noticed, triumphant notions put together in these considerations. Then, as far as the transfer of European know-how and exportation of an integration model in the case of the institutionalization of a regional parliament in South America (Parlasur) are concerned, despite the good intentions and practices, the limits of replicating a similar political organization are evident. And these are due not only to different social-economic-political contexts or to technical complexities that are very difficult to be exported,[39] but also to the apparent lack of reflexivity in the political intentions concerning the need and desire to impose or replicate political values and models.

Some more reflective positions, taking into consideration the negative or at least critical aspects of imposing the European model, nevertheless can be found, especially in the position of Latin American political leaders and a series of scholar analyses. Referring by now only to the latter, for many authors, typically those grouped under the 'postcolonial authors' term, the unfair, exploitative and dependent relationships established during the colonial times and continued thereafter would constitute the major critical aspect that informs us about the current relation. For these authors, the 'neo-imperial' attempts of the EU to derive benefits from imposing European ideologies and practices in Latin America is blameworthy on the historical grounds and paradigmatic similarities. Some other authors, manifesting their critical attitude, would focus their analyses on specific developments in relation with narrow sectors of social-political, social-cultural or socio-economic reality within which they would identify the same unbalanced relation, even without invoking the colonial paradigm.

Let me refer to a more neutral presentation of the EU–Latin America relations and, then, to these kinds of critical reactions from which I shall later derive some characteristic perceptions concerning the EU with reference to the difficulties of accepting its normative power in Latin America, in relation with some forms of identity construction.

Region-to-region dialogue, stalemate, actorness, post-hegemonic regionalism

A popular way of presenting the relations between two international actors is to focus on bilateral meetings. Given that the EU and Latin America (under the organizational umbrella of EU-LAC, then EU-CELAC summits) started to develop a program of regular summits in 1999, this is a common approach to understand the nature of this relation.[40] This is the major focus of Roberto Domínguez's book titled "EU Foreign Policy towards America".[41] This book is invaluable as it avoids the simple political discursivity exemplified previously, and instead, it formulates the relationship, from its very title, as a type of policy developed by one international actor in relation with another, i.e. it does not assume a horizontal relation (which in fact is unbalanced already at its discursive level, as noticed, apart from comparing the socio-political realities or the socio-economic indicators of the two regions), but an asymmetric one.[42] Accordingly, the presentation of this relation is largely impartial, observing also the critical and negative aspects within, even if they are mostly referring to the limits and failures to accomplish some goals established at the summits, and not specifically to the forms of constructing and imposing normative power.

Domínguez makes efforts in presenting the summits as a region-to-region dialogue, revealing the communicational aspect of the relationship, and thus inherently counteracting the unidirectional ideational-normative discourses coming from the EU's leaders exemplified previously. The summits have served several purposes:

> identifying the convergences and divergences in the interregional dialogue on a biannual basis; setting common positions on items of the international agenda; agreeing on broad mechanisms of cooperation; and evaluating the progress on negotiations between the European Union and sub-regions or individual countries in Latin America.[43]

but, probably, more importantly, helping to "take the pulse of the items on their agenda, which are constantly changing"[44] as a result of local political evolutions and events, which are difficult to anticipate, or set in a fixed normative setting, and of "the way both sides approach the international system".[45] Acknowledging and taking seriously the fact that political agendas are constantly changing and that the visions of international relations are distinct in the two regions, offer important additions to the analysis. Thus, beyond the factual presentation of the biannual summits, with their achievements or less fruitful outcomes, it is important to notice that the relationships should be seen beyond some schematic rules. On the other hand, besides the complex series of interconnections between the EU and Latin America reflected in Domínguez's book, including the presentation of the EU–Latin American inter-regionalism, EU policies developed towards Latin America, the association agreements, the alternative strategies, the regional partners (with Mercosur, CARIFORUM, the Andean Community) and the tense relationships (with Cuba, Venezuela, Argentina, in particular contexts), the overall picture creates an image of a rather inactive collaboration.

Referring to the previously mentioned summits, Celestino del Arenal noticed in 2009: "relations between the EU and Latin America have been practically stagnant since the second half of the 1990s. Despite the holding of five summits since 1999, no significant progress in them has been achieved".[46] And after that, following the international economic crisis and the recent crisis of the European Union itself, this situation remained largely unchanged, an aspect confirmed by a recent report: despite promises of establishing a stronger partnership between the EU and Latin America, "the progress that has been made in this area is not particularly impressive".[47] The latest 2018 report explains that "because, in the first place, there is no single approach to the region, and the majority of EU member states prioritise their relations with certain countries in accordance with an accumulation of bilateral and sectoral interests; and secondly because in general terms the EU has no clear idea of what it wants and expects of Latin America",[48] Arenal's paper suggests a more subtle typology regarding the standstill. Starting from characterizing it "a worrying stalemate" he further identifies several contexts and causes that explain the stagnation: changes on the global stage that "do not favour progress in relations between the EU and Latin America because they have placed the latter in a position of lesser relative importance for both the US and the EU",[49] changes in the European scenario that would not favour the development of bi-regional relations, at the expense of some type of relations with specific countries only,[50] and changes in the Latin American scenario, "in which different kinds of nationalism are returning to the fore with growing strength".[51] Despite these mutations, the relationship may develop well in the future, even for those less confident, Arenal included, in the form of a "new regionally-oriented strategy", comprising ongoing political dialogue, cooperation, and trade.[52]

With these remarks we may return to (the more recent evaluation made by) Roberto Domínguez and notice that the key analysis on inter-regionalism is developed in his book around the notion of *actorness*.[53] In a nutshell, it reveals 'high actorness' (i.e. effective participation of member states in a regional unit with a unitary policy), characterizing the EU, in stark contrast with the 'low level of actorness' (and 'fragmented regionalization')[54] characterizing Latin America. This is a key type of analysis which suggests, ultimately, that the culture and politics of regional construction in Latin America is fundamentally different from that developed in Europe, and, thus, difficult to be compatible with the latter. In addition, as Lincoln Bizzozero points out, the external models of regionalism for Latin America were and are not only European models, but *to the same extent* North American and Japanese models of regionalism.[55] Moreover, this may be combined with the critical idea that the Latin American regionalism, in itself, as demonstrated by Pía Rigiorzzi and Diana Tussie,[56] has a clear tendency towards establishing a post-hegemonic format: "this re-ignition of regionalism is not only post-liberal but also post-hegemonic. [. . .] Agenda-setting capacities have been set free. Changes are already under way shaping alternative spaces, relationships and *identities*".[57]

Surely this observation does not refer only to those anti-capitalist protectionist policies carried out in some countries of the region, such as Bolivia, Ecuador or Venezuela, that begun processes of renationalization of previously privatized companies, and thus acting against the interests of European companies (such as the decree of Bolivian president Evo Morales on nationalizing electrical companies owned by French or British interests),[58] but also to a mechanism of redefining politically the entire region. This forces us to reconsider the very significance of key concepts, including those of 'democracy' or 'development' and even 'Latin America', in an effort to deconstruct and reconstruct a reality that would distinguish itself from any other previous patterns, and thus constitute its own model. This analysis will reach the aspect of identity, and the way in which other identities are perceived.

Democracy, development, alternative visions

Typical political studies on Latin America have long revolved around the notions of 'democratic transition' or 'democratic consolidation'.[59] Since democracy in

Latin America never attained the level of performance encountered in North American and Western European democracies, one may venture to say that this kind of research shall continue. Nevertheless, new perspectives offered by Rigiorzzi and Tussie[60] suggest that the political developments should be assessed in the region through inner evolutions, as in the case of regional integration discussed previously, not within the framework of external standards. Surely there exists a set of features that allow us to recognize democratic practices and consolidated democracy, but beyond the theoretical level, in the world there are dozens of local versions, interpretations and forms put at work in ways that, ultimately, may constitute democratic practices or variants, typical for one region or another. In the case of Latin American countries, as already noted, this tendency towards particular evolutions, independent or contrasting external and international models, and even detaching from regional organizations, is rather its specificity than exception. In this sense, notions such 'political participation' or 'governance' acquire local flavours which are more than cultural exoticisms, resulting often in functional political realities. In this sense in Latin America, at both theoretical and political levels, not only Western democracy, but also the mechanisms through which it was meant to be imposed, such as liberal democracy and capitalist development, are frequently suspected and often rejected, only to be emulated differently on the local level. And this attitude is found not only in charismatic or populist leaders of indigenous, nationalist or communist background, but ultimately diffused at the level of larger acceptance (i.e. as diffused ideology) in both common people and elites.[61] These alternatives are described either as programs to be built up outside of global liberalism or pursuing an alliance between radical social movements and institutionalized political parties[62] while talking about democracy, or as alternative pathways to development, stressing the social and natural components at the expense of investment and profit scenario, when talking about development.[63] That these are not mere outside-the-box ideas is demonstrated by the international influence of some theoretical and practical models built up in (or in relation with) Latin America, including the *dependency theory*[64] and the *theory of post-development*,[65] or the practices of *participatory budgeting*, initially introduced in Brazil[66] or the notion of '*buen vivir*' (good life), expressing a genuine social philosophy and practice, originally rooted in the worldview of the Quechua peoples of the Andes.[67]

When put together, all these local contributions, alternative visions and discordant positions in the international system may appear disconnected from the usual theoretical, ideological and political scheme of European thought and thus they reinforce the preliminary observation about the difficult connection between the two regions. Yes, this is true, but only partially, because all these 'Latin American visions' can be seen as articulated within a larger post-colonial project in which such concepts as 'decoloniality of power'[68] fostered a typical Latin American critical approach following the post-colonial theory developed in Europe in relation with its cultural-political legacies in the former colonial territories throughout the world. Thus, the other side of this Latin American specificity is active in the processes of building a strong theoretical identity as well, and, subsequently, in reflecting other international identities, including European post-colonial identity. Let me refer now to this construction, and then to the perceptions of the EU's identity developed from the Latin American perspective.

Identities at play

A matter of identity: normative identity, post-colonial perspective

Latin America and European Union are subject to different processes, mechanisms and outcomes of identity construction. Considering the matter of 'identity construction' with its historical, cultural and theoretical contributions to identity problematization and critique, Latin America can be easily labelled as having a post-colonial identity. Even if its colonial past and legacy is not consensually considered by scholars its primary element of political recognition and central aspect influencing its political evolution,[69] it is nevertheless a strong factor of identity and identity (de)construction. When Walter Mignolo asked, in an influential contribution to contemporary Latin American studies, what Latin America means, he accounted for the 'colonial matrix of power' behind the invention of this name, and subsequently its political reality.[70] This paradigmatic perspective revealed that Latin America, as a political construction, has to be grasped beyond the theories of Eurocentrism or Third-worldism, towards a reconsideration of its identity. In this sense, 'postcolonial identity' represents a label which is deconstructed through its affirmation, in an attempt to recurrently 'de-colonialise' the representations. The previously quoted 'local contributions, alternative visions and discordant positions in the international system' set its paradigm exactly in this decolonial theory, which has some critical connections with European histories and ideologies, and, thus, is not so radically detached from Europe and the EU, as post-colonial construction of Europe, as we have already noticed.

On the other hand, even though it is a more openly political construction, the European Union has paradoxically a less firmly established and embedded identity, and when referred to as 'European identity' it offers a rather 'elusive meaning',[71] without clear conceptual understanding of its implications for foreign policy and international relations.[72] What is the major, unquestionable identity of European Union? This is still a matter of debate, which, significantly, reinforced the long-time dispute over Europe's boundaries, distinctiveness and mission. "Is Europe a project of Western Christendom? Is it the child of Roman law and empire? Or of the Greek rationality and democratic values? Or of Renaissance humanism and secularism? Or of Enlightenment universalism and cosmopolitanism?".[73] Then, in the last decades of the twentieth century, when the political continental union cemented, the theoretical paradigm within which the EU identity was increasingly more often formulated was a matter of regulations and political mechanisms, expressed through technical vocabulary involving such terms as treaties, enlargement, integration, enforcement, capacity etc. In this construction, the references to the roots of its political project were only rhetorically ascribed, reflecting a form of distant identification between the European heritages and the European Union values.

Furthermore, we may notice that in the case of Latin America, studies attempting to 'demonstrate' that it is a political construction are inevitably *critical* and preponderantly animated by insightful analyses revealing the geopolitical strategies and ideological mechanisms of that construction. In the second case, studies documenting that European Union is a political construction are inherently *descriptive* and plain presentations of banal, unsurprising political reality. And this may be the main reason why the European Union lacks a sense of theoretical dynamism when referring to its identity, as contrasting with the theoretically fruitful Latin American identity.

The two directions that I shall follow in the final sections of the chapter derive from these last observations on 'strong' identity (manifested in historical, cultural, political and theoretical perspectives) in the case of Latin America, and 'weak' (or at least 'unclear' and 'not consistent') identity in the case of Europe (and, by extension, the European Union). Firstly, as suggested by various authors dealing with the EU specificity in international relations, its *normative identity* should be adopted as an internationally valid identity, even if this would also contribute to deconstructing its normative power.[74] Secondly, as an attempt to interpret the Latin American viewpoint on the EU and its identity, its *post-colonial perspective*, derived from its identity outline and some of its more recent theoretical reconsiderations, would seem an appropriate method.[75]

EU identity through Latin American lens

It may be noticed that the EU lacks a strong universal identifier, comparable with the post-colonial identity of Latin America. If for Latin America its colonial history helped to construct such an identity, the European history only complicated the collective identification. The split during the Cold War, the little shared historical experiences (many European countries, including neighbouring states, who were long-time enemies), explicit competition between states in recent times (such as that reflected in the accession waves or the concentric circles) as well as the overall linguistic, religious and cultural fragmentation impeded the creation of a unifying identity within the EU. Moreover, for an external perception, the EU frequently appears as an artificial/bureaucratic organization. Nevertheless, because Latin American identity can be built around its post-colonial status, then maybe its post-colonial perspective should be regarded as important for understanding not only its positioning in international relations, but also its perception of the EU's identity. In this sense I refer to the post-colonial perspective when talking about the EU's identity through a Latin American lens.

A new kind of research dealing with European identity surfaced in European studies around 2008–2010 in the framework of such projects as "Normative Issues of Regional and Global Governance" or "The External Image of the European Union".[76] It differed from previous approaches in focusing on the external image of the EU, or as Lorenzo Fioramonti and Sonia Lucarelli directly asked themselves: 'How do the Others see us?'.[77] Their conclusion, "the EU does not seem to be widely regarded as a 'normative power'; besides the recognition of the EU as a model of regional integration, the EU tends to be regarded as a (neo-) liberal power, not too dissimilar from the USA",[78] suggests that further investigation of the EU's image in Latin America should take into consideration a distinction between its pragmatic and ideological underpinnings. The study on Mexico's views of the EU, published in a collection of studies about the "external perceptions of the European Union as a global actor", coordinated by the same Lucarelli and Fioramonti, demonstrates that the EU is viewed as a crucial partner by Mexico and the upgrading of their bilateral trade partnership is an important element of debate in this country.[79] Three ideas derive from the conjunction of the two perceptions: the prevalence of 'practical versus ideological' perception; the different levels of constructing perceptions; and the active characteristics of this construction.

Firstly, the practical aspects are highlighted mainly in bilateral relations, as revealed by those between the EU and an individual country, i.e. not at a regional or continental level. Secondly, the ideological perceptions tend to emerge when referring to geopolitical relations involving the continental or regional level. Then, contrary to the impression that Latin American public interest for the EU is weak or even absent, one may still notice that Mexicans, for example, are actively preoccupied with their country's European relations. And this is happening in a country where, more than in the case of other Latin American countries, news about the US are typical headlines. But the two aspects may be related. As Alejandro Chanona pointed out in his contribution to the previously mentioned book: "The Mexican public opinion's interest in the EU can be explained by the fact that most Mexicans feel an affinity for Europe and view it as an international counterweight to the USA".[80] This is the point where the pragmatic and ideological perceptions meet in a template of options from which Mexicans distribute their preferences in relationship with the two major international actors. In addition, there are political and global events and evolutions that may influence and counterbalance these perceptions. As Chanona explains, based on a public opinion barometer carried out between 1995 and 2005 (*Latinobarómetro*):[81]

> In 1995, only 12 per cent of Mexicans had a 'good' opinion of the EU. Yet, ten years later, this view was held by almost 60 per cent. It is in 1999, the year of the First EU-LAC Summit, that the first significant increase in favourable public opinion can be found, doubling the preferences of previous years. Since the turn of the millennium, favourable opinions of the EU continued to rise incrementally. This trend can be explained by two specific factors: first, the signing of the Global Agreement increased Mexicans' interest in and awareness of the EU; second, there was a convergence of values between the Mexican and the European society, especially around democracy and human rights.[82]

Certainly, the perception of the EU cannot be reduced to 'good opinions' and how numerous they have been over the years. As noticed in the previously quoted fragment it is more important to understand the factors that contribute to these perceptions. Besides the already mentioned aspects which affect perception, it is relevant then to consider different categories of *people* who express their opinions about the EU (Chanona presents, in corresponding subchapters, the perspectives of the Mexican governmental elites, political parties, business and civil society) and what elements are put together in building each group's perception about the EU, together with different categories of *topics* preoccupying Latin Americans that may be reflected in the EU's values and identity.

For the latter aspect a more useful approach is the analysis of the ways in which the two continents relate to the global agenda. For example, talking about the Brazil–EU relations, in a recent re-evaluating book on the subject, Gomes Saraiva concludes:

> it is possible to identify a coincidence of values in the global and regional agenda, such as those dealing with democracy and human rights (albeit in a minimalist sense); peacekeeping; the focus on global and regional multilateralism; the support for initiatives to build regional governance; regional stability, the fight against poverty and global and regional asymmetries; although the coincidences, the visions, the objectives and, above all, the tools to achieve them are different and the divergences are marked.[83]

This idea is then explicitly related with rejecting the EU normative power model: "while Brazil shares values with the European Union and follows Western standards internally, its diplomacy does not recognize the EU as a normative power of the international order".[84]

Moreover, in the case of the EU's articulation of power in inter-regional relations as well as in some specific policies, the EU's behaviour could be regarded as driven by imperial-like aspirations or practices. In this sense, for example, a study about the EU's active promotion of regional integration in Latin America, analyses the EU's external power projection in the logic of *imperial aspirations*,[85] and the research on the EU's external environmental policy characterizes its claims and strategies in the fields of deforestation and bio-fuels as *soft-imperial*.[86]

What is the EU? (a Latin American post-colonial response)

One should not expect a direct answer to this last question but, in the logic of the suggested post-colonial perspective, an indirect one. In many studies dealing with Latin America, the issue of its post-colonial identity is mirrored in the identity of other regions, typically – regions that exerted international influence and developed hegemonic policies in relation with Latin America, such as Europe or the US.

In a book titled *Territories of Difference*, Arturo Escobar places his analysis deliberately outside the hegemonic Euro–North American frame of reference in international geopolitics, by highlighting the importance and roles played by the Southern hemisphere, the Southern regions and countries, and the South–South relation.[87] Even the Atlantic ocean is intentionally decentred in his analysis, for which the Pacific region is seen more suitable for his political, economic and social commentary. Through this analytic process of differentiation, Escobar (re)constructs territories unknown, unnoticed or downplayed in international politics before, because of historical evolutions or modern strategies that placed Latin America in an inferior/subaltern position in the colonial/post-colonial history and on the current global North–South divide. Moreover, the analysis favours models of sub-national rather than supra-national governance, seeing in the indigenous movements, the Afro-Latino movements or the participatory practices of governance more suitable models for Latin American politics and Latin American identity, obviously different from the European ones. In this perspective, not only the EU's identity model is overlooked, but the EU's identity is indirectly (and negatively) revealed.

In the same vein, when Walter Mignolo debates the 'the idea of Latin America' he also throws the light on how Europe, the Euro-North American nexus and the European Union constructed a politically, economically, culturally and racially inferior counterpart: Latin America.[88] The interpretive efforts to deconstruct this mechanism disclose significant identity aspects of the constructor itself. Thus, the EU is perceived through these critical lens not only as racist, non-cooperative or possessing other similar superficial critical traits (paradoxical characteristics, because they contradict the EU's principles), but also as a user of a 'grammar of coloniality' that continues to be the logic of international relationships in post-colonial times.

The 'contrasting identities' anticipated in the previous sections of this chapter may be seen, therefore, not only as *a contrast* between two different constructivist discourses, but also as an analytical strategy, adopted by such authors as Escobar and Mignolo, *to contrast* between the two 'producers' and 'products' of discourses and their finality, in order to reveal differences that are useful for understanding the condition of both, in historical and contemporary perspectives. Ultimately, as Walter Mignolo highlights in another contribution, Latin America and the system of international relations need a 'grammar of decoloniality' that would 'delink' subaltern regions from the logic and mechanisms of coloniality.[89] Drawing on an idea originally put forward by the Peruvian sociologist Aníbal Quijano, Mignolo further deconstructs the very notion of identity as built on the still surviving colonial imagination.

Thus, Mignolo in this ultimate critical analysis of the fate of Latin America and the international identities at play, is not only against the Eurocentric model of civilization and modernity, as expressed in a preliminary criticism by Quijano,[90] or against the Western-liberal model of development as formulated in the theory of post-development by Escobar,[91] but also against the continuing identity construction of international actors on the basis of relationships and strategies reminding the colonial dominance and the coloniality of power.

Conclusions

The post-colonial paradigm illustrated by the authors discussed in the last section of this chapter is probably best suited to animate the reflexivity that Ian Manners talked about in his analysis of the EU's international identity myth.[92] The 'contrasting identities' approach, sketched in my chapter, adopted some ideas from these post-colonial Latin American perspectives, but principally built its arguments on noticing the different political integrative practices and discursive constructions. In the case of Latin America we could primarily notice some regional specificities, dissimilar from the EU's models, together with some specific political practices difficult to be compatible with the European ones. Europe is not something that the Latin American countries need, but rather an option they can take into consideration at their discretion. Surely, the local specificity and hesitation to embrace European models in the case of Latin America may be analysed as part of its post-colonial identity. Regarding the European Union identity, then, we saw that its normative power cannot generate enough discursive attraction and ideological solidity to forge an unquestionable international (normative) identity. Be it considered a myth, a utopian model, a too perfect model or a criticizable identity in the sense of post-colonial deconstruction, according to various authors' interpretations, the EU's identity is ultimately reflecting the fragile European collective identity, also revealed, as a matter of fact, by the recent EU crises. As already noticed in previous studies, the normative power construction may disempower the EU's political role as a global power.[93] I would add, based on my analysis, that this construction (and its deconstruction, as suggested by Latin American post-colonial scholars working on a project of decolonizing the Latin American identity) also debilitate its identity. The apparent paradox behind this assertion may be explained by the idea that a unified European identity still requires the figure of the 'colonial Other',[94] but also by the observation that universalistic and hegemonic values, as those put forward by the EU, diminished their international appeal. Ultimately, probably the EU would need to rebuild its foreign policy, international diplomacy and global strategy on different principles, other than that of exporting its values and model.

Notes

1 J. Barton, *A Political Geography of Latin America*, London-New York, Routledge, 2003, p. 23.
2 M. Gobat, 'The Invention of Latin America: A Transnational History of Anti-Imperialism, Democracy, and Race', *American Historical Review*, vol. 118, no. 5, 2013, p. 1349.
3 R. Burr, 'The Balance of Power in Nineteenth-Century South America: An Exploratory Essay', in J. Domínguez (ed.), *Latin America's International Relations and Their Domestic Consequences*, London-New York, Routledge, 1994, pp. 1–24.
4 T. O'Brien, 'Inter-American Relations in Historical Perspective', in P. Rigiorzzi and C. Wylde (eds.), *Handbook of South American Governance*, London-New York, Routledge, 2018, p. 86.
5 O'Brien, 'Inter-American Relations in Historical Perspective', p. 91.
6 Barton, *A Political Geography*, p. 96.
7 Barton, *A Political Geography*, pp. 23–28, 155–182.
8 M. Nilsson and J. Gustafsson (eds.), *Latin American Responses to Globalization in the 21st Century*, Basingstoke-New York, Palgrave Macmillan, 2012.
9 Barton, *A Political Geography*, p. 24.

10 H. Smith, 'Actually Existing Foreign Policy or Not?: The EU in Latin and Central America', in J. Peterson and H. Sjursen (eds.), *A Common Foreign Policy for Europe? Competing Visions of the CFSP*, London-New York, Routledge, 1998, pp. 166–167.
11 R. Domínguez, *EU Foreign Policy Towards Latin America*, Basingstoke-New York, Palgrave Macmillan, 2015, p. 55.
12 Domínguez, *EU Foreign Policy Towards Latin America*, p. 56.
13 ‚European External Action Service, *EU-CELAC Relations*, https://eeas.europa.eu/headquarters/headquarters-homepage_en/13042/EU-CELAC%20relations, (accessed 25 June 2018).
14 European External Action Service, *EU-CELAC Relations*.
15 Domínguez, *EU Foreign Policy Towards Latin America*, p. 127.
16 B. Luciano, 'Inter-Parliamentary European Union – Latin American Caribbean (EU-LAC) Relations and the Increasing Political Convergence among Latin American Regional Parliaments (2006–15)', *Parliaments, Estates and Representation*, vol. 37, no. 3, 2007, pp. 318–334.
17 M. Knodt and S. Princen (eds.), *Understanding the European Union's External Relations*, London-New York, Routledge, 2003.
18 S. Princen and M. Knodt, 'Understanding the EU's External Relations: The Move from Actors to Processes', in M. Knodt and S. Princen (eds.), *Understanding the European Union's External Relations*, London-New York, Routledge, 2003, pp. 193–206.
19 S. Gratius, 'Europe and Latin America: In Need of a New Paradigm', *Working Paper*, vol. 116, 2013, http://fride.org/download/wp_116_europe_and_latin_america.pdf, (accessed 25 June 2018), p. 2.
20 Gratius, 'Europe and Latin America', p. 18.
21 Gratius, 'Europe and Latin America', p. 8.
22 S. Santander et al., 'The EU-Latin American Strategic Partnership: State of Play and Ways Forward', European Parliament, Policy Department, Directorate-General for External Policies, 2017.
23 I. Manners, 'Normative Power Europe: A Contradiction in Terms?', *Journal of Common Market Studies*, vol. 40, no. 2, 2002, pp. 235–258; T. Forsberg, 'Normative Power, Once Again: A Conceptual Analysis of an Ideal-Type', *Journal of Common Market Studies*, vol. 49, no. 6, 2011, pp. 1183–1204.
24 I. Manners, 'Global Europa: Mythology of the European Union in World Politics', *Journal of Common Market Studies*, vol. 48, no. 1, 2010, pp. 67–87.
25 K. Nicolaïdis and R. Howse, 'This Is My EUtopia. . .: Narrative as Power', *Journal of Common Market Studies*, vol. 40, no. 4, 2002, pp. 767–792.
26 O. Ilany, 'The EU Was Too Perfect. That's Why It's Now Falling Apart', *Haaretz*, 10 November 2017, www.haaretz.com/opinion/.premium-the-eu-was-too-perfect-that-s-why-it-s-now-falling-apart-1.5464275, (accessed 25 June 2018).
27 European External Action Service, *Shared Vision, Common Action: A Stronger Europe. A Global Strategy for the European Union's Foreign and Security Policy*, Brussels, 2016, p. 37, http://eeas.europa.eu/archives/docs/top_stories/pdf/eugs_review_web.pdf, (accessed 25 June 2018).
28 For a more detailed discussion on this topic see our study Ş. Văetişi, 'Ideological Constructions and Sociological (Mis)Understandings in International Relations. The Case of "Transatlantic Community"', *Studia UBB Europaea*, vol. 62, no. 3, 2017, pp. 239–266.
29 Domínguez, *EU Foreign Policy Towards Latin America*, p. 3.
30 G. Wahlers (ed.), *América Latina y La Unión Europea*, Santiago de Chile, Konrad Adenauer Stiftung, 2007.
31 B. Vogel, 'Prólogo', in G. Wahlers (ed.), *América Latina y La Unión Europea*, Santiago de Chile, Konrad Adenauer Stiftung, 2007, p. 10.
32 H.-G. Pöttering, 'Prefacio', in G. Wahlers (ed.), *América Latina y La Unión Europea*, Santiago de Chile, Konrad Adenauer Stiftung, 2007, p. 18.

33 E. Brok, 'América Latina y sus relaciones con la Unión Europea', in G. Wahlers (ed.), *América Latina y La Unión Europea*, Santiago de Chile, Konrad Adenauer Stiftung, 2007, p. 64.
34 Brok, 'América Latina y sus relaciones con la Unión Europea', p. 69.
35 C. Dri, 'Limits of the Institutional Mimesis of the European Union: The Case of the Mercosur Parliament', *Latin American Policy*, vol. 1, no.1, 2010, pp. 52–77, see especially pp. 60–65.
36 Dri, 'Limits of the Institutional Mimesis of the European Union', p. 61.
37 Domínguez, *EU Foreign Policy Towards Latin America*, p. 127.
38 M. Contreras, P. de Lombaerde and A. Sampaio, 'El Mercosur y la Unión Europea: ¿Qué queda del poder normativo?', in G. Molano-Cruz (ed.), *La Unión Europea en América Latina y El Caribe: 1945–2012. Lógicas y Políticas de un Actor Global*, Bogotá, Universidad Sergio-Arboleda, 2015, p. 324.
39 Dri, 'Limits of the Institutional Mimesis of the European Union', p. 71.
40 Summits have been held biannually in different countries on both continents since 1999 except in 2017.
41 R. Domínguez, *EU Foreign Policy Towards Latin America*.
42 The asymmetry was also noticed by Clarissa Dri while comparing Parlasur and the European Parliament, see Dri, 'Limits of the Institutional Mimesis of the European Union', pp. 65–70.
43 Domínguez, *EU Foreign Policy Towards Latin America*, p. 52.
44 Domínguez, *EU Foreign Policy Towards Latin America*, p. 52.
45 Domínguez, *EU Foreign Policy Towards Latin America*, p. 52.
46 C. del Arenal, 'Relations Between the EU and Latin America: Abandoning Regionalism in Favour of a New Bilateral Strategy', *Working Paper*, vol. 39, 2009.
47 C. Malamud (coord.), 'Why Does Latin America Matter?', *Real Instituto Elcano*, vol. 22, 2018, www.realinstitutoelcano.org/wps/wcm/connect/508f77cc-f90e-42db-89e6-344155289971/informe-elcano-22-why-does-latin-america-matter.pdf?MOD=AJPERES&CACHEID=508f77cc-f90e-42db-89e6-344155289971, (accessed 25 June 2018), p. 65.
48 Malamud, 'Why Does Latin America Matter?', p. 65.
49 del Arenal, 'Relations Between the EU and Latin America', p. 4.
50 del Arenal, 'Relations Between the EU and Latin America', p. 8. This observation is reasserted and exemplified in a more recent FRIDE Report (Gratius, 2013), cited *supra*, on note no. 19.
51 del Arenal, 'Relations Between the EU and Latin America', p. 12.
52 del Arenal, 'Relations Between the EU and Latin America', pp. 18–26.
53 Domínguez, *EU Foreign Policy Towards Latin America*, pp. 8–27.
54 L. Bizzozero, 'América Latina a Inicios de la Segunda Década del Siglo XXI: Entre el Regionalismo Estratégico y la Regionalización Fragmentada', *Revista Brasileira de Política Internacional*, vol. 54, no. 1, 2011.
55 Bizzozero, 'América Latina a Inicios de la Segunda Década del Siglo XXI', pp. 31, 34, 38
56 P. Rigiorzzi and D. Tussie (eds.), *The Rise of Post-hegemonic Regionalism. The Case of Latin America*, Berlin, Springer, 2012.
57 Rigiorzzi and Tussie, *The Rise of Post-hegemonic Regionalism*, p. 10, my italics.
58 C. Malamud, 'Las relaciones entre la Unión Europea y América Latina en el Siglo XXI: Entre el Voluntarismo y la Realidad', *Working Paper*, vol. 6, 2010, p. 12, www.plataformademocratica.org/Arquivos/Las%20relaciones%20entre%20la%20union%20europea.pdf, (accessed 25 June 2018).
59 R. Millett, J. Holmes and O. Pérez, *Latin American Democracy: Emerging Reality or Endangered Species?*, London-New York, Routledge, 2014.
60 Rigiorzzi and Tussie, *The Rise of Post-hegemonic Regionalism*.
61 See Barton, *A Political Geography*, chapter. 5, for this idea.

62 L. Costilla, 'Revisitando al Estado. Las Especificidades Actuales del Estado en América Latina', in T. Castro Escudero and L. Costilla (eds.), *Poder y Política en América Latina*, México D.F. y Buenos Aires, Siglo XXI Editores, 2005, pp. 50–86, see p. 76.
63 J. Cupples, *Latin American Development*, London-New York, Routledge, 2013.
64 See M. Rivera-Quiñones, 'Dependency Theory and South American Governance in Post-Neoliberal Times', in P. Rigiorzzi and C. Wylde (eds.), *Handbook of South American Governance*, London-New York, Routledge, 2018, pp. 45–55.
65 A. Escobar, *Encountering Development: The Making and Unmaking of the Third World*, Princeton, Princeton University Press, 1995.
66 Certainly, the aim of participatory budgeting is not only economic, but it also attempts at "strengthening social actors and to thereby reinforce democracy" as explained by S. Donoso, 'Social Movements and Governance in South America', in P. Rigiorzzi and C. Wylde (eds.), *Handbook of South American Governance*, London-New York, Routledge, 2018, p. 336.
67 See A. Acosta, *El Buen Vivir: Sumak Kawsay, Una Oportunidad Para Imaginar Otro Mundo*, Barceona, Icaria, 2013. 'Buen vivir' is not only a manifesto or a theory of social practices, it is effectively utilized in jurisprudence in environmental regulations. Ecuador has a governmental secretariat for 'buen vivir' and was the first country in the world to include rights of nature in its constitution, in 2008, based on the same concept.
68 A. Quijano, 'Coloniality of Power, Eurocentrism, and Latin America', *Nepantla: Views from South*, vol. 1, no. 3, 2000, pp. 533–580; W. Mignolo and A. Escobar (eds.), *Globalization and the Decolonial Option*, London-New York, Routledge, 2010.
69 See J. Klor de Alva, 'The Postcolonization of the (Latin) American Experience: A Reconsideration of "Colonialism," "Postcolonialism," and "Mestizaje"', in G. Prakash (ed.), *After Colonialism: Imperial Histories and Postcolonial Displacements*, Princeton, 1995, pp. 241–275.
70 W. Mignolo, *The Idea of Latin America*, Hoboken, Blackwell Publishing, 2005.
71 U. Sedelmeier, 'Collective Identity', in W. Carlsnaes, H. Sjursen and B. White (eds.), *Contemporary European Foreign Policy*, London, Thousand Oaks-New Delhi, Sage, 2004, p. 123.
72 Sedelmeier, 'Collective Identity', p. 123.
73 A. Appadurai, 'Democracy Fatigue', in H. Geiselberger (ed.), *The Great Regression*, Cambridge, Polity Press, 2017, p. 12.
74 See I. Manners and R. Whitman, 'Towards Identifying the International Identity of the European Union: A Framework for Analysis of the EU's Network of Relationships', *Journal of European Integration*, vol. 21, no. 3, 1998, pp. 231–249.
75 Latin America's post-colonial identity as relevant identity in international relations was theorized among others by the previously mentioned Aníbal Quijano, Walter Mignolo and Arturo Escobar, who considered it a meaningful paradigm, especially in relation with the notions of development and modernity. As a theory and a method of interpretation in International Relations, the post-colonial paradigm already has a clear established position.
76 Projects developed within 'Global Governance, Regionalisation and Regulation: the Role of the EU (GARNET)', EU Sixth Framework Program, 2005–2010.
77 L. Fioramonti and S. Lucarelli, '"How Do the Others See Us?" European Political Identity and the External Image of the EU', in F. Cerutti and S. Lucarelli (eds.), *The Search for a European Identity. Values, Policies and Legitimacy of the European Union*, London-New York, Routledge, 2008, pp. 193–210.
78 Fioramonti and Lucarelli, 'How Do the Others See Us?', p. 207.
79 L. Fioramonti and S. Lucarelli, 'Conclusion. Self-Representations and External Perceptions – Can the EU Bridge the Gap?', in S. Lucarelli and L. Fioramonti (eds.), *External Perceptions of the European Union as a Global Actor*, London-New York, Routledge, 2010, p. 220.

80 A. Chanona, 'So Far, So Close? Mexico's Views of the EU', in S. Lucarelli and L. Fioramonti (eds.), *External Perceptions of the European Union as a Global Actor*, London-New York, Routledge, 2010, p. 124.
81 *Corporación Latinobarómetro*, www.latinobarometro.org, (accessed 25 June 2018).
82 Chanona, 'So Far, So Close?', p. 123.
83 M. Gomes Saraiva, 'Brasil, América Latina e a União Europeia Diante de Novas Agendas Globais', in F. Dane (ed.), *A União Europeia Alargada em Tempos de Novos Desafios*, Rio de Janeiro, Konrad Adenauer Stiftung, 2014, p. 162.
84 Gomes Saraiva, 'Brasil, América Latina e a União Europeia Diante', p. 157.
85 M. García, 'The European Union and Latin America: "Transformative Power Europe" versus the Realities of Economic Interests', *Cambridge Review of International Affairs*, vol. 28, no. 4, 2015, pp. 621–640.
86 S. Afionis and L. Stringer, 'The Environment as a Strategic Priority in the European Union–Brazil Partnership: Is the EU Behaving as a Normative Power or Soft Imperialist?', *International Environmental Agreements: Politics, Law and Economics*, vol. 14, no. 1, 2014, pp. 47–64.
87 A. Escobar, *Territories of Difference. Place, Movements, Life, Redes*, Durham, Duke University Press, 2008.
88 Mignolo, *The Idea of Latin America.*
89 W. Mignolo, 'Delinking. The Rhetoric of Modernity, the Logic of Coloniality and the Grammar of De-Coloniality', in W. Mignolo and A. Escobar (eds.), *Globalization and the Decolonial Option*, London-New York, Routledge, 2010, p. 307.
90 Quijano, 'Coloniality of Power'.
91 Escobar, *Encountering Development.*
92 Manners, 'Global Europa', p. 76.
93 M. Pace, 'The Construction of EU Normative Power', *Journal of Common Market Studies*, vol. 45, no. 5, 2007, p. 1043.
94 S. Castro-Gómez, 'The Missing Chapter of Empire: Postmodern Reorganization of Coloniality and Post-Fordist Capitalism', in W. Mignolo and A. Escobar (eds.), *Globalization and the Decolonial Option*, London-New York, Routledge, 2010, p. 284.

11 American think tanks' perspective of the European identity in foreign affairs

Bartosz M. Rydliński

Introduction

The relations between Europe and the United States are special. This is due to a certain political inability to separate both continents, resulting from Europe's perspective regarding the colonization of America, as well as the perspective of the US in relation to the European heritage. Also, the rebellion against the economic dependence from the Old Continent was a defining element of American political identity. The national anthem of the United States of America – "The Star-Spangled Banner" – refers to the British–American war and the heroic defense of Fort McHenry in Baltimore by the independence fighters. Currently one can say that relations with Europe have specific characteristics. This is the case when it comes to US foreign policy but also the American pop culture, in which we can frequently find references to European roots. A similar phenomenon is visible when it comes to politics, where Europe, and more specifically the European Union, is depicted as a unique example of totally different subjects of international relations, which even leads to new and specific theoretical depictions in terms of research. For example, there is a tension between the (neo)realistic approach (which is a popular way of understanding the international reality in the USA, assuming the primacy of national interest and the inevitability of conflicts with other countries) versus the liberal approach (which is almost idealistic and omnipresent in the European – here: in relation to the European Union – narration) to international relations.[1] It is characterized by the belief in the possibility of cooperation in international relations and the renunciation of violence in foreign policy. In a sense, the European identity in matters of foreign policy as seen by the Americans will be visible in the presentation of the reception of the idealism of the European Union by geopolitical neo-realists from the USA. This procedure will be more than interesting, as the time frame of this chapter will be marked by the beginning of the Russian–Ukrainian conflict (beginning on February 23rd, 2014) and the presidential elections in the USA (which ended on November 8th, 2016). Within those two years we witnessed many events of high importance in the international arena. They will help to analyze the role and significance of Europe on the international arena from an American perspective. We refer, inter alia, to the war in Ukraine, the nuclear agreement with Iran, the series of terrorist attacks in Paris, Brussels, Berlin and London, the refugee crisis and the war in Syria. Part of the previously mentioned topics will be a separate case study aimed at presenting the American evaluation of European Union politics.

The main hypotheses of this study refer to both normative and (neo)realistic approaches in international relations during the analyzed period. Both the European Union and the United States failed to prevent the Russian aggression on Ukraine or development of internal fights in Syria. Both the diplomatic and military capabilities of Europe and America failed in these situations. The United States did not even send its troops to these countries as it did many times in the past when facing similar decisions. We could assume that neither theory of international relations is applicable in reality.

The main aim of this chapter is to show the place and importance of Europe and its political identity in the global order of the American think-tank discourse. How do American institutions see the role of Europe in the modern global order? How is the EU's policy perceived? What European activity would be expected by the US? These are the main questions which will be answered in this chapter.

In this chapter the author aims to make a comparative study of three institutions based in Washington D.C. who deal with foreign policy in relation to the USA and the EU, namely the Brookings Institution, Carnegie Endowment for International Peace and the Atlantic Council. Each of these institutions has an acknowledged position among expert institutions dealing with the previously mentioned topics, both in the United States, and globally. By means of the comparative method, and the quality analysis of the content, the author will present how Europe, its international importance, and its identity, are perceived from the perspective of American expert institutions in terms of foreign policy. Is the foreign policy of the EU considered effective and providing measurable effects? How is the international activity of Europe regarded by these American think tanks who deal with foreign policy? What is the perception of the role and identity of the European Union among American analytical centers?

Why think tanks?

This question will be posed by many readers of this chapter. It will be natural and justified, as during the analyzed period we witnessed a number of political meetings of high rank, common US–EU activities on the international arena or concurrent opinions in the field of foreign and security policy. Also the election campaign in the United States, both within the Democratic Party and the Republican Party, as well as between the nominated candidates from those parties in the race to the White House could be used as a reference point and a source of research material. The author of this chapter focused on those think tanks in order to show the expert-analyst voice, which is seldom analyzed by political scientists.[2] Think tanks are niche and specific political bodies and their voice is often neglected both by the decision makers themselves and researchers of political science and international relations. The comparison of their perspective and the official opinions and actions of the US government will also allow us to make an inner American critical analysis and to answer the question to what extent the voice of Brookings Institution, Carnegie Endowment for International Peace and Atlantic Council had content-related values and whether their arguments or theses found confirmation in the politics of the American administration.

Think tanks have many definitions. For the use of this chapter we can quote the description provided by James McGann, who writes:

> Think tanks or public policy research, analysis, and engagement institutions are organizations that generate policy-oriented research, analysis, and advice on domestic and international issues in an effort to enable policymakers and the public to make informed decisions about public policy issues.[3]

The aspect of policy-oriented advice will be highly important to us, as at the end of this chapter we will be able to state not only how the European identity in international relations is described, but also to what extent opinions and suggestions formulated by think tanks were identical with the policy of the US Department of State.

The Brookings Institution

The Brookings Institution is one of the oldest American think tanks. It was founded in 1916. It is commonly considered to be not only the best and most influential think tank in the area of international relations in the United States of America, but also in the world.[4] From the very beginning of the Russian-Ukrainian crisis this think tank was extremely active in the field of analysis and held conferences on this topic. As far as the first phase of this conflict is concerned, analysts from Brookings were more focused on its significance for the foreign policy of the US and the global security system, but after some time they started to recognize the significance of their European partner in the whole process. After the signing of the EU–Ukraine Association Agreement Steven Pifer wrote: "The European Union wants stability on its borders. It can use the Association Agreement to help Ukraine build a more robust economy and democratic institutions. But EU officials will have to devote constant attention and resources to make that a reality".[5] The remark on the challenges which Europe will be facing in the future when it comes to helping Ukraine with structural reform is legitimate. Pifer also drew the readers' attention to how this step can be regarded by the Russian Federation as unambiguously hostile, which may be an obstacle for the Ukrainian side when it comes to the full implementation of the decisions anchored in the agreements.[6] The Brookings analyst marks his positive attitude towards the European project and points out clearly that the agreement between Brussels and Kiev provides a perfect opportunity to make a leap forward in civilization: "Implementation of the agreement will not only bring Ukraine's trade and customs rules into conformity with EU standards, it will help the country draw closer to EU democratic norms and 'Europeanize' other Ukrainian regulatory regimes".[7] We can therefore see that the European identity is in a sense identical with Western norms and standards indicating the development of the given country. According to Pifer's analysis, Europe is a symbol of modernity and political maturity which Ukraine could use so much.

Europe's condition in international politics was also discussed by Brookings during the refugee crisis, when hundreds of thousands refugees from war-plagued Syria and other unstable countries of the Middle East and North Africa stood at the gates of the European Union. Jessica Brandt focused on the fact that in the eyes of European politicians one of the biggest challenges for the European Union is that

> Almost every European leader passing through Washington uses the same phrase to describe the migrant crisis: 'existential threat'. They mean fear that the European Union could disintegrate as a result of the political, economic, and humanitarian stress caused by the most massive transfer of populations since World War II.[8]

The author also points at the weakness of Brussels in its relations with Ankara, which checkmates the European Union in a political sense. Turkey has extorted on the EU many political-economic concessions for the support in stopping the migration wave from Syria. Without this help Greece alone would not have been able to take thousands of refugees, which additionally could have worsened the situation in the whole Union:

> Taking swift action is also a political necessity. Bringing the flow of arrivals down to manageable levels is critical to keeping Europe's borders open and its right-wing parties in check. That will only happen if the deal is seen to be working, since only then will it have a deterrent effect.[9]

This example shows that Europe is regarded as a weak actor on the international arena. The dependence on Turkey, heading in an authoritarian direction, the inability to deal with the discussed crisis and the fear of the rise of populist tendencies, puts Europe in a bad light and shows its geopolitical handicap.

In the context of the importance of Europe in modern international relations, Brookings also discussed the role of the alliance with the United States. Constanze Stelzenmüller stated that especially during the presidential campaign mainly two strategies of the USA were discussed:

> As the U.S. presidential election campaign gears up and conflicts on the other side of the Atlantic multiply, two opposing views on what to do about European security compete for airspace in U.S. public debate. The first is essentially 'let's get out of there' – America no longer has any business being engaged in Europe's security. The opposing view is that Europe will collapse, implode, or be invaded (whether by the Islamic State or migrants) unless the United States steps in.[10]

Simultaneously the analyst warned that both opinions do not take into consideration the actual state of Euro–Atlantic relations. The cooperation between the main NATO states had not been that good for a long time, taking into account the common position regarding the Russian Federation and in regard to Iran, when it comes to the nuclear agreement. Stelzenmüller goes even further in her thesis about the role of Europe in these relations:

> While the outcomes of these efforts have been imperfect, it's safe to say that these concerted efforts at transatlantic diplomacy averted war. European governments – contrary to popular misconception, at least in the United States – often played leadership roles. Cooperation around Ukraine and Iran provides excellent examples of what close transatlantic security cooperation can achieve.[11]

Of course this opinion does not cover a number of internal problems which the EU is currently dealing with and which influence its foreign policy and importance in international relations. The division into Northern and Southern Europe, of which the former is dealing better with the economic crisis and the latter is struggling with debt, low economic growth, structural youth unemployment gives power to all Euro-skeptical groups.[12] All this contributes to the reduction of the role of the EU in their tandem with the USA. The faster Europe must conquer the analyzed vicissitudes, because, as Constanze Stelzenmüller writes: "One thing is certain: Only if Europe resolves its own security dilemmas will it ever be able to join the United States in providing stability and security on a more global level".[13]

The Carnegie Endowment for International Peace

The second analyzed think thank is the Carnegie Endowment for International Peace, founded in 1910 by Andrew Carnegie, a tycoon of the steal and metal industry, who spent most of his fortune on founding institutions with public and expert character. The Carnegie Endowment is being described as a "global think tank" having five offices around the World – in Washington, Brussels, Moscow, Beirut and Beijing. Due to this fact it is difficult to refer to this think tank in pure American categories; nevertheless the Washington office is still characterized as the "head office". The "Carnegie" brand, even with its transnational dimension, is still identified with American institutions.[14] As both the Washington and Brussels Office are dealing with European topics, it is difficult to state precisely which activities of the Carnegie Endowment are the most important or the most representative for the whole think tank, especially as analyses of the Brussels branch are also published on the Washington branch's homepage. With regard to this the author of the chapter will treat the publications of Carnegie Europe which were uploaded on the website of the Carnegie Endowment for International Peace as one subject of his research.

The first discussed topic on Europe was obviously connected with the illegal annexation of Crimea by the Russian Federation and the reaction of the European Union. Cornelius Adebahr praised the EU for its devotion to the main political principles since the beginning of the Russian-Ukrainian conflict: "Support for the rule of law, territorial integrity, and reform-oriented economic policies have always formed the core of the EU's approach to Ukraine. Those were the right policies before the events of the last several months, and they remain so today".[15] The author explains that the European Union is a special and untypical player in international relations and is also characterized by a rather untypical philosophy of its actions. This is more important, as during the discussed Russian-Ukrainian crisis many commentators of political life in the USA accused Brussels elites of sluggishness and the lack of determined actions both during the Euromaidan and after the beginning of aggressive actions. The analysis says:

> The EU is a different kind of global actor than the United States or Russia. Many pundits and policymakers alike resent the EU's administrative and technocratic – as opposed to energetic and strategic – approach to foreign policy. But it is precisely the EU's bureaucratic, norms-based policy of establishing contractual relationships focused on achieving mutual gains that fundamentally distinguishes its foreign policy from that of other nation-states.[16]

The European Union appears as a complicated global player, in which a number of administrative norms define its politics and actions on international arena. And it is this aspect which is extremely important to understand one of the dimensions of the European identity in its place on the international scene. The European Union, in comparison to the USA, is not a national country, but an international organization, which at the end cares about the interest of its member states and the general European national interest. The EU deserves recognition, so the author of the mentioned analysis points out:

> The EU has shown a degree of flexibility that has gone largely unnoticed. It has separated for the moment the economic and political parts of the association agreement, signing the political portion with Ukraine's interim president and holding out on the economic one until the presidential election scheduled for late May brings in a new – and broadly legitimate – leadership. Moreover, the EU has begun to refine the overall ENP in light of the lessons learned from the current crisis. This flexibility is indicative of the EU's significant ability to embrace self-criticism and work to correct past policy failures.[17]

Another aspect of the importance of the EU for the international community was the refugee crisis, which constituted the biggest challenge for Europe in 2015. Richard Youngs points out in his analysis that especially after the terror attacks in France in the same year the EU regarded their policy in sheer humanitarian categories:

> Until the terror attacks hit Paris, the main strand of European responses to the refugee surge was an increase in humanitarian aid. This increase is necessary and welcome. But it represents a policy of humanitarian containment – the use of aid to prevent a spillover of refugee pressures into Europe – not one

> aimed at tackling root causes like poor economic performance, bad governance, and social division.[18]

This shows that besides the praise on the general attitude of Europe, the think tank notices also some shortcomings in the migration policy of the EU. The analyst of Carnegie criticizes also the insufficient military engagement of Europe in fighting international terror:

> European governments tend to stress that they see no military solution to Syria's violence. Only France and the UK have undertaken military action within Syria. In September, France became the second Western country to join the United States in carrying out manned air strikes in Syria. Yet France is for the moment more heavily engaged in operations in Mali and the Central African Republic than it is in Syria or Iraq. Despite launching more air strikes and halting defense cuts, France is still well short of contemplating a large-scale military engagement, especially one involving ground troops.[19]

At the same time Youngs underlines the German reluctance towards any military solutions in Syria.[20] We can therefore see that from a perspective of an American analyst, the European Union and its policy are far from paradigms of realism and that inside the organization we can observe various actions. In the author's opinion, Germany and France have a rather different vision of not even the solution to the conflict, but their own engagement in it.

The discussed opinion may also help us to look at the external environment of the EU from another perspective. Youngs does not define the border area of the EU in sheer conflict-related categories. He also draws our attention to the political passiveness of some countries, which lately resigned from a number of modernization reforms:

> One of the most cited phrases in policymaking and think tank circles describes the EU's neighbourhood as a raging ring of fire. This widely used metaphor is, however, somewhat misleading. Beyond the Syrian war, Libya's implosion, and low-level fighting on a small part of Ukraine's territory, the rest of the neighbourhood is not beset by open conflict. Its problems are quite different. Most of the neighbourhood could be described more accurately as a ring of stagnation than a ring of fire. It is made up of countries in which reforms continually fail to materialize and long-present problems drag on without being addressed by feckless and self-serving regimes of different political hues.[21]

Atlantic Council

The last analyzed think tank is the Atlantic Council, founded in 1961 with the aim to improve the relations and to exchange ideas between the United States of America and Western Europe. This organization strongly differs both from the

Brookings Institutions and the Carnegie Endowment for International Peace. First of all, the institution is younger than the previously mentioned think tanks and less significant on the global scene of ideas.[22] However, the Atlantic Council has gained significance especially during the events in Ukraine 2014. It was the Office of the Atlantic Council, where the most important Ukrainian politicians, such as Prime Minister at that time Arseniy Yatsenyuk, were speaking. On March, 12th 2014 he came to the Atlantic Council directly from the meeting with President Barack Obama, Vice-President Joe Biden and Secretary of State John Kerry at the White House. During his dramatic speech he appealed to the audience in the office of the Atlantic Council for solidarity with Ukraine, which found itself in the state of an informal war with the Russian Federation.[23] This was an unprecedented event and the think tank provided an open space for meeting one of the main actors of global politics at that time.

In the framework of its activities, the Atlantic Council has an initiative dedicated to Europe, the *Future Europe Initiative*, within which the main challenges for the Old Continent are discussed. Some of their analyses have a different perspective than the one offered by other think tanks. Nicholas Dungan, in his text *What Europe Means*, which was published for the 70th anniversary of D-Day draws our attention to the fact that from the historical point of view the European project, in spite of many shortcomings, is a success and that the European Union flag remains a symbol also for others:

> Once the Berlin Wall fell and the reunification of Germany became inevitable, the impulsion to incorporate the former Comecon countries left no choice but to favor enlargement of the European Community. Recent events in Ukraine demonstrate how strong an appeal the European ideal exerts. The flags being waved in Maidan Nezalezhnosti were not the banners of the United States or the United Nations, but of the European Union.[24]

The author also stresses that Europe is currently outrunning the United States in many matters. We can refer even to economic issues, where EU standards of labor law may seem an unattainable norm for the American judiciary system, which we could witness with the big failure of the negotiations around TTIP. As Dungan states:

> In the United States, Europe is often wrongly considered a problem solved. To be sure, US sacrifices and statesmanship have contributed enormously to the building of Europe, but the current negotiations on the Trans-Atlantic Trade and Investment Partnership (TTIP), for example, have made it plain to Americans that Europe sees itself as a guardian of higher standards than the United States in areas such as food safety, personal privacy and worker protection.[25]

With regard to the existing analysis on how Europe was perceived by American experts, we can observe an important change of narration and perspective.

Another key issue for the European Foreign and Security Policy was mentioned by Henrik Breitenbauch in his text for the Atlantic Council, namely the lack of solidarity not only between NATO states, but also within the EU. This concerns above all the threat from the Russian Federation, which has tested European unity more than once. The analyst draws our attention to the institutional crisis of the EU as well as to its political significance:

> Institutions and ideology in the European Union make this growing European schism particularly dangerous. Institutionally, the absence of a European equivalent to the federal American government means that European unity is dependent upon both a sense of purpose in Brussels as well as support from European capitals and Washington, D.C. But over the last decade Brussels has run out of steam. Political relations in Europe have become increasingly 'rebilateralized'. Solutions are mostly sought among able, willing and relevant nations, rather than in a multilateral forum like the EU. This institutional weakening means that Russia can more easily pick off countries on the eastern flank, as in the case of Hungary, Slovakia and perhaps Greece.[26]

On the other side, though, the challenge for the European foreign policy is the attachment to legal acts and the legitimacy of the conducted activities. Breitenbach points at the fact that in the relation between the EU and Russia we are witnessing a huge asymmetry in this field, which also constitutes a large problem. Concluding his considerations, the author comes back to the significance of the EU bureaucracy and the sophisticated administration rules for conducting effective foreign policy:

> The EU bureaucratic world-view, unfortunately, is contagious and spills over into European capitals where if affects scarce strategic attention. Europe has a critical strategic blind spot, formed by the idea that there is no such thing as power politics, that strategic issues can be reduced to administrative security policy, and that dialogue and the magic attractiveness of the acquis communautaire are sufficient tools of foreign policy. This ideology makes it very hard for the EU and many European political leaders to acknowledge and address the hard geopolitics behind Russia's actions in Ukraine.[27]

This clearly shows that the European identity in international politics seems to be little effective, clichéd and tied up by the multitude of treaty regulations. Surely this may prove more of its weakness than strength in conducting foreign policy, especially when it comes to centralized and strong actions of Russian political decision makers, who, in comparison to their European peers, do not have to agree on the common position which has to consider the interest of 28 member states and the Brussels bureaucracy apparatus.

Conclusions

The analysis of how these three American think tanks perceive the European identity, in terms of international policy, allows us to draw three main conclusions. First of all, Europe, and more precisely the European Union, is regarded by American experts as a player at an impasse, whose role and importance in the global order is shrinking. According to the think tanks, both the Russian-Ukrainian crisis and the refugee crisis showcased Europe's incapability to take quick and determined actions to influence international security and external stability of the EU environment. The second conclusion concerns the European "Ring of Fire", namely the worsening situation in the countries which are part of the European Neighborhood Policy. War in Ukraine, frozen conflicts in Moldova, Georgia, Armenia and Azerbaijan, countries basically fallen apart like Syria and Libya, as well as highly unstable Egypt, prove that the policy of the EU towards their neighbors cannot be regarded as a success. Naturally one must not imply that the European Union is intentionally destabilizing its frontiers. Nevertheless, the chronic crisis in the European dimension has a direct impact on the weakness of the European Union itself. Thirdly, the EU is still regarded as a non-military and normative power. The values and attachment to the rules of international law are shaping its politics, its role and its geopolitical importance.

The hypotheses presented in the beginning of this chapter have been proved correct in this study. American think tanks rightly define European self-identity as a normative power in international relations; however, they mostly see this as the main weakness of the EU. This is especially visible during the analyzed period, which could be defined as the "renaissance" of the hard and brutal geopolitical game between the West and Russia. On the other hand, it can be stated that the policy of the United States was not characterized effectively, either, which unfortunately was not given its due attention in the analysis of these think tanks. It is also dubious that American analysts and their doubts about the effectiveness of European normative policy would affect the political leaders of the European Union. It could be stated that both components of the Euro–Atlantic world are currently in crisis, leading to the perception of them as declining powers.

In the author's opinion, despite the objective weaknesses resulting from the normative approach to international relations, Europe will not change its policy in the upcoming years. Equally, it will not affect the policy of the United States, which, despite the loud announcements of withdrawing its military forces from the Old Continent, is currently placing new units on NATO's so-called eastern flank in the "new" member states of the European Union.

It is worth mentioning that all the analyzed think tanks – Brookings Institution, Carnegie Endowment for International Peace, as well as Atlantic Council – had not designated a special place for Europe in their activities during the analyzed period. The topics connected with the situation in Ukraine, for example, left the agenda of the analyzed think tanks after a few months. The situation was similar when it came to the refugee crisis or terror attacks within Europe. In the analyzed time period we also witnessed other discussions on the war in Syria, the rise and fall of so-called Islamic State, tensions in Asia, and the possible Russian influence in the American presidential elections. All these topics caught the attention of the American public. It is worth noticing that the pan-European perspectives of these events were seldom taken. Certain analyses referred to how various member countries (Germany, France) deal with such problems, or how they influence their internal situation. The voices of experts mentioned in this chapter were an exception. It is also interesting that the authors dealing with the European topics were mainly Europeans. On one side it is not surprising that American think tanks are using the knowledge and language skills of EU citizens, but on the other hand, without their activities, American think tanks would have serious deficits in their analysis of the situation in Europe.

All three think tanks, despite their political and ideological backgrounds (both Carnegie Endowment for International Peace and the Atlantic Council are recognized as centrist think tanks, and Brookings Institution as a progressive one),[28] had a similar perspective of the European identity in foreign affairs. The liberal approach of the EU in finding peaceful resolution of the Ukrainian-Russian conflict or the refugee crisis was more than visible in the discussed American analyses. We could find a strong similarity between the mentioned organizations and that of the US administration in their understating of Europe's role in the US–EU alliance in the evaluated time frame. However, it is also hard to verify to what extent the activity of the described think tanks influences the politics within the White House in its perception of Europe. Literature on this subject underlines that the activities of external and non-governmental expert milieus do not have the same significance for political decision makers as they previously had, for example during the Cold War.[29] Furthermore, the power of think tanks lies within long-term activities through the sketching of various scenarios for any given policy. In the modern, globalized world, it is the speed of reactions and non-standard and interesting perspectives on a given topic which prove their strength of pull, or their popularity among political groups. In a sense the "technologicalization" of life, as well as the shallow analytical discourse in the Western world both influence the decreasing role of think tanks in the political decision making process. The author would like to contribute this chapter to a broader discussion about the condition of expert institutions in the modern world.

Notes

1 J. Rifkin, *The European Dream*, Cambridge, Polity Press, 2004.

2 Think tank studies are a domain of Northern American scholars. It is worth mentioning the work of Donald E. Abelson, see: D.E. Abelson, *Do Think Tanks Matter? Assessing the Impact of Public Policy Institutes*, Montreal-Kingston, McGill-Queen's University Press, 2002; D.E. Abelson, *A Capitol Idea: Think Tanks and US Foreign Policy*, Montreal-Kingston, McGill-Queen's University Press, 2006; and: James G. McGann, see: J.G. McGann, *Think Tanks and Policy Advice in the United State. Academics, Advisors and Advocates*, Abingdon, Routledge, 2007; J.G. McGann, *Global Think Tanks. Policy Networks and Governance*, Routledge, Abingdon, 2007.

3 McGann, *Think Tanks and Policy Advice in the United State*, p. 24.

4 J.G. McGann, *2016 Global Go Think Tank Index Report*, Philadelphia, 2017, p. 84, http://repository.upenn.edu/cgi/viewcontent.cgi?article=1011&context=think_tanks, (accessed 25 June 2018).

5 S. Pifer, 'Poroshenko Signs EU-Ukraine Association Agreement' *Brookings Institution*, 27 June 2014, www.brookings.edu/blog/up-front/2014/06/27/poroshenko-signs-eu-ukraine-association-agreement/, (accessed 25 June 2018).

6 Pifer, 'Poroshenko Signs EU-Ukraine Association Agreement'.
7 Pifer, 'Poroshenko Signs EU-Ukraine Association Agreement'.
8 J. Brandt, 'A Pivotal Moment for Europe', *Brookings Institution*, 13 June 2016, www.brookings.edu/blog/order-from-chaos/2016/06/13/a-pivotal-moment-for-europe/, (accessed 25 June 2018).
9 Brandt, 'A Pivotal Moment for Europe'.
10 C. Stelzenmüller, 'Why Europe Needs America, a Little', *Brookings Institution*, 29 September 2015, www.brookings.edu/blog/order-from-chaos/2015/09/29/why-europe-needs-america-a-little/, (accessed 25 June 2018).
11 Stelzenmüller, 'Why Europe Needs America, a Little'.
12 Stelzenmüller, 'Why Europe Needs America, a Little'.
13 Stelzenmüller, 'Why Europe Needs America, a Little'.
14 Russian forces often discuss the role of the Carnegie Moscow Center in categories of a so called "foreign agent". This denotes an institution which is not only financed externally, but can be also regarded by the Kremlin as a quasi-intelligence organization. Zob V. Ryzhkov, 'Russia's Foreign Agents Law Is Recipe for Disaster', The Moscow Times, 2 June 2015, https://themoscowtimes.com/articles/russias-foreign-agents-law-is-recipe-for-disaster-47062, (accessed 25 June 2018).
15 C. Adebahr, 'Europe's Decisive Role to Play in Ukraine', *Carnegie Europe*, 07 May 2014, http://carnegieeurope.eu/2014/05/07/europe-s-decisive-role-to-play-in-ukraine-pub-55515, (accessed 25 June 2018).
16 Adebahr, 'Europe's Decisive Role to Play in Ukraine'.
17 Adebahr, 'Europe's Decisive Role to Play in Ukraine'.
18 R. Youngs and J. Gutman, 'Is the EU Tackling the Root Causes of Middle Eastern Conflict?', *Carnegie Europe*, 1 December 2015, http://carnegieeurope.eu/2015/12/01/is-eu-tackling-root-causes-of-middle-eastern-conflict-pub-62138, (accessed 25 June 2018).
19 Youngs and Gutman, 'Is the EU Tackling the Root Causes of Middle Eastern Conflict?'.
20 Youngs and Gutman, 'Is the EU Tackling the Root Causes of Middle Eastern Conflict?'.
21 Youngs and Gutman, 'Is the EU Tackling the Root Causes of Middle Eastern Conflict?'.
22 The author means the previously mentioned think tank ranking: J.G. McGann, *2016 Global Go Think Tank Index Report*.
23 *Ukrainian Prime Minister Arseniy Yatsenyuk*, [online video], 2014, www.youtube.com/watch?v=ewdW0sbyA2g&feature=youtu.be, (accessed 25 June 2018).
24 N. Dungan, 'What Europe Means', *Atlantic Council*, 6 June 2014, www.atlanticcouncil.org/publications/articles/what-europe-means, (accessed 25 June 2018).
25 Dungan, 'What Europe Means'.
26 H. Breitenbauch, 'As Europe Breaks in Two, Putin Gains', *Atlantic Council*, 24 April 2015, www.atlanticcouncil.org/blogs/natosource/as-europe-breaks-in-two-putin-gains, (accessed 25 June 2018).
27 Breitenbauch, 'As Europe Breaks in Two, Putin Gains'.
28 'The 50 Most Influential Think Tanks in the United States', *The Best Schools*, https://thebestschools.org/features/most-influential-think-tanks/, (accessed 25 June 2018).
29 T. Medvetz, *Think Tanks in America*, Chicago, University of Chicago Press, 2012, pp. 70–71, 73; D. Stone and A. Denham (eds.), *Think Tank Traditions Policy Research and the Politics of Ideas*, Manchester-New York, Manchester University Press, 2004, p. 95; McGann, *Global Think Tanks*, p. 41.

12 Conclusions

Anna Skolimowska

The purpose of the book was to show the perception of the European Union's identity in international relations by 'Others' (third countries' political elites, civil society, think-tanks etc.) and the meaning of the third parties' discourse on the European Union's (EU's) identity in international relations, especially for the narration on its identity in international relations.

The objective of the book was to fill the gap in the subject literature by presenting a wide and consistent review of the existing surveys addressing the external perceptions of the EU. The innovative character of the survey refers to the theoretical assumption of the normative character of the European Union's identity and discursive practices in the third countries that legitimize (or not) narration among third parties and thus influence the European Union self-identification.

The book aims at depicting how the EU is perceived and understood outside its borders. In order to do that all the available relevant surveys have been collected and reviewed in order to have the widest possible and the most precise representation of others' perception of the EU under investigation.

Having conducted empirical analyses, in the form of case studies, we could observe that the definition of the European Union's identity in international relations as a normative actor has failed to gain common acceptance among participants of international relations. There might be several reasons for this, namely:

- the history of Europe's involvement in the world – its colonial past and imperial experience is a huge obstacle in building an image of a credible normative and altruistic actor, especially in Africa and Latin America. Here the EU is perceived rather as a protectionist and paternalistic actor with limited interest in local issues;
- the lack of a strong universal identifier as a consequence of incomplete, fragmented and impotent foreign policy;
- problems in communicating the European Union's international offer in the political issues (the case of India and lack of knowledge of the European Union specificity). Insufficient efforts in building the post-colonial image of Europe in this region;
- too bureaucratic and administrative approach to relations with third countries, which hinders the recognition of diversity, the significance of the geopolitical

and historical factor in relations with the European Union (the case of the Western Balkan countries);

- the lack of interest regarding the EaP countries' perceptions of the EU is rooted in the assumption that they are not influential enough in the EU policy-making and have little impact on political developments;
- some actors do not share the vision of the European Union as a normative actor, considering the content related to the EU as hostile to their own identity – the case of the Russian Federation;
- the political model offered by the European Union within its normative identity is not exceptional when compared to other entities which also refer to universal norms in the international space. This mainly concerns the so-called liberal democracies and international institutions, such as: the USA, Japan or the UN;
- there are entities which accept the normative identity of the European Union (e.g. Ukraine) for purely pragmatic reasons (expecting to be offered membership) rather than out of their conviction concerning the rightness of the European norms and values;
- the picture of the European Union as a normative actor, built by the European political elites, seems too ideal or even utopian. This, in turn, gives rise to a presumption that the concept of a normative power in reality constitutes a certain type of a meta-narrative, utopia, or a form of ideological measure relating to the identity of the European Union in international relations, the defects of which are easily revealed in the face of international crises such as wars and other conflicts;
- the international space contains competitors to the normative and even economic offer of the European Union (American, Russian and Chinese political and economic rivalry), which accounts for the fact that the European Union, as a non-state entity, having much smaller means of international influence, naturally cannot stand this competition and becomes less attractive for such states.

Nonetheless, since its formulation the concept of 'a normative power' has evolved within the field of European Studies and has been used to account for the transformation of institutional and legal circumstances and the conditions in which the European Union conducts its activity. One of the crucial challenges faced by the concept of normative power is the call for the militarization of the European project announced in the Treaty of Lisbon, which will entail the departure from a norms-based and values-based foreign policy and mark the return to the paradigm of military power in the international space.

Moreover, the described phenomenon of dissonance between the narration on its normative identity delivered by the European political leaders and the way in which the European Union is perceived in third countries, which see it more as an economic actor, the post-colonial empire, an incredible actor in human rights issues or international ethics with fragmentary and dispersed policy towards the international environment, may be described as 'normative gap'. This is a gap between the European Union's self-defined identity in international relations, namely that of a normative actor, and the perception of Europe's role and identity in some regions of the world. This gap translates into the crisis of the EU's place as an effective and credible actor in international relations. This stems from the assumption adopted by Constructivists, who claim that the character of European Unions' identity at the global scene, should depend on others' perception of actors' identity. In that sense the construction of the European Union's identity should include others' perception of its identity.

In addition, the survey showed that the identity of a normative actor adopted by the European Union in the international relations is in crisis. It is manifested *inter alia* in the lack of general acceptance of the normative role of the EU in international relations in the analyzed countries and the regions of the world. Within the discourse about the EU in the third countries we can observe the need for the EU to develop another identity in international relations as partners of the European Union do not perceive it as a normative power. They are more interested in an economic or political side of the cooperation with the European Union rather than in its normative attractiveness.

When it comes to the case studies:

- in the Western Balkans countries (Serbia, Montenegro, Former Yugoslav Republic of Macedonia, Bosnia and Herzegovian and Kosovo) – as Laura Maria Herţa and Adrian Corpădean wrote in their contribution – perceptions of the EU vary across countries. However, European integration is on the agenda of each of these countries and support for the EU is not falling dramatically, even though their integration is always postponed. The countries included in the Western Balkans region seem to be victims of the so-called 'enlargement fatigue' and EU accession sometimes seems to be elusive, even though, as shown previously, there is a growing support for the EU. Norm transference and norm internalization are processes that take time. For the Europeanization of the Western Balkans to operate properly, the EU should stay closer to countries from the region and consistently act on its commitments;
- within the Eastern Partnership countries (Armenia, Azerbaijan, Belarus, Georgia, Moldova, and Ukraine) – as Beata Piskorska wrote – the European Union was firstly perceived as a transformative power and as a donor or rarely as a security provider. Cooperation with the EU is perceived mostly as an opportunity for these countries. The EU was seen as a chance to put an end to economic and political hardships and improve almost all aspects of life mostly in Ukraine. In this context, the European Union is often portrayed as a transformative power, which through its insistence on political and economic reforms could trigger a positive change in these countries. Mostly the visa-free regime should be used by the EU as a leverage to enhance the fight against corruption in Ukraine and Moldova. However, the EU's attractiveness might be challenged by the rising Russian influence and its alternative regional project (the Eurasian Union). Moreover it is worth stressing that the cost-benefit calculations (economic dimension) were the dominant element

of the EaP European discourse. From the security point of view, the EU and the European integration are described as the only alternative to Russian influence in the region and the protection of national sovereignty;

- Russian Federation, as Olga Barburska wrote, perceives the European Union and its identity mainly from the perception angle of its own Russian identity, by establishing a direct opposition between European identity and Russian identity. In other words, Russians perceive the traits that characterize Europeans as mirroring their own traits, which is the consequence of the fact that in general terms the Russian world view is developed as the antithesis of the paradigms developed by the West, including Europe. By doing so, Russian élites and people reject vigorously the idea of the European Union as a normative power, considering this very notion as a direct threat to their own identity, as well as to Russia's vital national interests;
- African elites (mainly from Congo and Tanzania as well as from African Union in general) as analyzed by Anna Masłoń-Oracz and Iwona Janczyk, perceive the European Union both politically as the home of former colonial masters and the promoter of free trade and liberal democracy and economically as a body assisting the African Union in implementing its Agenda 2063 vision.[1] The colonial and slavish past and deep-rooted reasons for the mutual mistrust are still present in the relations between Europeans and Africans. In the eyes of the latter the EU countries are regarded as former colonial powers, and, although independence was gained by African states decades ago, colonialism has left a difficult legacy;
- in India, as Ana Pantea wrote, the EU is often perceived as a conservative and protectionist structure. The normativity of the EU is disadvantageous for the developing countries and simultaneously safeguards the European interests. The double standards of the Union make India and other players unwilling to take 'ethical lessons' in terms of human rights, democratic consolidation or the energy sector. As such, the goal for India would be to change its position in the international arena, from a norm-taker to a norm-setter;
- in Japan and South Korea, as Olga Barbasiewicz wrote, the economic ties seem to be crucial in both Asian countries' policy toward the EU. For sure, the Korean side represents the main interest in trade partnership with Europe, whereas Japan, whose politicians often raise economic issues concerning the EU policy in the Parliament, frequently refers to the norms and values, which are synonymous to the postwar Japanese attachment to peace and respect for human rights in negotiations with its European partners;
- for Latin America, as Şerban Văetişi, wrote, the EU is not something that the Latin American countries need, but rather an option they can take into consideration at their discretion. Surely, the local specificity and hesitation to embrace the European models in the case of Latin America may be analyzed as part of its post-colonial identity. Regarding the European Union's identity, then, we could see that its normative power cannot generate enough discursive attraction and ideological solidity to forge an unquestionable international (normative) identity. Be it considered a myth, a utopian model, a too-perfect

model or a criticizable identity in the sense of post-colonial deconstruction, according to various authors' interpretations, the EU's identity is ultimately reflecting the fragile European collective identity, also revealed, as a matter of fact, by the recent EU crises;
- the leading United States' think-tanks, as Bartosz M. Rydliński wrote, define European self-identity as a normative power in international relations; however, they mostly see this as the main weakness of the EU. This is especially visible at the times of the hard and brutal geopolitical game between the West and Russia. It is also dubious that American analysts and their doubts about the effectiveness of European normative policy would affect the political leaders of the European Union. It could be stated that both components of the Euro-Atlantic world are currently in crisis, leading to the perception of them as declining powers.

The detailed analyses conducted for this book prove the Constructivist hypothesis that identity in international relations is fluid, contextual and changeable. The European Union itself is perceived in various ways in many regions of the world and there is no single narration on its identity coming from the outside world. Some consider it as an economic actor (Asia), others as past colonial power (Africa and Latin America), while some discern weaknesses in the normative narration on the European identity (US) or see it as a threat to its own specificity (Russian Federation). In some regions the normative identity is accepted for pragmatic reasons while looking forward to the announced benefits, such as membership in the EU and stemming from the acceptance of the European political and legal norms (Western Balkans or Eastern Partnership countries).

What the empirical studies described in this book have in common is the questioning of the actions and the European self-narration on its own identity as a normative actor. These entities, when participating in the internal discourse on the European Union, often took up the issues of changes to the narration on the role and identity of the European Union in international relations, expecting the EU to be more realistic, pragmatic and effective in its actions in international relations.

Therefore, a question arises whether the European Union political elites have noticed such critical voices and reflected them in the narration on the European identity in international relations. The answer to this question seems positive, taking into account the debate on the strategic presence of the European Union in international relations in 2016 – the new document entitled: *Common vision, joint action: A stronger Europe – The global strategy for the foreign and security policy of the European Union.*

There are also other signs proving that the European Union is aware of the existence of the normative gap in its identity, in particular low acceptance of such narration on its identity in the international environment. This is manifested in political initiatives adopted in the EU relations with some regions of the world, consisting in changing the strategy of political relations in order to improve the attractiveness of the European offer for them. An example of this could be seen in actions aimed at changing the EU politics towards Africa, first expressed in the

Cotonou Agreements and now developed in Agenda 2063. Their essence lies in actions aimed at empowering African countries in their relations with the European Union through economic and political partnership. However, the undertaken activities are often insufficient and consolidate the image of Europe far from the normative ideal of identity it has created for itself.

Concerning the theoretical and methodological issues resulting from the conducted survey, the following conclusions could be drawn:

- the Constructivist assumption on the identity of international participants and the conceptual and methodological tools offered within this approach seem to have some potential for analyzing the EU identity in international relations. The post-structural version of Constructivism allows us to treat the EU as a specific unit of analysis, leaving the issue of its non-state nature in international relations aside;
- however, taking into account the fact that the post-structural epistemology does not offer the possibility of providing objective knowledge of the analyzed reality, but only a form of its interpretation, the results of this research do not claim the right to generalize or the status of objective knowledge.

The greatest challenge associated with the adopted research approach resulted from the methodology (discourse analysis). It is difficult to reach the true motives behind actions. However, if we follow the post-structural assumption that the language can reflect the reality, we assumed that the discourse on the European Union in third countries presented fragmentarily for selected social groups in specific time may provide knowledge of the specificity of the European Union identity in international relations.

In conclusion, it should be postulated, however, that further research be conducted in the way of constructing and deconstructing the research approach. A promising issue, though still requiring in-depth analysis, is that concerning changes to the narration on the EU identity influenced by information on the EU coming from the international environment. Our publication constituted the first attempt at dealing with this issue. Many issues, however, require further empirical studies, especially those that would allow us to develop analytical tools to demonstrate the change of the narration on the European identity as a result of interaction with the international environment. Currently we can only assume that such reflections exist among the European political elites, which is expressed in the debate and the content of the new global strategy of the European Union in international relations, where we can observe abandoning the narration of a normative actor concerning its identity and embracing a more pragmatic and realistic approach. Further scientific analyses and inquiries should focus on the extent to which this change stems from the awareness of the decreasing popularity of the concept of the European Union as a normative power in the international environment, and the extent to which it stems from the need to seek adequate instruments to defend one's own interests when facing activities of political and economic competitors (such as the USA, China or the Russian Federation).

Note

1 It is a strategic framework for the socio-economic transformation of the continent over the next 50 years. It builds on, and seeks to accelerate the implementation of past and existing continental initiatives for growth and sustainable development. Compare: African Union, *Agenda 2063*, https://au.int/agenda2063/about, (accessed 25 June 2018).

Index